D0368467

A Political History of Italy

A Political History of
ITALY

The Postwar Years

Norman Kogan

PRAEGER SPECIAL STUDIES • PRAEGER SCIENTIFIC

Library of Congress Cataloging in Publication Data

Kogan, Norman.
  A political history of Italy.

  Originally published as 2 separate works: A political
history of postwar Italy, 1966 and A political history
of postwar Italy: from the old to the new center-left,
1981.
    Bibliography: p.
    Includes index.
    1. Italy—Politics and government—1945–
2. Italy—Economic conditions—1945–1976.   3. Italy—
Economic conditions—1976–   I. Kogan, Norman.
Political history of postwar Italy.   II. Title.
DG577.5.K62   1983   945.092   83-3963

  ISBN 0-03-062959-4
  ISBN 0-03-062961-6 (pbk.)

DG
577.5
.K62
1983

Published in 1983 by Praeger Publishers
CBS Educational and Professional Publishing
A Division of CBS, Inc.
521 Fifth Avenue, New York, NY 10175 U.S.A.

3456789   052   98765432

Printed in the United States of America
on acid-free paper.

To Meryl

PREFACE

This book results from the encouragement of several friends who suggested I produce a one-volume survey of postwar Italy. It is the outgrowth of two earlier books that together cover most of the postwar period. I am grateful to the many people, American and Italian, who have provided me with ideas and suggestions, and who have stimulated my continuing interest in Italy. Most of all, my wife Meryl, to whom this volume is dedicated, has sustained me over the years.

The Italian people continue to draw me back to their fascinating peninsula, and I take this opportunity to thank them for their warmth and hospitality. They have suffered much and survived much in a long history but they have not lost their commitment to life. Whatever the future may bring, may they retain their ability to find satisfaction from the close ties of family and friends.

Norman Kogan
Storrs, Connecticut

CONTENTS

ix

TABLES

MAPS

GLOSSARY

Political Parties

CPSU	Communist Party of the Soviet Union
DC	Democrazia Cristiana / Christian Democracy
DP	Democrazia Proleteria / Proletarian Democracy
MSI	Movimento Sociale Italiano / Italian Social Movement
MSI-DN	Movimento Sociale Italiano-Destra Nazionale / Italian Social Movement-National Right
PCF	Parti Communist Français / French Communist Party
PCI	Partito Communista Italiano / Italian Communist Party
PDIUM	Partito Democratico Italiano di Unità Monarchica / Italian Democratic Party of Monarchist Unity
PDUP	Partito Democratico di Unità Proletaria / Democratic Party of Proletarian Unity
PLI	Partito Liberale Italiano / Italian Liberal Party
PR	Partito Radicale / Radical Party
PRI	Partito Repubblicano Italiano / Italian Republican Party
PSDI	Partito Social Democratico Italiano / Italian Social Democratic Party
PSI	Partito Socialista Italiano / Italian Socialist Party
PSIUP	Partito Socialista Italiano di Unità Proletaria / Italian Socialist Party of Proletarian Unity

PSU	Partito Socialista Unificato / Unified Socialist Party
SVP	Sud Tyroler Volkspartei / South Tyrol People's Party

International and Regional Organizations

CAP	Common Agricultural Program
EEC	European Economic Community
GATT	General Agreement on Tariffs and Trade
IMF	International Monetary Fund
NATO	North Atlantic Treaty Organization
OECD	Organization for Economic Cooperation and Development
OPEC	Organization of Petroleum Exporting Countries

Finance and Tax Terms

IGE	Imposta Generale sul Esercizio / General Multiple Step Sales Tax
IVA	Imposta sul Valore Aggiunto / Value Added Tax
SDR	Special Drawing Rights

Trade Unions, Workers Organizations, and Trade Associations

ACLI	Associazione Cristiana di Lavoratori Italiani / Christian Association of Italian Workers
CGIL	Confederazione Generale Italiana di Lavoro / Italian General Confederation of Labor
CISL	Confederazione Italiana di Sindacati Lavoratori / Italian Confederation of Workers' Unions
Confindustria	Confederation of Industries (Private Sector)
ECFTU	European Confederation of Free Trade Unions
Intersind	Confederation of Industries (Public Sector)
UIL	Unione Italiana di Lavoro / Italian Union of Labor

WFTU World Federation of Trade Unions

Government Holding Companies and Other Agencies

ENEL Ente Nazionale di Energia
Elettrica / National Electric Power
Agency

ENI Ente Nazionale Idrocarburi / National
Hydrocarbons Agency

IMI Istituto Mobiliare Italiano / Italian Real
Estate Investment Bank

IRI Istituto di Ricostruzione
Industriale / Institute for Industrial
Reconstruction

ISTAT Istituto Centrale di Statistica / Central
Statistical Institute

RAI Radiotelevisione Italiana / Italian
Radio and Television Company

CHRONOLOGY

April 29, 1945	World War II ends in Italy.
June 2, 1946	In a referendum, the Italian people choose a republic over the monarchy.
May, 1947	Communist and Socialist Parties ejected from the cabinet.
January 1, 1948	New republican constitution goes into effect.
April 18, 1948	First parliamentary election produces a major Christian Democratic victory.
1949	Italy joins NATO.
1952	Italy joins the European Coal and Steel Community.
1956-1959	Socialists and Communists diverge. Communists announce their program of the "Italian Way to Socialism."
1959-1963	The opening to the left emerges.
December, 1963	First center-left coalition government formed.
October, 1966	Socialists and Social Democrats temporarily united. Split again in July, 1969.
1968-1969	Eruption of the student movement.
October-December, 1969	"Hot Autumn" of the labor movement.
December, 1969	Emergence of terrorist violence.
Summer, 1970	Beginning of economic slowdown. Establishment of regular regional governments.
September, 1973	Berlinguer proposes the historic compromise.
October, 1973	Oil embargo with drastic

	increase in petroleum prices. Beginning of double-digit inflation.
May, 1974	Divorce referendum upholds the divorce law.
January, 1975	Socialists finally pull out of the center-left coalition.
June, 1975	Big Communist gains in the regional and local elections lead to a substantial increase in leftist governments below the national level.
June, 1976	These gains are repeated in parliamentary elections.
August, 1976	Andreotti forms a cabinet dependent on the abstention of the Communists and other parties. The PCI receives several important posts in Parliament.
March, 1978	Communists and Socialists become part of the majority supporting the government.
March-May, 1978	Aldo Moro kidnapped and then assassinated by Red Brigade terrorists.
January, 1979	Communists withdraw from the parliamentary majority, bringing down the government.
June, 1979	Communist vote declines in parliamentary elections for the first time.
March, 1980	Socialists join the government, re-creating the center-left coalition.
October, 1980	New four-party center-left coalition. The Socialists and Social Democrats agree to collaborate in the formulation of policy.

1
POSTWAR SETTLEMENTS

Two immediate postwar problems faced the Italian Government: to achieve a satisfactory peace settlement and to keep the population alive. The solutions of both depended on foreign, as well as Italian, intentions and deeds. Ever since the armistice in September, 1943, the Italian Government had sought to moderate the surrender terms and to obtain an acceptable peace settlement. The collaboration with the Allies during the period of economic, military, and political cobelligerency had undoubtedly achieved an amelioration of Allied controls by the end of the war. The military effort, especially, had earned the appreciation of the Allied military. Field Marshal Sir Harold Alexander, commander of the British forces in Italy, told a press conference on June 21, 1945, that in his opinion Italy had completely rehabilitated itself.[1] The American Army newspaper, *Stars & Stripes* (Mediterranean section), editorialized on the contributions of the northern partisans in the following language:

> Our advance guards and armored troops entered cities full of Italian patriots. They were there in an extraordinary number. The Allied soldiers have finally felt that they were fighting to liberate people who really wanted to be free. After long months of the winter war in the mud and the rain and the ruins, finally the Allied soldiers have seen another Italy.[2]

---

[1] *Il Progresso italo-americano* (New York), July 30, 1945.
[2] "Italian News Bulletin" (mimeographed; U.S. Office of War Information, May 2, 1945).

On August 23, 1945, General Mark W. Clark, commander of American forces in Italy, cabled Ferruccio Parri, who had succeeded Bonomi as Prime Minister the previous June:

> On leaving Italy after two years of hard campaigns in your country, I wish to salute your people and thank them for the help and collaboration they always gave me in driving the enemy out of your country. . . .
>
> It was a great satisfaction to me that your people—soldiers, partisans and civilians—gave me such cordial help and played such an important part in the final campaign of the Po Valley where they completely annihilated the enemy, thus liberating your country.[3]

Hardheaded European politicians, however, were not likely to permit themselves the luxury of gratitude or forgiveness. They had demands to make on a defeated Italy; they had their own power positions to establish or to reinforce; they had vivid memories of Fascist aggression. Britain, France, Yugoslavia, Greece, Russia, Albania, to say nothing of Ethiopia, had all felt the effects of Mussolini's expansionist ambitions. They had territorial or financial or colonial claims to present to Italy for payment.

In addition to its contribution to the war against the Nazis, post-Fascist Italy had two other important assets. America wanted nothing material from Italy and was committed to its rehabilitation. Inside the United States there were influential Italian-American and Roman Catholic forces to plead Italy's cause. This attitude was also held by a number of Latin American countries, although their voice at the peace conference would be modest.

There was also a fear, among the Western Allies at least, that a harsh peace settlement might wreck Italy's fragile political and economic structure, perhaps bringing chaos to be followed by Communism or a revival of Fascism. As the Cold War evolved in the postwar period, and as the internal strength of the Italian Communist Party was revealed in its full electoral force, these considerations would become more pressing. But in the early period of peace negotiations, the rancors and resentments of past depredations, and the jockeying for future power positions, would dominate among the victors.

---

3 *Nazioni unite* (New York), September 15, 1945, p. 2.

Italy participated in the peace conference but could not negotiate with the Allies. It was permitted to make oral and written
presentations of its position, but the peace conference was primarily a testing of strength among victors, not a settlement between victors and defeated. The Italians would, of course, try to
influence in any way possible the positions of the various victors,
through diplomatic and other channels, but in the end they
would have to accept the decision of the others.

Of the major issues of the peace settlement—boundaries, colonies, disarmament, and reparations—the drawing of territorial
boundaries was by far the most important. Yugoslavia, France,
and Austria demanded frontier revisions; the first two countries
were among the victors, the last was classified as a "liberated," not
an "enemy," state, although it had been absorbed by Germany
in 1938.

Before the end of the war, both the royal Yugoslav government-
in-exile and Marshal Tito's Communist partisan regime inside
Yugoslavia had publicly demanded all of the Italian region of
Venezia Giulia, including its key city of Trieste. In May, 1945,
Tito's partisans had overrun Trieste, occupying the city and most
of the surrounding region. Italy pleaded with the Allies to get the
Yugoslavs out, and under considerable British and American pressure, supplemented finally by Soviet advice, Tito reluctantly withdrew. A provisional occupation boundary, called the Morgan line,
was negotiated with Tito in June, 1945, leaving the cities of
Trieste and Pola (Pulj) in the hands of Anglo-American forces,
but most of the Istrian Peninsula under Yugoslav control.

All the Italian parties were behind the government's position.
Even the Communists, who had temporized for some time, publicly asserted the *Italianità* of Trieste in May, 1945. Count Sforza,
the most authoritative Italian foreign-affairs spokesman, had delivered a speech in August, 1944, that called for a return to the
1920 boundary, which he himself had negotiated, with Fiume
(Rieka) to be made a free city. By the summer of 1945, this position was no longer tenable. Foreign Minister Alcide De Gasperi
suggested in a letter to Secretary of State James F. Byrnes that the
Wilson line of 1919 would be an equitable boundary. He reaffirmed this position the following month in an address to the

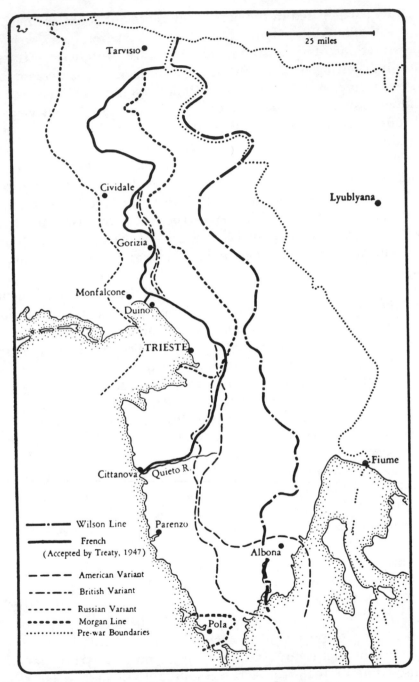

25 miles

Tarvisio

Cividale

Gorizia

Monfalcone

Duino

TRIESTE

Cittanova   Quieto R

Parenzo

Albona

Pola

Lyublyana

Fiume

Wilson Line
French
(Accepted by Treaty, 1947)
American Variant
British Variant
Russian Variant
Morgan Line
Pre-war Boundaries

VENEZIA GIULIA–BOUNDARY PROPOSALS

Council of Foreign Ministers.[4] The Yugoslavs, with Russian backing, were demanding the entire region, claiming that it was solidly inhabited by Slavs except for enclaves of Italians in the coastal towns.

The dispute dragged on and the Foreign Ministers finally decided to send a four-power committee of experts to establish a boundary. The experts were instructed to draw a frontier relying mainly on the ethnic principle which would take into account local geographic and economic factors. The goal was to minimize the minorities that would inevitably remain. The committee, however, returned in April, 1946, with four different boundaries. None of them recommended the Wilson line, although the American boundary came closest to it. The Russian expert ignored instructions and drew a line equivalent to the extreme Yugoslav claim. The British and French lines lay in between. In May, 1946, the Italians retreated to the American line.

The Americans and the British retreated to the French line over vigorous Italian protests, and in June, 1946, after the French suggested setting up the Free Territory of Trieste as an additional concession, the Russians agreed. The French line would be the eastern boundary of the Free Territory. Italy's protests went in vain: the settlement remained unsatisfactory, leaving major headaches for the future. The Free Territory was subdivided into two zones, A and B, with Zone A, including the city itself, under Anglo American occupation and Zone B under Yugoslav occupation. The occupation was supposed to be temporary, to last only until the United Nations Security Council could appoint a neutral governor for the Free Territory. The Council could not agree on a governor, however, so the occupation dragged on for years.

The Trieste settlement was Italy's biggest blow. Areas that were indisputably Italian were torn away. It left bitterness and rancor inside the country, for Trieste was the one foreign-policy issue

---

[4] The text of De Gasperi's letter to Brynes is printed in *United States and Italy, 1936–1946* ("Publications of the United States Department of State," No. 2669 [Washington, D.C.: Government Printing Office, 1946]), pp. 166–67; De Gasperi's statement to the Council of Foreign Ministers is reprinted in *Memorandum on the Italo-Yugoslav Frontier* (Rome: Ministry of Foreign Affairs, 1946), pp. 2–3.

really felt by large numbers of Italians, even those in small villages and remote rural areas. It became a weapon with which right-wing nationalist forces inside Italy attacked the Italian Government for its weakness, and the British and American governments for having sold out Italy's interests. And even though Russia forced the concessions that culminated in the Anglo-American retreat to the French line, the Italian Communists did not suffer. They pointed out that Russia knew how to fight for its friends and that if Italy were more friendly, it would benefit too.[5]

On February 28, 1945, Italy and France resumed diplomatic relations. At that time the French asserted they had no claims on Italian metropolitan territory. Nevertheless, in April, 1945, French troops crossed the Alps to occupy adjacent territory in Piedmont and the Val d'Aosta. French agents tried to win the French-speaking *Valdostani* over to the idea of annexation. Allied agreements made with Charles de Gaulle had permitted a restricted French occupation of Italian soil, but de Gaulle's troops had gone beyond the agreed limits. The British and the Americans could not permit a French occupation at the same time they were trying to push the Yugoslavs out of Trieste. De Gaulle was ordered to pull his troops out. He hesitated and President Truman threatened to cut off all supplies to France. De Gaulle retreated and by July, 1945, French troops were behind the frontier. The Italian Government immediately announced that linguistic autonomy would be granted to the Val d'Aosta (reversing Mussolini's policy of forcible Italianization) and that French-language schools would be instituted along with a limited degree of administrative autonomy.

At the Council of Foreign Ministers, the French gave up claims to the Aosta Valley and to stretches of the Italian Riviera, but demanded minor boundary rectifications in the Maritime Alps. The size of the territory demanded was not large, and the number of inhabitants was quite small, but several of the desired valleys were of both strategic and economic importance.

The Italian position was that the boundary should follow the

---

5 During this period, bilateral negotiations between Italy and Yugoslavia were conducted with the aim of reaching a settlement, but they also failed.

watershed of the Alps. The French demands, if realized, would bring France down onto the Italian side of the mountains and eliminate natural barriers to invasion routes into the Po Valley. Also on French soil would be some major hydroelectric-power installations that provided substantial portions of electric current to such cities as Genoa and Turin.

Italian objections were overridden and the peace conference approved the French requests except for a few very minor territorial rectifications. Provisions were inserted in the final document to protect Italian rights to the water and electric power from the detached territories. In later years, the French Government was willing to return some of the seized territories, but the French Assembly refused to ratify a bill for their return.

Even more vexatious than the issue of French territorial claims was the clash over the South Tyrol. In 1919, at the end of World War I, Italy had acquired both the province of Trento and the province of Bolzano (South Tyrol) from Austria. The population of Trento was overwhelmingly Italian; the South Tyrol was predominately Austro-German in culture and language and less heavily populated. During the Fascist period, Mussolini had made efforts to Italianize the South Tyrol by importing Italian industries and labor into the province and by attempting to impose Italian language and culture on the indigenous inhabitants.

The South Tyrolese were rabid German nationalists and were later Nazi in orientation. But Hitler abandoned them in 1939 when he and Mussolini agreed that since the South Tyrol was "forever Italian," a plebiscite should be held among the German-speaking inhabitants that would require them to opt for Italy or the Third Reich. (It must be remembered that Austria had already been absorbed by Germany.) Those choosing Italy would accept Italianization; the others would be transferred to the Reich. Of the 266,885 persons who voted in the plebiscite the following year, 185,365—or almost 70 per cent—opted for transfer to Nazi Germany. The outbreak of the war slowed down the transfer of population, so that only 77,772 people had left the South Tyrol by 1943. The Italian surrender in September, 1943, led to a *de facto* German annexation of the area and the return of many of the optants.[6] Because of their bilingual capacities, the South Tyrolese Germans played a crucial part in the German rule over northern Italy in the next twenty months, earning the bitter hatred of partisans and other inhabitants alike. Austria, also, was unpopular, because ten of the Nazi divisions operating in Italy after September, 1943, were composed primarily of Austrians.

The main Italian claim to the South Tyrol was that Italy had fought toward the end of the war on the side of the victors, while Austria had stayed with Germany all the way. Even before November, 1945, when Austria put forth its claim for the return of the South Tyrol, the Italian position had been fully developed. The fundamental point was to play down the ethnic issue, which was the major Italian thesis in the Trieste dispute, and to substitute other arguments—strategic, economic, and geographic—as the controlling bases for debate. Therefore, at the same time the Italian Government thought the loss of some 350,000 Italians in the provinces of Trieste and Istria an outrage, it considered the inclusion of some 200,000 German-speaking inhabitants in Italy "a matter of minor importance."[7]

The Allies accepted these Italian arguments (not necessarily because of their compelling logic) and in March, 1946, the foreign ministers' deputies decided that the ethnic claim would not be controlling in the South Tyrol dispute. The Austrian Government then asked for border rectifications, but later these were also denied. The 1919 boundary was left untouched—the major Italian victory of the peace conference—although about two-thirds of the population of the South Tyrol was, and still is, ethnically German.

On September 5, 1946, the Italian and Austrian governments entered into an agreement concerning guarantees for the administrative, cultural, and economic autonomy of the South Tyrol.

---

6 After September, 1943, the Germans also conducted a *de facto* annexation of Trieste and the Istrian Peninsula. There are indications that a German victory in the war would have led to the Italian loss of Venezia Giulia and the South Tyrol despite the fact that Hitler and Mussolini were allies.

7 "Memorandum on the Question of the Italian Northern Frontier," in *The Italo-Austrian Frontier*, Vol. I: *Official Statements and Other Documents Presented to the Council of Foreign Ministers (February–June, 1946), with Foreword* (Rome: Ministero degli Affari Esteri, 1946), pp. 2–4.

Known as the De Gasperi–Gruber Accord, it became Annex IV of the final peace treaty. Ambiguities in the language, put in to help Foreign Minister Karl Gruber make it acceptable to the Austrians, however reluctantly, as well as disputes over its subsequent application by Italy, would lead to a revival of conflict in the area in the 1950's and 1960's. The conflict would be accompanied by acts of terrorism on the part of South Tyrolese extremists and severe repression on the part of Italian authorities.

The Italian positions on Trieste and the South Tyrol were completely contradictory. The arguments used in one case refuted the arguments used in the other. Aware of this, the Italians did not call for a plebiscite as a suitable means of resolving conflicting territorial claims in Venezia Giulia until after the South Tyrol agreement had been reached, in order to avoid justifying the Austrian request for a plebiscite in the province of Bolzano. The logic of Italy's position lay in its ambition to hold fast to all it could reasonably save. It was more powerful vis-à-vis Austria than a vis-à-vis France or Yugoslavia, so the Austrians lost their claim. From the Allied point of view, the South Tyrol was a compensation for some of the losses Italy was required to suffer elsewhere.

In the colonies, Italy's losses were practically total. All of its colonies were taken away from it. This, however, may have been the best thing that happened to Italy in the postwar period. When the agonies of the liquidation of the French, British, and other overseas empires are recalled, the Italians may be considered fortunate to have escaped them. In 1945 and 1946, however, no Italian government (and no other colonial power) saw the situation in this light. Although Italy's colonies had been an economic and financial drain on the limited resources of a chronically poor country, all efforts were made to hang on to them.

The Italians made a distinction between those colonies acquired before Fascism and those acquired by Mussolini. As early as August, 1944, Count Sforza had announced that Italy renounced the Fascist acquisitions of Albania and Ethiopia and would give the Dodecanese to Greece. He stated that Italy would claim the pre-Fascist colonies, however, unless other colonial powers turned over their colonies to an international organization. One year later, August, 1945, in his letter to United States Secretary of State James Byrnes, Foreign Minister Alcide De-Gasperi again claimed the pre-Fascist colonies of Eritrea, Italian Somaliland, and Libya, preferably under direct Italian sovereignty, but at least as trusteeships. He was ready to grant England strategic bases in Libya and to rectify the Eritrean frontier to provide Ethiopia with an outlet to the sea. His main argument was that the colonies were necessary to relieve Italy's surplus population, although they had failed miserably in this function in preceding decades.

England was unalterably opposed to the return of the colonies to Italy and had committed itself on this issue to various African chiefs, especially in Libya. Nor were the Russians and the Americans much more favorably disposed. Only France was on Italy's side, for fear of the repercussions on its own colonial system. The victorious Allies could not agree on how to dispose of the colonies, however, and the peace treaty took them away from Italy without a definitive solution. The United Nations General Assembly wrestled with the problem for several years. During those years, Italy pleaded, negotiated, and bargained in order to regain control of them and finally a piecemeal solution was reached. The U.N. turned Eritrea over to Ethiopia, Libya was given independence under British sponsorship, advice, and assistance, and Somaliland was granted to Italy as a United Nations trusteeship for ten years. For that decade, Italy continued to pour some of its limited resources into Somaliland's desolate and economically backward land, and in return received only trouble, scandal, and inferior bananas.[8]

The long-drawn-out colonial struggle, to a considerable extent a question of *amour-propre* for Italy, had negative repercussions on domestic Italian politics. Like the Trieste boundary settlement, it provided opportunities for nationalist, monarchist, and neo-Fascist attacks on the government and on Italy's Western

---

[8] The Italian banana monopoly later became the object of Italian judicial and parliamentary investigation for corruption and was abolished on January 1, 1965.

allies. It was the shortsightedness of the Italian Government in pursuing an unworthy and futile cause which opened it to these attacks. Even the Communists were able to parade as patriotic Italian nationalists once Russia abandoned its efforts to get a trusteeship for Tripolitania (part of Italian Libya). Unlike Trieste, however, there was little evidence that the colonies had any deeply felt meaning for the great masses of the peasants and workers, the inhabitants of rural and small-town Italy. The hullabaloo in Italy was due mainly to the exploitation of the issue by former colonial officials, political opportunists, and sufferers from nostalgia.

The commitment of the United States and Britain in September, 1944, to the postwar rehabilitation of the Italian economy logically implied the renunciation of demands for reparation as a part of the peace settlement. In 1945, the United States, Britain, and France formally renounced reparation claims. The Soviet Union and other, smaller victims of Fascist aggression—Yugoslavia, Greece, Albania, and Ethiopia—persisted, however, in demanding economic reparation for damage suffered.

Italy did not argue against the principle of reparation payments, for it had its own claims against Germany for damage sustained after September, 1943. It argued that its economic contribution to the war against the Nazis, and the economic damage suffered after September, 1943, valued at $5,543,900,000 and $13,-462,200,000 respectively, should be accepted as a more than adequate economic contribution to the war. It pointed out, in addition, that a reconstruction and rehabilitation program could only be hindered by a requirement to make financial reparation, whether in money or goods and services.

Neither American pressure nor Italian arguments moved the Soviet Union and the other claimants. The final peace treaty imposed a bill on Italy of $5 million to Albania, $25 million to Ethiopia, $100 million to Russia, $105 million to Greece, and $125 million to Yugoslavia. The U.S.S.R. was allowed to seize Italian assets in Hungary, Bulgaria, and Rumania as part payment. (Italy would have lost these assets in any case, because of the nationalization policies followed by Eastern European countries in the postwar period.) In effect, the United States paid the Italian reparation bills through its postwar loans, grants, and gifts to Italy.

In addition to the reparation payments, the peace treaty granted the victors the right to confiscate Italian property in their own countries as compensation for the claims of their private citizens for property damage and unpaid debts. Britain, the United States, and France did not confiscate the property of Italian nationals permanently resident on their own soil. They waived the right to confiscate foreign assets of Italian individuals and firms resident in Italy by accepting flat payments from the Italian Government: $5 million to the United States and 15 billion lire to France, while Britain settled for the payment of debts owed by Italians to private persons and firms in the United Kingdom. The Italian Government paid the debts and then had the difficult job of collecting from the Italian debtors. As a result, all Italian assets abroad were saved, except those in Ethiopia and Eastern Europe.

Italy's claim to reparation from Germany was rejected. The Germans had seized Italy's entire gold reserve, and though it was recaptured by the Allies intact, Italy was forced to accept, instead of full restitution, a proportionate share of the total gold stolen by the Nazis from all occupied countries.

On the whole, the financial burden imposed on Italy by the peace settlement was moderate, and as mentioned above, it was largely borne by the United States. It is true that Italy indirectly made a substantial economic contribution to the Allies by bearing the burden of domestic inflation caused partly by the expenditure of Allied military lire inside the country. Again, the United States gave Italy a credit for some of these lire spent by American servicemen on Italian soil during the war.

The last major issue of the peace settlement was disarmament and demilitarization. The Allies were in unanimous agreement that the size of the postwar Italian armed forces was to be strictly limited to the minimum required for the local defense of the boundaries and for maintenance of domestic law and order.

Italian claims as to the number of the armed manpower necessary for effective defense were based on the general principles that a nation's power had to be relative to the power of its neighbors and that, therefore, no final figures could ever be established as to the "adequate" number of a country's armed manpower. Italy presented some provisional figures on the proposed size of its Army and asked to be permitted to retain whatever of its Navy and Air Force it had left. The Navy was a crucial issue: next to the boundary questions, it touched the sentiments and hearts of the Italian people. The Italians argued correctly that the remnants of the Navy had not surrendered in September, 1943, but had passed to the side of the Allies with flags flying: the Navy was not available for disposal.

These Italian arguments carried no weight. The major Allies had already agreed at the Teheran Conference to take the Italian Navy; and the peace treaty left Italy with two old battleships, four cruisers, four destroyers, sixteen torpedo boats, and twenty corvettes. Italy was forbidden in the future to build or buy battleships, aircraft carriers, and submarines. Personnel was to be limited to 25,000 men. The Army was limited to 250,000 men, including the Carabinieri (part of the domestic police force in peacetime). The Air Force was limited to 200 combat and 150 noncombat planes, bombers were prohibited, and personnel was limited to 25,000. Italy was required to destroy all fixed fortifications within twenty kilometers of its boundaries with France and Yugoslavia, and was prohibited from constructing new ones that could fire on these nations or their territorial waters. With the boundary changes that have already been mentioned, which eliminated the natural defenses of the mountain barriers, Italy was left vulnerable to invasion by land.

In addition, Italy was prohibited from constructing military installations on the Apulian coast, opposite Yugoslavia, Albania, and Greece. The coasts of Sicily and Sardinia were to be unfortified, and smaller islands, such as the base of Pantelleria, were to be demilitarized. Thus Italy was left vulnerable to invasion by sea. Since the British had been dominant in the Mediterranean in the past, and erroneously expected to be dominant in the future, the demilitarization of the Italian coastlines was conceived as an integral part of British postwar strategy for the reassertion of a pre-eminent role in that part of the world.

The Americans and the British later returned their share of the Italian fleet to Italy for scrap, as they had surplus vessels of their own. The gesture was received gratefully. France returned some of its spoils, but kept its best acquisitions. Greece, Yugoslavia and Russia returned nothing.

De Gasperi did not hesitate to point out to the peace conference that in its efforts to guard against future Italian aggression, it was leaving Italy defenseless. But the whole postwar balance of power was so changed that Italy could no longer be considered even nominally a first-class power. Any probable future aggression by Italy would most likely be part of a larger struggle; and the same could be said for any future attack against it.

For Italy was dependent on others for its security. American troops remained in occupation until the peace treaty was ratified by the victors in the autumn of 1947. And at the time of their withdrawal, President Truman publicly warned that the United States would not be indifferent to any threat to Italy's security. Two years later, Italy was a member of the North Atlantic Treaty Organization. Its allies then attempted to get the Soviet Union to agree to a revision of the clauses on armament, but the Russians demanded the exodus of Italy from NATO as their price for consenting to revision. At the peak of the Cold War, the Italian Government claimed that the Soviet refusal to approve Italy's admission to the United Nations justified Italy's escape from the obligations of the peace treaty. Thus, on February 8, 1952, Italy announced its intention to rearm beyond the treaty limitations. It was so economically and politically weak, however, that its rearmament was dependent on external—primarily American—military aid, which had already begun and which was continuing a decade and a half later.

The peace treaty was not finally signed until February 10, 1947, and not ratified until the autumn of that year. During the two years that had elapsed between the end of hostilities and the completion of the treaty, Italy's international position had changed drastically. In September, 1945, in his first appearance before the Council of Foreign Ministers, De Gasperi had entered a hall filled with hostility and rancor. Only Secretary of State Byrnes demonstrated any kindliness toward him. Memories of Fascist aggression were still sharp among Europeans and Africans. By 1947, the emerging Cold War and the internal Italian vulnerability to the extreme left had changed the international picture. Although England was still wavering between a policy of keeping Italy weak and therefore less of a threat in the Mediterranean and a policy of bolstering Italy the better to enable it to resist internal and external pressures, France and the United States were firmly engaged in rebuilding Italy's international position. France was negotiating with Italy for an alliance and a customs union. The United States, with French help, was putting pressure on a reluctant England to accept Italian membership in the European Recovery Program (the Marshall Plan).

Italy had remained officially neutral in the Cold War for the duration of the peace-treaty negotiations. It could not afford to antagonize any of the powerful victors. Unofficially, of course, most Italians sympathized with the West (except for the extreme left), although there was considerable resentment at the hard British position. And Italy was fundamentally dependent on American good will.

The peace treaty was accepted with considerable bitterness by Italian anti-Fascists. They felt that they had staked not only their personal futures but, more importantly, the political future of the country on collaboration with the Allies, who had then let them down. When the treaty was presented to the Italian Government for signature, there were voices raised against signing it. The United States, however, warned the government that economic aid would be cut off if it did not sign. When it was presented to the Constituent Assembly for ratification, distinguished anti-Fascists—such as the philosopher Benedetto Croce and the pre-Fascist Prime Minister Francesco S. Nitti—denounced its harshness. But Italy had no choice. It ratified, protesting that the treaty was unduly harsh, that it did not take into account the anti-Fascist resurgence of the Italian people or their contributions to the final struggle against Germany. It ratified, to enable it to be present at the Marshall Plan Conference of July, 1947, to bring an end to the occupation, to finish off a dark chapter in the history of modern Italy.

2
POLITICAL AND
ECONOMIC REVIVAL

Political parties suppressed by Fascism had been gradually reforming, and new ones developing, even before the overthrow of
Mussolini. Although they were still illegal in the summer of 1943,
the Badoglio government of technicians had made no effort to
suppress them. On the contrary, it had maintained informal contacts with the principal party leaders and had released political
prisoners of Fascism. After September 8, 1943, the parties in central and northern Italy were forced again into the underground.
Behind the Anglo-American lines in the south, however, although
still technically illegal, they were actually in open operation and
engaged in recruitment and discussions, held congresses, and
formed ranks. The top leadership was composed of older men
who had been active in the pre-Fascist period. Beneath them was
a group of younger men, products of the Italian universities of the
1930's and 1940's who threw themselves into the struggle to build
a new and better world.

Although no elections were held, it was apparent, even in this
early period, that the principal postwar parties would be the
Christian Democratic, Communist, and Socialist parties. The
Action Party had a brilliant intellectual leadership, but no mass
base. The Liberal Party mainly comprised the old notables of
pre-Fascist days. The southern Liberals in particular had long
since been cut off from contact with the emerging world of workers and peasants who were indifferent to upper-class nineteenth-

century paternal benevolence. Thus the party, again especially in the south, became an elite party representing the powerful landowners and the respectable practitioners of the free professions.

The Socialist and Popular parties had been the two largest parties in the final years of the pre-Fascist period. Fascism hurt the Socialists badly; they had neither the skills and techniques to survive in the underground nor the protection of the Vatican. As the earliest of the mass parties, however, they had a long, solid tradition on which they could hope to build in the post-Fascist future.

The Communist Party, founded in 1921 as an extreme left-wing splinter of the Socialists, had only a few years to develop before the Fascists outlawed all competing parties. It was able to survive by going underground, nevertheless, and in spite of some splits among its leaders inside Italy and in exile, it emerged in 1943 with a small but very tight base in the industrial cities and in the countryside of central and northern Italy. From about 10,000 adherents in 1943, it grew to a membership of 400,000 card-carrying Communists by the beginning of 1945. Skillfully organized and adequately financed, the Party rapidly established an elaborate system of sections and cells throughout the whole country. Within a few years, this communications network made the Italian Communist Party the largest Communist Party in the Western world.

The Christian Democratic Party emerged after the fall of Fascism as the successor to the old Popular Party, which had been founded in 1919 by the Sicilian priest Don Luigi Sturzo. During the 1920's, the Vatican had sacrificed both the party and Don Sturzo in order to come to terms with Fascism. Some of the leaders, Don Sturzo included, went into exile. Others found asylum and protection in the Vatican, where Alcide De Gasperi, for example, worked as a librarian. A small core of Christian Democrats continued to exist in Italy under Church patronage, in case the situation changed and there might be a role for them once more. A younger group found opportunities for organizational experience in the youth and adult groups of the Italian Catholic Action Society, a lay organization under Church direction. When Fascism fell, these men were ready to step into the political world, and would, in fact, furnish a large share of the party's cadres.

Even in its early years, the Popular Party had been a collection of disparate groups with widely differing orientations. Only a common confessional bond and Catholic Church discipline held them together, and schism even then was potentially present. But under Don Sturzo's direction, the Popular Party had a predominantly progressive and reformist policy and had succeeded in bringing large numbers of Catholic rural and village men into the Italian political arena, from which they had been excluded in the past both by the Liberals' upper-class disdain and by Vatican prohibitions. It is true that, like the Socialists, the Populists brought their masses into the political arena only as voters, not as activists, for politics then, as now, was a game for a "ruling class" that manipulated the large masses.

After 1943, the Christian Democrats retained this disparate agglomeration of supporters who ranged from left to right, from radical workers to conservative landowners and industrialists. The conservative elements, however, were far more prominent, for the fear of postwar left-wing extremism had led the formerly laic and liberal middle and upper classes to turn to the Church and to the party identified with it as their best defense. The Church, like the monarchy, symbolized authority, order, and stability, all seriously menaced; but the Church, unlike the monarchy, was not too incriminated in the Fascist catastrophe, and was, moreover, in a far better position to survive it. So the Christian Democratic Party had not only a large popular base demanding postwar progress and substantial reform but also important lay and clerical influences, fearful of radical innovation and concerned mainly with stabilization and restoration. In addition the party was weak in organization and communications; it would have to depend on the network of Catholic parishes spread throughout Italy to reach its electorate, and upon the efforts of the parish priests and diocesan bishops to mobilize money, activists, and voters.

A simplified description of Italy at the end of hostilities would therefore seem to be that of a country caught in a struggle between the forces of revolution and those of restoration. In May and June of 1945, superficial appearances indicated the victory of revolution. The liberation of the Po Valley unleashed upon the country the "wind from the north," and the wind appeared to be blowing from the far left. The danger of direct revolutionary action having been minimized, the question became: Could the forces of revolution gain their ends through party and political maneuvers and economic seizures?

Partisan bands had taken over many of the factories and plants in the north, Italy's major industrial area. In numerous cases the management was expelled on grounds of collaboration with the Nazi occupiers and Il Duce's Fascist Social Republic. Factory councils were set up to operate the firms. This was a *de facto* purge, but one conducted with relative restraint. Managers and owners with clean records were members of the councils and active in plant administration. Nevertheless, the threat to private property and capitalistic ownership was evident.[1]

The threat was further magnified by the financial purge attempted by the central government to punish those who had profited from Fascism. All of Italian big business was potentially vulnerable, for large firms had been a principal beneficiary of Fascist economic policy. In addition, in November, 1945, the government drew up a new economic plan that called for a capital levy and a discriminatory allocation of raw materials, both of which favored small firms rather than the large trusts. The purge, the levy, and the allocations were part of a twofold objective: economic reconstruction and the redistribution of wealth.

Resistance to these economic operations was both internal and external. Right-wing Liberals and conservative Christian Democrats considered them an attack on the economic structure of society. Allied occupation officials (the Allied Military Government was still in control in the north) considered them in the same light, and also as a substantial hindrance to the rehabilitation of the economy. The Economic Section of the Allied Commission threatened to withhold coal and other raw materials unless they were used efficiently. The argument of efficiency was used to break the factory councils and restore former managers. Allied

---

[1] Riccardo Levi, "L'azione economica e sociale dei CLN dell' alta Italia," *Il Ponte*, November–December, 1947, pp. 994–1000.

officers protested against the capital levy and the allocation policy that were aimed at redistributing the wealth.[2]

The government in power at the time was led by Ferruccio Parri, Action Party leader and partisan hero. He had become Prime Minister in June, 1945, not because of his party's strength, but as a compromise between the competing candidacies of Alcide De Gasperi and Pietro Nenni, leader of the Socialist Party. Nenni represented the wing of his party advocating close unity of action with the Communists.[3] He believed that divisions among the left had been responsible for the past victories of Fascism and Nazism and that the workers could not afford to be divided in the future if the triumph of reaction were to be prevented. This outlook, however sincere, would make the Socialists vulnerable to Communist strategy. Naturally, neither the Allies nor the conservative forces in the Italian Government could look to a Nenni victory with equanimity. The Christian Democrats imposed an effective veto, but failing to get the prime ministry for their own candidate, they consented to the Parri compromise. All six parties of the Committee of National Liberation participated in Parri's cabinet.

The Allied Military Government blocked the CLN committees in northern Italy from taking over provincial and communal governments. Local officials were appointed by Allied Commissioners. Many of them were CLN leaders, but their authority came from the Allied occupation officials, not from the CLN committees. Thus the northern attempt for a degree of autonomy and independence from domination by Rome was thwarted.

The negotiations to form the Parri cabinet had taken so long that the spirit of revolt attendant on the liberation of the north was quickly diluted. In the autumn of 1945, a miasma of doubt, hesitation, and disillusion settled over the country. The conferences for a peace settlement were going badly, and Italian political leaders were being made aware of what was in store for the country. Economic reconstruction, dependent on always insufficient external supplies, was limping along. Inflation was rampant.

---

2 *Economist* (London), November 24, 1945, p. 752.

3 The party's full name was the Italian Socialist Party of Proletarian Unity.

Food was in short supply. The parties and the government seemed to be bogged down in conflicts and maneuvers which had little relevance to the needs of the vast majority of the population. Law and order were difficult to enforce. Fear and hostility were widespread.

In this atmosphere, it was not surprising that there emerged political movements of a turbid and negative nature. Separatist organizations had begun to operate in Sardinia and especially Sicily after the liberation of these two major islands of Italy. Conservative and reactionary forces feared that radicals would take over the central government on the mainland. The more substantial landowners believed they could better protect their holdings by separation. Although in 1944 the Americans and British had both repudiated the separatists' claims of Allied support,[4] the agitation nevertheless continued. Its peak was reached in the immediate postwar period.

Another development of concern was the ambiguous movement called Uomo Qualunque (Any Man), led by the journalist Guglielmo Giannini. It was a party that attacked all parties, a reaction against the complications, hesitations, compromises, and problems of a struggling party system. Its point of view was, "Down with politicians—Down with talk," and it was able to find support in the difficult postwar years when everything appeared to be going wrong.

A major issue to be resolved was the disposition of the monarchy, or, as the Italians called it, the Institutional Question. The truce established in April, 1944, had provided that King Victor Emmanuel III would nominate his son, Humbert, as Lieutenant-General of the Realm, retiring then to private life, and that at the end of the war, the people would have the opportunity to decide their form of political organization, monarchy or republic. When the Allies occupied Rome in 1944, the American Government had insisted that Victor Emmanuel live up to his pledge before returning to his capital. Humbert had, in subsequent months,

---

[4] Alleged British complicity with the separatist movements was based on an assumption that the British policy of keeping Italy weak and of dominating the Mediterranean would be advanced through creating new states tied to England by treaties and, perhaps, the granting of bases.

played a formally correct role, but had tried to use the various crises of the CLN to insert conservative forces and personages outside that group into the political arena.

The end of the war had brought a tremendous surge of republican enthusiasm, especially in the north, where the King's flight from Rome was bitterly remembered. As time passed, however, and all the troubles and difficulties had wrought their influence on the evolution of opinion, monarchist sentiment revived. The parties committed to republicanism, mainly on the left, wanted to settle the issue as quickly as possible, while the public mood was still in their favor. The monarchists, conversely, wanted to delay the decision, hoping that the passage of time would work to their benefit and that the influence of authority and tradition would increase as the shock of the war receded into the background.

Within the cabinet, the Christian Democratic and Liberal leaders represented divided parties, containing both monarchists and republicans in their ranks. The Action, Socialist, and Communist parties were decisively republican, although the Communists would have had no hesitation in supporting a king, as long as he might be useful to their game. During the war, in fact, Palmiro Togliatti had backed both Victor Emmanuel and Marshal Badoglio. Prime Minister Parri's drive to get a constituent assembly elected to settle the issue and to draft a new constitution, in combination with the economic plan of November, 1945, led to an open attack on the government by conservative Liberal leaders of the south. The Liberal cabinet ministers resigned. Although northern Liberals came to Parri's defense, the Christian Democrats saw their opportunity to get the prime ministry they had wanted the previous May. Then the Communists, interested in making a deal with the Catholics (both the Church and the Christian Democratic Party), shifted their support. Parri's government fell.

In December, 1945, a new six-party cabinet was formed with Alcide De Gasperi as Prime Minister. But the internal equilibrium of the cabinet had definitely shifted to the right. De Gasperi was not personally a conservative, but powerful pressures from within his own party and from the Church forced him to move in that direction. The British and the Americans, concerned over the power of the extreme left, were eager to reinforce his position. The day after the new cabinet was formed, they announced that at the end of December, the north—still under Allied Military Government supervision—would be turned back to the control of the Italian Government. Exclusion from the north had been one of the weaknesses in the position of De Gasperi's predecessor.

A few days later, De Gasperi announced that officials such as career prefects and police chiefs would replace CLN appointees as of January 1, 1946. At the same time, he proclaimed that the High Commission for Sanctions Against Fascism would be dissolved not later than March 31, 1946. Its functions would be turned over to the courts, and these were manned by judges who, for the most part, had been in office during the period of Fascism. The speed with which a restoration was accomplished was remarkable.

It must be remembered, however, that it was not a simple restoration of Fascism. If it is true that most of the business leaders, military and civil bureaucrats, professors, and journalists who regained or maintained their posts had worked or made careers under Fascism, it is also true that most of them were hardly dyed-in-the-wool Fascists. Many were half-Fascists, opportunists who held party cards to get ahead, or ordinary professionals who had to take out party cards in order to keep their positions. A number of them had always remained anti-Fascist; others saved their honor by their contributions to the overthrow of the regime and to the resistance movement. The catastrophe which Fascism brought on Italy shook many of them to the core. All of them, however, whether true converts or opportunists, could thank the Christian Democrats for saving them from a purge, and De Gasperi's party was the principal beneficiary of their gratitude.

Not the only one, however. The extreme left was also willing to accept former Fascists. As Minister of Justice, Togliatti would later be responsible for promoting a widespread amnesty for political prisoners, and the Communist Party would have some success in attracting ex-Fascists, intellectuals, and trade-unionists. Except for the top-ranking Fascist hierarchs, most of those who had made careers under Fascism found that there was still a future for them.

The new De Gasperi government also made dispositions to settle the problem of the monarchy. The decisions reflected the predominance of conservative influence. The Liberals had not been the only party working for delay. Leaders of both the Christian Democratic and the Labor Democratic parties (the Labor Democrats were nonexistent in the north and minimal in the south) played the monarchist game. They proposed that local elections be held first, to postpone settlement of the Institutional Question. Officially, the Allies were neutral, unofficially they supported the monarchy, the British more strongly than the Americans.[5] Administrative (communal and provincial) elections were scheduled for the spring of 1946, while the political election was postponed to June 2, 1946. The final choice was to be left to the people in the form of a referendum, to be held at the same time that the Constituent Assembly would be elected to draft a new constitution for either a republic or a monarchy. The left-wing parties had wanted the Constituent Assembly to make the decision. Women would be voting for the first time in the history of Italy, and the parties of the left feared the traditionalist outlook of Italian women, almost always attracted to the panoply and social snobbery of monarchy and aristocracy, and generally susceptible to the influence of the priests. And it was becoming ever more obvious that the Church was in large part promonarchist.

In another decision, the cabinet decreed that since the negotiations for a peace settlement were in progress, the Constituent Assembly would be restricted to drafting a constitution, elaborating election laws, and ratifying treaties. The left-wing parties had wanted the Assembly to function as a parliament also, establishing and supporting a government, passing laws, appropriating funds, and carrying on all the functions of a legislature. If such a body had a left-wing majority, major reforms could be enacted before a constitution came into effect. But in a multiparty cabinet not dependent on a parliamentary majority and ruling instead by

---

5 De Gasperi claimed that the United States wanted the local elections to be held first to insure the establishment of democracy in the towns and villages.

decree, the conservatives could, in effect, defeat any attempt at reform.

The administrative election returns showed the Christian Democratic, Communist, and Socialist parties to be the three largest, as had been suspected all along. The last two were definitely republican. A poll of Christian Democratic Party cardholders in April, 1946, found 73 per cent to be republican. This poll represented a sample of party activists—the most politically conscious party workers—not the large masses of Christian Democratic voters who held no party cards, were rural, female, or generally apolitical. Nevertheless, the reviving monarchist forces were panic-stricken. They bombarded the Allied Commission with pleas to postpone the referendum. The Allied Commission refused: it had not set the date, the cabinet had. The monarchists persuaded King Victor Emmanuel III to abdicate on May 10, 1946, in favor of his son, who became Humbert II. The left charged that the Institutional truce that had established the Lieutenancy in 1944 was thus violated. It, too, appealed to the Allied Commission, which refused to intervene.

The Church was openly enlisted in the monarchist cause. The Vatican remained neutral, but the Italian clergy intervened, which they had a right to do as citizens, but not as priests. The issue was shifted from Monarchy *vs.* Republic to Monarchy *vs.* Communism, to Christianity *vs.* Communism. On June 1, 1946, the day before the referendum, Pope Pius XII himself addressed the Italian people. Without mentioning republic or monarchy, he called on the voters to choose between materialism and Christianity, between the supporters and the enemies of Christian civilization.[6] Given the context of the campaign, it would be difficult to misunderstand the plea.

The following day, the referendum and elections revealed the wide divisions in the population. The republic was endorsed by a ratio of 54 per cent to 46 per cent, 12,717,923 votes to 10,719,284, but the south had given its strong support to the monarchist cause, and only in the center and north had the republic gained substantial backing. For a few days, Humbert appeared ready to

_____
[6] The English translation of the text appears in the *New York Times,* June 2, 1946.

plunge the country into a crisis of the first order by claiming procedural irregularities in the voting. But he could get no support from the Allied Commission, and Prime Minister De Gasperi told him to go. The threat collapsed and Humbert, King for three weeks, left for exile in Portugal. Thus the House of Savoy paid for the errors committed by Victor Emmanuel III between 1922 and 1946.

The big monarchist vote did not mean that large masses of the population were true legitimists. Any possibility of a restoration of the House of Savoy quickly disappeared, and within a few years, except to nostalgic members of the upper class and impressionable middle-class women, the idea of a return to monarchy seemed extremely remote. A monarchist party would run candidates for office with substantial success in Naples, and it would even expand its voting base in the early 1950's, but the foundation of the party's strength was a combination of the corruption of the poverty-stricken southern subproletariat and the retaliatory bitterness against the center and north. It became, in part, another protest party, and to some degree a calculating seller of support to the Christian Democrats in return for patronage and favors.

The election of members to the Constituent Assembly verified the previous electoral indications. The Christian Democrats received 35.1 per cent of the vote, the Socialists 20.7 per cent, and the Communists 18.9 per cent. None of the others received as much as 10 per cent. The Liberals, who had a long pre-Fascist tradition of rule, were reduced to 6.8 per cent of the vote. The Action Party, which had played a noble role in the resistance, was again shown to have no mass base. It had suffered a preliminary split in February, and a short time after the election it dissolved, its members entering other parties of the center and left. Uomo Qualunque, fundamentally Fascist in tone, attained minor representation, receiving a small but visible 5.3 per cent of the vote.

Thus was the Institutional Question resolved. The trend toward restoration that was operative in Italian society had not saved the monarchy. The Fascist inheritance was not so much the political organization that would be re-created to glorify Fascism's tarnished image as it was the mentality of autocratic disdain for equalitarian principles, the contempt for parliamentary institutions, and the subservience to hierarchy that was still prevalent among large parts of the populace who did not vote for Uomo Qualunque. But these persistent attitudes derived from centuries-old traditions that even the liberalizing movements of the Risorgimento had failed to destroy.

The Constituent Assembly was racked by the varying pressures for economic and social reform and the strong resistance offered by powerful forces of moderation and conservation. The Constitution it produced, reflecting these countervailing forces, contained a mixture of Marxist, Catholic, and Liberal doctrines. It went into effect on January 1, 1948, with its bundle of compromises.[7] Obeisance was made to the principle of private property and, at the same time, to the principle of social and political controls over the economy. In effect, the document sanctioned the mixed economy actually in existence in the country. Along with articles guaranteeing the basic freedoms of thought, speech, and writing were articles permitting censorship. An article guaranteeing freedom of religion was juxtaposed with the famous Article 7, in which the Lateran Pacts of 1929 were, in effect, written into the Constitution. These pacts gave the Roman Catholic Church a privileged position in the life of the country, the state, and public education. Communist votes were crucial in getting Article 7 through the Constituent Assembly. While provisions were made for the maintenance of the centralized Italian state, other provisions aimed at creating a decentralized system of considerable regional autonomy.

Some of the articles of the Constitution were normative; they would become legally binding automatically. Others were programmatic, expressing hopes for the future. An example is Article 4, which proclaimed, in face of mass unemployment (that would continue for a decade), the right of all citizens to work. Many of the articles could be made effective only by implemental legislation, which was often long delayed. Some fundamental organs of the state that were created by the Constitution took years to become established. The Constitutional Court did not come into

---

[7] An English translation can be found in Norman Kogan, *The Government of Italy* (New York: Thomas Y. Crowell Co., 1962), pp. 188–215.

existence until 1955, and the Superior Council of the Judiciary not until 1958. In 1965, the regular regions had yet to be created,[8] and the legislation to establish procedures for holding referenda had yet to be passed.

That a constitution was drafted at all was due to the fact that the second and third largest groups in the Constituent Assembly, the Socialists and the Communists, took a relatively moderate position on crucial economic and religious issues. Neither of them pushed for a socialized economy. Pietro Nenni argued merely for social control of economic activity, to be exercised in a democratic, decentralized, and efficient manner. Togliatti's position was that "the Constitution is not a Socialist constitution but represents a transition period in which there exists a struggle for an economic regime in which there exist economic forces that tend to spill over into each other."[9] In spite of a powerful left in the Constituent Assembly, including part of the Christian Democratic Party itself, the Constitution was not even a very reformist document. What can be said is that it did not prevent reform in the future. A judgment of the work of the Constituent Assembly was expressed by the ideological leader of the left-wing Christian Democrats, Giuseppe Dossetti:[10] "In just a few short months, the propulsion toward reform was contained. And in a few years, progressively compressed up to the point of being practically wiped out for now."[11]

De Gasperi was primarily concerned with re-creating the political institutions of democracy, halting the drastic inflation, and reviving, not changing, the economy. This meant reviving existing businesses and economic organizations. Power over the key industries was concentrated in the hands of a few powerful individuals and groups, whether ownership was public or private. To accomplish revival, foreign help was indispensable, and this was mainly available from the United States, which itself had no

---

[8] Special regions to accommodate linguistic minorities or separatist movements were established early. Trentino–Alto Adige, Val d'Aosta, Sicily, and Sardinia.

[9] Quoted in Joseph LaPalombara, "The Politics of Economic Planning in Italy" (mimeographed essay, 1964), p. 25.

[10] He later abandoned politics for the priesthood.

[11] Quoted in LaPalombara, op. cit., pp. 25–26.

fondness for left-wing economic doctrines. At the end of hostilities in Italy, a joint Allied-Italian program had been drafted. Relief supplies were provided by the Allied forces as a military responsibility while the war against Japan was still in progress. These were cut off after the Japanese surrender in September, 1945, but the American Government granted a substitute credit of $100 million for the acquisition of food and other relief supplies from the United States. Rehabilitation of the economy was to be borne initially by the Italian Government with dollars acquired from the lire spent by American troops in Italy, from emigrants' remittances, and from the small amount of exports Italy could send to the United States. The restoration of the communications and transportation systems had been partly achieved by the Allies during the war; afterward, Italy was able to get the Allied war surplus located on its soil, principally port machinery and railroad equipment. In June, 1945, Italy received permission to trade with Allied and neutral countries. This consent was meaningless until the end of the year, when the Allies gave up control of the north, the principal commercial and trading area.

Financial claims were settled between Italy and the British and American governments in the following years. In October, 1946, the United States granted a credit for the lire spent by American governmental agencies in the purchase of supplies in Italy, and waived charges for the supplies it had brought in during the war to keep the population alive. In January, 1947, De Gasperi came to America and arranged for a major loan. In April, 1947, the United Kingdom credited to Italy the value of lire spent by British forces in the peninsula after June 1, 1946, and of all services and supplies furnished by Italy to British forces after that date. Italy paid for British military equipment transferred to its forces and for the war surplus that the British had left in the course of their war operations. All in all, between 1943 and 1947, foreign aid totaled approximately $2 billion, of which almost $1.75 billion came from the United States.[12]

In spite of the weakness of the Italian Government and its dis-

---

[12] Bruno Foa, *Monetary Reconstruction in Italy* (New York: King's Crown Press, 1949), p. 35.

integrated public administration, certain kinds of rehabilitation were handled very quickly and effectively. Within a few months after the end of hostilities, essential services had been restored throughout the country. Italian hard work and Allied equipment got roads, bridges, harbors, railroads, and utilities into operating order, and by the end of 1945, it was again possible to move by rail and road from one end of the peninsula to the other. Railroad rolling stock, trucks, and merchant marine were badly wrecked and would take much longer to replace. In contrast to transportation and communications facilities, the Italian industrial plant survived the war without extensive damage. The textile industries were among those to get back into full action most quickly, while heavier industries—dependent on large-scale imports of foreign coal and other raw materials—took longer.

Revival of the economy was left essentially to the operations of a system of laissez faire. This was congenial to the outlook of the postwar Minister of the Treasury Epicarmo Corbino, a Liberal in politics and economics. Nor did the left-wing Marxist parties make any serious demands for a reconstruction based on controls and allocations, such as the Labor government was executing in England. They limited their drive for drastic reforms to the verbal level. They used their positions in the government to gain some concessions, such as sliding wage scales designed to help workers keep up with the declining value of the lira. They obtained the freezing of industrial employment. This latter policy, which was in essence a way of hiding the real unemployment in the country, had the consequence of making production costs very high. Another high-cost factor—the obsolescence and expensiveness of many traditionally protected machine industries—further reduced Italy's competitiveness in foreign markets. In effect, agreement was reached on a practical, if not openly stated, compromise that gave Italy a period of relative social peace.

The laissez faire policy actually pursued, which imitated American postwar decontrol measures, aggravated an already drastic inflation. The lira had been declining throughout the war, and fell even faster after hostilities ended. No real attempts were made to reintroduce rationing except for some basic foodstuffs, such as bread, sugar, and olive oil. A black market was in widespread operation, and the rationing system was progressively slackened to the point of losing almost all effectiveness.

Fundamentally, the wartime and postwar inflation was due to the drastic drop in production. In 1945, industrial production was 23 per cent of the last prewar year, 1938. Agricultural production was dislocated. Fertilizers and machinery were lacking. The wheat harvest in 1945/46 was only half of the normal requirement, and extensive hoarding and maldistribution aggravated the shortage. The people in the cities suffered terribly. But inflation was due also to the huge amount of currency in circulation, much of it the lire of the Allied Military Government. Even though the United States eventually gave the Italians credit for American expenditures of such lire, the fundamental solution to inflation was, of course, to increase the supply of goods and services and to reduce the supply of money in circulation. "By the midsummer of 1947, the extreme shortages of coal and other key materials had, to a large extent, disappeared and all-around recovery of production was well on its way."[13] But the currency and credit crises were coming to a peak.

The official exchange rate of 100 lire to the dollar and 400 to the pound sterling, established at the end of the war, had long since become obsolete. In early 1946, the government was permitting exporters and importers to use a special rate of 225 lire to the dollar. While limited, this permission drove the official rate out of effective use by the end of 1946. Black-market rates for foreign currencies were even higher, because of demand by importers capable of making exorbitant profits and because of a capital flight caused by wealthy businessmen who were fearful of possible radical socialization at home. The government, however, declined to practice open devaluation for fear of psychological and political repercussions. In 1946, exporters were permitted to use 50 per cent of the foreign exchange they acquired on the free market instead of turning all their foreign currencies over to the exchange-control authorities. This further reduced the unofficial value of the lira. By early 1947, Italian prices had become so high on the international market that the remarkable recovery of the

13 *Ibid.*, pp. 46–47.

export trade came to an end. Furthermore, the sterling crisis of August, 1947, tied up Italian sterling balances and depressed international purchasing power. Since a good share of Italian exports went to the sterling market, the repercussions in Italy were sizable.

The amount of money in circulation inside Italy (and probably also its turnover) had been increasing throughout the last half of 1946 and the first half of 1947, so that the revival of production did not bring about a decline in prices. On the contrary, prices kept rising rapidly, forcing another round of wage increases based on the cost-of-living sliding scales. While union labor in the large plants was thus able to protect its real income to a certain degree, the numerous artisans, workers in family-sized firms, and white-collar employees suffered enormous decreases in real income. The currency inflation was a consequence of extensive deficit financing by the government, inevitable considering the many burdens of relief and rehabilitation—of subsidies and social welfare payments—it had to bear. Its ability to collect taxes and elicit hoarded savings was limited. The Bank of Italy made banknotes available to the government to finance public operations. Commercial banks were advancing credit to the government (which owned the biggest of the banks already), and also to private business to cover payrolls expanded by inflationary wage increases and by reviving production. By the middle of 1947, coincident with the foreign-exchange crisis, the policy of laissez faire and the absence of effective controls brought fiscal difficulties to a head.

At this point, Professor Luigi Einaudi was made Deputy Prime Minister, as well as Minister of the Budget. An outstanding economist of the classical school, he became the "dictator" of the country's financial policies. His strategy was the powerful application of credit control. Reserve requirements of the Bank of Italy were raised. Bank loans were cut back ruthlessly. The stock market boom collapsed. Prices fell, and the value of the lira rose on foreign exchanges. Exchange controls were relaxed to permit more imports, further reducing prices. The announcement of the Marshall Plan in the summer of 1947 gave a psychological impetus toward promoting financial stability. In November, 1947, the official exchange rate was abolished as being meaningless. From that time, the rates in the market reflected a realistic evaluation of the lira's international position. The wild inflation was over.

The merits of Einaudi's tight credit policy were undoubted; its demerits should be mentioned also. It brought about a substantial recession. Unemployment increased somewhat, although the freeze on firings and layoffs was still in effect. Businessmen were caught with large payrolls and dropping prices; the government had to extend its areas of intervention to come to their rescue. Interest rates, always high in Italy, became even higher. The reconstruction of the Italian economy was brought to a halt and production actually declined. Production revived the following year, however, after the April, 1948, election victory of the Christian Democrats and the coming into effect of the European Recovery Program. By 1949, Italian productivity, as a whole, regained prewar levels and in some sectors rose far beyond them.

Since the major gainers were the large monopolies, which had flourished under Fascism, it can be argued that a more austere and equitable method of reviving the Italian economy could and should have been pursued, one that did not depend so much on the greed, speculation, and unabashed self-interest that the system of laissez faire permitted, one that would have been fairer to the masses of the population. By 1949, the economy was restored, but the national averages could only superficially conceal the vast discrepancies in wealth, the extreme poverty of large parts of the population being made all the more irksome by the lack of self-denial and the conspicuous consumption of the fortunate minority. New and old wealth was visibly on display; sharp operators had made killings in all kinds of markets—black, gray, and white. The Italian people had worked very hard, but only a small number of them had been substantial beneficiaries of the revival.

Yet it must be admitted that the cabinets of the period were too weak to have been able to manage successfully a system of priorities and controls. They had too little command over their own bureaucracy, to say nothing of their command over the people as a whole. And the people had too little faith in, or respect for, their own government to have collaborated with a rationing system. But these deficiencies and attitudes of the government and the people in the immediate postwar period were only extreme manifestations of more deep-rooted and fundamental problems. Even in "normal" times, both before and after the war, the governments of Italy have lacked the support and consensus of the people, who themselves have lacked the social solidarity necessary to accept common sacrifices for common goals.

The inflation during the war and immediate postwar periods had made a strong impact on the behavior of the masses and the political class. The "defense of the lira" became a political slogan to be reckoned with. Fear of even a slight inflation provided ammunition for political parties to use against reforms and reformers. In the early 1950's, new production was held back on the grounds that it would cause the price level to rise. The implementation of the Constitution was opposed with the argument that the economy could not afford the budget deficits that implementation might bring.

Since the Constituent Assembly was not a full-fledged legislative body, the cabinets continued to govern essentially by decree, as they had been doing ever since the Fascist period. The composition of the cabinet was changed, however, to reflect the results of the 1946 election. De Gasperi no longer felt obliged to include the representatives of parties that had practically ceased to exist, i.e., the Action Party and the Labor Democratic Party. The Liberals were unwilling to collaborate, so De Gasperi constructed a four-party government that included representatives from the three largest parties—Christian Democrats, Socialists, and Communists—and from the small Republican Party, which had obtained 4.4 per cent of the vote. The Republicans, the inheritors of the nineteenth-century traditions of the democratic radicals Giuseppe Mazzini and Carlo Cattaneo, had refused to participate in any government under a monarchy. With the establishment of a republic, this obstacle was removed and they entered the cabinet. Their most prestigious leader was Count Carlo Sforza, who would soon become Foreign Minister.

The Constituent Assembly met on June 25, 1946. Two days later it elected Enrico De Nicola, the eminent Neapolitan jurist and politician, as Provisional President of the Republic, thus replacing a displaced king with an outstanding monarchist, a man ready, nevertheless, to support the fledgling republic loyally. This was a wise move to conciliate the monarchist south. His presence as provisional head of the state was, in its limited way, an attempt to reunite a badly divided people.

The Italians were disunited in many ways, and the poverty-stricken masses were susceptible to Communist-Socialist manipulation. The frightened middle and upper classes thus demanded more police protection and the enforcement of order. They took out their resentments against the Christian Democrats (who were in a cabinet with Communists and Socialists) and the workers by voting for Uomo Qualunque in a number of local elections in the fall of 1946, especially in provinces from Rome southward.

The electoral losses to the extreme right made the Christian Democrats more restive about the government coalition with the extreme left. The growing intensity of the Cold War at the international level brought American pressures to bear against the continuation of the cabinet. (It has been claimed that an American condition for the loan granted to Italy during De Gasperi's visit to Washington in January, 1947, was the ejection of the Communists and Socialists from the government.) The same month, those Socialists who opposed continued unity of action with the Communists (they were led by Giuseppe Saragat) walked out of the Socialist Party.[14] The Socialist schism widened the gap between the Christian Democrats and their left-wing allies. The combination of pressures and circumstances made it only a question of a short time before a pretext was found that would topple the government. In May, 1947, the pretext was created and De Gasperi resigned as Prime Minister. In the negotiations for the succeeding cabinet, the Communists and Socialists were dropped.

While a substantial percentage of Socialist parliamentarians had followed Saragat in the schism, a far smaller percentage among the rank and file had done so. In subsequent months, other splits from Socialist ranks would occur, but it took several

---

[14] After the split, the remaining Socialists resumed their historic name, the Italian Socialist Party.

years before the various schismatic groups could unite in what finally became the Italian Social Democratic Party.

Until May, 1947, the Communists and Socialists approved of the economic aid received from the West. Their attitude changed after their expulsion from the government. When in the summer of 1947 the Marshall Plan Conference was called to establish a European-wide organization for reconstruction, and after the Soviet Union rejected the American invitation to participate, the extreme left began a campaign against American aid, charging that it was a tool of American economic imperialism. Political strikes were called, in the autumn of 1947, to protest against the Marshall Plan and to prevent supplies from being delivered. The atmosphere of the country was one of intense excitement, but the strikes were only sporadic successes economically, and failures politically. For they showed that the Italian worker was reluctant to demonstrate over issues which were not directly concerned with immediate, tangible objectives, and that Communist manipulation of the working class and its organizations had its limitations. That the strikes were even occasionally successful was due to the Communist domination of the united labor movement. This domination was crucial to the Communist displacement of the Socialists after 1946 as the principal party of the extreme left. The splintering of the Socialists and the break between the Christian Democrats and the far left had, among the trade unions, repercussions that the political strikes called by the Communists served to magnify.

Politically oriented, Italian unionism before the advent of the Fascist regime had been divided among Socialist, Catholic, and Anarchist union federations (plus independents). Under Fascism, the party and the regime had taken control of the entire union movement. During the war, Allied officials in southern Italy encouraged the creation of one nonpolitical trade-union confederation, and in Rome—behind the German lines—Communist, Socialist, and Christian Democratic labor leaders were also thinking of unity. They had all paid a bitter price for the divisions of the working class in the past. On June 4, 1944, one day before the Allies entered the capital, a pact had been signed that created the

Italian General Confederation of Labor (CGIL). While claiming to be independent of all political parties, and proclaiming that workers of differing faiths and ideologies could collaborate for common goals, the CGIL established three secretaries-general (a premature troika?): Communist, Socialist, and Christian Democratic. From the very beginning, it was not, therefore, an apolitical organization. This tripartite division of offices was carried all the way down to the provincial and local levels.

The Communists rather quickly established their domination of the CGIL. They had organizational experience and personal leadership that the others could not match. The principal Communist trade-union leader, Giuseppe Di Vittorio, was undoubtedly an outstandingly dynamic and charismatic leader and a true son of the masses. By 1945, when the north was brought into the CGIL, the Communists were definitely the strongest group.

At the end of 1945, the Christian Democratic labor leaders were beginning to react against Communist exploitation of the CGIL for their own ends. As the strains in the political coalition increased, these were transferred to the trade-union movement. By 1947, the Christian Democrats were engaged in open polemics against the domination of the other two parties, and the Cold War was being increasingly injected into the Italian labor scene. With the calling of political strikes against the Marshall Plan, the conflicts were further increased. The CGIL was a member of the World Federation of Trade Unions, and its behavior was strongly influenced by this Soviet-controlled body. If it could control Italian labor effectively, the chances for the Marshall Plan to succeed in Italy would be considerably reduced. But these strikes turned into political failures. The final straw came, however, when the CGIL called a general strike to protest the attempted assassination of Palmiro Togliatti in July, 1948. Some of the rank-and-file Communist workers were under the mistaken impression that the Party was a revolutionary party, and in some central and northern provinces they actually seized control of local governments and key communications points. The Party quickly brought them under control and dampened whatever revolutionary fervor they might have had. As a reaction to the strike, the leaders of the Christian Democratic and Catholic Action workers announced that a new, nonpolitical labor confederation would be created. It was formally set up in October, bearing the cumbersome title, Free Italian General Confederation of Labor (LCGIL).

The Communists claim that the American Government, the Vatican, and the Christian Democratic Party forced the split, and therefore bear the responsibility for dividing and weakening the Italian labor movement. There cannot be much doubt that all three welcomed the split. The Christian Democratic Party and the Americans unquestionably helped to finance the new confederation, which, however, did not acquire any reputation for nonpolitical identification. Republican and Social Democratic labor leaders and workers were, on the whole, reluctant to join what had every appearance of an organization sponsored by Catholics and Christian Democrats. They remained in the CGIL a while longer. By May, 1949, however, they too withdrew, and on June 4, 1949, they created a new federation, the Italian Federation of Labor (FIL). The new organization was under substantial American and Italian pressure to merge with the LCGIL, and in fact, at a FIL conference in Naples, some of the FIL leaders succeeded in forcing a vote on fusion with the LCGIL. The vast majority of the rank and file refused to go along, however, and in March, 1950, created still another federation, the Italian Union of Labor (UIL). Several weeks later, the formal fusion of the LCGIL and the remnants of the FIL took place. The new organization was given the title of Italian Confederation of Workers' Unions (CISL). Supposedly free of any party or ideological domination, it was recognized in fact as a Catholic labor federation, and it operated as a faction in the faction-ridden Christian Democratic Party. With very few exceptions, its leadership was drawn from Christian Democratic Labor elements or from the Christian Associations of Italian Workers (ACLI), a branch of Catholic Action.

By 1950, consequently, the three major labor confederations were formed. The CGIL was still the largest and still under Communist and Socialist leadership, with the Communists dominant; the CISL was next in size and clearly Catholic; while the UIL was the smallest and clearly Social Democratic and Republican.[15] This splitting seriously weakened the effective economic and political power of the union movement. The maneuvering and jockeying for position of trade union leaders antagonized many of the rank and file, for all sorts of personal animosities and rivalries were involved—as well as questions of domestic and international politics—and none of it appeared to have anything to do with the immediate, daily problems of the ordinary workingman. In disgust, many of them left organized labor completely, thus weakening its position still further.

The first election of a parliament under the new Constitution was scheduled for April 18, 1948. The preceding winter had been bitter. The 1947 split in the Socialist Party had left it more firmly in the hands of those committed to unity of action with the Communists. The two parties agreed to present a common list for the election, and this aggravated the fears of the other parties.[16] In the early spring of 1948, tension mounted. The single event that brought it to its peak, however, occurred outside the country: the February, 1948, *coup d'état* in Prague, which led to the Communist takeover of Czechoslovakia. The Italian election campaign was immediately turned into a struggle of apocalyptic proportions, and the vote was depicted as a telling climax in the battle between Christ and Antichrist, between Rome and Moscow.

The United States mobilized its economic and political weapons to stem the apparent red tide. On March 15, 1948, the State Department announced that all economic aid would be cut off if the Communist-Socialist slate won.[17] The U.S. persuaded the French and British governments to join in a tripartite declaration favoring the return to Italy of the entire Free Territory of Trieste, including both Zones A and B. Americans of Italian origin or extraction were encouraged to bombard their relatives in Italy with letters urging them to vote for the government parties. In

---

[15] A neo-Fascist federation, CISNAL, would be formed in 1952, and there are also many independent unions. CISNAL has never amounted to much.

[16] The election system was a list system of proportional representation, modified by the right of the voter to choose his preferences within the party list.

[17] Text in the *New York Times*, March 16, 1948.

American Catholic churches, priests encouraged their parishioners to write to any Italian friends or connections. In Italy, various cardinals and bishops were ordering their priests not to administer sacraments to anyone voting for the pro-Soviet slate.

The danger was exaggerated, although many honest and serious people were convinced by its reality. It served, however, on the international level, to commit more American resources to Italy. When the election was over and the returns were in, the percentage of the vote received by the Marxist parties was slightly less than their vote in the election of 1946. Adding the Social Democratic vote (which did not exist in 1946) to the Communist-Socialist vote makes this result readily evident. The election returns are shown in Table 1.

TABLE 1
ELECTION RESULTS, 1946 AND 1948

	1946		1948	
Parties	Popular Vote (Per Cent)	Assembly Seats	Popular Vote (Per Cent)	Chamber Seats
Uomo Qualunque	5.3	30	2.0	6
Monarchist	2.8	16	2.8	14
Liberal	6.8	41	3.8	19
Christian Democratic	35.2	207	48.5	305
South Tyrol Populist			0.5	3
Republican	4.4	23	2.5	9
Social Democratic			7.1	33
Socialist	20.7	115 ⎱	31.0	183
Communist	19.0	104 ⎰		
Other	5.8	20	1.8	2
Total	100.0	556	100.0	574

Source: Italia, Istituto Centrale di Statistica.

Internally, the scare drew large numbers of conservative and moderate voters into the Christian Democratic Party, which they thought was the most effective bulwark against an apparent Communist seizure. The campaign had weakened, not the left, but the smaller parties of the center and right. The influx of right-wing elements was so marked that on the morrow of the election De

Gasperi found it necessary to affirm that the Christian Democratic Party was and remained a democratic party with progressive social goals.

Although the Christian Democratic Party had received less than half the popular vote, it had an absolute majority of the seats in Parliament. The Vatican put tremendous pressure on De Gasperi to form a one-party Catholic government. This he resolutely refused to do, deeply fearing the consequences of a sharp Catholic-secularist division. He had no desire to revive the bitter clerical-anticlerical splits of the late nineteenth century. Instead he re-formed a coalition government of four parties, taking parties to the left and to the right as allies, but all formally committed to principles of democratic parliamentary government. Joining the coalition were the Liberal, Republican, and Social Democratic parties, and this center coalition, as it came to be called, was the basis of future governments for seven years.

De Gasperi was also subject to tremendous pressure, this time from America as well, to outlaw the Communist and Socialist parties. He refused to countenance such an action, thereby demonstrating an independence from American pressure in crucial areas of domestic political choice.

In foreign affairs, however, there gradually evolved a close relationship between the two countries. During the negotiation of the peace settlement, Italy had refrained from overtly siding with the West in the growing split between the Soviet and non-Soviet worlds. It could not afford to antagonize one of the principal victors and thereby provoke a further hardening of attitude toward the defeated state. Even after the peace treaty was signed, the Italians were slow to side politically with the Western victors for several reasons. The government sought to avoid further aggravation of domestic antagonism. The British, who were still uncertain as to their commitment to Italy, displayed a distinct coolness toward it. And, finally, Italians hoped that their country, singly or with France, might play a mediating or conciliatory role in the sharpening rivalry between the superpowers. This conception of a "third force" between East and West was felt to be consistent with full Italian participation in the Marshall Plan. Count Carlo

Sforza, the Foreign Minister, made no hesitation in arguing their compatibility.[18]

Then, in late 1948 and early 1949, under the impact of the Berlin air-lift crisis, the United States evolved the idea of a Western military alliance in the form of the North Atlantic Treaty Organization. The U.S. wanted Italian membership in NATO and exerted pressure to get it. Resistance, however, was encountered both inside and outside Italy. Outside, the British raised objections to Italian participation. Inside, the extreme left and extreme right opposed such participation. This internal opposition was based on historical, and relatively logical, grounds. The neo-Fascists opposed NATO because they considered the British and the Americans to be enemies of Italy. They were especially Anglophobic, for they blamed on the British the loss of their colonies and of Trieste. On the left, the Communists opposed NATO simply because it was anti-Soviet. The Socialist position was more complicated. Socialists had a historic aversion to balance-of-power politics, which they regarded as the major cause of war. They disliked a world divided into blocs. They had a tradition of neutralism and anti-imperialism and were too easily and superficially persuaded by their Communist allies that NATO was an imperialist alliance. So Nenni justified Socialist opposition to Italian membership in NATO on the grounds that his party was applying the policy of its predecessors, who had opposed Italian membership in the Triple Alliance and later in the Triple Entente.

Both extremes were in the opposition, however, and the government had a solid majority in Parliament. It was not the opposition that made the government hold back, but uncertainty within the governing coalition. Sforza's hopes that Italy could play a third-force role gradually evaporated under the combined influence of a deteriorating international situation and the repeated warnings from his ambassador in Washington, Alberto Tarchiani, that the American Congress could not be expected to finance Italian economic recovery and receive in return nothing more than neutralism. In 1949, this was a fair argument, although the late

---

18 See Carlo Sforza, "Italy, the Marshall Plan, and the 'Third Force.'" *Foreign Affairs*, April, 1948, p. 455.

1950's would show that Asian and African states could exchange nonalignment for American dollars very nicely. After Sforza's conversion, it was still necessary to convince De Gasperi, whose reservations reflected a variety of opinions in his party. Many Christian Democrats felt that Italy, as the home of the Catholic Church, should stay out of the East-West political conflict in order to protect the Church, a universal body not tied to any blocs, cultures, or economic or political systems. Other left-wing Christian Democrats identified NATO as the foreign counterpart of domestic conservatism, an instrument for blocking domestic social reform and freezing the internal, as well as the international, status quo.

De Gasperi was finally convinced by Sforza that Italy could not afford to remain isolated from the other nations of the West. De Gasperi however, when confronted by strong opposition within both his party and the ecclesiastical circles, brought himself around to doing something to which he was opposed in principle: to call on the Church for help. He took Sforza to see Pope Pius XII to explain the case for NATO. Sforza convinced the Pope and the Catholic opposition collapsed.

In the spring of 1949, the NATO treaty was submitted to Parliament. In his arguments, De Gasperi rejected the idea that NATO was necessary to halt potential Soviet military aggression. He publicly doubted that war was likely or even conceivable in Western Europe. He argued instead that Italy had to join NATO to guarantee continued economic aid and to assure the continued possibility for Italians to emigrate. He assured Parliament that such participation would be no hindrance to trading with the states of the Soviet bloc and announced that he was sending an economic mission to Moscow to negotiate a new trade agreement.[19] Parliament ratified the treaty and Italy was a member of NATO.

The year 1949 may be said to have marked the end of a period in postwar Italian life. In that year was completed the liquidation of the most obvious political and economic consequences of the war. The economy was restored to prewar levels. The country was again an active participant in the international community, a member of all the organizations existing in Western international

---

19 *Atti parlamentari, 1948–1949*, Senato della Repubblica (Italy), 1st Legislature, pp. 6534–44.

life, with the exception of the United Nations.[20] The domestic
political system appeared relatively stable, with a four-party coalition commanding a clear majority in Parliament. The dangers
and fears of the immediate postwar period seemed to have been
successfully overcome.

---

[20] Italy was prevented, by successive Soviet vetoes, from joining the United
Nations until 1955. The Russian Government announced that it had no objection to Italian membership but would block it as long as the United States
and its friends opposed the admission of Communist states of Eastern Europe.
Italy supported the "package deal" of 1955, by which a large number of Communist and non-Communist states gained admission to the United Nations.

3
ECONOMIC INNOVATIONS

The revival of the economy to prewar levels was hardly a goal to satisfy either the people or their political leaders. In fact, the contrary happened: relief from the most abject misery stimulated further demands. This was particularly true in agriculture, where low productivity, in general, and backward forms of landholding, especially in the south, became a focus of renewed agitation on the part of a dissatisfied peasantry. Stimulated by political movements and sincerely interested in alleviating centuries-old poverty as well as in using peasant unrest as a political weapon against the economic and political status quo, propertyless southern peasants were seizing unused lands that were part of the vast holdings, the latifundia, of southern aristocratic owners. Often these were absentee landlords living in metropolitan areas while their local agents exploited a helpless mass of farm laborers who at best might not have more than 100 or 150 days of work per year.

Concern over the economic and social disabilities of the south had been expressed by both southerners (Giustino Fortunato, Gaetano Salvemini, Francesco Nitti) and northerners (Sidney Sonnino, Umberto Zanotti-Bianco) since the last decades of the nineteenth century. The governments of both pre-Fascist and Fascist Italy had attempted sporadically and inconclusively to rehabilitate southern agriculture and social life through land-reclamation projects, mosquito control, reforestation, and other means. None of these efforts had been serious enough or sustained enough to change agricultural and social patterns fundamentally. Mussolini had drained the Pontine Marshes south of Rome to use as a show piece of Fascist achievement, but then he became diverted to policies of imperialistic aggrandizement. The post-Fascist governments after 1944 seized some of the landed properties of prominent Fascists as part of the financial purge of those who had profited from Fascism. This was a first step in expropriating land, but it could not furnish the basis for more general agricultural reform.

In 1949, farm laborers went on strike under CGIL leadership. The hue and cry that resulted, the tensions raised, not only in rural areas but in political headquarters in Rome, forced the government to take some alleviatory action. American pressure, expressed through Marshall Plan administrators located in Rome, added to the growing feeling that something had to be done. De Gasperi and his Minister of Agriculture, Antonio Segni, a Sardinian landholder and university professor, prepared legislation for the breakup of large, backward landed estates. (Modern agricultural operators using advanced techniques were excluded from the legislation, no matter how large their holdings.) In April, 1949, De Gasperi proposed the redistribution of 3.7 million acres of neglected farmland. The bill went into an interministerial committee for examination. Confagricoltura (Confederation of Agriculture), the agricultural organization of the large landowners, put such pressure on the ministers that the bill was stalled in committee. In the fall of 1949 and spring of 1950, landless peasants in Calabria and Apulia, and later in the Roman *campagna,* stimulated by Communist agitators for the most part, seized unworked tracts of land. These seizures produced further political agitation and finally prodded the government into action.

De Gasperi's bill had been moderate. It would have left the landowners with substantial holdings, and the government would have compensated them for their losses partly in cash and partly in government securities. In turn, the peasants were to pay the government for the land they received, in installments over thirty years. Nevertheless, delay in Parliament induced the government to compromise—and to split up—its proposals. In May, 1950, a special bill for the Sila area of Calabria, where the peasant outbreaks had been particularly sharp, was pushed through Parliament. The *stralcio* ("pruning") law, intended as an advance installment of the main act, was passed in October of the same year. This covered certain areas of the Po Delta, the Tuscan Maremma, Sardinia, and various sections of the southern mainland. (Sicily was excluded; its land reform was placed under the aegis of the new Sicilian regional government.) Then the cabinet quietly proceeded to abandon the main law, so that only one-third to one-half of the land originally scheduled for distribution ever went to the peasants.

The government's responsibilities did not end with the partition of the land. Administrative agencies set up in each land-reform area not only were responsible for the reassignment of holdings but were also involved in supplying animals, constructing houses and barns, educating the new holders, and doing other kinds of social welfare work. In some cases they became paternalistic, treating the peasants like incapable children who would be in need of constant tutelage.

Some weaknesses of the reform were apparent immediately. The landowners kept their best land and got rid of their marginal or useless holdings by giving it to the reform agencies. Much of the land turned over to the peasants was not suitable for intensive farming. Other weaknesses became apparent later. Under pressure to provide land and incapable of conceiving of a situation other than permanent rural overpopulation, administrators allocated tiny plots to too many families; even under the best of circumstances, farming them would involve a bitter struggle to make a bare living. After 1959, when a rural exodus of substantial proportions would take place, the fallacious assumption of permanent rural overpopulation would be exposed, and the worst land abandoned. Another weakness was that the beneficiaries were picked by lot, rather than by presumed potential ability to run a farm, and some of them proved to be absolutely incapable. Although it was charged that favoritism and influence were used in making the allotments, there seems to be little evidence that voting Christian Democratic helped anyone obtain land. There is plenty of evidence, however, that the reform agencies themselves were instruments of Christian Democratic patronage.

The land reform was an economic revolution in the areas where it took effect, but appeared in the following years to have been of little political consequence. Whatever hopes might have been held that the creation of a large number of new peasant proprietors would break the influence of the extreme left on the beneficiaries were not borne out by subsequent elections. The Christian Democratic Party did not gain many votes in the reform areas. On the other hand, the party earned the enmity of landowners and conservative middle and upper classes, especially in the south, who threw their political support to the reviving Monarchists and to the neo-Fascists. At this time, the latter were organized in the Italian Social Movement (Movimento Sociale Italiano, MSI), which had been created in 1949 out of some sections of the disintegrating Uomo Qualunque.

Redistribution of land was by itself not enough to convert the impoverished and retarded south into a modern society. Development of nonagricultural resources was also required, and in 1950 the government introduced a bill for the creation of a development agency, the Cassa per il Mezzogiorno (Southern Italy Fund). It was to spend 1,200 billion lire over ten years (later prolonged several times with more funds) for the purpose of creating the prerequisites for a developing economy. Half of the original appropriation came from counterpart funds of the European Recovery Program. The Fund was related to agricultural reform in its concern with dams, aqueducts, roads, irrigation, and other elements of economic development that together are generally classified as infrastructure. But it was hoped that this infrastructure would provide a basis for industrial and commercial, as well as agricultural, development. It was anticipated that private initiative would step in to take advantage of the public investment. To stimulate private investment, a whole series of special credit facilities were established to make loans at exceptionally low interest rates. In addition, special tax waivers were authorized.

The operations of the Southern Italy Fund provided much material for controversial discussion. Enemies charged that it lost considerable effectiveness because of graft and corruption. These are difficult charges to prove, and most Italians take graft and corruption for granted, assuming them to exist even when they do not. Some things are fairly clear, however. The selection of sites and projects were often influenced by political considerations. The central government was subjected to tremendous pressure by local political organizations to locate a project here rather than there, to support the political ambitions of candidate or faction X rather than Y, to reward the commune or province that provided a nice majority and to punish the one that supported the opposition. As public works and the jobs resulting therefrom were (and are) important electoral factors—especially in the south, where clientelism remains strong—these practices were perhaps inevitable. They are not peculiar to Italy, but they did reduce the effectiveness of the programs.

An additional cause of ineffectiveness lay in the behavior and reaction of the traditional government departments. Some of them tried to get their hands on the Fund to aid in the building of departmental empires, but the Fund had been created outside the old-line departments precisely because of the low opinion of their ability to operate a strikingly new project. The departments then reduced their own regular spending in the zones where the Fund was operating, so that what was conceived as an extraordinary supplement to government investments became, to a certain degree, a substitute. In 1951, public works constructed in the south by the regular government departments represented 45.8 per cent of the national total. Five years later, the percentage had declined to 41.5 per cent. By 1959, it was down to 29.7 per cent; in 1961, it rose slightly to 31.7 per cent.

Another unquestioned result of the institution of the Southern Italy Fund was the impetus it gave to northern industry. Especially in the Fund's initial stages, the north gained perhaps more than the south. While unskilled southern peasants could be used on road building, dam building, and other projects, the heavy equipment, the earth-moving and road-grading machinery, was of necessity manufactured in northern plants. Tractors and other farm machinery purchased to modernize agriculture came from the same source. It is not surprising, consequently, that the Southern Italy Fund helped to contribute to northern industrial expansion.

In the early 1950's, hopes for a rapid expansion of private industry in the south were not realized to any significant extent.

The south appeared to lack substantial entrepreneurial tradition. The land, rather than industry, had been the traditional focus of southerners with savings to invest, for land was the established source of prestige and social status. Existing favorable tax laws encouraged speculation in real estate, and it remained more attractive than unfamiliar industrial development, in spite of the special incentives offered. The unusual credit facilities made available by the creation of new governmental loan agencies for the southern mainland, Sicily, and Sardinia (separate ones were created for each of these areas) did not have powerful capacities for attraction. In the mid-1950's, the large northern and central industrial firms, capable of self-financing out of their own profits, did not need to borrow extensively for expansion. Consequently, hopes that northern industrialists would locate plants in the south in large numbers went unfulfilled. Some of them certainly did—Olivetti, for example, constructed an office-machine factory in the Naples area—but most were cautious. They had doubts about southern markets for their products and about the capacities of southern labor. The national wage contracts negotiated by the unions provided for lower wages in the south, but these were not sufficiently lower to offset the many attractions of the north. The result was that the expansion of Italian industry remained concentrated in the north.

In spite of the difficulties and drawbacks, the land reforms and Fund programs are still among the most striking developments in postwar—or even modern—Italian history. Progress was made in attacking a whole pattern of living, shaking up age-old habits and customs, in order to permit the unification of the country economically, socially, and culturally. This move toward unity was slow in starting and remains far from complete.

Marshall Plan aid had been geared originally to promote economic recovery, which was essentially accomplished by 1949. The aid was not halted at that time but was continued until 1952, when the European Recovery Program was declared completed. Substantial portions of the counterpart funds accumulated under Marshall Plan operations had been used to help finance the Southern Italy Fund. The question now was whether northern business would be stimulated to continue the general economic expansion. This was not necessarily to be taken for granted.

Italian business was traditionally based on small and protected markets. Both public and private business enterprises had been operated with a mentality oriented toward securing an agreed slice of a small pie, rather than toward competing for a larger share of a bigger pie. Pre-Fascist and Fascist regimes had encouraged protection, controls, and cartel arrangements, and had discouraged competition. Italy had been, and still was, so poor a country that it was difficult to conceive of the nation providing a growing and vital market. There was no certainty these habits of long standing could be shaken.

They were, but it was not easy. It required a political leadership determined to engage in a program of development. It required a good dose of fear of the consequences of the failure to develop. The fear was, and is, present. All Italian society, all social classes, are pervaded with fear: the poor fear misery, unemployment, and abuse of power by those above them; the middle classes fear for their social and economic status; the rich fear loss of their wealth and privileges. Fear was nothing new in Italian history, but in the atmosphere of the Cold War of the early 1950's, with large and active Communist and Socialist parties spurring the disinherited to advance more and more claims on society, the only answer was to enlarge the pie. Determined men in the government pushed the hesitant private industrialists along.

One impetus was the realization by private industry that its failure to expand would threaten it with seizure by the government. Not that extreme Marxist parties of the left would come to power by revolution—certainly after 1948 they were recognized as being of little direct danger—but there was little moral or ideological commitment to private enterprise throughout most of Italian society. During the first half of the twentieth century, the Italian state had acquired major economic assets, such as railroads, insurance firms, coal mines, mechanical enterprises, and banks. In the 1930's, in its attempt to bail out many firms and banks grievously hurt by the great depression, Mussolini's government had ended up by acquiring a controlling stock interest in substantial parts of the economy. Many of these firms were grouped by Mussolini into a large holding company, the Institute for Industrial Reconstruction (IRI), which the republic inherited. Many groups described as center in Italian politics, inside and outside the Christian Democratic Party, would always be ready to demand that the state step in wherever and whenever private enterprise showed unwillingness to exercise dynamic initiative.

It was assumed not only that the domestic market was expandable but also that foreign markets could be made available through political cooperation. Count Carlo Sforza, the Foreign Minister between 1947 and 1951, when he retired because of ill health, was a Europeanist of long standing. While he avoided wrestling with the hard issues of regional integration and preferred to talk in generalities and aphorisms (one of his favorite was: "Boundaries must be written in pencil, not ink!"), he stimulated the at first uninterested and later reluctant De Gasperi to realize the advantages to Italy of European unity.

Sforza had begun his program with a failure. He negotiated, in 1948, a customs-union agreement with France behind the backs of unsuspecting Italian businessmen, who only later awoke to the fact that they might have to face French competition. Sforza had foreign-policy, as well as economic, goals in mind and thought that Franco-Italian unity would increase the political power of the two countries throughout the world, thus enabling them to play better the third-force role he then had in mind. The Italian business community was saved by the more alert French business, agricultural, and labor interests—equally protectionist in mentality—who proceeded to exercise enough pressure on the French Parliament to prevent ratification of the treaty.

The next opportunity came in 1951 and 1952, when the French Government, through Maurice Schumann, proposed the establishment of the Coal and Steel Community. Italy's coal industry is minor and in the hands of the government. Its resources of iron ore are insignificant. Its steel industry had been developed in the latter part of the nineteenth century under the protection of governments determined to make Italy a great power. Without this protection it never could have met the competition of Western

European producers, for it was dependent on imports of its basic raw materials. During the 1930's, many steel firms failed and were taken over by the Fascist government through the mechanism of the IRI. At the beginning of the 1950's, they were technologically backward, compared to foreign competitors, and would have been unable to withstand the strain of an unprotected situation.

For these reasons, the private steel producers opposed Italian participation in the Coal and Steel Community. Their objections would have carried more weight if they had been dominant in the industry, but they were not. The major steel producers were government-owned, but the government could not ignore the consequences of unrestricted foreign competition either, for it could not afford to add to the already existing mass of unemployed. It was committed to operating all of its enterprises at a loss in order to keep men at work. Desirous of participating in the initiation of a new economic community, it found, with the toleration of the other European members, a compromise path. Italy was permitted to join with a five-year period of grace before its steel industry would be exposed to the full effects of foreign competition. During those five years, it would have to modernize its plant to prepare for the day of reckoning. In an earlier period, the Italians would not have prepared, but would have drifted along and then requested an extension of the special exemption. That this was not done points up the difference in the atmosphere and attitudes of the 1950's. Under the dynamic and driving leadership of the engineer Oscar Sinigaglia, the Italian steel industry was converted in five years into a modern and efficient producer, capable of competing with the best in the world. Its production expanded dramatically, and when the grace period expired, instead of collapsing it surged on to further advances.

The performance of the steel industry was imitated by the other branches of industry in which large-scale firms were the order, such as the mechanical, chemical, and petroleum plants. In the five years between 1950 and 1955, the Italian gross national product increased at an average annual rate of between 5 and 6 per cent. The increase was actually fluctuating from year to year, as the figures in Table 2 indicate. The main reason for the fluctuations was the varying harvests in agriculture, which still employed

TABLE 2
GROWTH RATE OF GROSS NATIONAL PRODUCT, 1951–55
(*In Per Cents*)

Year	Increase
1951	5.9
1952	2.9
1953	7.3
1954	4.4
1955	7.5

Source: Bank of Italy, *Relazione 1958*, p. 197.

close to 40 per cent of the labor force. Industrial output increased on an average of nearly 10 per cent per year during this period. The early discovery of large reserves of natural gas in the Po Valley, and of smaller reserves of petroleum, created a major new source of the energy in which Italy was traditionally deficient. Located near the principal centers of industry, these discoveries provided a further stimulus to economic expansion. They had been made by the state-owned petroleum company, AGIP (Italian General Petroleum Agency), which was incorporated in 1952 into the newly created National Hydrocarbons Trust, the ENI. Under the leadership of the dynamic left-wing Christian Democrat Enrico Mattei, the ENI was created to unify the state-controlled properties in the petroleum industry. It became a major public holding company, comparable to the IRI.

The dramatic increases in productivity in the advanced parts of the economy were due primarily to technological improvements and modernization of the existing plant. In these years, Italian industry caught up with the rest of the world. In addition, the Italians brought into full productivity the existing surplus plant and labor. The ending of quantitative controls and the liberalization of imports, carried through after 1949 by the Minister of Foreign Trade, Ugo La Malfa, gave Italian industry access to the most modern foreign machinery and equipment, from which it had previously been cut off by the operation of exchange controls and quotas. The increases in efficiency due to modernization, coupled with the low wages due to the divisions within the labor movement and the debilitating effects of mass unemployment, led to declines in labor costs that served to make Italian prices competitive in foreign markets and to a substantial expansion of exports. The economic recovery and development of the other advanced countries of the Western world not only increased the demand for Italian products but provided the basis for the beginnings of a mass tourism from which Italy would profit greatly in subsequent years.

This happy picture was not the total portrait, however. It applied only to the part of the economy more or less advanced and ready for still further evolution. Whole sectors of Italian economic life were outside this zone, in a state of underdevelopment. Agriculture, which was still the largest area of manpower absorption, struggled along in its efforts to improve, with only marginal success. The numerous tiny artisan and retail enterprises, employing the members of one family, or perhaps one or two outside assistants, had no dramatic increases in efficiency or in profits. The increased wealth resulting from development and modernization was poured back into more investment or into the increased consumption of the business and commercial circles of the increasingly prosperous cities. The workers in the advanced industries enjoyed increases in real wages, although not comparable to the increases in productivity and profits. The result was that during the 1950's the gap between the two Italys was enlarged, rather than diminished.

The absence of a significant increase in employment was striking. Increased efficiency was the principal goal. The surplus labor kept on the payrolls in the late 1940's because of legal requirements could now be fully used. While there was some increase in nonagricultural employment, more of it probably went into the low-paid, small-scale artisan and distribution sectors than into industry. There was, in addition, a small exodus from agriculture. It has been estimated that between 1950 and 1959, larger industry absorbed only about 120,000 workers, while construction and transportation accounted for 400,000 to 500,000 more. At the same time, new elements—youths reaching working age and housewives seeking to enlarge the family income—were entering the labor market.[1] Thus, neither unemployment nor underemployment diminished substantially.

In the first half of the 1950's, unemployment was actually increasing. While Italian unemployment figures are debatable from both statistical and political standpoints, they are the only ones we have, and the broad picture they present is dramatic enough. The statistics of Table 3 are revealing. It can be seen that 1954

TABLE 3
UNEMPLOYED REGISTERED AT LABOR EXCHANGES, 1950–55

Year	Number of Registrants
1950	1,860,100
1951	1,938,300
1952	2,073,400
1953	2,181,300
1954	2,197,300
1955	2,161,000

Source: Italian Ministry of Labor.[2]

was the worst year for unemployment—and the figures do not show the underemployment, which is difficult to measure. Considering that the total labor force of that period was approximately 20 million persons, they indicate that roughly 10 per cent of the working population was unemployed during the first half of the 1950's.

That the figures were not worse was due to the vigorous emigration policy followed by the government. After the war, the Foreign Office invested a tremendous amount of time and energy in promoting arrangements for both permanent and temporary emigration. Its success was limited. Italian emigrants had to compete with millions of racial, religious, and political refugees fleeing from various types of persecution. Immigrant quota systems, such as those of the United States, were discriminatory. Many receiving countries were selective on the basis of skills (including literacy) that were in short supply in Italy. Failure of adjustment

[1] Vera Lutz, *Italy: A Study in Economic Development* (London: Oxford University Press, 1962), p. 75.

[2] *Ibid.*, p. 64.

abroad, or the completion of contracts when the emigration was temporary, meant a steady stream of returners. The result was a net emigration over these years of about 150,000 per annum.

The failure to make greater inroads on poverty and unemployment led to demands both inside and outside Italy that the government take steps to push the rate of development even faster. In 1952, Parliament established an investigating commission named for its chairman, the Social Democrat Roberto Tremelloni, to make a thorough investigation of unemployment. Officials of the American aid program urged the government to ease the tight monetary and credit policies in order to expand production and employment. The memory of the inflation of 1946/47 was so sharp, however, and the "defense of the lira" was so imbedded in the political mythology of the dominant economic ministers, mainly right-wing Liberals or Christian Democrats, that the hard-money policies were continued.

Political unrest was the consequence, and the voting power of the two extremes actually increased. The pressures generated led to strains within the ruling coalition, with demands by important groups for a revision of political alliances.

4
THE DIFFICULTIES
OF CENTRISM

The political and economic strains of the years after 1948 made the life of the four-party coalition difficult. The unrest generated by increasing unemployment and peasant seizures of the land led to frightened demands by middle- and upper-class spokesmen for stern repressive action. Under the instructions of the Christian Democratic Minister of the Interior, Mario Scelba, mobile flying squads (*celeri*) of national police, often recruited from ex-Fascist elements, were generous in their use of such weapons as rubber truncheons and wooden clubs. Although the extreme left was manipulating the unrest, the moderate left was genuinely disturbed by the brutality. In addition, the Social Democrats felt that the reform measures enacted were too compromised by concessions to the conservatives, especially as represented by the Liberal Party.[1]

On the opposite side, however, the conservatives felt that the Christian Democrats had not been firm enough in handling the unrest. They resented De Gasperi's refusal to outlaw the Communist and Socialist parties. They resented the agricultural reforms that had been instituted, in spite of their limited nature. They considered the reforms a symbolic attack on their whole

---

[1] In later years, Giuseppe Saragat admitted that "in the years of centrism, the Italian Social Democratic Party had to sacrifice part of its program because of the social blindness of the Liberals." *Corriere della sera* (Milan), November 2, 1964.

structure of prestige, status, and economic power, for their absolute right to their own possessions was thereby contested. They felt that the government was ineffective in challenging American and British inaction on the Trieste problem, and resented Italy's close link to the Atlantic alliance and to the United States.

A good part of De Gasperi's time and effort was involved in trying to maintain a balance between progressive and conservative elements inside his own party and within the coalition. He had less and less success in these efforts, so that by 1951 both the Social Democrats and the Liberals had left the government, although they continued generally to support it in Parliament. Since the Christian Democrats in any case had a majority by themselves (the 48.5 per cent of the votes received in 1948 had given them by law over 53 per cent of the seats in the Chamber of Deputies), the votes of the minor parties were not absolutely necessary, but were welcome when forthcoming.

An additional source of friction was the manipulation of patronage by the Christian Democrats at the expense of their small coalition partners. Almost all of the government-controlled corporations were put into the hands of Christian Democratic executives. The various appointments to public and semipublic agencies were also monopolized by the dominant party. Even academic appointments became subject to political manipulation.

The Catholic Church and its principal lay organ, the Italian Catholic Action Society, became increasingly aggressive in public life. Recommendations by high clerics, whether on personnel or on policy, not only brought about increasing resentment from the lay parties but frequently caused embarrassment to the Christian Democrats. De Gasperi had a very strong sense of the independence of the state from the Church, and he fought a hard battle against the clericalization of Italian life. When he retired from the political scene, his successors were in a much weaker position, and Church intervention in lay affairs expanded rapidly. To a considerable degree, this was the fault of the party itself. De Gasperi had never built up a strong party organization at the local level. The party depended on the clergy to support it at election time and to tell the voters for whom to vote. Parish churches were often converted into political headquarters. The Civic Committees, established by the Catholic Action Society, supplied the campaign workers and election agents. If priests and Catholic Action leaders were crucial to success, it is not surprising that they demanded their say after the elections were over. Naturally, they did not all speak with one voice, but in the early 1950's the predominant voice of the Church was conservative, if not reactionary. This was a further strain on Christian Democratic relations with the lay allies, especially the Republicans and the Social Democrats.

The combination of factors leading to discontent with the Christian Democrats was revealed in the results of the administrative elections held in 1951 and 1952. The Christian Democrats lost over 4 million votes (compared to the parliamentary election of April, 1948), a drop from 48.5 per cent to 35.1 per cent. While some of these votes were lost to the left, the Socialists having made some gains, most were lost to the right, to the rising Monarchist and neo-Fascist (MSI) parties. These two parties practically tripled their vote, gaining especially from Rome southward. The elections demonstrated that the Christian Democrats had never been as strong as the 1948 election had indicated them to be, but had merely been able to exploit a temporary situation—the *coup d'état* in Czechoslovakia—that was no longer repeatable.

The 1952 election had been especially crucial in Rome itself. The city had a strong neo-Fascist core, but was surrounded by a belt of poverty-stricken slum areas that were strongholds of the extreme left. It was doubtful that the Christian Democrats and their minor centrist allies would get enough votes to acquire a majority in the communal government of the capital. In this situation, Luigi Gedda, autocratic president of the Civic Committees of Catholic Action, precipitated a political crisis by demanding of De Gasperi that the Christian Democrats ally with the Monarchists and the MSI in Rome and further south, to stave off the possibility of a left-wing victory. Gedda threatened to organize an "outright Catholic party" pledged to carry out a program of "authoritative democracy" if De Gasperi refused.[2] In

2 The Christian Democrats are not formally a "confessional" party and reject any attribution that they are the representatives of the Church in political life. The effort to promote a çenter-right coalition in Rome was known as

addition, the Civic Committee of Rome advocated to the Christian Democrats the detachment of the peripheral areas of the commune from the central city, with the "red belt" to be made into a number of subcommunes. This latter proposal, designed to guarantee right-wing control of the city itself, was rejected by the party.

De Gasperi put up a bitter battle against allying with the extreme right. He knew that a center-right government in Rome, the capital, would become the basis for similar demands at the national level. He felt that the only long-run solution to Italy's problems was for the party of Christian Democracy, like the British Labour Party, to be progressively oriented with a strong social commitment. He had already described his party as a "center party looking toward the left." He had to fight not only Catholic Action but also the whole right wing of his party and a substantial body of opinion in the Vatican led by Pope Pius XII, who threatened to publish, in the Vatican paper, *L'Osservatore romano,* an endorsement of a separate list of Catholic candidates. In May, 1952, De Gasperi's position prevailed, the Pope retreated, and the coalition for Rome was composed of Christian Democrats, Social Democrats, Republicans, and Liberals. But to many conservative Catholic voters, it was obvious that the Church had no prejudices against the Monarchists and the MSI, both claiming to be good Catholic parties, and the increase in their vote has already been noted.

In Italy it is commonly believed that De Gasperi was supported by Monsignor Giovanni Battista Montini, then a Prosecretary of State and later Pope Paul VI. It should not be inferred that all members of Catholic Action shared Gedda's views or supported his demand for an opening to the right. Especially in the youth

---

the "Sturzo Operation." Don Luigi Sturzo, the founder of the Popular Party in 1919, had returned to Italy after the war and was made a senator for life. He had become rather conservative in his old age, but he was a republican and democrat always. How his name got attached to the affair is unclear, but it is hard to conceive of him advocating an alliance with Monarchists and Fascists. In the summer of 1965, Giulio Andreotti, one of De Gasperi's principal aides, wrote that Pope Pius XII was directly involved in the "Sturzo Operation." See Andreotti's journal, *Concretezza,* August 14, 1965, as reported in the *New York Herald Tribune* (Paris Edition), August 16, 1965.

organization, he met considerable resistance, which, however, was crushed. After the failure of Gedda's offensive against De Gasperi, the leaders of the Catholic Action youth group faced a purge at the hands of the Church conservatives. Carlo Carretto, president of the youth organization, left for Africa as a missionary on the basis of "authoritative suggestions." Don Arturo Paoli, who had warned Pius XII of the Fascist danger in the south, left Italy as a chaplain to emigrants. Mario Rossi, Carretto's successor, was purged two years later as a "left-wing deviationist."

Although the Christian Democrats suffered large over-all losses, together with the centrist parties they were able to hold and to gain control of a number of major cities in the center and north, including Rome itself. This success was due to changes in the election laws for the 1951/52 elections. In communes of over 10,000 in population, a premium of two-thirds of the seats in the communal council was given to the alliance obtaining a plurality of the votes. For the provincial councils, a prize of two-thirds of the seats was given to the alliance list that elected a simple majority of the council. It was by these devices that the center parties gained control in a number of formerly left-controlled cities, such as Florence and Turin.

The rise of the Monarchists and neo-Fascists had been particularly noticeable from Rome southward. Both of these parties had grown after the disintegration of the Uomo Qualunque, which had received its death blow in the election of 1948. The Monarchists were led by two southerners, Alfredo Covelli, of Benevento, and Achille Lauro, a wealthy shipowner of Naples. The formal goal of the party was the restoration of the monarchy. Since Article 139 of the Constitution states that the republican form of government is not subject to constitutional amendment, the party's goal could be achieved only through revolution. In fact, it was not a revolutionary party, but rather a conservative or reactionary one. Its appeal was to nostalgic members of the upper class and to those of all classes who spend their time reading magazines filled with gossip of princesses, aristocrats, and movie stars. This audience could never give it many votes; however, it was able to gather the votes of a mass of poverty-stricken southern subproletarians. Its greatest success was in Naples, where it was able to demonstrate the effectiveness of personality (Lauro's), corruption, and a feudal and absolutist past on the sensibilities of a semiliterate, miserable population. The party's conception of social consciousness was the distribution of a paternalistic largess to the unfortunate.

The MSI, the Italian Social Movement, is generally called neo-Fascist, but the prefix "neo" is inappropriate because the MSI was composed mainly of relics of the immediate past. Its leadership came from secondary levels of Mussolini's National Fascist Party, which was outlawed by the republican Constitution. In its early years, the intransigent elements who had remained loyal to Mussolini's Fascist Social Republic, the Republic of Salò, anti-monarchist and anticapitalist, had controlled the MSI. Later, after a number of violent internal wrangles, these groups were superseded by the more moderate elements from the south, who favored collaboration with the Monarchists, conservative Liberals, and Christian Democrats. It attracted some of the youth, especially secondary-school students, who had had no direct experience with Fascism. They were available to carry out destructive raids on meeting halls and section headquarters of the left-wing opposition and to beat up Communists and Socialists who were caught out alone (for the *Missini* were always careful to outnumber their opponents). Like the Monarchists, the MSI employed nationalist and anti-Communist themes, combined with pious displays of devotion to the Church. The party held its first national congress in 1952.

Like the extreme left, the Monarchists and Fascists represented a protest against the conditions of Italian society. The Fascist protest was the more ideological and uncompromising, however, and was able to resist the erosion that would eventually sap Monarchist strength in the late 1950's. But in the meantime, these two right-wing parties were flourishing in their southern strongholds, available to join with Christian Democrats and Liberals to form majorities in southern communal and provincial governments. They demanded their price, a share in the *sottogoverno*—the corruption and patronage.

The election results of 1951/52 were a warning of what might be expected in the parliamentary election scheduled for 1953. A stable government based on a solid majority possessed by the center parties appeared highly unlikely. This unfavorable forecast led to the desperate decision to tamper with the election laws. A combination of proportional representation and a special premium was to be substituted for the existing proportional representation system of election to the Chamber of Deputies. Specifically, any alliance of parties that received one vote more than 50 per cent of the votes in the nation would gain two-thirds of the seats in the Chamber. The law would convert a nominal majority among the people into a powerful one in Parliament. That it was a very undemocratic device was disregarded by its proponents. That it resembled the Acerbo Law of 1923, by which Mussolini had achieved his first Fascist majority in the Chamber, was obvious to everyone with any knowledge of Italian history.[3] Yet it was put forward by men who had been personal victims of the results of the Fascist juggling of election laws.

The introduction of the bill created an uproar in Parliament. The Communists immediately baptized it the "swindle law." The three small allies of the Christian Democrats—Liberals, Social Democrats, and Republicans—reluctantly supported the changes, fearful that their failure to do so would mean an alliance between the Christian Democrats and the extreme right after the election, yet knowing that if the juggling succeeded, the Christian Democrats would again gain an absolute majority in the Chamber and could then proceed to govern with or without them at will. Individual members of the three parties refused to go along, however. They formed a new group, Unità Popolare, led by such men as former Prime Minister Ferruccio Parri and the distinguished lawyer Piero Calamandrei, a former rector of the University of Florence, but the group did not attract enough members to prevent the stormy passage of the bill.

The election campaign was fought out on two major issues: the "swindle law" and the land reform. A minor issue was the still-open Trieste dispute. The United States again intervened

---

3 The Acerbo Law provided that the party receiving 25 per cent of the votes would receive two-thirds of the seats. It was through the use of this law, plus threats and other means of "persuasion," that Mussolini got his parliamentary majority from the 1924 election.

through its ambassador, Clare Boothe Luce, who publicly warned of the unfavorable consequences for Italy—in terms of American support—if the center coalition lost. A reaction to this foreign intervention, stimulated by nationalistic resentments, caused the statement by Mrs. Luce to be widely criticized, and her words probably did De Gasperi more harm than good. The Church again repeated its warnings, and the Civic Committees again launched their campaigns.

On June 7, 1953, the election was held for both houses.[4] The vote for the Chamber, shown in Table 4, gives the important re-

TABLE 4
VOTE FOR THE CHAMBER OF DEPUTIES, JUNE 7, 1953

Parties	Popular Votes	Seats Won
Christian Democratic	10,834,466	261
Liberal	815,929	14
Republican	438,149	5
Social Democratic	1,222,957	19
Communist	6,120,709	143
Socialist	3,441,014	75
Monarchist	1,854,850	40
Fascist (MSI)	1,579,880	29
Other	693,505	4

Source: Italia, Istituto Centrale di Statistica.

sults. The four center parties received 49.85 per cent of the votes, 57,000 short of the 50 per cent plus one vote required to earn the extra premium.[5] The defection of Unità Popolare, which did not win any seats but gained 171,099 votes, had cost the center coalition its prize. The Christian Democrats, while gaining from their low point in the 1951/52 local elections, received 40 per cent of the vote, much less than their 1948 sweep. Their three small allies suffered serious losses also, far more than the votes picked up by the Unità Popolare. The big gainers were the extremes, the

---

[4] Although the Senate then had a six-year maximum term, it was dissolved at the same time as the Chamber. In 1962, the Constitution was amended to give the Senate a five-year maximum term coincident with that of the Chamber.

[5] The "swindle law" was abolished the following year, and the election to the Chamber was again based on proportional representation.

Communists and Socialists on the left, the Monarchists and Fascists on the right. The latter two improved on their performance in the administrative elections of the previous year. The Communists made major gains in the south, as that part of the country gradually became politicized.

The election of 1953 marked the end of De Gasperi's political career. Although the four center parties had a slight margin in Parliament (proportional representation is never perfect), De Gasperi's efforts to form a new four-party government broke down. The Social Democrats were smarting from their losses. The left wing within the party reproached it for having gone along with the "swindle law" and having, in general, covered the center, which had moved more and more to the right. De Gasperi then tried to put forward a one-party minority government but failed to get the support of Parliament. He retired from politics and died a year later.

It was during this time that a new alignment was proposed. Pietro Nenni suggested during the Chamber debate that his party was available for an "opening to the left," that is, a coalition extending from the Christian Democrats through the Socialists. The suggestion evidenced the beginnings of the separation of the Socialists from Communist tutelage. (In the 1953 campaign, the Socialists had run their own slate, rather than combine with the Communists as in 1948.) De Gasperi had considered Nenni's proposal and then shelved it as premature. But there were left-wing Christian Democrats and Social Democrats who were interested, and the idea would grow until it became the dominant issue at the end of the decade.

This account has been centered on the policies, actions, and maneuvers of the political elite, the "ruling class," as Italian scholars and journalists define it. In the life of the "popular masses"—again an Italian phrase—the hue and cry over the "swindle law," American intervention, capitalism, socialism, and legality made hardly a ripple. In the medium-sized and small towns, in the villages and rural areas, the debates of the politicians and intellectuals were ignored, although the Trieste issue appears to have made a small impact. A study made by International Research Associates in communes in which substantial shifts of votes had occurred in 1953 from the Christian Democrats to the Communists, or vice versa, showed that local economic issues, local jobs, local public works, favors, improvements, and clientelism were the important influences on voting behavior, not the big national issues and ideological rivalries.

5
THE DECLINE
OF CENTRISM

De Gasperi's failure to organize a government reflected the troubled nature of the second legislature from 1953 to 1958. The reformist urge that had marked the early years of the preceding legislature was further diluted by the energy absorbed in finding majorities that would then collapse and have to be re-created. In many cases, the cabinets of the next five years were minority governments dependent on the abstention of the right-wing parties or the occasional support of the left wing on determinate issues. The tendency was to postpone solutions to major issues, such as the revision of the principal legal codes inherited from Fascism and the establishment of a regulatory system for the development of atomic power.[1] Postponement was due to the succession of cabinet crises and to the dependence of the Christian Democrats on right-wing support on various issues, the price paid being one of delay. The second legislature has therefore often been described as the "legislature of immobilism."

---

[1] The Civil Law Code, the Criminal Law Code, the Codes of Civil and Criminal Procedure, were all Fascist in origin. At the beginning of 1965, commissions established by the third legislature had not yet completed the drafting of new codes.

As Italy is deficient in coal and petroleum and had practically exhausted the available sources of water power, atomic power was commercially feasible earlier in Italy than elsewhere. Regulation was delayed, however, by the bitter battle over public *vs.* private control of atomic plants. Not until 1962, when the electric-power industry was nationalized, was the issue settled.

This generalization is valid for the major questions of domestic politics; it is invalid for foreign affairs and for business development. Economic production continued to expand at a good rate, and after 1954 the level of unemployment declined slightly, as the growth of employment began to be greater than the growth of the labor force.

It was in the area of foreign affairs, however, that the most dramatic events took place. Here, first attention must be given to the Trieste problem, an issue left unresolved by the peace settlement. It will be recalled that the peace treaty had assigned most of Venezia Giulia and the Istrian Peninsula to Yugoslavia. The area around the city of Trieste was detached from Italy and made into the independent Free Territory of Trieste. The peace treaty provided that the Security Council of the United Nations would select a governor to supervise—in the name of the international community—an elected government of the Free Territory. Until the governor was chosen, the Free Territory would remain under the occupation of the victorious Allies. The growth of the Cold War in the late 1940's made it impossible for the Security Council to agree on a governor, so the military occupation continued.

The Free Territory had been divided into two occupation zones, A and B. Zone A was under Anglo-American military administration, Zone B under the Yugoslavs. The city of Trieste and a stretch of territory west of the city were included in Zone A. The population, totaling over 300,000 people, was overwhelmingly Italian in ethnic origin, with a small Slovenian minority. Although Zone B extended over more than twice the territory of Zone A, it had only about 75,000 inhabitants, most of whom were Slovenians. The Italian population in the coastal villages of Zone B had left their homes in the early years of the Yugoslav occupation. The Communist government of Marshal Tito had in effect integrated the area into the Yugoslav federation.[2]

It will be remembered that the United States, France, and the United Kingdom, to help De Gasperi in the 1948 election campaign, had issued a public declaration that called for the return of the Free Territory, including both zones, to Italy. This declara-

---

[2] Zone A was Italianized to some degree also, in currency and administrative systems, but it was not integrated into Italy.

tion immediately became the minimum basis for all Italian claims to the area. A few months later, however, the dramatic split between Stalin and Tito occurred. To support Tito's independence and to widen the first rift in the unity of the Soviet bloc, the Western Allies dropped their pressure for a Trieste solution, and the divided occupation continued. Italian nationalists became more and more bitter at the Allies for sacrificing Italian interests to larger considerations of power politics. In subsequent years, riots occurred in Zone A, as well as in Italy proper, and were encouraged by right-wing elements condemning the Italian Government for its subservience to its Western allies. Since a British general commanded and British troops were in the majority in the occupation of Zone A, the already existing undercurrent of anti-English feeling was aggravated by the measures used by the occupation forces to restore order.[3]

Again to aid the Christian Democrats in the electoral campaign of 1953, the United States proposed to De Gasperi that Italy accept a solution to the Trieste dispute on the basis of a partition of the Free Territory along the lines of the two zones, with some slight modifications of the border in favor of Yugoslavia. The United States pledged to use all of its considerable influence on Marshal Tito to get him to accept the partition. Although there was strong support in the Italian Foreign Office for this solution as the best available, De Gasperi, at that time both Prime Minister and Foreign Minister, rejected the American offer.

After De Gasperi's failure to form a new government in the summer of 1953, the Christian Democrats turned in desperation to other men, but none had any more success. As the country had now been without a government for several months, the party conceived the idea of a provisional nonpolitical, or "administrative," cabinet to tide the country over until a new majority in Parliament could be negotiated. This administrative cabinet was formed by Giuseppe Pella, a right-wing Christian Democrat with no

---

[3] Anti-English sentiment had been built up by Fascist propaganda from the time of the Ethiopian War and the sanctions imposed against Italy by the League of Nations under British urging. The hard line taken by Britain after World War II, especially against the restoration of the pre-Fascist colonies to Italy, had caused more bitterness.

strong following in the party, but with close ties to northern business and financial circles. His cabinet was composed of Christian Democrats and a few independent technicians. In presenting his government to Parliament, he emphasized its provisional and limited nature, although the tone of his remarks on foreign policy indicated a somewhat independent attitude toward Italy's allies. This was calculated to get right-wing support and it worked, for only the Communists and Socialists voted against him a few days later when he received his vote of confidence. The Social Democrats and MSI abstained.

Pella now sensed his opportunity to convert his administrative and temporary government into a political one, and seized the Trieste issue as his vehicle to real power. Adopting a nationalist and belligerent tone in a speech on September 13, 1953, he proposed that a plebiscite be held in the whole Free Territory. At the same time, he indicated that Italy's ratification of the European Defense Community Treaty might depend on satisfaction received on Trieste.

The creation of the Coal and Steel Community in 1952 had stimulated further efforts toward European integration. In the political sphere, the Europeanists worked to draft a constitution for a European federation, but their effort made slow progress. The idea of adding West Germany's weight to the defense of Europe—while avoiding the creation of a new German army—led at this time to the evolution of the concept of a European army. The United States threw its influence behind the scheme, and in due course the principal countries of Western Europe signed a treaty creating a European Defense Community. In both France and Italy, there were considerable reservations, however, and not only among those of the extreme left. In both countries, doubt existed as to whether the treaty would be ratified by their respective parliaments. Pella was now claiming compensation on Trieste as the price of Italy's participation in the EDC.

England and America responded to Italian pressure by offering to let Italy replace them in the administration of Zone A. The Italian press was enthusiastic and Pella's reputation increased strikingly. But Tito reacted violently, and on October 10, 1953, he warned that Yugoslavia would consider Italian entry into

Trieste an act of aggression. The tension increased on both sides and the British and the Americans backed down. Demonstrations took place in subsequent weeks in both contending countries and in Trieste itself. On November 6, local police forces under Allied Administration fired upon demonstrators in that port city; six people were killed and many more wounded. This led to hostile demonstrations in Italy against its two allies, especially against the British Embassy in Rome. Pella wanted to go to Trieste to be present at the funeral of the victims. It would have been magnificent politics, but the Allies refused permission. His presence would have stirred up another demonstration. At this point, Pella sent two Italian divisions to the border area near Gorizia. The Yugoslavs countered immediately. The situation was less serious than it appeared, for Pella—and probably Tito—was bluffing. The British and the Americans proposed a conference, which Tito rejected because Pella stipulated that the tripartite declaration of 1948 had to be the minimum basis for discussion. A few days later, both sides withdrew their troops from the border area and the tension was reduced, but the issue was left unresolved.

Pella's behavior had alarmed Christian Democratic leaders, who were aware of his domestic political motivations. De Gasperi criticized him more and more openly, as did Scelba. By January, 1954, Pella was running into trouble with the party secretariat, which was gradually moving to the left. Amintore Fanfani, an economic historian by profession who had been associated in the late 1940's with Giuseppe Dossetti in the Catholic intellectual group around the magazine *Cronache sociali,* had organized a new current within the Christian Democratic Party, the Iniziativa Democratica. Less extreme than the *Cronache sociali* group in its leftist social and economic principles, and less integralist in its Catholic philosophy,[4] the Iniziativa Democratica proclaimed a progressive pro-

---

4 Catholic integralism may be described briefly as a movement aiming to have all human activities, especially political and social activities, impregnated by a Catholic inspiration. It seeks to achieve a Catholic social order that would minimize and, in the long run, eliminate all social and political movements based on different inspirations, such as Marxism, liberalism, secular humanism. It is antipluralist in its ultimate objectives, although it can collaborate with groups of non-Catholic inspiration for pragmatic political objectives. Integralists may be right or left wing in their economic

gram aimed at the popular masses, rather than at the upper classes. Fanfani, the most practical politician of the old *Cronache sociali* group, was building up the Iniziativa Democratica influence within the party secretariat. Thus attacked from a number of sides, Pella was forced to resign as Prime Minister.

For two weeks, Fanfani tried to form a single-party (*monocolore*) government. He was looked upon with considerable suspicion both inside and outside his party. The right wing, within and without Christian Democracy, distrusted his anticapitalism. The democratic lay parties of the left had reservations because of his background of associations with corporatism and integralism. Having finally put a Christian Democratic cabinet together, Fanfani saw it defeated by Parliament. It was one of the very few times in the history of postwar Italy that a government was overthrown in a formal vote of no confidence. Fanfani's defeat led him to concentrate on building up the position of his faction within his party. Here, he had more success. At the Christian Democratic Party congress held in the summer of 1954, the Iniziativa Democratica emerged as the principal current. Fanfani was elected Secretary-General of the party.

After Fanfani's failure to form a government in January, 1954, the Christian Democrats decided to return to the earlier center coalition. Their negotiations with their former allies were difficult, but were finally concluded successfully by means of contradictory promises. To the Social Democrats, they promised a series of social reforms; to the Liberals, the Ministry of Industry and Commerce, in order to reassure private business that the reforms would not amount to much in practice. The Republicans remained outside the cabinet but promised to support it in Parliament. On this basis, Mario Scelba, former Minister of the Interior, hated by the left parties for his mobile police squads and strong-arm tactics, succeeded in forming a government.

Scelba was plagued from the beginning by scandals, in which he had no direct part. The most crucial of these was the Wilma Montesi affair, which got the government involved in a sordid

---

orientations. The *Cronache sociali* integralists were left wing, and enamored of corporatist ideas. Luigi Gedda would be a right-wing integralist.

intrigue of rivalries. Foreign Minister Attilio Piccioni, a Christian Democrat, learned that his son was implicated in the scandal. Piccioni was forced to resign, his career ruined.[5] Factions of the Christian Democratic party used the scandal to embarrass and undercut other factions. The Carabinieri were rivals of the national police (the Pubblica Sicurezza of the Ministry of the Interior). Scelba was also the Minister of the Interior. The whole business revealed a web of collusion, corruption, and rivalry among colleagues, and threw the public administration and the government into the worst possible position.

Heir to the unresolved Trieste issue, Scelba also tried to use the EDC treaty as a means of resolving it. He knew that the EDC was unpopular with some groups within his own party and among his allied Social Democrats, who feared even indirect German rearmament. He might have pushed EDC through Parliament if he were able to tie it in with a diplomatic success on Trieste; otherwise, he was doubtful of the effects on his own majority of a parliamentary debate. The French Parliament resolved the EDC issue by voting it down, thereby eliminating the necessity for the Italians to act upon it.

Scelba did succeed in settling the Trieste question independently. Through the insistence of President Einaudi, Piccioni had been replaced at the Foreign Ministry by a man who would be willing to accept the partition of the Free Territory, Gaetano Martino of the Liberal Party. In the autumn of 1954, England and America revived the earlier scheme of dividing the Free Territory between Zones A and B. They proposed the same boundary rectifications in favor of Yugoslavia that De Gasperi had turned down in the spring of 1953. In the fall of that year, Pella had reasserted the claim to the whole Free Territory. One year later the Italians accepted the Anglo-American proposal, and the rectifications in favor of Yugoslavia were even greater than those rejected by De Gasperi. This time, Tito was more tractable and agreement was reached in October, 1954. Technically, Italy merely replaced the British and the Americans in the administration of Zone A; thus, the Italians could assert that their claim to Zone B was not

---

5 Piccioni had been considered De Gasperi's political heir. Three years later, the courts found his son to be completely innocent.

renounced. Actually, everyone knew it was a partition of the Free Territory, and in fact Trieste was incorporated into Italy in subsequent years.

This solution was a bitter pill for the Italians to swallow, and the government did not feel equal to presenting the agreement to Parliament for consent to presidential ratification of it as a treaty. Instead, the government called the accord a "memorandum of understanding," taking the position that since it was an interim measure, not a definitive treaty, parliamentary approval for ratification was unnecessary. Scelba announced to the Senate, however, that President Einaudi had already given his approval of the memorandum. In fact, Einaudi had done more than give approval; he had actively backed it behind the scenes. Scelba then asked for, and received from both houses, resolutions endorsing the work of his government. The problem of treaty ratification was thus side-stepped.

Resolution of the Trieste problem led to the expansion of economic relations between the two claimants to the territory, so that in future years Italy became Yugoslavia's most important foreign supplier and best customer. In addition, a weapon that had been used with some success to poison internal politics was removed from the hands of Italian nationalists. One negative consequence of the years of agitation over Trieste was the stimulation of Austro-German agitation over the South Tyrol. If Italians were outraged that their compatriots were forcibly deprived of their irredentist rights, the South Tyrolese in the Alto Adige and the North Tyrolese in Innsbruck were similarly outraged. The Italians refused to recognize the similarity between the two agitations, but from the mid-1950's onward, the South Tyrol problem would grow to create another difficulty in foreign affairs.

It is evident that the Trieste issue, no matter how sincerely felt, had been manipulated to build up domestic political positions and to appeal to nationalistic and right-wing sentiments. These were the years of reaction and obscurantism in Italian public life. Anti-Fascists were called saboteurs of Italian national honor. The resistance movement was denigrated; partisans were characterized as bandits, murderers, and even Communists. The Communists had been trying to take all the credit for the resistance, but now the opposite extremists just granted them the credit as a favor.

Interest in ideas and in political action had drastically declined. Compared to the heated and tense atmosphere of the immediate postwar years, this decline might be interpreted as a growing acceptance by the general public of the institutions of the new republic, and of the political system. This would be an incorrect inference, however. The decline of political commitment was no indication of any such consensus, rather it marked a privatization of personal and family life, signifying an exclusive concern with immediate, materialistic goals. The phenomenon was apparent in the universities, historic home of the militant and committed youth of Italy. In the mid-1950's, the youth, in their preoccupation with private careers, seemed to have forgotten all about the struggle for a better world. The gradually widening market for professional skills created by a developing economy provided opportunities for young men as long as they avoided any identification as political extremists.

On the whole, the business community had always been naturally conservative, but a combination of fear and opportunism had led it to meet, with a policy of compromise, both the social demands of the times and the social commitments of the Christian Democratic Party. As insurance against left-wing political victories, business firms had even found it useful to collaborate with the CGIL and to provide some financing for the Socialist and Communist parties. The principal organization of the business community, Confindustria (Confederation of Industry), led by the Genoese Angelo Costa, had followed this cautious and moderate line throughout the late 1940's and early 1950's.

By 1954, business attitudes were hardening. Encouraged by the political expansion of the right-wing parties in the previous year, by the Republican victory in the United States, by the atmosphere emerging in Italy, Confindustria decided on an aggressive campaign against both the left and the center. Under the stimulation of the large electrical corporations located in Milan, Angelo Costa was replaced by Alighiero De Micheli, president of Assolombardo (Lombard Business Association). Instead of giving most of their support to the Christian Democrats, they put more and more money into the Liberal Party.

In the spring of 1954, Giovanni Malagodi became Secretary-General of the Liberal Party. An able and dynamic man, he was openly identified with the large industries of the north. His party had been divided between conservative and progressive wings. The progressive wing did not identify liberalism with unrestrained free enterprise and rugged nineteenth-century laissez faire capitalism. Reformist in the American New Deal sense, the progressives felt that the party had not been sufficiently firm in defending the principle of the separation of Church and state from the increasing pressure of Catholic confessionalism and the Church on their major ally, the Christian Democratic Party.

Under Malagodi's leadership, the Liberal Party became more and more openly the spokesman for big business and the opponent of any economic reformism or public intervention in the market place. The success in capturing the Liberal Party further encouraged the "economic right" in their attacks on the center coalition. The progressive wing of the party attempted to counter these trends without much success, and after a year and a half, finally split off to found the Radical Party, in the fall of 1955.

The Radical Party had a numerically weak base, and in its short life (it was practically defunct by 1962), it never elected any candidates to Parliament, although it was able to elect some members to local and provincial councils. It had an influence, however, far beyond its membership. Two weeklies identified with the Radical point of view, Il Mondo and L'Espresso, had a circulation and impact among intellectual and political leaders far beyond the confines of the party, and the various study groups, research congresses, and debates promoted by these organs of opinion provided a stimulus to political thought that contributed to the activity of the democratic left. For the Radicals became ardent exponents of the replacement of centrism by a coalition of parties from the Christian Democrats to and including the Socialists.

But the opening to the left could not become a reality in the atmosphere then prevailing. It has already been noted that Confindustria's position was hardening to the right.[6] It launched an ever more aggressive attack on the divided labor movement. Workers were becoming more cynical and less disposed to back their union leaders. Membership was declining. Those workers in the elite group—the employees of the large and expanding firms— were benefiting from higher salaries and improved real incomes. Under the influence of this combination of pressures and benefits, the most exposed of the labor federations, the CGIL, was in trouble: still the largest of the federations, it was now to be openly besieged by the American Government. American labor advisers, as part of the policy of weakening Communist influence, had supported the schisms in the CGIL that had occurred in the late 1940's. They had favored the CISL and had discouraged the UIL in subsequent years. In 1955, Mrs. Luce, the American ambassador in Rome, promoted a new policy to undermine the CGIL still further. The United States Department of Defense used to award "off-shore" contracts to European manufacturers for the production of military equipment that the United States Government was furnishing its allies. Mrs. Luce succeeded in having the Defense Department proclaim that no further contracts would be awarded to Italian firms in which the CGIL candidates won over 50 per cent of the votes in the election to the internal commissions.[7] Since these contracts were important to several major industries, the profits and jobs of a large number of people were at stake.

The test of the new American policy came in the plant elections of the Fiat Company in April, 1955. Fiat, the largest private business in Italy and the major producer of automotive vehicles and other heavy equipment, had a substantial number of off-shore contracts. In 1954, the CGIL had received 60 per cent of the votes for the internal commission; now, in 1955, it dropped to 38 per cent. Comparable results occurred in other large firms. The American policy appeared to be successful. Appearances can be deceptive, however. Many workers, often encouraged by their CGIL

---

6 Confindustria does not control all of Italian industry, and a number of firms are not guided by its policies.

7 The internal commission represents the workers in a plant in all dealings with the management regarding the application of work rules, etc.

leaders, voted for the other labor federations but remained basically Communist or Socialist in their orientation. They were voting for their jobs, not for a different union. In later political elections, the Communist and Socialist vote increased. The CISL was only a temporary beneficiary of the American pressure. Italian employers used the situation to erode all the unions, not only the CGIL. In 1958, the CISL was split wide open in the Fiat plant by the appearance of a splinter union, led by dissident CISL leaders, that was suspected of having company support. The consequence was that the democratic, as well as the Marxist, labor movement suffered substantial setbacks.

Other setbacks were suffered by the forces of democratic liberalism during this same period. The Catholic Church appeared to be enduring a period of reaction, and this had some influence on the domestic scene. The political eclipse of De Gasperi removed a barrier to clerical and integralist forces within Catholic circles. After 1952, Pope Pius XII was a sick man. During this time, a group of conservative Curia cardinals, of whom Alfredo Cardinal Ottaviani was the most voluble, if not the most important, appeared to get the upper hand in the Vatican and to use it heavily in Italy and France.[8] Under Cardinal Ottaviani's direction, the Holy Office smashed the worker-priest movement in France. In Italy, young Catholic Action intellectuals were careful not to get caught when reading the works of such French Catholic thinkers as Teilhard de Chardin, Jacques Maritain, or Emmanuel Mounier.

Under Church pressure, censorship became more vexatious. Article 21 of the Constitution prohibits publications and entertainments "contrary to good morals." While some constitutionalists insisted that only post-censorship was permissible under this article, in fact pre-censorship of moving-picture scenarios, stage plays, and radio and television scripts was exercised by a bureau in the executive office of the Prime Minister. (In later years, after the creation of the Ministry of Tourism and Spectacles, the bureau was transferred to this ministry.) The censorship was exer-

---

8 Carlo Falconi, an Italian expert on Vatican affairs, called this group *Il Pentagono* ("The Pentagon").

cised so arbitrarily that while many salacious films got through, scripts of social and political criticism were blocked.

Freedom of religion, although guaranteed by Article 8 of the Constitution, was under fire. Protestant evangelical denominations, especially the Church of Christ, found that the police harried all their activities, closed their meeting halls on a variety of pretexts, and generally made life difficult. The Fascist law of public security of 1931 was still in effect and was used to ban a wide variety of different activities.[9]

A further oppression of the period was the restraint on freedom of movement. A gradual exodus from the countryside was taking place, for peasants were going to the cities in search of jobs. Article 16 of the Constitution guarantees freedom of movement, but still in effect was an old Fascist law that prohibited anyone from moving to another locality unless he had the guarantee of a job; on the other hand, jobs could be offered only to individuals officially registered as residents of the locality. The law was not enforced effectively, and the peasants continued their influx into the urban slums. Since they were illegal residents, however, they could not register to vote or register in the unemployment exchanges. They could not even demand rights and social welfare payments from their employers, for they could not afford to expose themselves. They were the helpless victims of abuse and exploitation. The Constitutional Court finally denounced the Fascist law as unconstitutional, but it was not until February 18, 1961, that the old decree was superseded by new legislation. The indifferent enforcement of this Fascist decree indicates some of the saving graces in Italian life during this period of reaction. Through inefficiency, whether natural or deliberate, and through a certain sense of human compassion, some of the more vexatious aspects of the period were softened and made more tolerable.

Some of the reformist zeal still present at the end of 1954 had led to the passage of a law extending pensions to peasant farmers. Motives other than reform were behind its passage: it was an instrument for consolidating the control of the Christian Democratic

---

9 A full discussion of many of these cases was provided by the outstanding civil rights lawyer Piero Calamandrei. See *Dieci anni dopo* (Bari: Laterza, 1955).

farm federation, the Coltivatori Diretti, over peasant proprietors. It was a measure welcome to all concerned, no matter what political motives were behind it.

Another positive act was the passage of the Vanoni Plan in 1955, formally entitled, "Ten-Year Plan for the Development of Employment and Income." It was introduced and fought for by the Christian Democratic Budget Minister, Ezio Vanoni, supported by the left wing of his own party and the other parties of the left. There were six fundamental goals: (1) an increase of annual investments to 25 per cent of gross national product; (2) a growth rate averaging 5 per cent per year in gross national income; (3) a moderate increase in consumption, but not enough to deprive the economy of increased savings for investment; (4) a balance in Italy's international payments to maintain adequate foreign exchange reserves and reasonable price stability; (5) elimination of structural unemployment over ten years; and (6) a reduction in the wide gaps in levels of income between north and south, industry and agriculture, upper- and lower-income groups.

The motivations behind the Vanoni Plan were revealed by the evidence that the economic growth of the previous years had made little appreciable impact on unemployment or on poverty in those areas of the country that were traditionally backward. The pressure of right-wing interests inside and outside the government, while insufficient to block passage of the bill in Parliament, was adequate to undermine the "planning" aspects of the project. Scelba was Prime Minister when the Vanoni Plan was put through Parliament, but he and his successors, Segni and Zoli, reduced the plan until it was nothing more than a series of projections of future economic developments. Both private and public firms went ahead their own way, making decisions based on their calculations of their own best interests, without any commitments or obligations to accede to broad goals laid down by a national agency.

As a set of projections, the Vanoni Plan appeared audacious. Yet events proved that some of these forecasts were actually conservative. The growth of gross national income in the following years of the 1950's was closer to 6 than to 5 per cent per annum, one of the highest growth rates in the Western world. Italy's balance of international payments became very favorable indeed, due to the expansion of exports and of the tourist industry, so that the lira became a hard currency and Italy accumulated a substantial gold and foreign-exchange reserve. Price rises were kept moderate until the early 1960's and thus the real incomes of those who were working and making profits did increase substantially.

On the other hand, unemployment did not decline significantly until the end of the decade. The economic gap between contrasting sectors of Italian society widened rather than narrowed, with the north advancing more rapidly than the south, industry more rapidly than agriculture, profits and wages more rapidly in the modernized large-scale sector than in the traditionally artisan, handicraft, and small-scale merchant sectors.

It is not surprising, therefore, that political tensions thrived as they had in the past, and became even more acute. At the Christian Democratic congress of 1954, the center-left section of the party—the Iniziativa Democratica—had won control of the party organization, and Amintore Fanfani was elected Secretary-General. Fanfani was actually more conservative than his reputation, but he appeared as a dangerous symbol to the right wing of Italian society. His election had been one of the factors disenchanting Confindustria with the Christian Democrats and inducing that business organization to concentrate even more of its hopes on the Liberals.

Fanfani was more interested in power than policy, at least in the short run, and his first efforts were directed toward building up his party as an organization. Under De Gasperi, the party had had little in the way of an effective grass-roots organization and had depended on related Catholic groups—such as the Civic Committees of Catholic Action, the Coltivatori Diretti, the CISL and the Church network of parishes—to carry out the election campaigns and round up the voters. Fanfani now engaged in an effort to create a wide and strong party base that would leave his party somewhat more independent of these related organizations. He even made an effort to establish a network of party cells in the factories. Since a large number of politicians, inside as well as outside the party, had a strong stake in preventing the rise of a more integrated Christian Democratic Party, Fanfani had only partial success. Undoubtedly, the party as such was developed considerably in the following four years, and the influence of the *partitocrazia,* the party bureaucracy, rose, as it did in all other parties except the Communist, where it had always been dominant. But Fanfani was never able to make his organization dominant, and at best it became one more faction in the shifting league of interests which composed the Christian Democratic Party.

A transition of a different nature was at work inside the Socialist Party. Ever since the electoral defeat of 1948, there had been Socialists who questioned the pact of unity of action with the Communists. They recognized that they could accomplish little for their supporters, mainly workers, if they did nothing but protest the inequities of Italian life from outside the governing coalition. They recognized that neither the conditions of life nor the line followed by the Communists provided opportunity for successful revolution. Reluctance to undermine the "unity of the working class" had retarded the development of this point of view, and in the intervening years, the Socialists had suffered heavily through internal schisms and the loss of their electorate. By the early 1950's, at least two identifiable currents were apparent in the party: the "autonomists," led by Giovanni Pieraccini and Riccardo Lombardi, called for more independence of action, while the *carristi* defended the line of close cooperation with the Communists. The *carristi* were particularly strong among the Socialists in the CGIL, who were in close working contact with the dominant Communist leadership of the labor federation.

In the 1951 and 1952 local elections and in the 1953 parliamentary election, the Socialists had already run independent tickets wherever proportional representation was used. During the parliamentary election, Nenni, who was straddling the factional differences among his followers, had enunciated publicly for the first time the concept of the opening to the left. This was, in effect, the assertion of a reformist, rather than maximalist, position; it was also the recognition of Socialist willingness to collaborate with bourgeois parties within the political framework of the democratic republic if a common program of social benefits and economic reforms could be agreed upon.

Foreign policy had ceased to be a divisive issue. Although the

Socialists had originally opposed Italy's entry into NATO, by 1955 they were ready to accept the alliance—provided that it was used for defensive purposes only (they had originally condemned it as aggressive in intent) and provided that the emphasis in the alliance shifted from military to economic and political cooperation. Since the Christian Democrats were also primarily concerned with NATO as a means of aiding Italian economic development, the two parties were not too far apart. As the intensity of the Cold War spirit was moderated by a growing atmosphere of *détente,* which finally led to the 1955 Geneva understanding between the United States and Russia, the Socialist reconciliation with Atlanticism in the "spirit of Geneva" was promoted. The Socialists were now willing to accept the Western alliance if it followed a policy of rapprochement with the Soviet bloc.

At the Turin congress of the Socialist Party in the spring of 1955, Nenni made it clear that he was repeating his offer of an opening to the left and that his party was ready to test the possibility of collaboration with the Christian Democrats. This renewed offer, combined with the growing conservatism of the Liberals and the shift to the left among the Christian Democrats, made the center coalition of Prime Minister Scelba ever more precarious.

President Luigi Einaudi's term of office had come to an end, and his advanced age led him to refuse to run for a second term. The two houses of Parliament elect the president in joint session. For the first three ballots, a two-thirds majority is required; after the third ballot, a simple majority is sufficient. The Christian Democrats not only did not have the necessary majority, but as it turned out, could not keep control over their own parliamentarians. The official candidate of the party organization and of the cabinet, Cesare Merzagora, President of the Senate, was a rather conservative man, and a small left-wing group of Christian Democrats put forward the name of Giovanni Gronchi, President of the Chamber of Deputies, in competition. Fanfani tried to hold his party in line for its official candidate, but a group of right-wing Christian Democrats led by Guido Gonnella undercut Fanfani and threw their support to Gronchi. It was obvious that they were less interested in the person of Gronchi than in the opportunity to set Fanfani back in his efforts to build up a disciplined, integrated party.

At this point, Nenni saw the opportunity to insert the Socialists into the struggle. Gronchi was known to be sympathetic to the idea of collaboration between Christian Democrats and Socialists. He was known to have a more elastic conception of the Atlantic alliance than the official government position—involving less subservience to the United States than Gaetano Martino's conception —although Gronchi was not a neutralist, as his enemies claimed. There were so many rumors to the effect that Mrs. Luce opposed Gronchi that Prime Minister Scelba was obliged to announce publicly that the United States was not exerting pressure for or against anyone. In fact, the rumors aided Gronchi by bringing to him the backing of nationalists of the right. Once Nenni was able to mobilize his own party's support behind Gronchi and to negotiate with right-wing Christian Democrats and other conservatives, the battle was won. The Communists swung over, and the Christian Democratic government leaders, faced with the prospect of having a president from their own party elected by the extreme left and the extreme right against the center, released their supporters, who all voted for Gronchi and made his election overwhelming.

The presidential election had produced strains on the government and on the parties, especially the Christian Democratic Party. Nenni's skillful maneuvering had enabled him to insert an opposition party, considered beyond the pale, in all respectable circles, into the victorious presidential majority. Fanfani's failure to hold the Christian Democrats together in support of the party's candidate had exacerbated differences among various factional leaders. Scelba had been a vigorous opponent of Gronchi's election to the presidency of the republic. It is not surprising, consequently, that when the Prime Minister submitted his government's routine resignation to the new President, Gronchi did not invite him to form a new government. Instead, the head of the state called upon Antonio Segni. This action was the first indication that an enlarged conception of the presidency was to emerge in the Italian political system.

From the very beginning of his seven-year term of office, Gronchi made it clear that he did not conceive of his role as that of a mere ceremonial figurehead who wrote and spoke only at his government's dictation. He had his own ideas about policy and personnel, and about the broad goals of Italian political evolution. In his inaugural address to Parliament, he condemned a social order that left large sections of the population estranged from it, referring to "those working masses and middle classes whom universal suffrage has conducted to the doorstep of the state's edifice without introducing them effectively to where political direction is exercised." And he defined the goal of government policy to be "the reconciliation of the people with the state about which we dream and toward which we work."[10]

Dreams and work are both necessary, but in the Italy of 1955, there was still a long way to go before that reconciliation dreamed of by Gronchi could be realized. The government was so bogged down in contradictions that it was practically impossible for it to move in any direction, right or left. It was in fact stalemated. Outside of Italy, events were occurring, however, which would have an additional impact on the country's internal political alliances.

---

[10] Giovanni Gronchi, *Discorsi d'America* (Milan: Garzanti, 1956), pp. 39, 99.

6
STIRRINGS OF
REVISIONISM

The explosion that rocked the Italian left in the spring of 1956 was Nikita Khrushchev's report to the Twentieth Congress of the Communist Party of the Soviet Union, *The Crimes of the Stalin Era*. The "secret" report, once it was translated and published by the American State Department and thereby exposed to the rest of the world, aggravated all the stresses and strains inherent in the evolution of the Communist and Socialist parties in Italy.

Within the Communist Party, stirrings for a revision of policies and attitudes were confined to the intellectual elite and the leadership. The defense of all the past policies of the Soviet Union seemed hardly justified now that Russian leaders were themselves openly condemning them. Khrushchev's attack on the "cult of personality" threatened Palmiro Togliatti's position among his own colleagues. Togliatti maneuvered skillfully, however, and was able to isolate his critics effectively by using a combination of ideological concessions and toleration of criticism, while at the same time rallying all the personal interests of his followers to preserve the party's unity as the condition of political effectiveness. Administrative elections were due in June, 1956, and all Communist leaders who had positions in communal or provincial governments had a stake in their posts and in maintaining the unity of the Party organization.

To soften the impact of Khrushchev's exposures, Togliatti openly adopted a position of criticism of his Soviet comrades. While endorsing the elimination of the cult of personality, he questioned the past behavior of some of the current Russian leaders and demanded to know what they had failed to do to prevent some of the crimes of the Stalin era. Most importantly, however, Togliatti seized upon Khrushchev's assertion of the legitimacy of "various paths to Socialism" as an endorsement of the actual policy of the Italian Communists, who were claiming their own "Italian way to Socialism." Their submission to Soviet policy had been limited to international affairs; inside Italy, from the very beginning of the post-Mussolini era, they had always determined their own strategy and tactics.[1] Togliatti now openly asserted the doctrine that the Soviet Union and the Soviet Party were no longer the "guiding state" and "guiding Party" for the world Communist movement. Every Party was free to follow its own course; there were a number of centers of power and policy; "polycentrism" was the term he used. The following year, before a meeting of his own Central Committee, he asserted that the unity of the international Communist movement was based on the "common goals and ideals" of the several national parties, not on a system of hierarchical discipline, and he re-emphasized that each Party was completely independent in the formulation of its own Party line.

By these verbal measures and concessions, Togliatti succeeded in keeping the internal unrest minimal, and his position was reinforced by the results of the administrative elections held that summer. While the Communists suffered some losses in the major northern cities of Genoa, Turin, and Milan, they continued to make small but steady gains in the country as a whole, and especially in the south and the islands. The elections confirmed once again that the overwhelming majority of Italians who voted Communist did so because of the conditions of their personal daily lives, not because of dogmatic issues or events occurring thousands of miles away.

---

[1] For example, Stalin had opposed the Italian Party's policy of opening ranks to anyone, whether or not he was a knowledgeable and believing Communist. The Party had done so in spite of Stalin's objections, and this rejection of any ideological qualification for membership can be found in the Party's Constitution.

The effect of Khrushchev's exposures on the Italian Socialists was far greater. All their past sacrifices on the altar of "proletarian unity" seemed hardly justified by the abuses now revealed. The autonomist wing of the party received major reinforcement from these events, and the policy of seeking a reinsertion into the Italian constitutional political game was buttressed. The open affirmation that the sacrifice of political democracy was too high a price to pay for socialism, and that the one was not to be subordinated to the other under any circumstances, would not be long in coming. Within a few months of the Twentieth Congress of the CPSU, Pietro Nenni wrote in one of the Socialist Party's journals that the defects revealed by Khrushchev were not the results of the errors of one man, but were due to the degeneration of the Soviet political and legal system. It was the method of dictatorship that had to be abandoned; the mere replacement of one man by some others was not enough.

Logically, the Socialist reaction further encouraged their assertion of electoral independence from the Communists. In the 1956 administrative elections, therefore, the Socialists, along with the Social Democrats and Republicans, successfully urged a return to the method of proportional representation for electing councilmen in all communes over 10,000 in population.[2] This enabled the smaller parties to run their own independent slates; the Socialists separately from the Communists, the Republicans and Social Democrats separately from the Christian Democrats. The Socialist slates made a number of electoral gains that furthered their autonomy.

Growing Socialist autonomy laid the logical premises for reunification of the two Socialist parties. In August, 1956, Pietro Nenni and Giuseppe Saragat met at the resort town of Pralognan to discuss the issue. There is little information yet available as to what was said, but the conclusion was negative and the two political parties continued to go their independent ways.[3] Strong fac-

[2] Success in getting the election law revised was due to the Social Democrats and Republicans, who threatened the Christian Democrats with a government crisis at the national level if the changes were not made.

[3] Nenni has hinted that Saragat was the one who was unready for reunification, but until more is known any judgment is premature.

tions within each, however, would make the reunification issue an important question of policy from that time.

The shocks reserved for the Italian left in the year 1956 were not yet over. Even more dramatic than Khrushchev's revelations in the spring were the Polish and Hungarian uprisings of the following October. The Hungarian revolt was the real blow, especially to the Italian Communist Party. The Party's leadership abandoned any attempt to give a unified explanation of events. The official Party paper, *Unità*, lamely called the Hungarian uprising a counter-revolution organized by foreign and domestic reactionaries, while the interpretation published in other pro-Communist papers was notably different. The Communist leadership of the CGIL openly sided with the Hungarian insurrectionists, and Communist intellectuals signed manifestoes of protest against the Party leadership.

But discipline was slowly restored and the Party ranks were reunited. The Anglo-French-Israeli attack on Egypt helped divert attention from Hungary and enabled the leadership to launch an attack on Western imperialism. The efforts of the government of Imre Nagy to detach Hungary from the Soviet bloc were used to justify the Russian intervention. Even some dissident Communists could accept the necessity for the Soviet Union to guard its defenses and prevent disintegration of its East European alliance, and could thus overlook any mistakes the former Stalinist-type Hungarian leadership had made in handling Hungarian workers.

Nevertheless, the Communist losses were not negligible. It has been estimated that approximately 300,000 members left the Italian Communist Party at that time, and among them were some important political and intellectual leaders whose prestige would be missed. The Party's capacity to attract new intellectual leadership from among Italian youth declined considerably. Events appeared to confirm the benefits that ambitious young men might derive by avoiding political identification and commitment. The Communist youth federations, Party schools, training programs, all had to be scaled down in view of the reduced number of new recruits. The curious phenomenon of a declining Party membership coupled with an increasing voting support would characterize the Communist Party's future, for the 1958 and subsequent elections demonstrated that the Party could still function efficiently as an electoral machine.

The effects of the Hungarian uprising were dramatic among the Socialists. Nenni denounced the circumstances and conditions that had caused the Hungarian revolt, insisting again in public and in private that they represented the failure of a system, not of a man.[4] The Socialist Party, rejecting the Russian interpretation of the uprising as a counter-revolutionary plot, asserted the rights of the Hungarian workers and condemned the Soviet intervention. Nenni returned the Stalin Peace Prize he had received in an earlier year.

A few months later, in February, 1957, a Socialist Party congress met at Venice to assess party policy. Angelo Roncalli, the Archbishop of Venice, later Pope John XXIII, wished the Socialists a successful congress. Nenni's speech and the confirming resolutions later adopted by the delegates reasserted the interpretation given to the events of the previous year: Stalinist degeneration was inherent in the system and in the political and legal institutions of the Soviet Union more than in the man. The values of democracy and of liberty were as important as socialization of the means of production. The Socialists accepted the practices of parliamentary democracy, including the multiplicity of parties, and free elections, not only as means to social justice but as ends in themselves. The unity-of-action pact, which, in fact, had been moribund at the national level for a number of years, was practically, if not formally, finished.

But the results of the Socialist congress were not so clear-cut. Alongside these verbal statements and unanimously adopted resolutions was the contradictory fact that a substantial number of the incoming party directorate elected by the congress came from the extreme left-wing faction, the *carristi,* who favored continued collaboration with the Communists. In the election of

---

[4] In an exchange of letters with Mikhail Suslov, who had written in August, 1956, to complain about Nenni's condemnation of the Soviet system rather than one man, Nenni reiterated in October that the Hungarian events proved that the defects were due to the system. The letters were published in *Avanti,* October 25, 1964, after the defenestration of Khrushchev.

delegates, carried out in the party sections preparatory to the national congress, the secretariat had maneuvered the voting in such a way as to produce delegations suspicious of, if not antagonistic to, Nenni's thesis.[5] They voted for his resolutions, and then they elected to the principal party organs a number of men who were loath to carry them out. Thus, Nenni was obliged to work with many men who were not yet ready to follow his leadership. While the *carristi* were in an over-all numerical minority, they held key positions in the party, the CGIL, and the cooperatives. Some of them were accused of being on the Communist payroll, an accusation difficult to prove.

In every respect, the Socialist position remained ambiguous, and the ambiguity was exploited by the right wing of the Italian political spectrum. The continued association of Socialists and Communists in local governments and in the CGIL led these right-wing forces to assert that the proclamations of Socialist autonomy were all fraudulent, nothing more than a Marxist scheme to achieve power by a different tactic. This line of attack made life more difficult for those Social Democrats, Republicans, and left-wing Christian Democrats who were arguing that Socialist cooperation was necessary to achieve stable and progressive government. The evolution of the Socialist position could not be rapid. It had to overcome many years of past association with the Communists and to disregard the tempting hope that the Italian Communists were not unrecoverable for a progressive democracy. It had to fight its way against all the obstacles raised by external conservative forces who preferred to keep the Socialists in a position of sterile protest outside the effective centers of political power, rather than have them join and reinforce the democratic left.

The outcome of the Socialist congress revived a variety of attacks on the political parties, attacks that had persisted with various degrees of intensity throughout the postwar period. Uomo

---

[5] In the elections of the delegates to the party congresses held in the various sections, there was often little participation by the mass of party cardholders. In many cases only an insignificant minority of members came to section meetings, thereby making it easy for the local secretaries to get their own friends elected.

Qualunque, flourishing temporarily in the early years, had been one type of attack against party politics. Another type had taken the form of criticism of party control over parliamentarians. It was charged that the party organizations outside the chambers made policy and determined the voting positions of their parliamentary delegations, but since almost all national party leaders were also parliamentarians, the lines of influence were not that simple. Yet there was no question that the most influential parliamentary leaders derived their positions from the roles they played in their national party organizations. In the search for a means of breaking external party control, some critics advocated, without effect, the abandonment of proportional representation and its replacement by single-member districts.

A different line of attack was leveled at the full-time party bureaucrats, the *partitocrazia*. They were accused of manipulating parties to build their own power and fortunes, thus undermining —when they did not falsify—the wishes of the rank-and-file party members. They were charged with being the enemies of freedom, the crushers of internal party debate, the stultifying and rigid opponents of the evolution of new ideas. The results of the Socialist congress had appeared to verify these criticisms.

The critics came from many positions within the political spectrum and advanced their charges from a variety of motives. Some critics, such as the novelist Ignazio Silone, were sincere democrats anxious to improve the operations of the parties and to strengthen internal party democracy. Others used their attacks on party organizations as a decoy for assaults on political parties as such and, more fundamentally, on parliamentary democracy itself. The defense of permanent party organizers came from one who was himself a leading member of a *partitocrazia*, Giovanni Malagodi, Secretary-General of the Liberal Party. He argued, in Silone's own review, *Tempo presente,* that politics in the middle of the twentieth century was a full-time job, that all aspects of life were becoming bureaucratized, that the old world of the local notables was dying. In a world of many nationwide mass organizations that are, in reality, nationally organized interest groups, he argued, only a nationally organized party can stand up to them and mediate among the entrenched interests—only the party organization, structured at a national level, has some kind of vision of the national interest.[6]

In fact, the party bureaucrats were not so powerful as their critics maintained. Even the most formidable of the *partitocrazie,* that of the Communist Party, could not successfully suppress all internal debate and discussion all of the time, nor could it block the evolution of ideas nor avoid the challenging impact of external events. As for the most important of Italian parties, the Christian Democratic, it was so torn by factions, so pressured by extraparty confessional and economic interests—such as the Church hierarchy, the Catholic Action Society, and the Coltivatori Diretti —that the party secretariat at best was just one more competitor for power within the party. There was no dictatorial leadership; on the contrary, Italy, lacking effective leadership, was forced to muddle through a number of difficult economic and political issues.

One of the most controversial of the economic problems of the period was the disposition of exploration rights for petroleum and natural gas in the Po Valley. A dynamic left-wing Christian Democratic politician, Enrico Mattei, had built up a small government-owned oil corporation, AGIP, inherited by the republic from Fascism, into the large and aggressive National Hydrocarbons Trust (*Ente Nazionale Idrocarburi,* commonly known as ENI). The four-party Segni cabinet, which succeeded Scelba's government in the latter months of 1955, inherited a running dispute (dating back to 1949) between AGIP and the foreign international oil corporations. The ENI wanted exclusive exploration rights in the Po Valley, while the foreign corporations wanted private enterprise to participate in the search for additional sources of methane gas and petroleum. Mattei had tried to break into the international oil consortium in the past, but had been rebuffed, and he was now reacting vigorously. He could mobilize the left wing of his own party—and other parties of a Socialist orientation—to support the principle of state control of fundamental sources of energy. Behind the foreign corporations stood domestic Italian business interests, conservative Christian

---

[6] Giovanni Malagodi, "Il segretario e gli 'apparati,'" *Tempo presente,* February, 1959, pp. 137–41.

Democratic, Monarchist, and Liberal politicians, and the American and British governments. The American ambassador, Mrs. Luce, was particularly aggressive in fighting the ENI's effort to get exclusive control, and her attempt probably boomeranged by stimulating the Italian's nationalist feelings. The final political battle lasted for over a year, and in the end Mattei won. Parliament passed legislation giving exclusive exploration rights to the ENI.[7]

This was only one of the battles lost by Italian business interests during the time of the Segni cabinet. Another one involved the reorganization and coordination of all government-owned businesses. Attempts to get the government at least partly out of business failed: no private firms wanted to buy the weak, inefficient government companies, and the strong, dynamic ones were not for sale. These latter had many powerful friends and interests behind them. The Ministry of State Participations was created in January, 1956, to supervise the many existing publicly owned firms, coordinate their plans, and develop their possibilities. Confindustria fought its creation violently, but the fears of this business organization that the new ministry would prove to be the rallying point for a widespread attack on private enterprise turned out to be groundless. The ministry's powers were limited by law, and even more so by the facts of their existence. The many public corporations were, in reality, private empires with their own vested interests and political and economic connections. The Italian Government was too weak to control effectively its own creatures, who carried out their own commercial policies, sometimes in collaboration with, and sometimes in opposition to, private enterprises.

Two additional battles lost by Confindustria involved its control over its public member firms and influence over development

---

[7] It must be emphasized that the ENI monopoly was limited to the Po Valley and to exploration and production rights. It was given no monopoly on production in the rest of Italy. The Gulf Oil Company is producing oil from concessions in Sicily. In addition, other foreign firms, such as Shell, Esso, and British Petroleum, distribute Middle Eastern petroleum products throughout the country. The ENI's marketing subsidiary, AGIP, distributes supplies obtained from foreign, as well as domestic, sources. A major foreign source has been the Soviet Union.

policies in the south. The publicly owned firms, which came under the vast IRI complex, were regular dues-paying members of Confindustria, and it, of course, was dominated by the large private industrialists. Confindustria, in bargaining with labor organizations, reached nationwide agreements binding on all its members, including the state-owned businesses. Thus, a private-interest group controlled many policies of public firms. In addition, the funds collected by Confindustria from its members were used to attack the government and the principle of government ownership of productive enterprise.

The parties of Socialist orientation had always objected to this situation, claiming that public ownership was thus stripped of all social content and that the IRI firms, in acting for purely selfish purposes, behaved like the private monopolists. As early as 1954, De Gasperi had come around to this point of view. In the fall of 1954, a resolution calling for the withdrawal of all publicly controlled firms from Confindustria was introduced by Giulio Pastore, left-wing Christian Democratic Deputy and president of the CISL, and passed by Parliament. This was merely a resolution, not a law, and three more years of legislative battle were required before it was implemented by legislation. The final detachment of the public firms came in 1957, and was related to the creation of the Ministry of State Participations, which would presumably replace Confindustria in speaking for public enterprise. The detachment (*sganciamento*), however, did not have the awful consequences feared by private-business groups. The administrators of the public firms maintained their old contacts with their private counterparts, even though the public firms no longer paid dues to Confindustria or were bound by its contracts. Eventually, a new association of publicly owned companies was created, Intersind, to represent public management and to negotiate labor contracts in behalf of public firms.

A more significant struggle raged over the evolution of governmental policies for the development of the south. Originally, the program had restricted the government's role to agricultural reform and—through the instrument of the Cassa per il Mezzogiorno—to the provision of the fundamental infrastructure to lay the foundations for subsequent industrialization. It was left to private business, encouraged by special credit benefits and tax concessions, to carry out the actual industrialization. As it turned out, private industry, both southern and northern, moved very slowly to take advantage of the supposed opportunities. Industrialization was lagging behind seriously. Under the circumstances, there was more and more agitation by economic planners and southern interests for the Fund (Cassa) to engage in direct industrial investment and for the state-owned firms to expand their southern operations. Confindustria fought this pressure bitterly, arguing that the public sector should be restricted to infrastructure and that industrialization should be left to private business. This battle it also lost. In 1957, legislation was passed that required all firms owned or dominated by the state to locate 60 per cent of their new investments in the south and to work toward the eventual goal of having 40 per cent of their total investments located in that area. But legislation is one thing and performance is another. Although, in subsequent years, the ENI reached the percentages required by the 1957 legislation, many of the IRI corporations did not.

Through its principal spokesman, Confindustria, private business lost a number of legislative battles in the years following 1955: detachment of the public firms, the Ministry of State Participations, southern industrialization, the Po Valley petroleum monopoly. The defeats were due to a variety of reasons. In the legislature, it was obvious that important factions in the Christian Democratic Party were becoming less responsive to the pressures of big business. In addition, the business community itself was not unified; many firms failed to follow the Confindustria position when they had no direct stake in the issues involved. In the fight over the legislation for southern industrialization, there were wholesale desertions by southern business and commercial interests from the Confindustria line laid down by northern industrialists. The Neapolitan and Sicilian Chambers of Commerce and industrial groups welcomed more money flowing into their areas and had no ideological preconceptions concerning the source of the money, public or private. Their views were reflected in the voting behavior of southern Christian Democratic legislators.

Another factor in the Confindustria defeats was the growing injection of new money into politics. Enrico Mattei was actively bracing his position by buying and supporting newspapers and financing various parties, especially the left wing of the Christian Democratic Party. As Confindustria became more embittered at Christian Democratic progressives and shifted more support to the Liberals, the contributions from public firms to Christian Democrats would compensate for the reduction of private money. Both private and public contributors tended to give their funds, not to any party as a whole, but to the factions and individuals within the parties who best supported their interests. This was especially true of the Christian Democrats, and a consequence was a further undermining of Fanfani's efforts to gain organizational control over his party.

Before the 1956 administrative elections, Confindustria had approached the Confederation of Agriculture (Confagricoltura) and the Confederation of Merchants (Confcommercio) with a proposal for joint and open support of those candidates and parties that would defend the interests of private enterprise. They created a new political group, Confintesa, to finance and endorse publicly individual candidates ready to accept such backing. The effort failed magnificently. The public endorsement by Confintesa was practically valueless for collecting votes. Almost all of the endorsed candidates were defeated in 1956. In 1958, businessmen would return to working behind the scenes through factional party leaders and governmental bureaucracies for the protection of their interests.

A major success for big business was the establishment of the European Common Market. The French defeat of the European Defense Community in 1953 had brought the movement for European integration to a temporary halt. Efforts to revive the integration process were launched in 1956 and crowned with victory with the Treaty of Rome in March, 1957, the final act of the expiring Segni government. For the large-scale modern businesses of Italy, penetration into the markets of the advanced countries of northwestern Europe was a much more attractive prospect than penetration of the backward and underdeveloped Italian south. Rationalization and modernization of their operations, plus low wage costs, made many of them effective competitors in European markets. Since the reduction of tariffs contemplated by the Common Market treaty was to be gradual and subject to brakes in case of necessity, the representatives of Italian big business felt that the dangers of opening their domestic market to foreign competitors could be minimized. And, since the underlying economic principles of the European Economic Community emphasized a market economy and private enterprise, they hoped that Italy's membership in this community would protect them from socializers and planners in their own country.[8] It was anticipated that the Common Market would provide an alternative to a too rapid expansion of the domestic market, for the latter would result in a social and economic upgrading of the most poverty-stricken people, causing them to increase their political claims, and would thus bring instability.[9] The Common Market, like the policy of promoting emigration abroad, could function as a partial escape from facing some harsh realities at home.

These calculations were not, of course, the only reasons for Italian interest in the European Economic Community. A minority of the intellectuals were true Europeanists who looked upon the Common Market as a step toward the political and cultural integration of the continent. Others saw in such unification the means to a revival of the international power position of Italy and of Europe. There were Italian supporters of the Gaullist third-force concept. Still others opposed the third force but looked upon economic unification as a means of increasing Europe's relative weight within the Atlantic alliance, which they considered dominated by American power. Some emphasized the common moral and spiritual patrimony of the Western European

---

[8] Since the prospects for socialization and government planning would be increased if the Socialists were brought into the governing coalition, the Common Market could be used as an argument against this danger. Thus, Gaetano Martino of the Liberal Party argued during the election campaign of 1958 that the Christian Democrats were not free to choose an opening-to-the-left policy because the Common Market treaties prohibited policies of government direction and control over the economy. See *Il Corriere lombardo* (Milan), April 28, 1958.

[9] In Italy, as elsewhere, the initial effects of economic development were increased political radicalism and an expansion of the electoral strength of the extreme left.

countries. But unquestionably crucial was the hope and expectation that a Common Market could help to protect Italy from the internal dangers of an aggressive and growing left.

In the autumn of 1957, Parliament authorized ratification of the treaties to establish the European Community. Not surprisingly, the Communists voted against authorization. The Socialists voted in favor of the establishment of Euratom and abstained on the Common Market. They emphasized, in their publications, that they did not oppose European federalism in principle: they were suspicious of the role and influence of large cartels and capitalistic interests in the projected economic community, but they thought that vital Socialist movements in the Common Market countries might effectively counter them. One of their principal leaders, Riccardo Lombardi, wrote that the Common Market could do Italy positive good if it forced those Italian firms that were backward and inefficient to modernize as the price of survival.

The Common Market not only divided the Socialists from the Communists but temporarily divided the Communist Party internally. The trade-union wing of the Communist Party, with Giuseppe Di Vittorio of the CGIL taking the lead, saw in the European Economic Community an institution of potential benefit to the Italian worker. Socialist influence within the labor confederation was having 'some impact on the Communist comrades in this respect. For a short time, Di Vittorio led a battle to change the minds of his Party colleagues. Party discipline prevailed, and Di Vittorio and other Communist trade-union leaders were brought back into line. In subsequent years, however, the regional community would have its effect on Communist thinking, and in 1963 the Communists would openly endorse the Common Market.

During this whole period, Italy was experiencing contradictory demands in international affairs. Men working for greater Italian integration into the Western system were countered by other men working for more independence. President Gronchi felt that Italy was far too subservient to, and underrated by, its allies, especially the United States, and argued that a more direct pursuit of Italy's national interests was compatible with loyalty to the Atlantic alliance. The Socialists, who disliked military blocs, made known that they would be more interested in the Atlantic orientation if its military aspects could be de-emphasized in favor of economic and political aid. The troubles of European colonial empires in Africa and the Near East opened up prospects for Italian business and political penetration at the expense of Great Britain and France.

The policy of a more independent stance by Italy received the name "neo-Atlanticism." The title was first used in 1955 by Foreign Minister Giuseppe Pella, in connection with the launching of a more active policy among the Arab and North African states, and quickly got confused with the idea of a "Mediterranean Vocation." Both of these policies were denounced: some proclaimed them to constitute disloyalty to Italy's allies; others ridiculed the idea that economically and militarily poor Italy could have much influence in new states, which mainly wanted guns and money. Their supporters argued that Italy could represent the Western world better than England, France, and the United States, since these countries, for a variety of reasons, were looked upon with suspicion and in some cases hatred in the "emerging countries."[10]

The Mediterranean Vocation idea was later taken up by left-wing Christian Democrats, Social Democrats, Socialists, and others who advocated cultivation of the countries of the "third world." It was also compatible with the thaw in Soviet-Western relations after the Geneva Conference of 1955, which reduced the pressures on the Western countries to maintain absolute solidarity. It corresponded to a drive by Enrico Mattei and the ENI to break into the Middle Eastern oil markets. Mattei cared nothing for Italy's official foreign policy or for the Ministry of Foreign Affairs. He negotiated his own agreements and dealt directly with foreign governments. In the autumn of 1957, his first major break-through in the Middle East was announced: a concession agreement with

---

[10] There was no doubt that the great majority of Italians had looked upon the defeat of England and France in the Suez Crisis at the end of 1956 with bitter pleasure. England had run Italy out of Africa, and now its turn had come. Since these two Italian allies had also been opposed by the United States and most of the members of the United Nations at the time of the crisis, it was a safe position for Italy to take. But these underlying attitudes were hardly compatible with the spirit of Europeanism.

the government of Iran that was based on the formula of 75%: 25%, with the larger return going to the host country. This upset the 50% : 50% policy employed by the international oil concerns in their Middle Eastern contracts and antagonized Italy's important allies—the United States, Great Britain, and France. The agreement with Iran was followed by others in the Middle East and in North and Central Africa, often made with the new governments of former British and French colonies.

The policy of Italian penetration of the Near East and Africa won the endorsement of the left-wing parties. It was another point of contact between the Socialists, on the one hand, and the Christian Democrats and Social Democrats, on the other. It was another possible basis of unification between the two Socialist parties, or of bringing the Socialists out of the opposition into collaboration with the government. As a consequence, the issue of neo-Atlanticism lost its exclusively foreign-policy associations and became involved in the whole problem of domestic realignments. Pella, who had originated the policy and the phrase in 1955, dropped it when the debate between Atlanticists and neo-Atlanticists was converted into a conflict between the opponents and proponents of the opening to the left.

The interest in expanded trade relations with the countries of the Soviet bloc and the third world was not confined to the ENI or to other publicly controlled businesses. Private firms were just as anxious to pursue increased opportunities for profit. In this pursuit, they were not bothered by political or ideological preclusions. They would buy from, and sell to, any variety of regime: Communist, Fascist—no matter the country or the political system. This had been the policy of all Italian governments in the entire postwar period, but the thaw in international politics after 1955 and the decline of colonial empires with their protected markets opened new opportunities to Italian trade. In 1957 and 1958, Confindustria was pressuring the government to use all its influence with its allies to eliminate, or drastically reduce, the NATO embargo lists of items forbidden for export to the Soviet bloc. Conservative politicians and businessmen, such as Baron Raffaele Guariglia, the Monarchist Senator, or Teresio Guglielmone, the Christian Democratic Senator, were heading private economic missions to Moscow and Peking. Out of consideration for its ally—the United States—Italy did not recognize Communist China, but did not let nonrecognition stand in the way of business.[11]

---

[11] An agreement between Italy and Communist China, reached at the end of 1964, led to the opening of commercial offices by the two countries (in Rome and Peking, beginning in January, 1965). At the time of the agreement, Foreign Minister Giuseppe Saragat announced in Parliament that the Italian Government favored recognition of Communist China but would take action only in accordance with its allies, not unilaterally, as France had done.

7
CONSTITUTIONAL AND
POLITICAL EVOLUTION

The republican Constitution of 1948 provided for the creation of a number of new regional, judicial, and economic institutions. With the intention of limiting the exclusive power of a centralized and hierarchical political system, it was planned that the new institutions should be set up as independent centers of authority, protected from the domination of the cabinet and Parliament. In the late 1940's, the extreme left had opposed this constitutional trend on the grounds that it would limit the sovereignty of the people as expressed through the supremacy of Parliament. In plain words, as long as the Communists had some hope of capturing the central government, they did not want any limitations on that government's authority. The Christian Democrats, on the other hand, had a political tradition, extending back to the years before Fascism, that favored decentralization and federalism.

With the coming into effect of the Constitution, the positions of the principal parties became reversed. After the April, 1948 election, the Christian Democrats had an absolute majority in Parliament and dominated the cabinet. They postponed the implementation of those constitutional provisions that would have set up relatively independent judicial institutions and regional governments. Only the special regional governments were created —in those peripheral areas of the country where independence movements or linguistic minorities were present and where temporary autonomy had already been granted. These were Sicily, Sardinia, the Val d'Aosta (French-speaking), and Trentino–Alto Adige (with a German-speaking majority in the Alto Adige).[1] The Christian Democrats simply neglected to create governments for the rest of the regions.

The Communists and Socialists, on the other hand, became supporters of regionalism and judicial independence. Cut off from the government, in opposition to, and excluded from, all positions of power in Rome, they controlled 20 to 25 per cent of the local and provincial governments throughout Italy. Since they were especially strong in the central regions—Tuscany, Emilia-Romagna, Umbria—there was a good possibility they would win electoral control over regional governments in those areas if the regular regions were created. So the Christian Democrats and their allies continued to ignore the Constitution, and in precisely those parts of the country where the left opposition was strongest, strengthened and reinforced the powers of the Ministry of the Interior and the prefects.

For a number of years, the implementation of judicial reform was likewise postponed. Legislation to supplant the Fascist legal codes under which the country was still living was pigeonholed. Civil codes, criminal codes, and security laws that dated from the time of Mussolini were still in force. Two new judicial institutions provided for by the Constitution—the Constitutional Court and the Superior Council of the Judiciary—remained unimplemented.

In the 1950's, pressures from the professional associations and law schools, as well as from the democratic parties within the cabinet and the opposition, led the government to undertake, reluctantly and slowly, the establishment of these judicial institutions. The Constitutional Court was perhaps the most revolutionary in its implications. The Constitution of prerepublican Italy, the *Statuto albertino*, inherited from the Kingdom of Sardinia upon unification of the country in the nineteenth century, was an open constitution. Any act of Parliament passed by a simple majority was legal. Once Mussolini had obtained control over

[1] In 1963, a fifth special region, Friuli–Venezia Giulia, was created, with its capital at Trieste.

Parliament, he was able to put through any bill he wanted without constitutional obstacles. To prevent a repetition of this situation, insofar as a dictatorship can be prevented by legalistic devices, the framers of the 1948 Constitution had created a special amending process, and a Constitutional Court to pass on the constitutionality of legislation and decrees having the force of law. Failure to appoint the judges had been a way of avoiding the establishment of the Court.

In 1953, De Gasperi had finally decided to take action, but the creation of the Court was delayed for two more years by disputes over the filling of its positions. Article 135, paragraph 1, of the Constitution provided for a fifteen-judge Court, five nominated by the President of the Republic, five elected by the two houses of Parliament in joint session, five elected by the members of the highest regular and administrative courts (the Court of Cassation, the Court of Accounts, and the Council of State). President Einaudi insisted that the Constitution assigned to him the exclusive right to name the first group of five judges; the cabinet, controlled by Christian Democrats, claimed that the President must accept the five nominees suggested to him by the Council of Ministers. Einaudi finally won his battle, and his nominees were his own choices. But the delay was not yet over. Implemental legislation already passed required that the five judges to be elected by Parliament receive a three-fifths majority. After the 1953 parliamentary election, the Christian Democrats and their allies had no such majority. To elect the judges required logrolling with the opposition. The Communists held out for a fair share, one out of the five. It took until the end of 1955 for the Court to be constituted. It began functioning in April, 1956. Under the Constitution, the Court elects its presiding officers from among its own members; the judges chose Enrico De Nicola, the former Provisional President of Italy, as the first President of the Constitutional Court.

In the interim, a debate had raged over the limits of the Court's jurisdiction. Minimalist legal thinkers maintained that the Court was limited to judging the constitutionality of legislation and decrees enacted only after April, 1956, not of pre-existing law. This thesis would have preserved a whole body of Fascist law, as well as laws and decrees put into force in the years after Mussolini's downfall. The Court disposed of the argument in its very first decision, asserting that prior laws were subject to judicial review, and could be nullified if found contrary to the preceptive norms of the Constitution. With this decision, the Court did not automatically throw out the Fascist legal codes and legislative inheritance. They remained in effect until replaced by new codes, legislation, and decrees, or until the Court modified or destroyed them in whole or in part as particular cases on particular issues came before it for decision.[2] As of 1965, the major Fascist codes of criminal and civil law had not been superseded by new codes and were still in effect. A few of their articles had been replaced by subsequent legislation and a few others had been thrown out by the Constitutional Court. The behavior of the Court has been cautious, rather than daring.

In two broad areas of constitutional interest—civil rights and centralization—the Court soon had many cases to hear. Generally, it defended the important personal freedoms of speech, the press, and religion. Also it usually upheld the central government in controversies with the special regions, especially with the Sicilian regional government.

The problem of enforceability of the Court's decisions was a difficult one. As mentioned earlier, the Italian executive branch, historically, had not been accustomed to being checked. The result was that a number of Court decisions were ignored by administrative and political officials. Enrico De Nicola resigned in protest when a cabinet minister refused to adhere to the Court's decisions. His successor, Gaetano Azzariti, would also complain of the same problem.

If an independent Constitutional Court bothered executive officials, a really independent regular magistracy was potentially a greater source of concern. In the long run, the ordinary courts, handling the routine daily judging of litigation, would have more impact on the social system than the courts at the apex of the

---

2 A case comes to the Constitutional Court when the judges of the regular courts conclude that a constitutional issue is in controversy in a case they are hearing. Only they can transfer the case to the Constitutional Court.

judicial hierarchy. The doctrine of the independence of the magistracy had roots going back to the nineteenth century. Even before Fascism, however, the courts were often held to be subservient to the government in practice. Under Fascism, of course, the situation degenerated, although the judges fought a losing battle to maintain their professional standards.

The judiciary in Italy was (and is) a career service into which a young man entered after finishing law school and passing the competitive examination. (Not until 1964 did a woman enter the judiciary branch in Italy.) Assignments and promotions had traditionally depended on the Ministry of Justice, and the knowledge that a magistrate's career was at the mercy of a political minister, and of the higher judges who could influence the minister, had undermined the backbone of many magistrates in the past. The framers of the Constitution, aware of these historic conditions, had attempted to reinforce the doctrine of judicial independence by taking control of the magistracy away from the Ministry of Justice and vesting it in a new institution, the Superior Council of the Judiciary. Article 105 of the Constitution gave the Superior Council the following powers over judges: appointment, assignment and transfer, promotion, and discipline.

For eight years, the successive governments, and Parliament, had withheld the necessary enabling legislation to implement this part of the Constitution. In the middle of the 1950's, agitation was building up, especially among the younger magistrates themselves. In 1956, inside the National Association of Magistrates, the younger judges began to organize, and within two years took control of the association from the older senior judges who had dominated it. Their pressure on Parliament, together with that of the political parties and of the bar associations, finally led to the establishment of the Superior Council of the Judiciary in 1958.

The 1958 act was subject to vigorous criticism by the magistrates' association. The Constitution provides that two-thirds of the Superior Council be elected by the Judges from among their own members, one-third by Parliament in joint session from among law professors and practicing lawyers. The 1958 enabling act divided the judges, of whom there were then about 5,300, into three categories for the purpose of electing the judicial members of the Superior Council. As a consequence, the judges on the Superior Council that represented about 300 of the highest-ranking magistrates equaled those that represented the remaining 5,000. In addition, the 1958 act assigned disciplinary functions to a Superior Council committee that was to be composed almost exclusively of the representatives elected by the high-ranking magistrates. The younger judges protested, citing the constitutional dictum: "Judges differ only in diversity of function [Article 107, paragraph 3]." The 1958 act also continued the traditional method of setting higher salaries for the judges of the higher courts. The magistrates' association argued that Article 107 was thus violated and that salaries should be equal regardless of the type of judgeship, with increments based on seniority alone. In the opinion of the younger judges, the legislature's implementation of the Constitution on this question was defective. It left the judges open to fear of their superiors and to the temptations of economic careerism, both factors being capable of undermining judicial independence. They continued to protest, through their magistrates' association, but without avail. In 1960, the small minority of high-court judges split off to form their own association, from which the younger judges were excluded. The struggle was a conflict of generations, as well as a conflict of hierarchy, with the postwar generation of the lower courts arraigned against some of the holdovers of the Fascist period.

Another controversy, one that finally brought about the collapse of political centrism, was the debate over the agrarian pacts. The land reform of the early 1950's had created a number of new peasant proprietors, but had done little or nothing about the problem of sharecropping—*mezzadria*. Sharecropping was particularly prevalent in central Italy—in Tuscany, Emilia, and Umbria—and the sharecroppers provided a major source of voting power for the Communist Party in those areas. The struggles over constitutional reform, over detachment of the public firms, over public investments in southern industry, had been eroding the Segni cabinet between 1955 and 1957. During these two years, Segni, whose reputation as a moderate leftist was based on the fact that he was Minister of Agriculture at the time of the passage of the land-reform legislation (1950), was moving steadily to the right.

Moderate revision of the legislation concerning the *mezzadria* had been undertaken during the war and the immediate postwar period. The share of the income to go to the sharecroppers was increased, and they had been given greater security against eviction. Their situation was still an extremely difficult one, which explained the Communist gains, and the left parties and the left wing of the Christian Democratic Party were now negotiating for further improvements. Meanwhile, through the influence of the landowners on the Liberals and on the moderate and conservative factions of the Christian Democrats, a bill was introduced in early 1957 to increase the number of "just causes" available to a landowner to justify eviction, thus weakening the peasant's power to bargain with the landowner.

On February 28, 1957, the Republican Party, in protest, withdrew from the majority. With the support of the Monarchists and neo-Fascists (MSI), the cabinet was able to continue in existence for two months, but was reduced to routine administration. The situation became increasingly embarrassing for the Social Democrats. In May, 1957, Giuseppe Saragat publicly attacked the government, of which his party was a member, and Segni presented the cabinet's resignation to the President of the Republic. The bill to reform the agrarian pacts was discussed for another year, straining the discipline within the Christian Democratic Party. In a rare display of rebellion in Parliament, the trade-union Christian Democrats openly voted against the bill in the spring of 1958, when it came up again. It was finally dropped and the whole problem was postponed for five years more.

Segni's cabinet was followed by a one-party (*monocolore*) minority government of Christian Democrats that was headed by the Tuscan anti-Fascist Adone Zoli. It had no agreed majority in Parliament and was intended to function as an interim cabinet until the parliamentary elections scheduled for 1958. The Monarchists and neo-Fascists decided to support Zoli, certain that his government would not do anything in the way of reforms. These votes were extremely embarrassing. Zoli decided to accept the

Monarchist votes, but rejected the neo-Fascist support as "neither necessary nor desirable." The day following the vote of confidence, however, a recount showed that the MSI votes were necessary for a majority. Zoli handed in his resignation. Before accepting it, President Gronchi surveyed the situation with the political leaders. The only alternative was an opening to the left. But *L'Osservatore romano* editorialized clearly against such an alternative. Gronchi then refused to accept Zoli's resignation; the Prime Minister swallowed his objection to the Fascist support and the cabinet received a new vote of confidence. In view of the coming elections, the Christian Democrats were anxious not to be identified with Fascism. Zoli was a weak man and the party and government were being run by Fanfani, the Secretary-General of the party. The cabinet's position was strengthened by the general knowledge that if it were overthrown, the only remaining choice would be for the President to dissolve Parliament and call for immediate elections. And the parties did not want the election— for which they were as yet unprepared—pushed forward in time.

During Zoli's government, there were a few accomplishments of minor importance. The government completed its absorption of the national telephone system, over which the state already had majority stock control through the IRI. Legislation for the Cassa per il Mezzogiorno was extended. The final touches to the controversial bill establishing the Superior Council of the Judiciary were added. The Common Market treaties, negotiated by the preceding cabinet, were routinely ratified. Fanfani broke Communist-Socialist control over the Republic of San Marino.

Most attention was concentrated on the coming election, and to prepare for it the Christian Democrats who were under Fanfani chose to emphasize their relatively progressive tendencies. Their attacks against the Liberals on their right became stronger and were reciprocated. In February, 1958, the Minister of the Interior, Fernando Tambroni, dissolved the Monarchist government of the city of Naples, charging it with corruption. Some thought this was a tactical mistake that would make a martyr of Achille Lauro, the Monarchist leader and Neapolitan mayor. At the same time, the Christian Democrats continued to reassure their supporters of their own moderation by carrying on an anti-Communist barrage, reinforced by Catholic Action posters showing Russian tanks in the streets of Budapest and Communist and Socialist parties manacled together indissolubly.

Relations between Church and state became a major election issue, especially in Tuscany. The Bishop of Prato, an industrial city north of Florence, had publicly declared and written that a young couple of his diocese were "sinners" and "public concubines" for having been married in a civil, rather than religious, ceremony. The couple sued the Bishop for slander and defamation, and the court in Florence accepted jurisdiction of the suit. On March 1, 1958, it found the Bishop guilty and assessed a small fine. The Vatican reacted violently: for the first time since 1929, a bishop had been tried in an Italian court. The next day, in protest, Pope Pius XII canceled a forthcoming celebration of the nineteenth anniversary of his ascension to the papacy. The day after this, the Vatican announced the excommunication of all those responsible for the Bishop's trial and sentencing. The case had become a *cause célèbre*. While some Catholic circles attempted to make a martyr of the Bishop, comparing him to the persecuted clergy of China, the popular sentiment sided with the couple. The Bishop had demonstrated a fanaticism and extremism out of all proportion, which rebounded against him not only in court but in the public squares. The assertion of the jurisdiction of the state appeared to be a rebuff to the idea that Italy was becoming a *repubblica papalina,* a little papal republic, in which clergymen were beyond the law. The decision became a campaign issue.[3]

More important was the promulgation on May 3, 1958, of a letter in the name of the Italian Bishops' Conference calling on all Catholics to "vote united" for the Christian Democrats. The letter was posted on church doors and read at masses all over Italy. There was no evidence that the Italian bishops had met in conference to approve such a letter. It appeared that a small num-

---

[3] A year later, a court of appeals reversed the sentence and stated that the courts did not have jurisdiction. By that time, little attention was focused on the incident and the reversal had no political repercussions.

ber of cardinals and archbishops had drafted and issued it in the name of the entire conference. This was the first time such open and public election instructions had been given. In July, 1949, Pius XII had issued a general excommunication of believing Marxists. Now all the other parties, including the non-Marxist ones, were more or less pushed beyond the pale. The purpose of the open letter appears to have been, not to attack the left—whose constituency was more or less immune to such orders—but rather to prevent certain bishops and other clergymen in the south from openly endorsing either the neo-Fascists or the Monarchists, who had by then split into two parties, the National Monarchist Party and the Popular Monarchist Party.

The other parties, especially the Radicals and the Republicans, who had allied for the election campaign, immediately protested this clerical intervention in the campaign, an intervention that was a violation of the Concordat of 1929. These protests proved useless, since the predominant Christian Democrats would never openly rebuff the Church, and were happy to get support in any case. The practice became standard, and the Bishops' Conference issued similar appeals in subsequent parliamentary and administrative elections. But little attention would be given to them, and their electoral consequences became negligible.

The parliamentary election of May 25, 1958, came at the end of a period of economic advance. In the early months of the year, however, the growth of the economy had slowed down, reflecting the current American recession in a limited way. The Christian Democrats could point to the progress made on the economic front, even if political affairs had been stalled for some time. Its election slogan was "Progress without adventures," to reassure its more conservative voters that the problem of relations with the Socialists was not to worry them.

The election produced small increases for both the Christian Democrats and the Socialists over their 1953 representation. The results in the Chamber are shown for both elections in Table 5. These national figures do not give a real indication of the electoral consequences. A breakdown by electoral districts would demonstrate that the parties' positions had remained relatively stable in the north and that the gains and losses occurred prin-

TABLE 5

VOTE FOR THE CHAMBER OF DEPUTIES, 1953 AND 1958

| | 1953 | | 1958 | |
Parties	Seats	Votes (Per Cent)	Seats	Votes (Per Cent)
Fascist	29	5.8	25	4.7
Monarchist	40	6.9	23*	4.8*
Liberal	14	3.1	16	3.5
Christian Democratic	261	40.1	273	42.2
Republican	5	1.6	7	1.4
Social Democratic	19	4.5	23	4.6
Socialist	75	12.7	84	14.2
Communist	143	22.7	140	22.7
South Tyrol People's	3	0.3	3	0.5
Other	1	2.3	2	1.4
Total	590	100.0	596	100.0

* These figures represent the totals of the two Monarchist parties. They reunited in 1960.

Source: Italia, Istituto Centrale di Statistica.

cipally in the south.[4] The big losers were the two Monarchist parties, whose strength had been mainly in the south and who now demonstrated that they were entering a decline. The economic transformations occurring in Italy had made their political impact. The southern subproletariat was becoming less susceptible to traditionalist Monarchist appeals and gifts of *pasta* or clothing to buy their votes. They now wanted more than pa-

[4] Two weeks before the Italian election, the French Fourth Republic fell as a result of the Algerian crisis, and General de Gaulle took over the government with emergency powers. The Italian Christian Democrats immediately seized upon the French crisis to argue that France's troubles were due to the failure of any party to get a majority, and called on the Italian electorate to rally around the largest party to ensure stability "without adventures." The Communists blamed France's troubles on the failure of the working class to remain united, an obvious attack on the autonomists among the Socialists. Some observers considered that this event influenced the Italian electorate, especially to the benefit of the Christian Democrats. I doubt it. The Italians most interested in, and affected by, French events were the inhabitants of the large northern cities. The Christian Democratic and Communist gains were largely in the south, among voters who knew little and cared less about what was happening in Paris.

ternalistic charity. The Christian Democrats were the principal beneficiaries of the Monarchist decline, but Communists, Socialists, Liberals, and Fascists also profited. Communist votes increased in the south to compensate for slight percentage losses in the north. (Since there was a large increase in the number of voters, the parties would have to gain votes just to remain in the same relative position.) The election proved once more that the political earthquakes of 1956 outside of Italy—de-Stalinization and Hungary—had little effect on the mass of Communist supporters.

On the whole, the election indicated a shift to the moderate left. The Communists had held their own; both Socialists and Social Democrats had gained. Even more interesting, however, were the shifts inside the parties, the result of the preference votes cast by the party electorate. The left-wing Christian Democrats made considerable gains, as did the autonomist Socialists. A new alternative to the stalemate of the previous year now appeared. But the apprehensions on the part of both these parties were still so strong that the deadlock would persist for more than three years, leading in the interval to new crises.

8
FANFANI'S FAILURE

Fanfani, having directed the electoral campaign toward widening the gap between his party and the three parties to his right—the Liberal and the two Monarchist parties—now faced the problem of forming a new cabinet oriented toward the left. This involved overcoming strong resistance from within his own party and among the Liberals, the political groups committed to a relaunching of the old centrism. The immediate vehicle which these groups hoped to use was the Hungarian government's execution of three imprisoned leaders of the ill-fated 1956 revolt. Giuseppe Pella, the right-wing Christian Democratic Foreign Minister in the previous cabinet (which stayed on in a caretaker capacity until a new one was formed), denounced the executions in the most violent language, and as a sign of protest, summoned to Rome the Italian ambassador in Budapest. The large northern newspapers supporting the Liberal Party behaved in an identical manner. Pella's play for reappointment as Foreign Minister failed, however, since Fanfani's ambitions proved strong enough to resist these pressures.

Fanfani proceeded to construct a coalition of Christian Democrats and Social Democrats, taking for himself the portfolios of both the Prime Minister and Foreign Minister. The two-party coalition did not have a majority, but succeeded in obtaining the abstention of the seven Republicans as the condition for its accession to office. Fanfani made no serious effort to obtain Socialist support. He knew that important persons in his own party were opposed to it, as were influential Catholic groups outside the party, such as the Catholic Action Society and powerful ecclesiastical figures within the Church hierarchy. He himself was not yet ready to accept Socialist participation. With his integralist conception of Catholic politics, he envisioned social justice brought to the masses as part of the Catholic conquest of the whole society, not as justice achieved within a pluralistic society. Pietro Nenni stated, however, that the Socialists would not raise a general prejudicial opposition to the coalition, but would support or oppose each policy or bill on its merits.

Events outside of Italy did nothing to make the Socialists eager to participate in the government. In July, 1958, the Americans and the British invaded Lebanon to prevent the overthrow of the Lebanese Government from ending in a Communist takeover. The Italian Government supported its allies and defended their motives. The Anglo-American forces used the airport at Capodichino, outside Naples, as a transit station to move troops to the Middle East. The Communists naturally denounced the whole operation, while the Socialists criticized it on two grounds: It was, they charged, a classical example of the economic imperialism of English and American oil companies; second, it was intervention in the internal affairs of a foreign country. The Socialists, in the words of spokesmen such as Riccardo Lombardi, had opposed Soviet intervention in Hungary, and now opposed American intervention in Lebanon. All efforts by the far left to mobilize large demonstrations against American intervention met with little success. The government discouraged mass open-air meetings and parades. It permitted some speeches in theaters and meeting halls, but the turnouts were not impressive. The Communists tried to blame their weak showing on government "oppression," but it was perfectly obvious that the days were over when they could rally thousands of activists into the squares over issues that seemed remote from their supporters' immediate interests. Some commentators blamed the weak response on the heat wave that Italy was then suffering. Whatever the cause, the general indifference to the event was a conspicuous consequence.

Fanfani was convinced that Italy could and should play a more active role in international affairs, with a greater display of independence. Like President Gronchi, he did not believe that membership in the Atlantic alliance was identical with sub-servience to Italy's allies. They both saw that the decline of British and French power in Africa and the Middle East opened up the possibility for Italian political and economic penetration into those parts of the world. They approved of, and gave further backing to, Enrico Mattei in his search for exploration concessions and marketing deals for his state-owned oil-and-gas combine in the territories of the developing countries. And while they justified their politically motivated explorations as helping to maintain Western influence in Africa, their primary concern was with enlarging the Italian "presence" in the world.

A minor move made in the foreign-policy field was related to the ENI's expanding international operations. In the autumn of 1958, Mattei was working out an agreement with the Egyptian Government to create a jointly owned petroleum corporation. The 75% : 25% ratio of returns was again to be the basis of the agreement, as against the 50% : 50% ratio used by the large international Anglo-American oil consortium operating in the Near East. The agreement came roughly two years after the Anglo-French-Israeli political defeat over the Suez, and therefore rankled Italy's European allies politically as well as economically. Cyrus L. Sulzberger, the *New York Times* foreign-affairs columnist, charged that Fanfani was weakening NATO ties with his efforts to cultivate the Socialists at home and the Arab countries abroad. The Italian Government protested, and on November 26, 1958, United States Secretary of State John Foster Dulles publicly denied that Italy was weakening NATO.

One month after this little flurry, the Egyptian Government publicly announced the granting of an oil concession in the Sinai peninsula to the jointly owned subsidiary. A few days later, Fanfani made a formal visit to Cairo, and on January 8, 1959, a joint communiqué announced the signing of an economic and technical accord. On returning home, Fanfani found himself criticized for his apparent support of Arab neutralism.

Charging Fanfani with accepting or supporting Arab neutralism was not the same as charging that he embraced Italian neutralism, which was what his domestic enemies really wanted to claim. There is no evidence to substantiate the second charge, which was derived from the first, and much evidence to the contrary. On October 25, 1958, Italy had come out in opposition to de Gaulle's plan to create a "Big Three" directorate in NATO, but this can hardly serve as a basis for declaring that Fanfani was undermining the Western alliance. In fact, for the previous half-year he had been collaborating with his Western allies by quietly consenting to the construction on Italian soil of bases for American intermediate-range ballistic missiles with atomic warheads. Italy was to control the bases and missiles, the United States the warheads.

News of these negotiations had been leaking out ever since early 1958. At that time, Fanfani was not Prime Minister and Foreign Minister, but he was the dominant policy-maker behind Zoli's *monocolore* cabinet. The Italian Government had moved very cautiously on the issue, not only in view of the forthcoming elections but also in the knowledge that there was considerable opposition, by political figures as well as among the general public, to the installation of missile bases. A sample survey of opinion, taken in March, 1958, is given in Table 6. This indication of opinion

TABLE 6
ITALIAN ATTITUDES TOWARD MISSILE BASES, 1958
(In Per Cents)

Question: Do you favor the establishment of long-range-missile bases [in Italy] by the United States?				
Response	*Favor*	*Oppose*	*Don't Know*	*Depends*
Total sample	30	39	29	2
By education level:				
Primary or less	25	39	34	2
Secondary	39	39	19	3
Superior, university	48	33	15	4

Source: Istituto Italiano dell' Opinione Pubblica, poll of March, 1958.

may provide some insight into the Italian Government's caution. By the summer of 1958, and after the elections were over, the Fanfani ministry could move a little more openly. In the Chamber of Deputies on September 30, an administration spokesman implied —though did not admit in so many words—that Italy would probably agree to the construction of the missile bases. On November 2, the Soviet Union protested this probability, a protest which the Italian Government rejected. This is the background for Dulles' rebuttal of Sulzberger's charge.

The final agreement on the bases was not completed until the following spring, after Fanfani's government had fallen. A communiqué from Washington on March 30, 1959, notified the world that Italy was the first of the Continental allies of the United States to accept construction of the bases. On April 21 and April 28, the Soviet Government again made public protests to Italy. Khrushchev warned that Italy would be among the first targets for atomic destruction in case of war. The next month, at the suggestion of the Italian Communist Party, he offered to create a Balkan Peace Zone in compensation for the de-atomization of Italy. The offer was repeated again in June, to be rejected once more.

The missile-base accords between Italy and the United States were never submitted to Parliament for approval and were never formally debated or voted upon. Consequently, the parties were never required to take a formal position on the issue, a requirement that would have strained the internal unity of several of them.[1]

It was not foreign policy, however, that made the life of the Fanfani government brief and difficult. At the time of its creation, predictions were made that finally things in Italy were really going to change and that the government would have a life of at least two years (compared to an average life for cabinets in postwar Italy of about nine months). It is true that in his capacity as Foreign Minister, Fanfani carried out a major reshuffling of the top levels of the Foreign Office hierarchy, putting his supporters among the career diplomats into the key positions.[2] His domestic

[1] In an interview with Guglielmo Negri on November 5, 1963, former President Gronchi declared that he was never officially informed by the government that an agreement with the United States had been concluded to construct the IRBM bases, nor was he ever officially informed of the 1962 decision to dismantle them: Guglielmo Negri, *La direzione della politica estera nelle grandi democrazie* (Milan: Giuffrè, 1964), p. 49, n. 100.

[2] Over the years, the career officers of the diplomatic corps, as in other ministries, had become factionalized into groups supporting various currents in the Christian Democratic Party.

problems, however, frustrated his hopes of carrying out a more dynamic foreign policy, and it was a combination of religious, economic, and party conflicts that finally brought him down. Although they were all occurring at the same time, it will be convenient to take them up separately.

In the Veneto and Emilia-Romagna regions, a financial scandal of vast proportions that had been brewing for some time finally burst into the open. A certain Commendatore Giuffrè had been involved in a number of get-rich-quick schemes and financial speculations, promising individuals and groups exaggerated returns (90 to 100 per cent) in a year for money they deposited with him. To cover his tracks and protect his position, he had become a generous supporter of Catholic charities and had cultivated close friendships with several members of the hierarchy of those regions. As it turned out, various clergymen, including high-ranking bishops, greedy or ingenuous or both, had put their own money and that of their parishes, dioceses, or orders into Giuffrè's hands, dazzled by the prospect of large earnings. The cabinet ordered an investigation, the results of which not only embarrassed the Christian Democratic Party and the Catholic Church but also strained relations with the allied Social Democrats.

Another religious issue involved government harassment of minor Protestant evangelical sects, usually stimulated by local priests in the areas where the sects were proselytizing. The police often broke up their meetings on the grounds that the sects were not provided with the necessary authorization for their meeting halls or churches, or that they were not led by authorized ministers. These issues had finally arrived in the Constitutional Court. On November 24, 1958, the Court ruled that Protestant sects could operate churches without police authorization. It also held, however, that Protestant ministers must have official recognition as ministers by the state. A number of the groups were led by lay preachers who were not so recognized. While the government had no control over the Court's decisions, it was nevertheless blamed by many conservative Catholics for failing to defend the interests of the Catholic Church adequately. There has never been much understanding or appreciation in Italy of the doctrines of separation of powers or checks and balances. The government is blamed and held responsible for everything, even rain. Fanfani was considered deficient in the handling of the Giuffrè scandal, as well as of other issues that brought embarrassment to Catholics.

His economic problems resulted from his sense of social justice, the economic requirements of the time, and the suspicion of him that was widespread among the leaders of private business. The price of wheat in Italy was being supported at a rate well above the international market price (although below the German market price). The importance of wheat in the Italian diet meant not only that the poor suffered but that labor costs throughout the economy were pushed up. Foodstuffs had more than 50 per cent of the weight in the cost-of-living index, and most union contracts had sliding-scale clauses that provided for automatic wage increases if the cost of living went up. Fanfani wanted to reduce the support price of wheat but found himself in trouble with the powerful Coltivatori Diretti, who claimed control of some sixty Christian Democratic deputies in the Third Legislature. In principle, Paolo Bonomi, their leader, accepted the idea that support prices were too high and would have to come down, but in practice he opposed their reduction. His function was to protect his clients' income.

An additional economic dispute involved the construction of atomic electric-power plants. The expanding demand for electric power in the country could not be met by additional hydroelectric plants since almost all the possible water sources were already exploited. Imported coal and fuel oil were expensive, and as a result it was felt that atomic power would be economically feasible in Italy—especially in the center and south—earlier than in many other countries. For years, a debate had raged inside the country between the supporters of privately owned atomic plants and the champions of public ownership. The issue had divided the Christian Democrats and prevented the establishment of an atomic policy for the country. The privately owned utilities wanted government support and subsidy of the initial atomic construction, which would be very costly. For them, it was a life-and-death issue, for they regarded atomic power as the dominant source of energy in Italy's future, and unless they could participate in shaping an atomic policy, their days were numbered. The supporters of privately owned utilities mobilized all their propaganda resources and political influence, as did the opposition. Television debates, newspaper articles, and party resolutions were all directed to the issue. Fanfani, spurred on by the left wing of his own party, by the Social Democratic allies, and by Enrico Mattei, made the choice for public atomic power. Two atomic plants were announced for construction, one by Agip-Nucleare, a subsidiary of the ENI, the other by SENN, a subsidiary of the IRI. On November 20, 1958, Agip-Nucleare began construction of its plant at Latina, south of Rome.

But the most serious of Fanfani's troubles was organizational. The issue of independent party power probably was the most damaging to the life of his government. In the fall of 1958, Fanfani was Prime Minister and Foreign Minister, as well as Secretary-General of his party. There was no doubt that he was trying to establish a degree of authoritative leadership such as no Christian Democratic politician had been able to exercise since the heyday of Alcide De Gasperi. He was even going beyond De Gasperi, in that he had for four years been engaged in constructing an effective party organization, something that De Gasperi had neglected. Fanfani did not want to be dependent on the Civic Committees of Catholic Action and on parish priests to round up and bring in the voters. It was not surprising that all those groups whose political power depended on their influence over a voting clientele viewed the creation of a strong party organization with fear.

If organization is one source of party strength, finances are another. In the late 1940's and early 1950's, during the period of De Gasperi's leadership, relations between the Christian Democrats and Confindustria had been amicable, and the party's financing had come mainly from big business. Church funds were directed toward those groups and individuals, such as Catholic Action and the clergy, that provided "free services" (in the financial, not political, sense) to the party. In the later 1950's Fanfani had found the contributions of big business reduced as Confindustria threw more support to the Liberals. By the time of the 1958 election campaign, the Liberals were receiving massive financial aid from the business community. The decline in large private contributions to the Christian Democratic Party organization (they were diverted to those right-wing factions and individuals within the party whose viewpoints were most congenial to business interests), coupled with Fanfani's goal of making his party less dependent on outside interests, had led him to seek other sources of funds. He found them in the publicly owned holding corporations, which derived their legal source of authority from the national state itself. But as *de facto imperia in imperium,* the IRI and the ENI were becoming major contributors to political parties to protect their own interests. Most of their money was going into Christian Democracy, although other parties were also beneficiaries. Undoubtedly, these contributions were a consideration in Fanfani's decision in favor of publicly owned atomic-power plants.

Thus, the Civic Committees, important Church leaders, and large-scale business all had reason to fear the direction of political events, which presaged a decline of their influence in Italian political life. And although Fanfani's actual policies and behavior were far less radical than his statements, these groups were perturbed over the possibility of an eventual coalition between Christian Democrats and Socialists, and the price that might have to be paid for bringing the Socialists into the government.

Added to these fears was the disgruntlement of other Christian Democratic notables over Fanfani's monopoly of the top governmental and party posts. All that was needed was the right occasion to move to the counterattack, and the tribulations of the Sicilian regional government provided the occasion. Sicilian resentments over neglect by Rome, historical feelings for local autonomy, the instability of the coalition in control of the regional government, all led certain Sicilian Christian Democrats to resist instructions emanating from central party headquarters in Rome. In October, 1958, Silvio Milazzo, a former protégé of Don Luigi Sturzo and now the Sicilian Christian Democratic leader, engaged in wrangling with Fanfani's Sicilian supporters. In order to form a regional government, he negotiated a new coalition, accepting support from the Communists and Socialists of the far left, and from Monarchists and *Missini* on the far right. Orders came from the national Christian Democratic headquarters for him to resign, but he refused. His followers were ordered to stop supporting him, which they refused to do. Milazzo was expelled from the party. On November 6, 1958, he founded a splinter Catholic party, the Sicilian Christian Social Union, which acquired local support.

At the Vatican and in Palermo, the Catholic Church had backed Fanfani's attacks on Milazzo's insubordination. The formation of the splinter party led to even more violent clerical criticism, especially on the part of Ernesto Cardinal Ruffini, Archbishop of Palermo. The growing local support of Milazzo's schismatic political behavior indicates, however, that behind the scenes Milazzo must have had some backing from sectors of the local Sicilian clergy, who were happy to spite the Cardinal, a northerner.[3]

Fanfani's defeat in Sicily weakened his whole position in Rome. With increasing boldness, his conservative enemies within the party broke party discipline in Parliament by voting against their own cabinet. On November 24 and December 4, the cabinet was defeated in secret votes on a bill to continue a special surtax imposed during the Suez Crisis of 1956 on the sale of gasoline. It was easy to deduce that Christian Democratic snipers had used this minor issue to put their own government in the minority. On December 6, Fanfani called for a roll-call vote and the snipers fell back into line. The government won by a vote of 294 to 286.[4] The Christmas-holiday recess postponed the disintegration of the government, but in January the attack was renewed.

The internal strains of the Christian Democratic Party during the fall and winter months of 1958 had been matched by similar strains among the Socialists. The struggle between autonomists and *carristi* continued. At an October, 1958, meeting of the Socialist Central Committee, Nenni found himself and his support-

---

[3] There have been charges, unproven but not out of the question, that Milazzo's original insubordination was encouraged by Mario Scelba, also a Sicilian, as a means of undermining Fanfani's position at the national level. It is hardly likely, however, that Scelba would have endorsed either the later alliance with the Communists and Socialists or the open schism within the Christian Democratic Party in Sicily.

[4] Under the Italian Constitution (Article 94), a defeat on a bill in Parliament is not the equivalent of a vote of no confidence, and the cabinet is not required to resign. A formal request for a confidence vote must be made by the government or by an opposition party, and this formal vote cannot take place sooner than three days after the motion is filed.

ers temporarily in the minority in their opposition to a resolution calling for continued close alliance with the Italian Communist Party. On October 30, Nenni resigned the secretary-generalship of his party in protest, but the Central Committee refused to accept his resignation. A party congress to face the question was called for January, 1959. As a result of careful prior electioneering, Nenni arrived at the congress with a majority of the delegates behind him. Three resolutions were offered to the delegates: the first, by Nenni, called for complete independence of the Socialists and the final rupture of the unity-of-action pact with the Communists; the second, offered by Tullio Vecchietti, leader of the *carristi*, called for renewal of the unity-of-action pact; the third, submitted by Lelio Basso, was a compromise between the two. Nenni's resolution won, the other two were rejected, and on January 19, Nenni was re-elected Secretary-General. He pledged himself to carry out a policy of Socialist independence and to remain, for the time being, in opposition to the government.

The Socialist decision strained relations within the Social Democratic Party, which shared the government with the Christian Democrats. Left-wing Social Democrats asserted that the decisions of the Socialist Party congress laid the basis for the immediate reunification of the two Socialist parties. Giuseppe Saragat considered reunification premature. The supporters of reunification, however, jeopardized the life of the government, for it was at this critical juncture that the snipers inside Christian Democracy renewed their attacks on Fanfani. In a secret vote on January 22, called to judge the government's handling of the Giuffrè scandal, enough of the snipers voted against the cabinet to leave Fanfani with only a one-vote margin in the Chamber of Deputies, 279 to 278. At this point, Ezio Vigorelli, a Social Democratic cabinet minister, resigned from the government to join the group advocating Socialist reunification.

Fanfani's majority had disappeared and he saw the possibility of nominally blaming another party for the cabinet crisis. On January 26, 1959, Fanfani submitted his government's resignation to President Gronchi. Five days later, in a personal crisis of nerves, he also resigned as Secretary-General of the Christian Democratic Party, bitterly criticizing the right wing of his party for deserting him.[5] Thus, January, 1959, marked the end of the first, hesitant approach to an opening to the left. President Gronchi delayed accepting Fanfani's resignation while he spent a week exploring alternative coalitions. Having found none, on February 3 he rejected Fanfani's resignation and asked the Prime Minister to resubmit his cabinet for a formal vote of confidence. Fanfani had no taste for this, however, and Gronchi was again required to construct a holding operation, to seek a routine administrative government until a new coalition could be found. And Antonio Segni was just the man for this kind of operation.

Segni's new government was a typical Christian Democratic *monocolore*, whose center of emphasis was shifted to the right. It was voted into office on February 15 with the support of his own party, as well as the Liberals, the two Monarchist parties, and the *Missini*. Since it had a majority without the support of the last group, the cabinet was not felt to be conditioned by the neo-Fascists. The restoration of a voting majority dependent on the Monarchists was a temporary encouragement to those two parties, and on April 3 they agreed to reunite, forming the Italian Democratic Party of Monarchist Unity. Earlier, on the opposite flank of the Christian Democratic Party, a minor schism had occurred when five Social Democratic deputies abandoned their party to form an autonomist Socialist initiative group, dedicated to reunification.

The re-establishment of a government, even a caretaker one, had the political significance of bringing the leftward evolution of Christian Democracy to a temporary halt. In organizational terms, the halt was more permanent. On March 16, Aldo Moro, a law professor from Bari, was elected Secretary-General of the Christian Democratic Party, filling the vacancy created by Fanfani's resignation. Moro made no attempt to reconstruct a tight party machine. Instead, he let the various factions, or "currents," as the Italians call them, have their own heads, trying to play the

---

[5] Fanfani's opponents within the Catholic world were not all party men. Ignazio Silone has written that Catholic bishops inside and outside of the Vatican supported the attacks on the energetic Tuscan. Silone specifically named Cardinals Tardini and Ottaviani: Ignazio Silone, "Apparati, religione, e politica," *Tempo presente*, March, 1959, p. 228.

role of mediator among them. In the following years, the currents would become parties within the party, each with its own organization, its own offices, its own press service and publications, its own finances. An exception to this broad generalization, however, was a center grouping of Christian Democratic notables and their followers. In the process of realignment of factions after Fanfani's fall and the disintegration of his Iniziativa Democratica, a meeting of leading Christian Democratic politicians was held in March, 1959, at the Convent of St. Dorothy. A loose coalition of these notables emerged, led by the party secretary, Aldo Moro, and the deputy secretary, Mariano Rumor (who comes from the Veneto region, a Christian Democratic stronghold that delivers a substantial number of deputies to Parliament). The grouping became known as the *Dorotei*, after the location of their meeting. Later, as Moro built up his personal following, it became known as the *Moro-Dorotei*, with Moro taking a slightly more progressive position than the moderate *Dorotei*. Further governments would hinge on the shiftings of these moderates right- or leftward, and they would always manage to have some of their key men become the crucial economic ministers, such as Emilio Colombo, later Minister of the Treasury.

The reactions of the general public to the political infighting were either those of contempt or of indifference. During the interregnum in February and March, Randolfo Pacciardi, a colorful leader of the small Republican Party, launched a movement to change the form of government from a parliamentary republic to a "presidential" regime, à la de Gaulle's Fifth Republic. Pacciardi was reacting to his political failures within his own party—it was gradually accepting the policy of an opening to the left while he was shifting to the right. His movement would remain small in subsequent years, but its open launching provided a pretext for the Communist Party on March 10, 1959, to call again for a popular front with Socialists and Catholics to defend the parliamentary system. The times were against a popular front, and the Communist appeal fell on deaf ears. Italian parliamentary government, however, was to face more serious dangers than Pacciardi in the near future.

9
THE ECONOMIC BOOM

The year 1958 had been one of relative economic stability, if not quite stagnation. Although the American recession of that year did not effect an inversion of the Italian upward economic trend, there was, nevertheless, a considerable slowdown in economic growth. In the summer of 1959, the growth rate spurted again, and until the end of 1963 Italy experienced an economic boom on a scale never before known in its history, surpassing in speed and in intensity the growth during the years prior to World War I, in which were felt the first major impact of industrialism.

A few relevant statistics may indicate the scope of this economic drama. By the end of 1963, the gross national product, which had been increasing steadily throughout the period, stood at 23,669 billion lire, or 138 per cent of the 17,114 billion lire figure for 1958.[1] New investment, from which results the construction of new facilities or the modernization of existing ones, was averaging close to 25 per cent of gross national product, slightly less in 1959/60, slightly more in 1961/62. And Table 7 shows the strikingly large increase in total investment from year to year. That total investments in the Italian economy in 1959 were 10 per cent greater than those of 1958 would seem to be sufficiently dramatic,

---

[1] Computation based on figures adjusted to 1958 market prices, in *Economic Surveys by the OECD: Italy, 1963* (Paris: Organization for Economic Cooperation and Development), p. 37; and *Economic Surveys by the OECD: Italy, 1965*, p. 39.

TABLE 7

ANNUAL INCREASE IN GROSS INVESTMENTS, 1958–62

(*In Per Cents*)

Year	Increase Over Previous Year
1958	1.6
1959	10.0
1960	20.3
1961	13.7
1962	13.4

Source: Giuseppe Scimone, "The Italian Miracle," in Hennessy, Lutz, and Scimone, *Economic "Miracles"* (London: The Institute of Economic Affairs, 1964), p. 176.

but that until the end of 1962, at the least, each percentage increase is itself not only larger but is moreover calculated each year on an ever larger base surely validates the term "economic miracle."

Naturally, the resultant increases in production varied in different sectors of the economy. Generally, the growth rate in agriculture was lower than in industry and services, so that agriculture's share of the total productivity declined steadily. By 1962, it had dropped to 16 per cent of gross national product, whereas in 1953/54 it had been over 25 per cent. Industrial growth was the highest of all three major sectors of the economy, and there the biggest increases occurred in the manufacture of automotive vehicles, household appliances, chemicals, petroleum products, and artificial fibers. The increases were due not only to the expansion of the domestic market but, even more, to a rapid growth of exports. This was a result of both the general prosperity of the international economy and the advantages Italy possessed in comparative prices and in design. Traditional Italian exports, such as citrus fruits, marbles, and textiles, were surpassed by the rapid growth of exports in manufactured items and machine tools.

The Italian boom continues to deserve the name "miracle" when compared with the economic activity for other countries in the Common Market, the EEC. In Table 8, it can be seen that for all the countries of the EEC, the over-all industrial growth rate for

TABLE 8

INDICES OF INDUSTRIAL PRODUCTION FOR EEC COUNTRIES, 1961–63

(1958 = 100)

Country	1961	1962	1963
Belgium	122	130	138
Luxembourg	117	112	114
France	116	123	129
West Germany	126	132	136
Netherlands	126	133	139
Italy	142	156	170

Source: *New York Herald Tribune* (Paris edition), December 9, 1964.

Italy was the highest. This growth was matched by expansion of foreign trade, higher for Italy than for all the European members of the Organization for Economic Cooperation and Development. Table 9 indicates the comparative foreign-trade expansion of

TABLE 9

OECD VOLUME INDICES OF FOREIGN TRADE, 1961

(1957 = 100)

Country	Imports	Exports
Italy	181	189
European member countries combined	140	136
France	126	154
West Germany	166	143
Netherlands	135	144

Source: *Economic Surveys by the OECD: Italy, 1963* (Paris: Organization for Economic Cooperation and Development), p. 22.

these countries for 1961.

A major source of revenue for Italy was the tourist boom, a result of the combination of general prosperity abroad and of the rapid increase in accommodations in Italy at relatively attractive prices. By the end of the period, however, Italian prices had so risen that the country was becoming exceedingly expensive for foreigners. As a consequence, the growth rate of foreign tourism slowed down, for other southern European countries—such as Yugoslavia, Greece, Spain, and Portugal—became more attractive

to the budget-conscious vacationer from the north. A further de-
pressant was the crowding of the principal Italian tourist centers,
with the ensuing traffic jams and noise.

The growth of Italy's foreign trade was the result of an expansion of exports and imports to all parts of the world: the Soviet
bloc, North and South America, Asia, and Africa. But it was especially the result of the large increase in Italian trade with the
other countries of Europe, the other members of the EEC. The
EEC had come into operation on January 1, 1958, and its first
consequence was a reduction of tariffs in several stages among the
six members—Italy, France, West Germany, the Netherlands, Belgium, and Luxembourg. This gave them preferential access to
each other's markets. As a result, Italy's trade with its fellow EEC
members rose more rapidly than its trade with the rest of the
world. Exports to other EEC countries rose from 28 per cent of
total exports in 1959 to 34.8 per cent of total exports in 1962. For
imports, the change was from 26.8 per cent to 31.2 per cent for the
same years.[2] Among the six member states, Italy had the largest
increase in intra-EEC trade, as is indicated by Table 10.

Not only had Italy been the major beneficiary from the expan-

TABLE 10
INTRA-EEC TRADE, 1958 AND 1963
(*In Millions of U.S. Dollars*)

	Imports			Exports		
Country	1958	1963	Increase (Per Cent)	1958	1963	Increase (Per Cent)
Belgium-Luxembourg	$1,462	$ 2,661	82	$1,377	$ 2,950	114
France	1,227	3,103	153	1,136	3,065	170
West Germany	1,896	4,275	125	2,406	5,279	119
Netherlands	1,518	3,059	109	1,337	2,662	99
Italy	687	2,491	263	608	1,788	194
Total	$6,790	$15,589	130	$6,864	$15,744	129

Source: Scimone, "The Italian Miracle," p. 198.

---

2 Giuseppe Scimone, "The Italian Miracle," in Hennessy, Lutz and Scimone,
Economic "Miracles" (London: The Institute of Economic Affairs, 1964),
p. 197.

sion of trade within the Common Market, it had also been the prime beneficiary of other EEC institutions. The European Investment Bank, created to grant loans for economic development within the European Community, put more money into Italy than into any other member country. This is understandable, for among the six nations Italy contains the largest underdeveloped area. In 1961, Italian development projects received 54 per cent of the Bank's investments, while French projects received 24 per cent and West German projects 17 per cent. In 1962, Italy received 64 per cent of the Bank's total annual investments, while France received 12 per cent and West Germany 11 per cent.[3] The European Social Fund, created to promote employment opportunities and to retrain and resettle workers, was more helpful to Italy than to the other countries. Again, Italy was the major source of excess and unskilled labor within the EEC; the other countries had labor shortages. During two years of the Social Fund's life, Italy received grants worth $1.3 million, or about twice the amount that went to France or the Netherlands.[4]

One major goal that Italy failed to achieve was the free movement of labor within the Common Market. Although Italian workers were emigrating to other EEC countries—on either a time-contract or permanent basis—such emigration was accomplished under the legal authority of bilateral agreements worked out by the respective foreign offices. Italian emigration to Switzerland, not a member of the EEC, was as high (until Switzerland imposed restrictions in 1965) as to France or West Germany.

It can be seen why Italy would have been a more enthusiastic supporter of the Common Market than some of the other member countries, and more willing than some of the others, especially France, to convert the economic community into a political community. Yet, Italy did not refrain from behaving nationalistically when it was to its interest to do so, and to act independently of its Common Market partners, even in economic affairs. When, in early 1964, Italy encountered serious balance-of-payment difficulties, it negotiated a credit of more than $1 billion from the United States, which was granted on March 14, 1964. Italy had dealt

---

[3] *Ibid.*, p. 195.
[4] *Loc. cit.*

directly with the Americans. When the American credit was announced, the EEC Executive Commission publicly objected on the grounds that Italy had gone to the United States without informing the European Community, instead of working out its foreign-exchange problems with its partners through Common Market institutions.

The repercussions of the Common Market's success on Italy were political, as well as economic. If the Italian Government was more anxious than some others to convert the EEC into a political community, an important reason was due to the recognition that the other member countries had more stable and conservative populations than did Italy. Nowhere else in the EEC was there such a strong Communist Party, or even a Socialist Party as extremist as the left wing of the Italian Socialist Party. Within the larger community, consequently, the extreme left would be a much weaker minority than inside Italy. The moderate and conservative elements inside Italy would thus have their positions reinforced. This had been an original attraction of the EEC to them, and naturally a reason for the original hostility of the extreme left.

But the progress of the Common Market served to erode even that hostility, and eventually the last significant internal left-wing opposition to the European Community disappeared. The CGIL had been interested in the Common Market in 1957 (when it was first proposed), and Giuseppe Di Vittorio's then favorable reaction had had to be suppressed by a call to discipline within the Communist Party. By 1962, four years of EEC successes had also overcome Socialist hesitations (it will be recalled that they had abstained in the parliamentary vote of ratification), and had converted not only the CGIL but the Italian Communist Party itself. In the summer of 1962, the Communists took a public position in favor of the Common Market, and had to admit that the European Economic Community was forcing the party to reexamine its concepts about the "inevitable decadence of capitalism." Palmiro Togliatti speculated that the international class struggle might no longer make sense in Western Europe. In preparation for an autumn congress of the World Federation of Trade Unions, the CGIL announced that it was ready to go to the congress and openly defend the Community. The congress had been called by the Soviet-bloc trade-union federations to attack the Common Market, and the CGIL announcement created a furor. The congress was canceled, while at the same time the CGIL asked for representation at Common Market headquarters, a request opposed by the CISL.

Italian foreign trade continued to expand, apart from its growth within the Common Market. Trade with the Soviet bloc was developed, especially with the Soviet Union. Italian importation of Soviet crude petroleum expanded considerably on the basis of barter arrangements: Italian pipe line, manufacturing equipment, and petrochemical machinery were exchanged for the crude oil. Enrico Mattei first made this major agreement with the Soviet Government in 1959, paying a price for the oil calculated at roughly one dollar less per barrel than the price of Middle Eastern oil posted by the large international oil consortium. The deal caused an economic and political stir inside and outside Italy. The Italians were warned of the dangers inherent in becoming too dependent on Soviet sources of supply. Actually, Soviet crude oil amounted to about 30 per cent of all Italian petroleum imports.

The contract was renewed in November, 1963, for an additional six years at about the same average prices and quantities as in the previous agreement. This was concluded by Mattei's successors after his death in an airplane crash in 1962. However, in early 1963, his successors had negotiated an agreement with Esso International for the importation of additional crude oil from the Middle East. This appeared to indicate that the new ENI management was less committed to continuing the feud with the international oil consortium than Mattei had been. Italian oil consumption was increasing steadily, and while the 1963 agreement with the Soviet Government continued the average quantities purchased under the earlier contract, Soviet crude oil would occupy a declining percentage of total Italian consumption in subsequent years.

The increase in petroleum imports, and in the consumption of other raw materials, indicated the rapid expansion in the use of motor traffic and of power by both consumers and industry. More people were on the move than ever before, both in terms of getting on the highways and streets and in terms of shifting jobs and residences. In the former category, the dramatic increase is illustrated by Table 11, which lists the annual number of driver's

TABLE 11

DRIVER'S LICENSES ISSUED IN ITALY, 1952–62

Year	Licenses Issued
1952	225,090
1953	270,099
1954	292,957
1955	316,931
1956	319,431
1957	335,348
1958	358,760
1959	380,891
1960	500,581
1961	719,200
1962	1,250,400

Source: La Stampa, February 24, 1965.

licenses issued in the eleven-year period from 1952 to 1962. It can be seen that in the year 1962 alone, 531,200 new licenses were issued, more than the total number of licensed drivers in the country as late as 1960. The roads and streets of Italy were absolutely inadequate for the increased traffic, and the problem was aggravated by the growing number of tourists who arrived by car and by past urban construction patterns that choked traffic into narrow ways. In the countryside, a road-building program (of modest dimensions on the whole) was complemented by the construction of a few superhighways, the most spectacular of which was the toll road Autostrada del Sole. It linked northern and southern Italy, from Milan to Salerno. By the time of its completion in October, 1964, work had already begun on its extension from Salerno to Reggio di Calabria at the toe of Italy, and other new superhighways were on the drawing boards, at the contract stage, or in construction. The new system of highways could be expected to break down much of the isolation of one part of the country from the other, reducing provincialism and localism.

People were on the move not only in automobiles but in trains and buses, and many of them were looking for new jobs. During the five-year period of the boom, roughly 1.38 million persons abandoned agriculture to find jobs in industry or in services, about double the number that had fled from the land during the previous decade. The largest number came from the south, but there was also an exodus from central and northern rural areas. They moved to local towns of their own region, to the principal regional cities, to other regions of Italy, and to foreign countries. They came generally from the poorest agricultural areas, and for the first time in modern Italian history, they were not replaced by a quickly growing population. The consequence was that marginal mountain and hill farms were left abandoned, as well as others that lacked good soil or adequate water. This could permit conversion of such land to other agricultural uses, such as grazing, or to reforestation.

By the end of 1963, the proportion of the labor force engaged in agriculture had declined to 25.5 per cent. The exodus revealed the weaknesses of the land-reform program established a decade earlier. Almost 40 per cent of those peasants who were originally awarded land had left agriculture. Some of them sold out to fellow farmers, others among the new proprietors became so poverty-stricken that they simply abandoned previously expropriated lands. The success of the reforms was dependent to some extent on cooperation among the beneficiaries, but the highly individualistic and suspicious Italians—exaggeratedly so in the south—found it difficult, if not impossible, to develop the behavior patterns necessary for successful cooperative ventures.

The Sicilian land-reform program, promulgated by the regional, instead of the national, government, was the most dramatic failure. It had taken the form of "model" agricultural villages, and these proved to have little holding power over the assignees. When nonagricultural jobs became available elsewhere, they abandoned their allotments, with the consequence that by 1964 fifty of the fifty-four model villages were either almost or completely deserted.

The rural exodus led to a reversal of farm policy by the government. Whereas the original land-reform program of 1950 had been based on the policy of breaking up farms (on the assumption of permanent rural overpopulation), the new agricultural policy, adopted near the end of 1959 under the name Green Plan (Piano Verde), had as one of its goals the consolidation of farms. The Green Plan was not a plan, in the sense of real planning, but a system of authorized subsidies and easy credit for the agricultural sector, to be added to the already existing system of high agricultural price supports. The institution and elaboration of the plan, however, did little to encourage the peasants to remain on the land, and as jobs became available in urban areas, the desertion of agriculture continued. It was the young men who were naturally the most mobile and most willing to abandon traditional occupations, but their economic motivations were reinforced by sociological ones, for more and more peasant girls made it clear that they had no intention of marrying men who expected to remain peasants for the rest of their lives.

The industrial aspects of southern development left much to be desired. The 1957 law requiring state firms to direct 60 per cent of their new investments to the south was adhered to by some, not by others. The government did not have enough control over its subordinate agencies to impose its will effectively. The Cassa per il Mezzogiorno made commitments upon the basis of its own plans, which, in some cases, did not accord with changing cabinet policies. It had developed various local clienteles, and these used political influence to prevent effective implementation of new government policies.

The major change in cabinet policy was the decision to create "developmental poles" in the south. It was decided that instead of trying to implement a generalized program of development over the whole area, better economic sense was made by concentrating investments in a few "poles," key zones where a variety of factors—location, local resources, existing industry—increased the likelihood that further concentration of investments would be fruitful. This meant a policy of selection, or discrimination. It meant deciding that certain places had a future while others did not. The political pressure exerted to influence these decisions can easily be imagined. Typical bureaucratic delays, the result of incompetence, if not deliberate sabotage, worked to hamper implementation of the policy. These "poles" would require large investments in infrastructure, but many of the ministries concerned failed to include in their budget requests the funds to implement the decisions made by their political superiors. To be effective, the program would also require local agencies capable of recognizing development opportunities and collaborating with outside business. So "local development consortia" were to be created. But these consortia in the south were filled with lame-duck Christian Democratic politicians, local notables, men without qualifications to direct or innovate modern industry.

In spite of difficulties and discouragements, the south continued to pull ahead. However, growth in southern productivity was slower than in the center and north except in 1961, when good weather produced unusually bountiful crops. But a striking inversion of income growth occurred. Prior to 1959, the rate of annual per capita income had grown on the average more slowly in the south than in the center and north—3.2 per cent to 5.2 per cent. From 1959, average per capita income rose more quickly in the south than in the center and north—6.5 per cent as against 5.6 per cent. Since income was rising faster than productivity, increases in the southern standard of living were, in effect, the result of transfers of income from outside the area: from other parts of the country, or from abroad, through investments, subsidies, or remittances.

The shifts of population from rural to urban areas, from mountains and hills to the valleys, plains and coasts, from south to north, created tremendous strains on the recipient communities. The increasing population flooded into slums in the old centers and outskirts of the cities, creating social, educational, and transportation problems of the first magnitude. The towns and cities, ill equipped and ill financed for such problems, turned more and more to the national state to help finance new school construction, new streets, new water lines, new sewerage lines, and new health and sanitation services. The increased returns derived from local taxes were insufficient. Between 1959 and 1963, local-government expenses increased 83 per cent, while local-government income increased only 55 per cent. The total deficit of local governments increased in five years from 329 billion lire (1959) to 834 billion lire (1963), a deficit covered by loans from agencies of the national state or by the direct assumption of certain bills by the national state.

Local governments obtained their principal incomes from consumption taxes and real estate taxes. In the major cities, which felt the pressure most severely, real estate became a major source of speculation and quick gain, often fed by money derived from the evasion of income taxes. Contractors and land speculators made fortunes, and some of them would proceed to lose them. The pressure to build was so great, and the profits were so large, that zoning laws were violated, parks invaded, city administrations corrupted on an even larger scale than before, and construction codes ignored, with predictable increases in the number of jerry-built structures. Prices skyrocketed: between 1953 and 1963, prices of new buildings tripled, while the average price of construction land multiplied ten times, the biggest increases taking place in the last half of that decade. This meant, naturally, that land costs became an ever larger proportion of total construction costs. The growth of total construction costs was less dramatic because most construction jobs in Italy are considered unskilled, and the industry became a major absorber of low-paid peasant workers emigrating from the countryside. The real estate boom naturally had its effects on already occupied land and buildings, whose prices rose proportionately. Most of the new residential building was constructed in the form of expensive apartments. Only a relatively small amount of public housing for low-income families was built. There was, consequently, a shift of people within the city from lower- to higher-cost housing as incomes improved, and rent-control laws were gradually eliminated.

The construction boom was not limited to the large cities. The countryside, especially the scenic areas of the coast and resort areas of mountains, was overrun. The national parks were invaded, with the connivance of overcompliant public officials. The natural and historic beauty of one of the most striking countries of the world was seriously damaged. Protests by enraged intellectuals, organized in such associations as Italia Nostra (Our Italy), or institutes of urbanism, had little effect for a number of years. By the end of the period, however, the boom was beginning to falter. Thousands of expensive apartments were vacant, lacking sufficient buyers or renters in the upper-income groups, while millions of poor people desperately needed decent housing. The protests of the outraged intellectuals were having some impact on the political parties, and as the national government and many local governments shifted to the left, more attention was paid to enforcement of zoning rules. More importantly, a general overhaul of the laws on urban development was put under study. Expropriation of building land by public agencies was advocated to prevent speculative profits, and some urbanists were proposing that the expropriation prices be set back to those prevailing in 1958. The resultant shiver throughout the real estate world was sufficient to pull down the left-wing Christian Democratic Minister of Public Works, Fiorentino Sullo. His enemies charged, wrongly, that he was going to nationalize all the real estate in Italy, but there was no question that a collapse in the price of land for new construction would have brought a general decline in the price of all land. When the real estate boom was brought to a temporary halt, it was due, not to Sullo, but to the tight squeeze on mortgages and other forms of credit that was established in late 1963 to contain the ever more insistent inflationary symptoms.

Prices had been rising slowly throughout the 1950's, more slowly than the general increase in productivity. In the early years of the miracle, the increase in prices continued, but it was during the period 1962 through 1964 that the cost of living rose drastically. In 1962, the cost of living rose 5.8 per cent over 1961, in 1963, 8.7 per cent over 1962, and in 1964, 6.5 per cent over 1963.[5] Part of the reason for the price increases was the growth of domestic and foreign demand. Another part was the wage-price spiral, which in the years 1962 and 1963 was pushed up through the aggressiveness of the unions. The unions were stronger because of the general prosperity, a more sympathetic center-left government, and most importantly, rising levels of employment. By the end of 1963, Italy, for the first time in modern history, was on the threshold of a full-employment economy. Unemployment was estimated at only 3.6 per cent of the labor force. There was still underemploy-

---

[5] *Economic Surveys by the OECD: Italy, 1965*, p. 17.

ment in southern agriculture and featherbedding throughout public agencies and private enterprise, but nevertheless the category of unemployed was approaching the category of unemployable (defined in terms of long-run incapacity to get a job).

With this favorable situation, it is not surprising that the unions made something of a comeback. This was especially true of the CGIL, which had been losing out to its major competitors—the CISL and the UIL—during the middle 1950's. In the boom years, the CGIL reversed the tide because the workers felt more secure against management pressure and because the CGIL changed its tactics. It used its connections with the Communist Party to take care of newly arrived workers from the rural areas—i.e., finding them jobs and a place to live and providing them with some social life and institutional contacts.[6] In its general approach, the CGIL abandoned its emphasis on mass collective struggles and directed its attention to the individual factories and firms, to the detailed demands and needs of particular categories of workers. In collaboration with the other confederations, it made aggressive demands for higher wages and better working conditions. Strike activity increased, in proportion to the workers' sense of confidence, and the results were generally satisfactory to them.

From 1958 through 1964, wages in Italy rose 80 per cent. This was the highest increase among all the countries of the Common Market, and far above the rate of wage increases in Britain and the United States. The comparative figures are given in Table 12. The increases in Italy were sharpest in the last three years of the period, and resulted from a combination of new wage agreements, automatic cost-of-living adjustments, and employer-offered extras.

---

[6] Naturally, the other major union confederations, the Church, the Christian Democrats, and the Christian Associations of Italian Workers competed with the Communists and the CGIL in these social-service and employment-agency functions, but without the same success. The Christian Associations of Italian Workers organized employment agencies for peasant women arriving in the cities, finding them positions as domestic help. One worthwhile objective accomplished by the union confederations during this period was the breaking of the power of labor contractors who had exploited the uneducated and unskilled southern rural migrants in an earlier period. These operators, usually early migrants themselves, would recruit newly arrived emigrants from their home areas, sell their labor to industries or construction companies, and collect a percentage of the workers' earnings.

TABLE 12

INCREASES IN WAGES AND PRODUCTION FOR SELECTED COUNTRIES, 1958–64

(*In Per Cents*)

Country	Increase in Wages per Worker	Increase in Production per Worker	Increase in Wage Cost per Unit Produced
Italy	80	32	36
West Germany	67	35	23
France	60	27	27
Netherlands	75	30	35
Belgium	35	32	3
United States	27	22	4
England	36	25	10

Source: "[European Economic Community] Quarterly Report on Business Cycles," April, 1965, as reported in *La Stampa*, April 10, 1965.

For, although Confindustria blamed the unions and the center-left government for the wage-price spiral that resulted, the fact was that employers were paying more than the contract rates in their efforts to raid other firms for workers and to keep their own workers from being raided by others. In a few specialized categories, the bidding was so extreme that wages surpassed the German rates and stimulated a limited return by expatriated Italians.

The largest increases were received by workers in the advanced sectors of the economy. The many workers in artisan shops, in agriculture, in retail stores, were less fortunate. The general rise in prices affected everyone, and it also hurt certain export industries. Several of these industries had depended in the past upon the low level of Italian wages for their competitive position in foreign and domestic markets. After 1962, however, wages were no longer low. Many industries—the textile industry furnishes a good example—had neglected recent modernization because there had been no incentive, and as the boom reached its peak, they found themselves with high wage costs and outdated production facilities. To sell abroad, they had to meet competition and cut their profits, making modernization even more difficult. The problem of technical modernization faced by Italian industry was a result of the constant necessity to match the continued modernization of plant and equipment taking place in other advanced industrial countries. Italy in the early 1960's was caught in the middle of a squeeze from both the advanced and the underdeveloped societies. With certain important exceptions, it was not yet a really advanced economy, but its salary levels were too high to stand the competition of the low-wage underdeveloped countries.

The difficulties of technical modernization in many industries were superseded by the difficulties of sociological modernization. Italian business had been organized in the past on a family basis, with the head of the family exercising autocratic, if not despotic, control. This pattern had begun to break down during the depression of the 1930's, when a number of families were forced to sell out to the IRI in order to survive. After World War II, as original founders died, the decline of family control continued, and the heirs were often incapable of managing the enterprises. For example, the Agnelli family, which had controlled Fiat, found it necessary to bring in Professor Vittorio Valletta to manage the firm after Senator Giovanni Agnelli died. By the 1960's, most large-scale businesses were no longer family-controlled, but rather were directed by executives who might have held little or no stock in the firm. The death of Adriano Olivetti in 1961 brought on a crisis in the following years in the Olivetti Corporation, the largest business-machine firm in Europe. The family was forced to sell its controlling stock holdings to a consortium of banks and other firms. The consortium brought in an outside manager to operate the business.

It is difficult to judge if Italian big business is still family-owned, even though not family-operated. The difficulty comes from the fact that, in spite of legislation to the contrary, concealment of stock holdings is still general. The apparent decline of family ownership, however, did not mean the decline of autocratic habits of authority. To a great extent, the "boss," whether the owner or a salaried executive, still ran the business as his private domain, tolerating little interference and delegating little authority. Huge firms with thousands of employees remained highly centralized, with all significant decisions, and many insignificant ones, kept in the hands of the few at the top. The inability, or refusal, to decentralize authority was a further handicap in the evolution of Italian industrial life to more modern forms of organization.

This failure was not unique to private industry. The publicly owned firms and the public administration, in the form of the traditional ministries, were cursed with the same oligarchic patterns of behavior. Enrico Mattei, for example, had run the huge ENI as a private empire, independent of both political superiors and his own subordinates, who were kept in the dark as to his plans. Many of his overseas investments—in the Middle East, North Africa, and Argentina, for example—turned out to be financial losses, the price paid for his drive for personal and national prestige. Before his untimely death, he was beginning to retrench, for the financial cost of his policies was becoming more apparent and his political opponents were becoming more vociferous in their attacks upon him. He turned to collaboration with the international oil industry, a shift continued and extended by his successors.

The distribution of wealth and power still remained lopsided, and the tax system did not redistribute income very satisfactorily. In 1964, 74 per cent of Italy's tax revenue was still being derived from indirect taxes and only 26 per cent from direct taxes. This was an improvement over 1958, when the corresponding figures had been 78 per cent and 22 per cent, but it was still the most regressive tax system in the EEC. Cheating and evasion of direct taxes was a general practice encouraged by the outmoded and rusty tax system.

By the end of the period, the country's spending spree was beginning to show its negative effects. In 1963, balance-of-payment difficulties were increasing rapidly as Italian imports climbed. The lira was becoming shaky. There was a capital flight, partly political in motivation. The spending spree on consumers' goods and luxuries was not matched by the necessary spending within the public-service sector. Appropriations for schools had increased in the years between 1958 and 1963, but the funds remained drastically inadequate. Ports, railroad networks, hospitals, public health services, urban renewal, had all been neglected. The repercussions on the economy were demonstrated by the shortage of qualified scientists, professional men, executives, and administrators, by the inadequate skills of a semitrained and semiliterate labor force, by the loss to North Sea ports of transit trade in goods for Central Europe, by the inadequate domestic transportation of goods.

The boom had carried into the modern world of well-being a larger number of Italians than ever before, but still a minority. About 25 per cent of the population had attained a decent level of comfort by Western European standards.[7] But a larger number remained far below that level, and an important segment still lived under conditions of marginal survival.

[7] The figure of 25 per cent is an estimate, used by former Minister of the Budget Ugo La Malfa in an address to the national congress of the Republican Party on March 29, 1965.

10
THE CRISIS OF PARLIAMENTARY DEMOCRACY

The Segni government, created in the spring of 1959 to provide a period of domestic *détente,* lasted for little more than a year. As a minority government, backed by a coalition of center-right parties, it provided a political breathing spell in which the extreme tensions that had been generated by the crisis of Fanfani's fall could be moderated and harnessed. The new Secretary-General of the Christian Democratic Party, Aldo Moro, proved to be an extremely skillful mediator among conflicting factions, prudent and accommodating, although he lacked the mastery and authority of a De Gasperi. The business community also felt more secure under a moderate government; this feeling was reflected in an upsurge of investment and a revival of real estate speculation. Only the left-wing parties and organized-labor confederations could feel no pleasure at the political stalemate. Their antagonism was manifested in a series of strikes that erupted in one industry after another during the early summer of 1959. While these strikes were primarily economic—rather than political—in motivation, they reflected the hostility to the political solution reached in earlier months.

With the minority status of the cabinet, there was no leeway for positive moves in the domestic political arena, and the cabinet followed a policy of routine administration. In foreign policy, it followed its traditional policy of close friendship with the United States and promotion of European collaboration. General de

Gaulle visited Rome from June 23 to June 27, 1959, but failed in his attempt to gain Italian support for a Mediterranean pact under French leadership. President Gronchi announced in the name of the government that Italy always wanted close ties with France, but not at the expense of other NATO members. The following year, Italy again rebuffed the French President: the Italian Government rejected de Gaulle's proposal of a three-power NATO directoráte, with France to speak for the Continental members. It objected to France's emphasis on "national independence within the alliance" and opposed the development of a national French nuclear deterrent. In the autumn of 1959, this loyalty to the United States and to NATO was rewarded by Italy's inclusion in the ten-member disarmament committee meeting at Geneva. The Italians had no original ideas for reaching a safe, controlled, and proportionate general disarmament agreement (neither had any other member country), but Italy's inclusion would give it a sense of participation in the larger events taking place in the world.

On Italy's own northeastern boundary, trouble that had been brewing for years erupted into open agitation and violence in the South Tyrol, the Italian province of Bolzano. The South Tyrol People's Party, representing the German-speaking majority in the province, felt that the majority's long-run existence was being threatened by the gradual emigration taking place in Italy from south to north. Early in 1959, the party began agitation against the De Gasperi–Gruber Accord of 1946. While its ostensible demand was the establishment of a separate autonomous region for the province of Bolzano, its real goal was the eventual secession of the province and its return to Austria. Only in this way could its ethnic character and way of life be preserved in the long run. The agitation in the South Tyrol provoked counteragitations in Rome and in other Italian cities. Segni stated firmly that Italy would not countenance any revision of the accord. The Austrian Government intervened in March, 1959, to charge Italy with violations of the De Gasperi–Gruber Accord and threatened to take the issue to the United Nations. Pro-Austrian terrorists initiated a policy of bombing, both inside and outside the South Tyrol, which produced more counterdemonstrations in other parts of Italy.

In September, 1959, in anticipation of the annual meeting of the United Nations General Assembly, anti-Italian demonstrations took place in Innsbruck, Austria, capital of the North Tyrol and the center of Tyrolese agitation and subversion. On September 21, Bruno Kreisky, the Austrian Foreign Minister, formally charged on the floor of the General Assembly that Italy was pursuing a policy of social and economic discrimination against the German-speaking population of Bolzano. He asked the United Nations for a resolution that would call on Italy to grant regional autonomy to the province.

Foreign Minister Pella, representing Italy, responded to the charges skillfully. The Italian Government knew it was leading from strength. Pella denied the charges of discrimination and countered with the claim that Italy was extremely liberal in its treatment of the German-speaking inhabitants, more so than the De Gasperi–Gruber agreement required. Pella argued that in any case the treatment of Italian citizens was a domestic question and outside the jurisdiction of the United Nations.

This last claim made no impact on the General Assembly, but in all other respects the Italian position was in effect upheld inside the United Nations. The General Assembly refused to condemn Italy or to make any specific recommendations to the two countries. Austria raised the issue again in a note sent to Italy on May 29, 1960. Asking for "true autonomy" for Bolzano, the Austrian Foreign Office stated that unless its demands were met, it would put the question on the United Nations agenda once more. Italy responded by offering to send the dispute to the International Court of Justice for a decision, or else to engage in direct negotiations. Austria rejected international adjudication, for it knew perfectly well that the creation of a separate regional government for the province of Bolzano was not required by the De Gasperi–Gruber Accord. On July 17, 1960, Austria inserted the problem once again on the agenda of the General Assembly. The General Assembly debated the issue in its autumn session and on October 27 passed a resolution recommending bilateral negotiations between the two countries as the best means of re-

solving the dispute. The solution could not have been more satisfactory to the Italians.

Bilateral negotiations between Italy and Austria were carried
on sporadically in the following years, but as of 1965 no conclu-
sive agreements had been reached; fundamentally, the status quo
in the province was maintained.[1]

Italy's international success was due to reasons other than the
persuasiveness of Italian arguments. None of Italy's allies in the
West wished to weaken further an already feeble Italian Government by inflicting a diplomatic defeat upon it. And, as the Italians
were ready to point out behind the scenes, encouraging Pan-German nationalism in the South Tyrol was not conducive to the
wider peace of Europe. If German revisionism were successful in
changing the Italian boundary, it would stimulate even further
all the German refugee movements and nationalist groups in Germany proper and thereby threaten the status of the German
eastern boundary. This was an argument that had appeal to the
Eastern European countries as well.

The Italian success on the South Tyrol issue at the international level was not matched at home in the province itself. In
subsequent years, the terrorist campaign expanded, rather than
subsided, and it continued to spread outside the provinces of Bolzano and Trento into other areas of northern Italy. The resentments and antagonisms in the zone directly affected became
further inflamed, making local attempts at accommodation more
difficult. Within the South Tyrol People's Party, moderate forces
were weakened and extremist elements bolstered. There was no
national party in Italy ready to do battle for the principle of self-
determination for the people of the South Tyrol.

The mixture of foreign and domestic concerns inherent in the
problem of the South Tyrol was reproduced in even greater degree in the ambivalence of Italian attitudes toward the larger
problems of East-West relations. The movement toward a *détente*

---

[1] There is some question as to Kreisky's personal commitment to the Austrian case. Certainly, the delicate balance between Catholics and Social Democrats in Austria would be upset if eventually the conservative, nationalist, and
Catholic peasants of the South Tyrol became Austrian voters. The Social
Democrats had nothing to gain.

in Soviet-American relations was accelerated by Premier Khrushchev's celebrated meetings with President Eisenhower at Camp David in September, 1959. International reconciliation had always been feared by right-wing groups within Italian politics, both lay and clerical, for they considered their domestic fortunes to be brightest within an international atmosphere of extreme tension. In its election propaganda, the Catholic Action Society always attempted to re-create the ambiance of the Czechoslovak *coup d'état* of early 1948 or the Budapest uprisings of 1956. Former Foreign Minister Gaetano Martino, in a Liberal Party campaign speech of early 1958, had warned that a relaxation of international tension would benefit left-wing elements in Europe and "make it possible in six months for Communist elements within the various countries to occupy positions of predominant power."[2]

Within the conservative group of cardinals in the Vatican, the visit of the Soviet Premier to the United States caused grave concern, and a series of unsigned editorials in *L'Osservatore romano* expressed serious criticism of the whole concept of East-West negotiations. The visit of the two leading world statesmen stimulated imitations, however, and in the fall it became known that President Gronchi had received an invitation to pay a state visit to Moscow, which he was eager to accept. Vatican pressure to prevent Gronchi's trip was enormous. It was pointed out that a reciprocating invitation would have to be extended to Khrushchev, which would bring the leader of the Communist world to the center of the Catholic world. The demonstration that the Italian Communist Party would organize to greet Khrushchev could easily be imagined. Gronchi was persistent, however, and he presumably threatened to go to Moscow whether or not the cabinet approved. Finally, the first week in November, the government authorized the trip for early 1960, after assurances had been received that Khrushchev would not make a return visit to Rome.

When President Eisenhower visited Rome in early December, 1959, he was greeted warmly by the government and enthusiastically by the Communists, Socialists, and other parties of the

---

2 Gaetano Martino, *L'idea liberale nella politica estera italiana* (Rome: Partito Liberale Italiano, 1958), pp. 13–14.

left and center who supported the reduction of international tension and the doctrine of peaceful coexistence. The next month, in burning indignation, Alfredo Cardinal Ottaviani publicly denounced "men of high responsibility in the West . . . who say that they are Christians [but] shake the hand that slapped Christ in the face."[3] Although Christian Democratic Gronchi was the direct target of Ottaviani's remarks, Eisenhower was the indirect one. Gronchi left for Russia in early February and soon learned that life in Moscow could be as difficult as in Rome. Apparently, his efforts to play the role of mediator between East and West were rather sharply discouraged. If Russians wanted to come to terms with Americans, they did not need Italian go-betweens.

At the domestic level, the minority government's incapacity to make basic policy decisions favored the status quo and was unquestionably one of the factors encouraging big business to proceed with its plan for expansion. But Italian political life was not quiescent. From both the right and the left, the respective attacks upon each other and upon the center continued. In May, 1959, the right-wing parties and press had opened up a barrage of criticism against Mattei, the ENI, and its principal newspaper organ, *Il Giorno* of Milan, accusing all of them of neutralism and, in some cases, of pro-Soviet bias. On June 1, Urbano Cioccetti, Mayor of Rome and a right-wing Christian Democrat, refused to approve a celebration of the fifteenth anniversary of the Allied liberation of Rome on June 4, 1944. His communal government was dependent on the votes of the *Missini* for its majority.

At the same time, the left was continuing to move forward electorally. Administrative elections for the regional governments of the Val d'Aosta and of Sicily, and for the provincial government of Ravenna, were scheduled for the late spring and summer of 1959. On April 13, the Vatican newspaper, *L'Osservatore romano,* issued a warning against voting for the Communist Party or for parties supported by the Communists. In Sicily, an excommunication decree was issued by the Archbishop of Palermo, Ernesto Ruffini, against anyone who would do so. Clerical intervention was ineffective in all cases. In the Val d'Aosta, a popular-front

---

3 *New York Times,* January 8, 1960.

coalition of Communists, Socialists, and the local Union Valdo-
taine won the regional election. On May 30, the Communist-
Socialist coalition governing the province of Ravenna won
re-election with an increase in votes over the previous majority.
And in July, in Sicily, Silvio Milazzo's schismatic Christian Social
Union improved its position, as did his left-wing allies. When
the Sicilian regional parliament met to elect a regional government, *L'Osservatore romano* issued a warning against re-electing
Milazzo as president of the region, but on July 28 the regional
parliament proceeded to do just that. Milazzo obtained the support of his own party, the Communists, the Socialists, and rebel
Christian Democrats.

The general trend of events, as indicated by the results of these
local elections, was not lost upon the national leadership of the
Christian Democratic Party. The shift to the left in the underlying strata of the population was apparent, and Aldo Moro, Secretary-General, felt that his party had to respond to this historic
trend if it were to have a long-run future. He finally convinced
the moderate and conservative leaders of his faction, the *Dorotei*,
that their party would have to approach the left. He and they felt
that if handled prudently and cautiously, the opening would not
be disastrous for them or for the party. At a national congress of
the Christian Democrats held in Florence at the end of October,
1959, Moro gradually unveiled his plans. In a major policy address, he defined the Christian Democratic Party as a "popular
and anti-Fascist" party, at a time when at the national level and
in many local governments his party was dependent on the votes
of Liberals, Monarchists, or *Missini*, who were spokesmen more
for the classes than the popular masses. Right-wing Christian
Democratic leaders, such as Pella, Andreotti, and Scelba, grudgingly went along with the new emphasis. The congress concluded
with an agreement between the *Dorotei* and the left wing of the
party, whose leadership was resumed by Fanfani, returned once
more to political activity. Moro would reject extremist support
from right-wing parties for any future government. Since the old
centrism was also impossible because the Social Democrats and
Republicans would no longer accept it, an opening to the left
appeared to be the only other choice.

If these conclusions appear clear in retrospect, they were not so clear at that time. It took several more months before the Liberals became convinced that under the cover of a government supported by the right, the *Dorotei* of the Christian Democrats were cautiously moving in the opposite direction. As the Liberals became aware of the development, their criticisms of the government increased, and in the major northern and central cities the large newspapers that supported them, such as *Il Corriere della Sera* of Milan and *La Nazione* of Florence, became more aggressive and violent. Large-scale industry threw its money and economic pressure behind the effort to block this evolution. ENI and IRI money was being similarly used, but for the opposite purpose. Fanfani's followers inside the Christian Democratic Party were increasing their attacks on the cabinet for relying on right-wing support. The Liberals finally withdrew their support of the government, and on February 24, 1960, Segni presented his cabinet's resignation to President Gronchi.

This resignation initiated a major crisis that lasted for months and threatened the very existence of democracy in Italy. Segni's resignation had come as the result of decisions reached by the *direzione* of the Christian Democratic Party, without having been preceded by any parliamentary debate or by any vote of no confidence. On February 29, Cesare Merzagora, Christian Democrat, resigned in protest from the presidency of the Senate, delivering a bitter speech in which he charged that Parliament had been reduced to an "organ without a voice at the crucial moments of Italian life."[4] He went on to condemn the "atmosphere of corruption [that] weighs on Italian political life, polluted by speculation and unlawful financial activities."[5] To many political commentators Merzagora's action appeared to be aiming toward the destruction of the party-parliamentary system and its replacement by a presidential one, as in France.

The parties were still struggling to reorganize a government, and with the endorsement of a majority within his own party's *direzione*, Moro began to negotiate for a revival of Segni's pro-

---

[4] The complete text of the statement can be found in Armando Saitta, *Storia e miti del '900* (Bari: Laterza, 1960), pp. 938–41.

[5] *Loc. cit.*

visional Christian Democratic *monocolore,* to be supported this time by the parties to the immediate left—the Social Democrats and the Republicans. Since the votes of all three parties would be insufficient to provide a parliamentary majority, Moro was prepared to negotiate for the Socialist Party's abstention, and Segni, who had accepted Liberal and Monarchist backing throughout the previous year, was willing to accept this indirect Socialist support. The Socialist price was the nationalization of the electric-power industry.

As the news of Moro's maneuvers leaked out, the conservative elements in Italian society, lay and clerical, moved to the attack. They were not yet ready to accept Moro's conviction that "historical inevitability" required Christian Democracy to open to the left. Under the stimulation of the private electric-power industry, Confindustria exerted its pressure. The Coltivatori Diretti did likewise. But the most effective restraints came from Church circles. The Catholic Action Society denounced the idea of the acceptability of Socialist support. Cardinals Ottaviani (Curia), Siri (Genoa), and Ruffini (Palermo) used their influence behind the scenes.[6] Faced with these pressures, Segni abandoned his efforts to form a government. Fanfani was willing to try in Segni's place, but clerical condemnation induced him to withdraw also.

Moro was confronted with the prospect of another cabinet dependent on the right, which he felt was both pragmatically and historically wrong. He refused to accept Liberal and Monarchist conditions and, instead, recommended a stopgap Christian Democratic administrative government that would not be identified with any political trend. It would be ready to accept votes from any source except Communist, on the grounds that the cabinet would be temporary and would have no political coloration. President Gronchi suggested that the man to lead the experiment was the Christian Democrat Fernando Tambroni, who had the reputation of being mildly leftist and who had had cabinet experience as the Minister of the Interior in several previous gov-

---

[6] Cardinal Siri was chairman of the Bishops' Commission for the Supervision of the Catholic Action Society. Ruffini was a leader of the conservative wing, as was Ottaviani, Prosecretary of the Holy Office.

ernments. Tambroni, ambitious and cynical, was more than ready to consent.

On March 25, one month and one day after Segni's original resignation, Tambroni's administrative cabinet was sworn in before President Gronchi, who gave it his endorsement. Tambroni asked Parliament for backing on the grounds that his cabinet was only temporary, that its functions would be limited to routine administration and to compliance with the constitutional requirement that the annual budget be passed by the end of June. On April 8, his cabinet received a vote of confidence from the Chamber of Deputies by a figure of 300 in favor to 293 opposed. Included in Tambroni's small majority were 271 Christian Democratic votes, 5 Monarchist votes, and 24 *Missini* votes. It was clear that the neo-Fascist votes had been determining; without them the government would have been rejected.

All Moro's efforts to present his maneuvers as nonpolitical could not gainsay the hard fact that for the first time since 1943 the Fascists were back in a crucial position of leverage at the national level. Left-wing Christian Democrats were not ready to accept the identification of their party with Fascism. Had not De Gasperi in 1948 defined Christian Democracy as a center party moving to the left? Had not Moro just six months ago called his party a "popular and anti-Fascist" party? Within two days, three left-wing Christian Democratic ministers—Giulio Pastore, Fiorentino Sullo, and Giorgio Bo—resigned rather than accept the Fascist votes. Others threatened to do likewise. On April 11, Tambroni submitted his government's resignation to the President of Italy. Gronchi held it in reserve while he explored the possibility of other choices.

Even before the vote in the Chamber, Fanfani had indicated his readiness to try for another agreement with the Socialists in case Tambroni failed to get a majority. Gronchi now let him go ahead informally, but Vatican cardinals again interposed what amounted to a veto. By April 22, Fanfani had given up once more, and the following day Gronchi rejected Tambroni's resignation. He told the Prime Minister to fill the vacancies in his Cabinet in order to govern.

The interference of the Catholic hierarchy had been behind

the scenes, but visible to active political and journalistic circles. To justify clerical intervention, *L'Osservatore romano* published an unsigned editorial (usually attributed to Cardinal Ottaviani or Cardinal Siri) entitled, "Basic Principles." It asserted the right of the Church to issue political instructions, arguing: "The Catholic can never overlook the teaching and instruction of the Church; in every field of his life he must base his private and public behavior on the guidance and instructions of the hierarchy."[7] The editorial went on to claim that collaboration with the Socialists was contrary to Catholic doctrine in principle. It added, inconsistently however, that "collaboration with those who do not admit religious principles may arise. In that case, it is up to the ecclesiastical authority, and not to the choice of the individual Catholic, to decide on the moral lawfulness of such collaboration."[8] This was, indeed, an open assertion of the right to dictate the choice of political alliances to Catholic politicians. The implication that collaboration with Fascists was morally acceptable, but collaboration with Socialists was not, was equally obvious. Of course, the Fascists claimed to be good Catholics, the heirs of the party of reconciliation between the Church and the Italian state.

More than two months had passed between the fall of the Segni cabinet and the final installation of Tambroni's administrative government. The Prime Minister now set about converting his stopgap, nonpolitical cabinet into an active political one. He already had the support of most business and industrial groups, which did not hesitate to praise him in their press. The stock market flourished. Now he announced a whole new spate of legislative bills, decrees, and executive orders hardly consonant with the role of a temporary place-saver that was pledged to step down in a few months. He proclaimed that bills would be introduced to reform the Senate, local finances, and the bureaucracy, to lower prices, and to increase government spending on highways, railways, and housing. He ordered reductions in the prices of sugar and bananas (controlled by government agencies), automobile

---

[7] An English translation of the editorial was published in *U.S. News & World Report*, May 30, 1960, pp. 73–74.

[8] *Loc. cit.*

gasoline (through ENI price leading), all designed to make himself popular with the public, especially with the middle classes, for whom the automobile was becoming a necessary status symbol. Later, price reductions were announced for bread, pharmaceuticals, fertilizers, cement, and automobile licenses. Postal and railroad workers received needed raises. He promised something for almost every group in Italian society: more government spending, more subsidies to industry and agriculture, to the south, to the islands, and to northern shipbuilding interests. And at the same time he promised to cut taxes. His Minister of Finance, Giuseppe Trabucchi, suggested that a law requiring the registration of stock transactions be repealed. He was not successful, but he had hoped to legalize the practice—then and still widespread—of concealing dividend income and capital gains. Tambroni's efforts to win popularity included the lavish distribution of honors: new *commendatori, cavalieri,* and *grand' ufficiali* were created on a scale and with a speed never known before or since.

Tambroni's demagoguery stimulated fears of his future ambitions, fears aggravated by the newly acquired respectability of Fascism. To press its advantage, the MSI announced its intention of holding its national congress in Genoa at the end of June. Genoa was a center of the resistance movement, where wartime partisan activity had been effective and widespread. It was easy to foresee possible trouble. The Italian governments of the past had often refused to permit meetings and conventions of left-wing parties on the grounds that they would lead to disturbances of the peace. The *Missini* knew, however, that Tambroni could not afford to stop a congress of a party upon which his government depended. On the contrary, they expected the police to provide them with the necessary protection. They were unquestionably engaged in a display of strength, anxious to demonstrate, if not to abuse, their newly acquired position.

On June 30, riots broke out in Genoa when groups of young anti-Fascists who were milling around the MSI meeting hall formed a protest demonstration that swelled rapidly, and by the following day, the area around the meeting hall was besieged. The demonstrators, who appeared to have joined together spontaneously, included individuals from a variety of parties and political groups. Later efforts to attribute the Genoa riots to the Communist Party do not appear to be justified. In fact, the Communists were caught unprepared at the outset. Some of them considered that an extreme right-wing pro-*Missini* government in Italy was the best one to further the Communist cause in the long run.

The Communist Party soon realized, however, that it would have to get on the anti-Fascist bandwagon. The Communists also saw in the situation the possibility of escaping from their progressive isolation by re-creating the wartime atmosphere and unity of the anti-Fascist popular front. It then quickly used its extensive network and party machine to organize demonstrations in other parts of Italy. A general strike was called in Reggio Emilia, in the "red belt." A number of deaths occurred in the ensuing violence. Protest rallies were held in numerous other cities, under Communist stimulation but often with the support of other political groups. By mid-July, ten demonstrators in various parts of the country had been killed and many others wounded.

Under Tambroni's orders, the police had been heavy-handed in their control of the unrest. As a former Minister of the Interior, he was prone to see police clubs as the solution to his problems. Visualizing himself as the object of conspiracies in which he felt many of his fellow Christian Democrats were participating, he appeared ready to use on his colleagues in his own party the dossiers that he had been able to accumulate during his years at the Ministry of the Interior. He also had been tapping the telephones and checking the mail of some of his own cabinet members.[9] When, however, he was challenged to produce the evidence of conspiracy, for some reason he backed down.

How far Tambroni went or was prepared to go is still debated. How seriously democracy in Italy was endangered remains a speculative subject. Phone tapping and mail checking had gone on before and have probably gone on since. What else was done in the way of threats or suppression of the press is uncertain. What became certain, however, was that the days of Tambroni's

---

[9] On the whole problem of the Tambroni episode, see K. Robert Nilsson, "Italy's 'Opening to the Right': The Tambroni Experiment of 1960" (Ph.D. dissertation, Columbia University, 1964).

government were numbered. The depth of anti-Fascist feeling in the country had turned out to be far more profound than was expected. On July 1, he had been forced to suspend the MSI congress. The following day, the *Missini* announced that they would no longer support his cabinet. And Aldo Moro could now use the crisis to demonstrate to an alarmed Church hierarchy and a concerned business community not only that Christian Democracy could not afford to be identified with Fascism but that Italy had no alternative but to move to the left.

11
THE OPENING TO THE LEFT

Before that alternative could be openly accomplished, however, two more years would elapse, in which the necessary adjustments in policy and attitude on the part of both Christian Democrats and Socialists would gradually, and in many cases, grudgingly, take place. In the meantime, the country needed a government, even if only an interim one, but a government free of any identification with Fascism.

Even before Tambroni's resignation, Moro had begun negotiations with the Social Democrats and Republicans for the formation of a "democratic coalition" to give parliamentary support to a new "administrative" cabinet. These parties, together with the Christian Democrats, did not have a sufficient majority, however, and because of the difficult and very special circumstances, the Liberals were approached for their support. The Liberal Party agreed, provided that the government not be used as a cover for an opening to the left. To insure further the security of the cabinet, negotiations were also opened with the Socialists for their abstention. The Socialist agreement to abstain, which was properly interpreted as a positive endorsement of the new government, provided the necessary condition for later developments.

The *direzione* of the Christian Democratic Party authorized Fanfani to head another *monocolore* interim cabinet, which in due course received the confidence of Parliament on the basis of the party agreements reached beforehand. Fanfani defined his government as one of "democratic restoration." This very description was an indication of the nature of its predecessor. While the four parties that voted in favor of the cabinet were precisely those that had composed the old centrist coalitions, it was not the intention of Moro and Fanfani to revive the old centrism. Fanfani defined the basis of his one-party cabinet as a system of "parallel convergences," without any policy agreement other than to "restore democracy."

The price of Socialist abstention was one that any proponent of the opening to the left would pay gladly. Administrative elections were scheduled for the fall of 1960. The electoral laws provided for proportional representation in all communes over 10,000 in population. In the election of the provincial councils, however, a prize of two-thirds of the seats was given to the list that elected a simple majority of the council, using single-member districts. This voting system exerted a strong pressure on the minor parties to merge (for the provincial election) with the major ones, and had been one factor in the Socialist-Communist presentations of joint tickets. The Socialists now asked that the provincial councils be elected by a system of proportional representation. Those Christian Democrats who were interested in the opening, knowing that the ability of the Socialists to run separate tickets would aid their gradual separation from the Communists at the local as well as the national level, got their party's consent. The Christian Democrats, also, would have to endure a separation, for other small parties that previously had participated in Christian Democratic provincial lists would now be able to run their own tickets. In the future, provincial governments would have to be constructed on the basis of coalitions formed after, rather than before, the election. In September, the law changing the provincial election to one of proportional representation was pushed through Parliament.[1]

An additional innovation of indeterminate, but potential, significance was the introduction of television campaigning. Televi-

---

1 In 1964, the electoral laws were further modified to extend the proportional representation system to communal elections for all communes over 5,000 in population.

sion was initiated in Italy in 1954 by the government, which controlled radio and television broadcasting through an IRI corporation. Unlike the British BBC, the Radio-Televisione Italiana delivered news and comments in such a form as to favor the party in power, always the Christian Democrats. Neither its minor allies nor the opposition parties had ever had a chance. They had protested over the years without effect, but finally in 1960 the television program "Tribuna politica" was introduced in the months preceding the administrative elections. Here the secretaries-general of all the parties had an opportunity to face the camera in a question-and-answer session conducted by both friendly and hostile journalists. Now they could present their respective points of view directly to a national audience. The program was continued in differing formats in subsequent years, so that television became another imponderable in the operations of Italian political life.

On November 6 and 7, 1960, the administrative elections were held. In Table 13, the over-all results for the provincial councils

TABLE 13
PROVINCIAL ELECTION RETURNS OF 1960 COMPARED WITH
1958 ELECTIONS TO THE CHAMBER OF DEPUTIES
(*In Per Cents*)

Party	1958	1960	Difference
Fascist	4.8	5.9	+1.1
Monarchist	4.8	2.9	−1.9
Liberal	3.5	4.0	+0.5
Christian Democratic	42.4	40.3	−2.1
Republican	1.4	1.3	−0.1
Social Democratic	4.5	5.8	+1.3
Socialist	14.2	14.4	+0.2
Communist	22.7	24.5	+1.8
Other	1.7		

Source: Italia, Istituto Centrale di Statistica.

are compared to the political elections of 1958. The principal gainer, in percentages, was the Communist Party, the main losers, the Christian Democrats and the Monarchists.

In an address to the Chamber on November 25, Nenni announced that with the elections of November 6 the "truce" established during the previous summer could be considered ended, and for all purposes the Socialists once more could be considered in the opposition. Nenni's intention was not to attempt an overthrow of the government, but rather to use the ending of the truce as a basis for negotiating openings to the left at the local level. Since Liberal Party support for the truce had been conditioned precisely on a pledge by the Christian Democrats not to negotiate an opening to the left at the national level under the cover of "parallel convergences," the Socialist attempt to end the truce could pave the way for a shift of alliances. The supporters of the opening were convinced that it could proceed better if attempted first at the local levels, and negotiations to this effect were begun once the election results were in.

Within each of the four parties directly concerned, there were minorities opposed to the attempted opening. On the left wing of the Socialist Party, the *carristi* and the followers of Lelio Basso, a left-wing dissident, considered any collaboration with bourgeois forces or Social Democrats a betrayal of the working class. On the right wing of both the Social Democratic and the Republican parties, there were minorities favoring the old centrism or even collaboration with the parties of the right. (Pacciardi had appeared on platforms with neo-Fascists; and he was a man who had once been a leader of the International Brigades in Spain.) And within and without the Christian Democratic Party, strong opposition to any deals with Socialists still existed. On November 23, however, two days before Nenni's speech, the *direzione* of the Christian Democrats had agreed that local alliances with the Socialists could be made where feasible. The only stipulation was that Christian Democrats could not form local governments which included or depended on the support of Communists or neo-Fascists.

It took months of negotiations and long, hard bargaining before many local center-left governments were brought into existence. On January 21, 1961, the first local center-left government was created for the city of Milan, to be followed in February and March by similar governments for Genoa and Florence. By the end of spring some forty such local governments had been formed in north and central Italy, in those areas where the left-wing groups within Christian Democracy and the autonomist forces within the Socialist Party were strongest. But many older-style alliances were in existence at the same time: centrist governments, Communist-Socialist governments, and center-right governments. These last flourished especially in the south, where Christian Democrats often continued collaboration with Monarchists and in some cases neo-Fascists, in spite of the prohibition laid down by the party's central executive board.

The northern local center-left governments had not been created without continued opposition from within Church circles. The Catholic Action Society fought the trend bitterly, as did high churchmen such as Cardinals Ottaviani and Siri. In the spring of 1961, Cardinal Siri of Genoa, chairman of the Italian Bishops' Commission for Supervision of the Catholic Action Society, wrote to Aldo Moro, warning against the formation of local coalitions that included Socialists.[2] But the power of Catholic Action and its leaders had declined considerably. Its president, Luigi Gedda, had bitterly fought the leftward evolution of the Christian Democratic Party throughout this whole period. His influence had been present in Fanfani's downfall in January, 1959. His publications had attacked Moro's declarations to the Christian Democratic congress of October, 1959. He had supported Tambroni's opening to the right in the spring of 1960. He had attempted to build up the Catholic Action Society as a counter-altar to the Christian Democratic Party, potentially its successor should the Church hierarchy ever decide to abandon the party. His war against the left-wing Christian Democrats was unconcealed from the autumn of 1959 on. He even attacked the moderate *Dorotei* for their apparent opportunism and lack of ideological rigidity. The collapse of Tambroni's government was a severe blow to Gedda. The refusal of even conservative Christian Democrats to follow him in his attacks upon the party was another one. These conservatives preferred to resist the center-left evolution from inside the party rather than to split from it. The failure of the intransigent wing

---

[2] See the *New York Times*, March 3, 1961.

of Catholic Action to induce large numbers of Catholics to vote "blank ballots" in the administrative elections of November, 1960, was another defeat.

From the beginning of 1961, the political power of Catholic Action was substantially on the decline, a regression due not only to its inability to halt the leftward direction of the Christian Democratic Party but also to changes in the atmosphere within the Church hierarchy. Pope John XXIII had succeeded Pope Pius XII in the autumn of 1958, but for the first two years of his pontificate he had been feeling his way slowly and moving cautiously. In 1960, he began to affirm his progressive views in a manner that was careful but that nevertheless enabled the leaders of Christian Democracy to stand up to the assault of conservative Catholic groups. It was John who, as Patriarch of Venice, had wished the Socialists a successful congress in 1957. In 1961, Pope John acted more vigorously. On April 11, the occasion of an official visit by Prime Minister Amintore Fanfani to the Vatican in connection with the celebrations of the centenary of Italy's unification, the Pope took the opportunity to express publicly his warm sympathies for the Prime Minister, the man most identified among Christian Democrats as the proponent of the opening to the left. In September, 1961, the Sicilian Christian Democrats accepted Socialist support in the regional legislature to obtain a majority capable of maintaining a Sicilian regional government. The move had been publicly condemned by Catholic Action and by Cardinal Ruffini of Palermo, as well as by the other Sicilian bishops. Threats of excommunication had been made broadly before the event, but when the alliance was formed no public reprisals ensued.

The publication in 1961 by Pope John XXIII of his first major encyclical, *Mater et magistra* (*Mother and Teacher*), was a further step in weakening the conservative wing of Catholic society. The encyclical's broad endorsement of a mixed economy, its rejection of the uncontrolled free market, its call to bring the disinherited into the social and political order, its emphasis on social justice and economic development, could all be legitimately deduced in its application to Italy as backing for the direction being pursued by Moro and Fanfani and as a rejection of the policies advocated by Catholic Action.

John XXIII was preparing for the Second Vatican Council, which would begin the following year, and he wanted to shift the focus of Church attention from Italian politics to the larger questions that the ecumenical council would face. In December, the Pope addressed Catholic Action leaders and advised them to concentrate on spiritual, rather than political, functions, advice repeated in an editorial in *L'Osservatore romano*.[3] Gedda was transferred from the presidency of Catholic Action to the presidency of the Civic Committees, replacing Ugo Sciascia in the latter post. While Gedda was succeeded by his close collaborator Agostino Maltarello, who shared his predecessor's outlook, the symbolic significance of Gedda's removal was not lost upon attentive political observers.

The weakening of the position of the right wing within the Catholic spectrum during 1961 also weakened the position of the right wing outside the Catholic world. The Liberal Party was faced with a dilemma as to the strategy it should pursue. It could accept Nenni's assertion that the administrative elections of November, 1960, brought to an end the special conditions of truce that had justified the Fanfani *monocolore* based on "parallel convergences." It could argue that the formation of the center-left local governments in early 1961 violated the conditions under which it had agreed to support the cabinet. If the Liberals wanted to precipitate a government crisis they had reasons to justify such an action. There were groups within the Liberal Party calling for this very step, but Giovanni Malagodi opposed such a policy and was able to get majority endorsement for continued Liberal backing of the cabinet. It was relatively easy for him to demonstrate that the minority cabinet was following a *de facto* centrist policy (which is what the Liberals advocated), even if it were more desirable to participate directly in the cabinet. The Socialists, in their party congress of February, 1961, still showed themselves to be bitterly divided over collaborating with the Christian Democrats and Social Democrats. The Christian Democrats, like the

---

[3] *L'Osservatore romano*, December 13, 1961.

Socialists, were not committed to the proposition that the center-left experiments at the local level must inevitably achieve a logical completion at the national level. The situation was still fluid, and the Liberals finally concluded that it was best to leave it that way.

Another factor inducing caution was the fear that pulling down the cabinet might bring about an early parliamentary election. The regular five-year term for the Chamber of Deputies would expire in 1963, but President Gronchi's seven-year term of office would end in 1962. Gronchi was understood to be eager for another term, but his reputation had been badly damaged by his original support of Tambroni in 1960. It was felt that he might seize upon a new crisis as an excuse for dissolving Parliament, in the hope that a new parliament might prove more favorably inclined toward him.[4] Article 88 of the Constitution prevents the President from exercising his power of dissolution within the last six months of his term. This meant that the potential danger would exist until November of 1961, and none of the parties desired an anticipation of elections.

So the cabinet of "parallel convergences" continued, but under its apparent immobility, action was being taken, at both the governmental and party levels, to work for a future center-left coalition. In February, 1961, an old Fascist law that prohibited both the migration of peasants to the city without a guarantee of a job and the offering of a job to anyone not a registered resident of the locality was finally abolished. The Constitutional Court had challenged this law years before, but it had taken time until the government finally eliminated it. The old law had been ignored in fact, and peasants had been on the move throughout the postwar period. By 1961, however, the flight from the land was reaching a peak, and hundreds of thousands of people were living in places where they had no legal residence. But they could not register to vote or register in unemployment offices in their new towns of residence. The left parties had fought for the abolition of the old law on both political and constitutional grounds. The Christian

---

[4] It must be recalled that the President of the Republic is elected by both houses of Parliament in joint session.

Democrats, fearful of how transplanted peasants would vote in the newly inhabited urban and suburban slums, had delayed for years, but finally gave in. The pressures of the left, and the mobility of a people in the midst of an economic boom, could not be resisted indefinitely.

Other steps were taken during the year to lay the groundwork for an eventual Christian Democratic–Socialist convergence. On March 24, a special parliamentary commission was formed to study the problem of the lack of economic competition. The Christian Democratic Party established a study group to examine the problems connected with national planning, or "programming," as the Italians preferred to call it (to make it sound less Marxist). In May, 1961, the government announced that equalization of electricity prices throughout the country would be imposed upon the electric-power industry, the first of two stages to begin the following September. A Christian Democratic study commission was established to analyze the problem of urban planning and zoning, one of the most chaotic and corrupt aspects of Italian life, and one that was becoming even more chaotic and corrupt because of the boom.

On July 11, 1961, Nenni presented to Parliament a Socialist motion of no confidence to prepare the way for restructuring the cabinet. He argued that the period of emergency was over, that in the year since July, 1960, democratic legality had been established, and that it was now time for the parties interested in the center-left to clarify their positions. Nenni's timing proved to be bad, and the vote was lost. The center parties were not yet ready to commit themselves, nor was his own party. The move boomeranged on him; he was condemned by his potential allies, and was subjected to renewed attacks from the Communists and the *carristi*.

In September, the Christian Democrats held a conference at San Pellegrino to discuss their ideology. The left wing dominated the conference and it was clear that an intellectual basis was being laid for an historic "meeting" with the Socialists. Professor Pasquale Saraceno, the most influential economist connected with the party, made a strong argument for national programming as the only means of eliminating the historic disequilibria of Italian society. He maintained that the natural forces of the market could not break through age-old underdevelopment, as the experience of the Italian south during the previous decade and the experience of other underdeveloped areas demonstrated. The following month, the National Council of the Christian Democratic Party issued a call for a party congress to settle fundamental policy. The date of the congress, set for the end of January, 1962, provided further time to organize for the internal battle that would take place and also provided another excuse for prolonging the life of the government now that the original one (fear of Gronchi's ambitions) had expired.

While the country waited for a decision in internal affairs, Fanfani busied himself in trying to play the role of mediator abroad. In the summer of 1961, he visited first the United States and then the Soviet Union. He arrived in Moscow during the Berlin crisis of August, 1961, but learned to his chagrin that the Russians were not any more disposed to take his suggestions than they had been earlier to take Gronchi's.

The national congress of the Christian Democratic Party began at Naples on January 27, 1962. A decision on opening to the left was the purpose of the congress, and Moro and Fanfani had prepared the ground carefully. To reduce the foreign-policy obstacles, Pietro Nenni had published an article in the January, 1962, issue of the American review *Foreign Affairs,* in which he announced to both the American and Italian interested publics that the Socialists, although opposing NATO in the past, had no intention of insisting on Italy's withdrawal from the alliance in the present. He wrote: ". . . we have never raised the question of withdrawal [from NATO] for two reasons. First, because to do so would convict us of demagoguery; and second, because to withdraw under present conditions would jeopardize the European equilibrium, which though it is dangerously unstable does contribute to the maintenance of a truce between the two opposing blocs."[5]

On January 11, 1962, the Central Committee of the Socialist Party voted a resolution stating that the party did not expect Italy

---

[5] Pietro Nenni, "Where the Italian Socialists Stand," *Foreign Affairs,* January, 1962, p. 221.

to desert its alliances, but merely insisted that NATO's obligations must be limited to Europe and given a "purely defensive interpretation." The Central Committee approved, by a majority vote, both the resolution and a report by Riccardo Lombardi in which a "defensive interpretation" was meant to include an absolute denial of atomic weapons to West Germany.

Reinforced by these Socialist pronouncements, Moro was able to concentrate the argument on domestic issues. While the right wing of the Christian Democrats, led by Mario Scelba, opposed the opening, the great majority of delegates was ready to try the policy on an experimental basis, without committing the party to it irrevocably. Tactical expediency required this approach, for the Social Democrats and Republicans had already announced that their support of Fanfani's cabinet of "parallel convergences" was to be considered terminated as soon as the results of the Christian Democratic congress were known. The announcement was intended to force the Christian Democrats to make a clear-cut choice, and to bolster Moro's position within his own party by cutting off the only other feasible alternative, a return to centrism. Moro was thus successful in carrying the large majority of the congress with him and emerged victorious with a final resolution authorizing the party executive directorate to construct a center-left government with the support though not the direct participation of the Socialist Party. The resolution promised continuation of a pro-Western foreign policy, and did not require that the Socialists split immediately with the Communists at local governmental levels, in the CGIL, or in various cooperatives. Moro had argued that a successful center-left policy would produce these splits as an eventual consequence.

The Christian Democratic congress ended on February 1. The next day, Fanfani presented his cabinet's resignation to President Gronchi. After three weeks of negotiations with the Social Democrats, Republicans, and Socialists, Fanfani presented a new government composed of his own and the two small parties. There had never been any intention to have Socialist participation, nor did the Socialists want it at this time. They were involved, however, in the elaboration of the program that Fanfani intended to present to Parliament and to the people of Italy. Both Mario

Scelba and Giuseppe Pella, the most prominent of the conservative Christian Democrats, refused posts in the cabinet.

Fanfani's program contained seven major policy declarations:
(1) establishment of governments for all nineteen regions of Italy
—fourteen regions were still without them (this was a somewhat
nebulous promise, however); (2) reform of the public administration; (3) a three-year program for school development, including
the establishment of a unified junior high school;[6] (4) the gradual
abolition of *mezzadria* ("sharecropping"); (5) the establishment of
economic programming for "just and harmonious social development," including new legislation for urban planning and zoning;
(6) elimination of the private electric-power industry; and (7)
fidelity to the North Atlantic Treaty Organization.

The program was unquestionably center-left, yet there were
elements in it that raised Socialist doubts. The commitment on
regional governments contained all kinds of hedging. The school
statement was a compromise that avoided the delicate issue of illegal state subsidies to private, mainly confessional, schools. There
were differences as to the method of eliminating the private electric-power industry; the Socialists argued for nationalization,
while some Christian Democrats preferred "IRIzation" (the buying up of a controlling stock interest by IRI corporations). For
these and other reasons—the most important of which was the
firm *carristi* disapproval of the whole idea of collaboration—the
Socialist Party decided to abstain, rather than vote for the government. Nenni announced in Parliament, however, that Socialist
abstention must be interpreted as favorable to the government.
The right-wing parties—Liberal, Monarchist, and *Missini*—voted
against the cabinet. The Communists did too, but Palmiro Togliatti justified their negative vote on the bases of the two issues of
fidelity to NATO and the vagueness of the commitment to regional governments. He insisted that the Communist opposition
was limited to these two issues, and was not a general opposition
to the center-left. In this respect, the Communists were more mod-

---

6 The establishment of the unified junior high school meant that the child's
future life was to be determined by a decision made at the age of fourteen,
rather than eleven, as had been the case previously. The choice of secondary
school determined the choice of future vocations open to the child.

erate than the Socialist *carristi,* who revealed anarcho-syndicalist orientations by charging their comrades with transformism[7] and desertion to the class enemy.

The establishment of the first center-left government created an uproar in the press and in business circles, especially within Confindustria. The intensity of the attacks, the barrage of accusations of betrayal, the predictions of economic disaster, knew no limitations. The stock market declined more drastically than before. Yet the government was moving slowly, with the *Dorotei* restraining precipitate action. Gronchi's term was expiring in May, and the *Dorotei* anticipated that in the battle over the succession they might need the votes of right-wing parties. This is precisely what they did need. While the Socialists, Republicans, Social Democrats, and some left-wing Christian Democrats insisted that the new President of the Republic should be identified with, and committed to, the center-left, the *Dorotei* imposed the choice of a conservative Christian Democrat upon their party. Antonio Segni was their man, and it was becoming apparent that this was a price Moro had had to pay the past January to get their support for his policy. The three lay parties put forward the candidacy of Giuseppe Saragat, the leader of the Social Democrats. A victory for him would remove one of the obstacles to the reunification of the two Socialist parties, since it would leave Nenni in an unchallengeable position of party leadership.

It took nine ballots before the *Dorotei* were able to get Segni elected. Insurgent left-wing Christian Democrats refused to support Segni in the early ballots, proposing instead their own candidates: Gronchi, Piccioni, Fanfani. They would never go over to Saragat, however. After the sixth ballot, Fanfani released his followers, and the insurgents came back into line. Then the *Dorotei* negotiated with the right-wing parties and Segni was finally elected on the ninth ballot with the support of the Liberals and the Monarchists. So in a very early stage of its existence, the new center-left coalition was racked with dissension.

The three-party coalition continued with its program. The pre-

---

[7] Transformism can be defined as a betrayal of ideological principles in return for power, prestige, or material rewards. Historically, it has been applied to the Italian left.

censorship of stage plays was abolished, but not of movies. A special parliamentary commission was established to investigate the Mafia. A withholding tax on stock dividends was passed in the hope that it not only would produce income-tax revenue that was escaping payment but would also smoke out the real ownership in Italian industry. Both hopes turned out to be unwarranted, however, and in 1964 it was "temporarily" suspended.

In May, 1962, Budget Minister Ugo La Malfa of the Republican Party presented the government's reasons for, and methods of, national programming. In an address on the state of the economy, he announced that the biggest economic boom ever known in Italy's history had failed to establish a balanced economic system but, on the contrary, had aggravated the gaps, between north and south, industry and agriculture, modern and backward industries, that were dividing Italian society. He insisted that continuation of current patterns would not overcome these disequilibria, that democratic government programming was the only solution. An interministerial committee on programming would be set up with the Minister of the Budget as its chairman. An assisting technical committee composed of experts—including representatives from the major categories of Italian economic life, industry, agriculture, commerce, and labor—started its work in September under the chairmanship of Professor Pasquale Saraceno.

On June 16, 1962, the cabinet presented to Parliament its bill on the electric-power industry. The bill provided for nationalization of the industry, including those firms already owned by the IRI and ENI. A new and separate agency, ENEL (Electrical Undertakings Trust), would be created to administer the plants. A generous cash price was to be paid to the firms in ten annual installments.[8] The short-run inflationary impact would be reduced by permitting the firms, most of which were diversified with large operations outside of electric utilities, to invest in other areas of business.

The decision to nationalize the electric-power industry had both economic and political motivations. Economic complainers against

---

[8] Municipalized electric-utility companies were given the option to sell out to ENEL or to continue independently. In subsequent years, most of them chose to continue operating independently.

the industry charged it with a reluctance to cooperate in the development of the south, and with noncompliance and evasion of the prices set for electric power by the Interministerial Committee on Prices (which fixed prices for the sale of energy and of other basic necessities, including medicines). Politically, the industry was felt to be responsible for the conservative and uncompromising line followed by Confindustria since 1955, and for the shift in financial and journalistic support away from the Christian Democrats to the Liberals. The decision of the majority of the Christian Democrats to support nationalization may very well have been the result of the party's reaction to this treatment in the previous years, rather than of ideological principle or economic conviction.

During the following months, the battle over nationalization held the center of political attention. The fight inside and outside Parliament was bitter. Led by the Liberals and by Confindustria, the battle was fought with a variety of techniques: parliamentary obstruction, stock-market decline, threats and intimidations, newspaper proclamations of disaster. The Christian Democrats promised that there would be no future nationalization of other industries; the Socialists announced that they would not insist on further nationalization on principle, but would examine and judge the future development of the various sectors of industry. The attempt on the part of Confindustria and the Liberals to forge a united front in defense of the ideological principle of private enterprise failed. Many large firms and industries not directly affected refused to rally to the cause. Such giants as Fiat and Montecatini (chemicals) stayed clear of the struggle.

In reality, there was little doubt about the outcome. Most Social Democrats, Republicans, Socialists, and left-wing Christian Democrats were committed to nationalization of the industry. The Communists, after criticizing the bill in detail and suggesting various amendments that were not accepted, announced their support of the government's measure. Thus, many more than enough votes existed to offset any potential sniping that conservative Christian Democrats might attempt. There was no possibility of repeating the events of January, 1959, which had brought Fanfani down. In the fall, nationalization was approved in the Chamber of Deputies by a vote of 404 to 74. The Senate vote was of similar proportions. A number of Christian Democrats abstained or absented themselves.

The nationalization bill did not consolidate the relationships between the two principal parties of the center-left. The fight over the presidency of the republic still rankled, for Fanfani's refusal to support Saragat was not yet forgotten. On the other hand, the dominant moderates within Christian Democracy, the *Dorotei,* were worried about the effects of the nationalization battle on their conservative supporters and were already hedging on the next major issue, the creation of regional governments for the regular regions. The reason they gave was the unwillingness of the Socialists to guarantee that they would never form coalitions with the Communists in those regions—Emilia-Romagna, Tuscany and Umbria—where there was a long experience of Communist-Socialist collaboration at local and provincial levels. Nenni responded by offering direct Socialist collaboration in a center-left national government after the 1963 parliamentary elections. The *carristi* objected violently. Later, Nenni offered to examine the question of regional center-left alliances (where the strength of the parties made such alliances possible) if the four parties would agree to, and pledge themselves to act together for the application of, a five-year program to be enacted after the election. The *carristi* threatened a split.

On November 10, the Christian Democrats turned Nenni's offer down. It was becoming obvious that they wanted to conduct the coming electoral campaign by emphasizing moderation and prudence, to stave off the Liberal Party attraction to the conservative wing of their electorate. The Socialists, on the other hand, were worried about losing support to the extreme left. Not only were the *carristi* of the Socialist Party threatening a split, but in October, 1962, the Communist Party had abandoned its cautious waiting and had launched an outright attack on the center-left, concentrating on the Socialist Party.

Communist hesitations had been the product of both domestic and international complications. The Party could not ignore the effects of the boom and of the Common Market on Italian society. An editorial by Togliatti in his weekly, *Rinascita,* on August 25, 1962, had openly accepted reformism as a suitable method to achieve socialism. He had argued that while his Party accepted the elaboration of gradual reforms, on a democratic basis, it did so with the goal of achieving a truly socialist society. His differences with the Social Democratic parties of Western Europe, he claimed, were not over the method of reform, but over their abandonment of socialism as the final goal. He speculated that the classical class struggle no longer made sense in Western Europe, and in September the Party openly reversed its former negative judgment of the European Economic Community.

These trends within Italian Communism were naturally not shared by all Party members. A more orthodox group, getting moral and perhaps financial support from Communist China, opposed the acceptance of this program. The growing public dispute between Russia and China over peaceful coexistence, and the Chinese charges of revisionism, became reflected in battles inside the Party. The reopening of the attack on the center-left and on the Socialists helped to limit internal Communist dissidence. At the Party congress held in Rome in December, 1962, Frol Kozlov, representing the Russian Party, openly attacked the Chinese Party. The Chinese delegate responded, attacking not only the Russians but also the Italians. Togliatti reacted by endorsing the Russian position and further recommending to the two major disputants that they handle their disagreements in private and resolve them by negotiation.

By the end of 1962, the positions being taken by all the parties were in anticipation of the coming parliamentary elections. In January, 1963, the tensions between the Christian Democrats and Socialists over the postponement of the commitment to regional governments almost precipitated a cabinet crisis. Aggravating the tension was a dispute over the assignments to the top posts of the new electric-power agency, ENEL; the Christian Democrats had skimmed the cream of the patronage, leaving their allies embittered. The Socialists, with an electorate that was traditionally "against the government," had no desire to be identified with it, especially when the benefits of such identification were negligible. The Christian Democrats preferred not to enter the campaign identified as an ally of the Socialists. An open crisis was avoided, however, when cooler heads within both parties argued that a crisis would just advance the election date and, more important, be an open admission that the policies of the two parties had failed. The crisis was postponed, and on February 18, 1963, Parliament was dissolved for elections scheduled for April 28.

12
THE TESTING OF THE CENTER-LEFT

The end of the third legislature inaugurated one of the strangest campaigns in Italian electoral history. The cabinet routinely remained in office until the elections were over, while the country, prosperous as never before, was subjected to an assault of unwarranted proportions from both extremes. One would have thought, from observing the propaganda of the parties of the right (with the Liberals in the forefront), that country, religion, morality, and Western civilization had been betrayed by unscrupulous Christian Democrats, subverted by alien ideologies. At the other extreme, the Communists were denouncing a perfidious Socialist Party that had betrayed the workers, better off than ever before, to the class enemy. These bombardments put the two principal parties of the center-left on the defensive. To meet the attacks, the Socialists announced that they were returning to a position of noncommitment for the future. The Christian Democrats likewise declared that their obligation was ended; they would feel free to decide which way to go after the election returns were in. The two minor parties warned, however, that they would support only a new center-left government.

Meanwhile, international events contributed to maintaining a future for the center-left. De Gaulle had vetoed Britain's entry into the Common Market the previous January. The Italian reaction the following month was a refusal to sign an agreement, already initialed, accepting the association of former French African colonies and protégés into the EEC. Anti-Gaullism was one thing all four center-left parties had in common. By June, 1963, however, Italian-French relations had been smoothed. The removal of the intermediate-range-missile bases from Italian soil, in the spring of 1963, undoubtedly helped to improve the Socialist attitude toward the government.[1] The decision of the Americans and Italians that Italian ports would not be needed for bases for the American Polaris submarines that were replacing the land-based missiles also pleased the Socialists

During the election campaign, two other events of international importance occurred that would have ramifications in internal affairs. On March 6, 1963, Pope John XXIII received Premier Khrushchev's daughter and son-in-law in private audience. The impact on the world and on Italian politics was stunning. Domestically, the gesture symbolized a reversal of the 1949 general excommunication of Marxists by Pope Pius XII. Although six days later the Italian Bishops' Conference published its by now routine pre-election instructions to Catholics to vote united for the Christian Democratic Party, this letter could not offset the impact of the visit. The wording attacked atheistic Communism specifically, rather than Marxism or socialism. Its intentions were interpreted to be as much an attempt to hold conservative Christian Democrats from the attractions of the Liberals as it was a warning against Communism.

On April 10, 1963, Pope John published his second major encyclical, *Pacem in terris* (*Peace on Earth*). The significance of the document was universal; its consequences for Italian life were apparent in three of its fundamental characteristics. First, it was addressed to "all men of good will," not just to Catholics. Second, it gave major emphasis to the principle of freedom of conscience. Third, it endorsed the possibility and rightness of collaboration for peace and social justice between men who differed on ideological grounds. Consequently, it was, in effect, reversing the *Osservatore romano* editorial of May 17, 1960, "Basic Principles," which

---

[1] While the decision to remove the missile bases was justified on the grounds of their obsolescence, it may have been related also to the American-Russian agreements that brought the Cuban crisis to an end in October of 1962.

had declared collaboration between Catholics and Marxists to be immoral. Inside Italy, it could easily be interpreted as an endorsement of the center-left. On a larger scale, along with the visit of Khrushchev's relatives, it could be considered an acceptance of the Communists as within the bounds of respectability.[2]

A little over two weeks later, on April 28, the elections for the fourth republican legislature took place. The results, compared with the 1958 vote, as shown in Table 14, clearly indicate the ad-

TABLE 14

VOTE FOR THE·CHAMBER OF DEPUTIES, 1958 AND 1963

	1958		1963	
Parties	Seats	Popular Vote (Per Cent)	Seats	Popular Vote (Per Cent)
Fascist	24	4.8	27	5.1
Monarchist*	25	4.8	8	1.7
Liberal	17	3.5	39	7.0
Christian Democratic	273	42.4	260	38.3
Republican	6	1.4	6	1.4
Social Democratic	22	4.5	33	6.1
Socialist	84	14.2	87	13.8
Communist	140	22.7	166	25.3
South Tyrol People's	3	0.5	3	0.4
Other	2	1.2	1	0.9
Total	596	100.0	630	100.0

* The Monarchist figure for 1958 represents the totals of the two Monarchist parties. They were reunited in 1960.
Source: Italia, Istituto Centrale di Statistica.

vances made by the Communists, who received more than one-fourth of the total vote after five years of the greatest and most widespread prosperity ever known in Italian history. The Liberals doubled their small vote. The Social Democrats made moderate gains; the Socialists ended with a small gain in absolute numbers,

2 In spite of the anti-Communist barrage of the previous decade, the Catholic and Communist groups inside Italy had always been in contact with each other, both inside and outside of the political sphere. The Communist Party was too large and too rooted in Italian society to have been kept at arm's length, on the margins of Italian life.

but a percentage loss because of the larger total vote. The Monarchists were the big losers, while the Christian Democrats also suffered a significant drop.

The recriminations began immediately, especially over the large increase in Communist votes, an increase registered throughout all parts of the country. It was evident, also, that the Christian Democrats had lost both to the right and to the left. Fanfani's center-left policy was blamed for the loss of votes to the right. Pope John was blamed by the conservatives for the Communist gains. They claimed his actions and statements had released the inhibitions of many voters, especially women, who voted Communist for the first time because they felt that they could now do so without fear of reprisals from the Church. These recriminations were politically motivated, of course, designed to influence the formation of a subsequent government. Aldo Moro, however, gave a more profound explanation of the results. He pointed out the significant transformations of a society in the midst of an industrial revolution. He mentioned the vast migration from the country to the city, from south to north; the urbanization and proletarianization of the peasants; the emancipation of women from the home and from age-old traditions and restrictions. He alluded to the specific causes of discontent, such as rising prices, the lack of housing, the inadequacy of public services in the mushrooming outskirts of the cities. He admitted that the Communists had been better able to exploit these discontents than had the other parties. They had gained support from urbanized peasants who, in their former villages, had previously voted Christian Democratic or, in the south, Monarchist. They had made inroads in the left wing of the Socialist electorate, especially in the "red-belt" areas of Emilia, Tuscany, and Umbria. They had gathered the mass of the protest vote.

The four parties that had supported the former center-left coalition still controlled over 60 per cent of the seats in Parliament, if they could agree on a program. In May, negotiations were begun for a new coalition, and Fanfani, pushed aside as the scapegoat for the Christian Democratic losses, was succeeded by Moro directly, who tried to form a new government. Fanfani was bitter at such treatment and refused to enter a new cabinet. Moro proceeded very deliberately with his negotiations. He hoped to strengthen his hand with a Christian Democratic success in the Sicilian regional election, which was scheduled for early June. His hopes were realized. Milazzo's schismatic party suffered a severe defeat, and the Christian Democrats felt more secure nationally. Then the death of Pope John delayed progress toward a cabinet until his successor, Pope Paul VI, the former Giovanni Battista Cardinal Montini, was installed. At this point, negotiations accelerated and the leaders of the four center-left parties arrived at an agreement which committed them to a relaunching of their program.

On the evening of June 16, Pietro Nenni brought the program to a meeting of the Central Committee of the Socialist Party. There he saw his autonomist majority split. The dissidents, led by Riccardo Lombardi, argued that the new program was deficient. The commitment to establish regional governments was too vague; the law on urban planning and zoning was not tough enough; the criteria for economic programming were too imprecise; the deadlines for the enactment of these bills were too loose. These were the official reasons. Unofficially, the *Lombardiani* were involved in a maneuver to scuttle Moro and restore Fanfani, in whom they had more confidence.

With his majority temporarily gone, Nenni and his secretariat presented their resignations to the Central Committee, which refused to accept them. Moro's attempt to form a cabinet had thereby collapsed, and the only course of action was to hold new elections, or else establish another caretaker government. The right-wing Christian Democrats, encouraged by the results of the Sicilian regional vote, wanted new national elections. This threat of new elections played into the hands of those who preferred a caretaker government, because the Socialists felt themselves in no condition to face such elections so soon. On June 19, Giovanni Leone, the Christian Democratic Speaker of the Chamber of Deputies, formed still another minority *monocolore*. Leone assured the Socialists that he had only two purposes: to get the budget passed by June 30 as required by law, and to provide the time for the Christian Democrats and Socialists to pull their respective parties together. The Socialists would hold a party congress in

October to decide on fundamental policy. All Leone asked of the Socialists was that they abstain on the vote of confidence.

The Socialists realized that to vote against Leone would practically guarantee new elections. Both Nenni and Lombardi apparently felt that Leone's pledges and his party's commitment to relaunch the center-left were honest. The autonomist majority inside the Socialist Central Committee was reconstituted and the party agreed to abstain. The Social Democrats and Republicans did likewise. Leone's *monocolore* was safe and his government was voted into office over the opposition of the Communists, Liberals, and *Missini*. The Monarchists, too, abstained.

During the summer, Moro pulled his party majority together by able maneuvering. In early August, the Christian Democratic National Council issued a strong call for the constitution of a four-party government of the center-left after the Socialist Party Congress. It was a specific invitation for direct Socialist cabinet participation; the purpose was to aid the autonomists within the Socialist Party in their campaigning prior to the congress. In foreign affairs, the international *détente* between the United States and the Soviet Union also helped to reduce points of friction between the prospective partners. The agreement between the two superpowers in June, 1963, to establish a "hot line" between Washington and Moscow was approved by the Italian Government. The moratorium on nuclear testing in the atmosphere, which Russia and America negotiated the next month, was endorsed by all Italian circles except extreme-right supporters of the Cold War. On only one foreign issue was there potential disagreement. The American proposal for a NATO multilateral atomic force was advocated by many as a way of providing a substitute for the proliferation of national atomic arsenals, and the Christian Democrats looked upon it in this light. The Socialists, however, considered this an indirect way for the Germans to get to the atomic trigger, and so were generally opposed. The Italian Government's agreement in 1963 to "study" the proposal postponed any final commitment and headed off a possible source of friction for the prospective coalition. Since France rejected the proposal and other NATO members were hesitant, a final Italian decision was not urgent.

During the summer and fall of 1963, the peak period of the boom, the price level was still rising and the Italian balance of payments was becoming shaky. A capital flight of substantial proportions occurred, principally to Switzerland. The conservative parties claimed the flight was due to stupid government economic policies; the left-wing parties claimed it was politically motivated to undermine a prospective relaunching of the center-left. In September, the Bank of Italy tightened credit policies. In October, the Leone government initiated cautious measures to control prices and rents and to stop the flight of capital. Together with the squeezing of profit margins, these measures served to discourage new investments.

On October 24, the party congress of the Socialist Party convened and within a brief time it became clear that the reconstituted autonomist group had a small but workable majority. Over the violent protests of the *carristi,* the congress voted to take the revolutionary step of participating directly in a bourgeois government. On November 6, the Leone cabinet resigned and Aldo Moro began negotiations for a four-party coalition. This time he succeeded and on December 4 his new cabinet was announced with himself as Prime Minister and Nenni as Deputy Prime Minister. After sixteen years, the Socialists were finally out of what Nenni called "the ghetto of isolation." The new Deputy Prime Minister pledged the enactment of a five-year program that would go into effect in June, 1964, the establishment of regional governments, and new reforms in education, city planning, and agriculture. On foreign policy, the Socialists reiterated that they considered Italy's obligations to NATO to be strictly defensive and limited to Europe.

Opponents of the agreement within both the major parties of the coalition were restive and unhappy. The right wing of the Christian Democrats, led by Scelba and Pella, threatened not to vote for the new government in the forthcoming vote of confidence. They controlled approximately thirty deputies. In justifying their insubordination, they claimed that too many reforms had been conceded to the Socialists without any guarantees that the Socialists would split with Communists in local, provincial, and future regional governments. On December 16, however, a sharp editorial in *L'Osservatore romano* condemned any breach of Catholic party discipline and unity. The potential dissidents retreated immediately.

In the Socialist Party, there was no higher outside authority to impose obedience on agitated and bitter minorities. Charging a betrayal of the working class, the *carristi* broke party discipline; about 20 per cent of the Socialist parliamentarians voted against granting confidence to the new government. Although the cabinet still had plenty of votes to spare, the Socialist Party had no choice but to punish the dissidents. In reaction, the *carristi* broke away, and in January, 1964, formed a third Socialist party, taking the name Italian Socialist Party of Proletarian Unity (PSIUP), which had been used by the Socialists during the war. Not all of the Socialist antagonists of the center-left policy split off, however, for a number of them preferred to fight their battle within their party. The parliamentary loss of about 20 per cent appeared to represent fairly accurately the Socialist loss among the rank-and-file supporters, for in elections in 1964—such as the one in May to establish a new government for the special region of Friuli–Venezia Giulia, and the administrative elections of November—the Socialists lost an over-all average of about 20 per cent of their voting support to the new party. In the trade unions, however, the Socialist loss was more serious. A substantial number of the top Socialist leaders of the CGIL, including Vittorio Foa, the president of the Metallurgical Workers' Federation and the theorist of syndicalism, were leading schismatics. Their dissidence gravely weakened the Socialist presence at the upper levels of the largest Italian labor confederation.

The new government and its program were under pressure and criticism from the very beginning of 1964. In January, Aldo Moro, the Prime Minister, resigned his post as Secretary-General of the Christian Democratic Party. The party did not want the same man to occupy the two key roles in Italian political life. Moro was replaced by his Deputy Secretary-General, Mariano Rumor, a leading *Dorotei*. In February, the agricultural reform bill was postponed in time and watered down in content when presented to Parliament, in an effort to placate disgruntled Christian Democratic conservatives. The inflation was spiraling, the heavy deficits in the country's balance of payments were still rising, the stock market was still declining, and the business community was demanding the jettison of reforms that would be not only expensive but negative in their effects on business confidence.

The initial and hesitant deflationary measures enacted by the interim Leone government the previous October had been inadequate. At the end of February, the cabinet issued new and severe regulations, raising interest rates, increasing consumption and excise taxes, instituting a new supertax on automobile sales, restricting installment buying, and suspending the new withholding tax on dividends from stocks. On March 14, the American Government granted a credit of over $1 billion to Italy to handle the loss of foreign-exchange reserves. It was a demonstration of faith in the future of the Italian economy and also an indication of American support for the center-left government.

Domestic assaults continued. In March and April, Amintore Fanfani, the original executor of the opening to the left, launched a series of attacks on his own offspring, claiming that the center-left was "not irreversible." In May, 1964, Guido Carli, the Governor of the Bank of Italy, called for a moratorium on new wage agreements, and a spreading-out of the cost-of-living increases built into existing union contracts. At the same time, the *Dorotei* Minister of the Treasury, Emilio Colombo, leaked sections of a private report that blamed the inflation on the wage-price spiral generated by the wage increases of the previous years. His report was also an indirect attack upon the five-year program being drawn up by his cabinet colleague Antonio Giolitti, the Socialist Budget Minister. Essentially, Colombo was arguing that a plan based on coercing the business community into behaving on a basis of social consciousness or civic duty could never work in Italy. Italian businessmen had to be accepted for what they were, and the kind of ambiance should be created that would restore their confidence and their profits. The implications were spelled out by Robert Marjolin, the French vice-president of the executive board of the EEC. He publicly criticized the Italians for not taking sufficiently drastic financial measures to counteract inflationary pressures, and he urged a balanced governmental budget and the dismissal of high-cost reforms.

All of the trade-union confederations refused to accept Carli's call for a wage freeze, especially when there was no freeze on profits and little effectual collection of income taxes. Colombo's leak had practically plunged the government into another crisis, and by June the coalition was disintegrating. In that month, Moro announced to the Chamber of Deputies that the sole object of his policy was stability—political, monetary, and fiscal. Reforms would have to be postponed twelve to eighteen months. It was at this point that it was learned, almost by accident, that the *Dorotei* Minister of Public Instruction, Luigi Gui, had inserted into his budget, behind the back of Socialist Budget Minister Giolitti, a small fund to begin the financing of Catholic parochial secondary schools.[3] The three lay parties immediately objected. Their ministers resigned and the government fell.

All efforts to form a different kind of coalition failed, and by the middle of July the four parties were negotiating once more. At the end of the month, an agreement was reached. Christian Democrats accepted the postponement of the school-aid problem. They repledged their commitment to the enactment of the agreed reforms, but later, and in a diluted form. It was a center-left program with some of its teeth filed down, if not pulled. The same ministers were back at their posts with few exceptions, the most conspicuous being the replacement of Antonio Giolitti, who had been a Communist until 1957, by the less controversial Socialist Giovanni Pieraccini. A few more outraged Socialist parliamentarians went over to PSIUP. A large number, led by Riccardo Lombardi, remained in the party but announced, in effect, that they no longer felt the center-left had any real life. They would oppose Socialist participation in the government from their minority position within the party, but accept the decisions of the majority. The potentiality of another schism was thus ever present.

The new cabinet was formed in time for the August vacations, and political activity was limited. Two personal misfortunes in that month laid the bases for future conflict. Antonio Segni was struck by a cerebral thrombosis early in August, and although he was out of danger after several weeks, it became apparent that he

---

[3] Catholic elementary schools, but not secondary schools, had been receiving public funds for years.

would be left semiparalyzed. A short time later, Palmiro Togliatti died of a stroke while visiting Russia. His deputy, Luigi Longo, moved smoothly into the succession, but Longo had neither the ability nor the authority of his predecessor, and rivalries among leading Communists for new positions would gradually emerge.

The major concern of both the general public and the government remained the business cycle. The anti-inflation policy had produced a recession. Prices kept rising, although less steeply. But in 1964 consumption started to fall, especially in hard goods, consumer durables, and investment goods, but also in textiles. The real estate market collapsed as high mortgage and interest rates, combined with uncertainty about future urban-planning legislation, served to induce both buyers and builders to delay. Unemployment rose as production declined. Layoffs were coupled with a failure to fill job vacancies when they occurred. Employment in industry declined by 325,000 workers for the year.[4] Underemployment figures rose even faster than those for unemployment as firms reduced their operations to three-quarter time, half time, or one-quarter time. The flow of peasants from the country to the city gradually slowed down to a trickle, and a flow in reverse even began to take place. The recession in 1964 was not as drastic as that in 1947. It began from a situation of almost full employment and from a much higher level of economic activity and standard of living. But people's expectations had risen and they were not much impressed with the argument, obvious but irrelevant, that they were still a lot better off than they had ever been before.

Two favorable factors in 1964 served to moderate the impact of the recession: crops were excellent as a result of favorable weather conditions and previous investments in increasing productivity, and exports expanded substantially while imports declined with domestic demand. The continued growth of exports was the result of general prosperity among Italy's principal foreign customers. It was also a consequence of the desire of Italian firms to maintain their hard-won positions in foreign markets.

---

4 (Italian) Istituto Centrale di Statistica, as quoted in *La Stampa*, March 30, 1965.

They were willing to see their profits squeezed in order to hold on. The combination of higher exports and lower imports brought about a sharp improvement in Italy's trade and payments balances. Whereas in 1963 Italy had a deficit of $1,250 million in its balance of payments, in 1964 it had a surplus of $764 million.[5]

While the improvements in Italy's international financial position had become apparent to its economic ministers and banking authorities by the summer of 1964, the declining domestic economy was becoming a matter of greater concern. The tight money policy began to be eased in September. The banks were encouraged to make loans. Public works, which had been slowed down in the past year to reduce budget deficits, were accelerated. A speedup was ordered in projects such as public-housing development and school construction. In November, the special supertax levied on the sale of automobiles was removed. The state took over some of the contributions previously paid by employers to social insurance funds in order to help cut labor costs. By the end of 1964, the government had definitely shifted from a restraining to a propulsive economic policy, while trying at the same time to keep the price level stable. Since the early months of 1965 showed only a slight increase in domestic business activity while prices remained fairly stable and exports continued high, the government issued a decree on March 15, 1965, incorporating a wide range of antirecession measures.[6] Local governments were authorized to borrow large sums from the central state for local improvements, schools, hospitals, streets, and water and sewer lines. National entities were given funds for highway, port, and railroad building and repairs. Procedures for implementing public-works projects were simplified and accelerated. State-owned corporations were urged to speed up their plans for expansion. More liberal credit facilities were authorized for private business. Social insurance payments, unemployment benefits, and family allowances were increased to put more money into circulation.

While all these efforts to improve the public sector were needed, and in fact long overdue, it took a sharp recession in the construc-

---

[5] *Economic Surveys of the OECD: Italy, 1965,* pp. 19–20.
[6] In May, Parliament converted the decree into law.

tion industry to get action. But the delays and inefficiencies of the public bureaucracy, the complicated procedures and system of review, the legal requirements of codes that were a half-century to a century out of date, all served to slow down the actual application of policy decisions made at the top. At the private level, easier credit did not mean a quick decision to engage in new investment. With plenty of existing plant and labor not being used full time, the availability of money was in itself not enough to induce new private investment. So although business was gradually reviving in 1965, there was little evidence that any significant dent was being made in the reserves of the unemployed.

The action taken in the last quarter of 1964 and the first quarter of 1965 had been almost completely the work of the executive branch. Parliament was practically at a standstill. At the beginning of November, it adjourned so that the parliamentarians could campaign in the administrative elections, scheduled for November 22. During the fall, however, Parliament had brought forth the second major reform which the center-left was able to accomplish. It passed a law that would gradually abolish sharecropping: existing sharecropping contracts would be allowed to expire, but no new contracts could be made or old ones renewed, and at the time of expiration, the landowner would have to sell, with the sharecropper having first option to buy. If the two could not agree on a price, the provincial agricultural agent was empowered to establish an arbitrated price. The law provided for forty-year loans at 1 per cent interest, to enable the sharecroppers to buy the land, and thirty-year loans at 2 per cent interest for equipment and supplies. Thus an ancient institution would be finally eliminated and an ancient ideal (the land to the peasants who work it) partially achieved. Whether the peasants would want the land if another industrial boom got under way would be determined only in the future.

Before the administrative election, the Bishops' Conference issued its standard call for all Catholics to vote united for the Christian Democratic Party. The returns in seventy-four provincial elections, compared to the previous year's parliamentary election returns in those provinces, are shown in Table 15. These over-all results hide some of the major trends, however. The

TABLE 15

ELECTION RETURNS IN 74 PROVINCES IN 1964 COMPARED WITH
1963 ELECTIONS TO THE CHAMBER OF DEPUTIES
(*In Per Cents*)

Parties	1963*	1964
Fascist	5.0	4.99
Monarchist	1.7	0.93
Liberal	7.0	7.96
Christian Democratic	38.2	37.36
Republican	1.3	1.17
Social Democratic	6.3	6.68
Socialist	14.2	11.30
PSIUP		2.91
Communist	25.6	26.02
Other	0.7	0.76
Total	100.0	100.00

* The 1963 results are for the 74 provinces in which elections were held in 1964; therefore, they do not coincide with the 1963 figures for the whole country.

Source: *La Stampa*, November 25, 1964.

Christian Democratic vote increased in the centers of the cities and in the north, while it declined in central and southern Italy, with the exception of Sicily.[7] The Communist vote increased in northern and central Italy and in the peripheries of the cities, while it also declined in the south. In the country as a whole, the Socialist decline was almost perfectly matched with the votes received by its left-wing splinter group, PSIUP. The Liberals continued their general increase throughout the country, but on a smaller scale. On the whole, the parties of the center-left coalition suffered a slight decline. Since the country was in the midst of a recession, it may be said that they survived fairly well, although the indications of widespread unrest could hardly be ignored.

On November 30, *L'Osservatore romano* sadly criticized those Catholics who had not voted Christian Democratic. Repeating its

---

[7] Unofficial explanations of the Sicilian increase are that the Mafia threw its support to the Christian Democrats in return for their burial of the parliamentary report on the Mafia.

condemnation of voters who mistakenly endorsed atheistic Communism, it used stronger language in attacking liberalism, insisting that the Catholic could not support the liberal theory of the separation of Church and State, in which religion becomes a private matter. It concluded that liberalism would never be able to weaken Communism.

This recognition of the lack of Catholic unity, of the temptations of Communism on the left and the Liberal Party on the right, was just one effort to hold together a bitterly divided party. During the preceding year, the factions within Christian Democracy had crystallized even further. On the extreme left, some Christian Democrats were engaged in a "dialogue" with the Communists, examining the possible areas of common belief, as well as the possible trends in their respective ideological orientations.[8] The most advanced Catholic group, in this respect, was centered, in Florence, around Christian Democratic Mayor Giorgio La Pira, who accepted the votes of the Communist members of the Communal Council in early 1964 in order to keep his center-left administration in office.

The Communist Party had been trying to escape from the political isolation, local and national, into which it had been placed by Socialist participation in the government. It was also engaged in a struggle to understand and to cope with the evolution of events in Italy and Western Europe. Divided by the reactions inside Italy to the Russian-Chinese dispute, by the efforts to cope with the postwar prosperity in the Western world—an economic phenomenon not easily explained by Marxist dialectic—by its declining ability to bring Italian youth into the Party in spite of its voting gains,[9] the party leadership had gradually moved to a verbal compliance with the more standard, if still qualified, procedures of political democracy. In 1963, it announced that if the Party came to power it would still accept the existence of opposi-

---

[8] The most elaborate result of this dialogue can be found in the volume edited by Mario Gozzini, *Il dialogo alla prova* (Florence: Vallechi, 1964).

[9] In 1965, Giorgio Amendola acknowledged that while over 50 per cent of the Italian workers were under thirty years of age, less than 10 per cent of Communist Party members were under thirty. The Party membership was aging. See Giorgio Amendola, "Il partito in fabbrica," *Rinascita*, May 29, 1965, p. 1.

tion parties (limited to those parties willing to participate in the construction of a Socialist society), and that it concurred in the principle of majority-and-minority votes and accepted the possibility of losing an election after once winning one. Its internal debates became more open to the external world, and various leaders were more willing to take contradictory positions in public. Giorgio Amendola went so far as to advocate majority-and-minority voting on specific issues inside the Party organs, although he rejected the open acknowledgment of organized factions, which existed in any case. While outsiders differed as to the sincerity and reality of these professions of democracy, it was evident, nevertheless, that the Party was alive and moving, that the internal dissatisfactions were real, that the political world could not wash its hands of the whole development by writing it off as fraudulent.

By 1964, the Communists had openly divided in a debate over the best means of escaping from isolation. One group, headed by Amendola, advocated launching a new drive for the creation of a united party of the working class. Amendola argued that neither Communism nor Social Democracy had succeeded, and could not succeed, in constructing a Socialist society in Western Europe, and he called for the creation of a new party "neither Leninist nor Social Democratic." The other group, led by Pietro Ingrao, argued for a direct Communist-Catholic dialogue, disregarding the Socialist parties for the time being, concentrating instead on attracting the Catholic masses, negotiating with the Catholic political, economic, and social organizations and with the Church itself.

These differing strategical conceptions were to be tested shortly. Although it had been apparent for months that Segni would never recover completely from his stroke, his resignation as President of the Republic had been delayed to save the Christian Democrats from an additional source of division before the elections. During this period, Cesare Merzagora, presiding officer of the Senate, had functioned as Acting President. With the administrative elections over, Segni resigned and Parliament was faced with choosing his successor. The three lay parties of the coalition again agreed on Giuseppe Saragat's candidacy for the office. The *Dorotei* imposed Giovanni Leone's name on the Christian Democratic Party without negotiating with other factional leaders. When the parliamentary balloting began, these two candidates quickly took the lead, while the other parties ran favorite sons. As one ballot succeeded another, it became apparent that Fanfani's supporters were not voting for Leone, while the left-wing Christian Democratic trade-unionists and intellectuals were throwing votes to Giulio Pastore, the former president of the CISL.[10] Then, slowly, it also became apparent that this time there would not be a repetition of the previous election. The *Dorotei* could not re-establish discipline, and together with the right-wing parties they did not have enough votes to win. The Socialists threw Nenni's hat into the ring. All the candidates were now negotiating with the Communists for their votes, which the latter refused to deliver while they themselves debated what to do. Amendola argued for support for the Socialist candidates. Ingrao argued that the Communists should vote for Fanfani. But Ingrao could not demonstrate that even with Communist support Fanfani could get enough votes from his own party. The Vatican successfully "advised" Fanfani to withdraw his candidacy. Nenni finally withdrew his name in favor of Saragat. The *Dorotei* eventually gave up and decided to accept Saragat. Amendola carried the debate in his own party and Saragat was elected President of the Republic. Dissident Christian Democrats refused to switch to the Social Democrat when the party leaders did, however, so that the Communist votes were necessary for Saragat's majority.

It had taken twenty-one ballots to elect a President of the Republic, during which time those who formed the interested and attentive public looked on, with fascination at first, and then with greater and greater disgust. The inadequacies of the parties, the ineffectiveness of Parliament, could not have been more

---

[10] In 1964, the Christian Democrats were organized in four major factions. On the right was *Centrismo Popolare*, the group led by Scelba, Pella, and Gonella; in the center was the largest faction (almost one-half the members of the party's National Council), the *Moro-Dorotei*, a loose coalition led by Moro, Rumor, Colombo, and Flaminio Piccoli. On the left were two groups, the *Nuove Cronache* or *Fanfaniani*, and the *Nuove Forze*, composed of Catholic trade-unionists and the intellectuals who came from an association known as the *Sinistra di Base*. Pastore was its most prominent spokesman.

graphically demonstrated. The principal party, Christian Democracy, had almost reached the point of disintegration. The political system itself appeared to be undermined. Monarchists used the spectacle to moralize about the virtues of monarchical succession. Pacciardi once more denounced the parliamentary system and called for a presidential regime, with the President to be directly elected by the voters. Some of the more fearful citizenry prepared themselves for a shift in allegiances in case the political system crumbled.

The new year saw a slow pulling together of the government. The Socialists thought they could utilize the temporary defeat of the *Dorotei* and the state of disarray of the major party to push it further to the left. This turned out to be a false hope. At the end of January, 1965, the Christian Democratic National Council issued a unity declaration. The declaration was an attack on Communism, practically the only subject the factions could agree on in public. *L'Osservatore romano* and other Catholic publications criticized the party severely. Pope Paul VI ostentatiously revived the Catholic Action Society, a warning to the Christian Democrats that the Church had other choices. He also attacked those Catholics who believed in dialogue with Communists. One after another, the principal Catholic organizations—Coltivatori Diretti, the ACLI, the CISL—issued denunciations of the "dialogue."

Under the circumstances, it was not surprising that Ingrao's strategy had suffered a failure. This did not mean a victory for Amendola's point of view, however. In April, 1965, the Communist Central Committee launched an appeal for a new "superparty" of the working class. On close examination, it turned out that the Communists were calling for a confederation of parties in which each would keep its identity. This was different from Amendola's original call for a new party that would not be Communist. It was a relaunching of the concept of the popular front. A large superparty could take up once more the task of negotiating with the Catholics, and on a more equal basis. The Social Democratic and the Socialist parties turned down the Communist call immediately. PSIUP expressed interest. In the meantime, in a number of local governments formed after the administrative elections, Socialist councilors had shifted away from the traditional alliance with the Communists to form center-left local administrations. Inside the CGIL, the Socialist trade-unionists were more restive and unhappy than ever before over that labor confederation's attacks on the government. By May, 1965, in a number of local Chambers of Labor, the Socialist union officials had organized an open minority opposition to the Communist leadership. The Socialists were not yet ready to abandon the CGIL, however, since they were fearful of losing what was left of their contact with their working-class base.

On the other side of the political spectrum, a different abandonment appeared to be in process. In the spring of 1965, Giovanni Malagodi announced that the Liberal Party accepted the social commitments of modern society, that programming was not an evil if carried out on a democratic and noncoercive basis, and that his party was ready to participate in the common effort to organize a better future for Italians. Liberal renunciation of the conception that all would be well if only the market economy and private entrepreneurs were left alone was taken with a considerable amount of disbelief by center-left protagonists. Malagodi, however, had overcome some strong opposition among very conservative Liberals to go even this far. The move was interpreted to mean the abandonment of the frontal assault on the center-left by Confindustria. The skeptics considered it merely a shift in tactics, others a recognition by some elements of the business community that nineteenth-century ideas were inadequate in a twentieth-century world. Gianni Agnelli, the son of the founder of Fiat, in arguing the importance of collaboration between business leaders and the government, admitted the difficulty for Italian business executives "to move out of the old defenses and behavior patterns, which have little relationship to the requirements and atmosphere of a modern enterprise, in a country that would like to be modern."[11]

In the spring of 1965, the four-party coalition was shaky. All major government activities had been in a state of semisuspension from the beginning of November, 1964, until the following March, when the cabinet could once more pull itself into working

---

[11] Quoted by Gianni Baldi, "I due poteri," *Il Mondo*, June 1, 1965, p. 2.

order. Fanfani replaced Saragat as Foreign Minister, and another Christian Democrat, Giuseppe Medici, resigned to make way for the Social Democrat Edgardo Lami Starnuti, so that the Social Democrats could have the representation in the cabinet to which they felt entitled. This minor reshuffle left a number of Christian Democrats and Socialists unhappy. The parties of the coalition were divided over issues of foreign policy and the meaning and timing of their program. The Socialists openly criticized the growing American military intervention in the war in Vietnam and the American military intervention in the uprising in the Dominican Republic. The Christian Democrats dutifully defended their American ally, although Foreign Minister Fanfani concentrated on calling for negotiated solutions, rather than on making justifications. At the end of 1965, Fanfani, as President of the United Nations General Assembly for the 1966 session, would transmit private messages to the United States Government from his friend Giorgio La Pira. This communication concerned the latter's interview with the leaders of North Vietnam. American publication of the messages led to a sarcastic attack by La Pira against the United States. Fanfani resigned in embarrassment, further weakening the Moro cabinet. On January 21, 1966, the government fell, again over a school issue.

In domestic affairs the Church's pressure on the government to close a Rome performance of the play *The Deputy*, which was critical of Pius XII, produced resentment among the lay parties. Since the Christian Democratic Minister of the Interior, Paolo Emilio Taviani, used the Concordat of 1929 to justify his closing of the play, the Socialists announced that revision of the Concordat would be one of the issues on their future agenda. Reform of the school system was another source of friction. A temporary compromise was reached that continued the public financing of confessional elementary schools, but excluded Catholic secondary schools from public funds.

Disputes over patronage and over the major economic issues strained relations within and among the coalition parties most seriously, however. The new five-year program set forth by the Socialist Budget Minister, Giovanni Pieraccini, in March, 1965, was attacked by the left wing of his own party, led by Riccardo

Lombardi, as insufficient and inadequate. Although the majority of the Socialist Central Committee finally approved it, the minority was a large one. In a meeting of the Christian Democratic National Council, Fanfani attacked the program as a "book of dreams," while his supporters were clamoring for more positions in the cabinet. From business and industry came criticisms of the program for not making economic efficiency the prime goal, while the political leaders insisted that relatively full employment must be the first goal. All the labor confederations rejected the program's assertion of an incomes policy in which future wage increases would be kept proportionate, in general, to increases in productivity. Although the CISL and the UIL proclaimed that their wage demands would be responsible ones, they would not accept the incomes policy in principle. The CGIL violently attacked the policy, thereby aggravating the dissension between Socialist union leaders on the one hand and the Communist and PSIUP leaders on the other. In fact, however, the unions were all too weak and the business conditions were too precarious to enable them to pursue effectively a higher goal.

Although business conditions were improving in the first part of 1965, the situation was still so uncertain that the dangers of renewed inflation preoccupied the economic and financial ministers. In June, it was announced that the five-year program and the reform of the schools would be postponed until 1966,[12] although Pieraccini claimed that the government was already making decisions according to the program. The activation of the regular regional governments was barely mentioned, and the bill on urban regulation appeared to be in suspension. The Governor of the Bank of Italy was calling for the containment of wage increases and the restoration of profits to induce new investment by entrepreneurs. He argued that public expenditures had to be controlled to avoid inflation. The Socialist Party could look ruefully at the apparent necessity to accept more delay for costly reforms, and its more impatient left wing could reassert its conclusion that

---

12 School reform would be costly and produce only long-run benefits. School construction put unemployed laborers to work immediately and therefore provided short-run benefits. However, educational reform was given first priority *after* economic revival.

the center-left had failed and that it was time for the Socialists to get out of the government.

The vast majority of the Socialists were not yet ready to accept this pessimistic conclusion. In addition, they had now received positions on almost every board, committee, agency, and bureau in government, at the national, provincial, and local levels. New vested interests had rapidly been created. As a result, at the Socialist Party congress of November, 1965, Lombardi and his supporters were in such a small minority that they dared not repeat their demand to abandon the government. Nor did they threaten to create still another schism. As a result, Nenni, who resumed the post of Secretary General, was able to lead a party more united than it had been in years, and to put through a resolution approving a policy of reunification with the Social Democrats.

The Communists could do little more than accuse the Socialists of betraying the working class. At their own party congress held at the end of January and beginning of February, 1966, the Communists concentrated on an appeal to the Catholics, praising the Ecumenical Council, denouncing state atheism, and applauding the efforts of Pope Paul, Foreign Minister Fanfani, and Giorgio La Pira to promote a peaceful settlement in Vietnam. Luigi Longo called for a direct dialogue with both the Christian Democratic Party and the Roman Catholic hierarchy. The Vatican rejected this effort to instrumentalize the Pope's efforts for peace. The Christian Democrats answered that the center-left government was the only possible one for Italy; even Scelba abandoned his opposition to it. The cabinet had fallen in January, 1966, after still another clash over schools, this time at the nursery level. But on February 23, 1966, a new center-left ministry was created, leaving both the Communists and Liberals again in opposition. Both were in increasing isolation, and both were increasingly unhappy. There were still more than two years until the next parliamentary election (1968), and perhaps a renewed prosperity could do what the last boom had not done—moderate the attractions of a powerful party of the extreme left and provide the necessary lubrication to keep Socialists and Christian Democrats together and to keep the internal feuds of the Christian Democrats within reasonable limits.

13
ECONOMIC RECOVERY

The revived economic growth lasted through the end of the decade. It differed in nature from earlier periods of expansion. Investments began increasing in the spring of 1965, but grew more slowly than in the past, or even in comparison to other Western countries during these same years. Government spending gradually increased. The Bank of Italy cautiously expanded the money supply, but more to sustain than to stimulate renewed economic growth. At all costs, it wanted to avoid inflationary excesses and to stabilize the exchange rate of the lira. The economy achieved gains in productivity and particularly in exports. Between 1963 and 1969 exports more than doubled. Steady reductions of trade barriers within the European Community and favorable Italian prices in comparison to those of competitors explain much of this expansion. In addition, Italian producers engaged in a major export drive to compensate for the slower growth of internal demand.

The automobile boom continued. By the end of the decade Italy was almost as motorized as the most advanced countries of Western Europe. Stimulating and reinforcing this rapid increase, a government road construction program gave primary emphasis to superhighways and toll roads. Smaller appropriations were directed to the extension and improvement of the ordinary road system. In the early 1970s Italy had a superhighway network that was a close second to that of West Germany. Public transportation, both urban and interurban, remained relatively neglected. The cities were jammed with cars. Meanwhile the railroads carried a declining proportion of passenger and freight traffic.

Employment had fallen during the brief setback and recovered only gradually. Productive capacity remained underutilized even after growth rates were resumed. At the end of 1969 industrial employment was only slightly above the 1963 level. At the same time the average industrial work week was somewhat reduced. The growth of production was the result of regular and continuing increases in hourly productivity.[1] Since additional workers were being added slowly, young people in search of jobs found few available. More students were staying in school longer, however, so that the labor force grew at a diminishing rate. In the south, furthermore, the slow growth of the economy discouraged many people, particularly women, from registering at the unemployment offices for jobs, or even from entering the labor force in the first place. At the same time the expansion of national pension systems encouraged retirements so that the industrial labor force was increasingly concentrated in the central age groups.

Labor costs gradually declined in the second half of the 1960s. A 1964 law transferring the costs of certain fringe benefits from the wage package to the public treasury reduced the employers' contributions to these social costs while increasing the burden on the public treasury. The salary increases achieved in the 1966 round of wage negotiations were moderate.* Put together with the required indexing of salaries to the cost of living (the *scala mobile*), which was also moderate because of the relative stability of prices, unit labor costs declined slightly. The increase in industrial productivity more than compensated for the increases in wages and fringe benefits. Raw material costs were stable or in decline, while wholesale prices rose slowly so that profits in private industry increased. Much of the profit was invested in reorganizing production and, to a lesser extent, in new technology. Another part was invested abroad. These were not the types of investments to create many new jobs in private industry. Had it not been for political pressure on public sector firms to expand employment, the growth of the industrial labor force would have been even slower. The excess labor foisted on public sector industries was one of the factors leading to their declining efficiency and reduced profits.

As surplus industrial capacity discouraged private investment, so did low interest rates. Both factors served to stimulate capital export in the late 1960s. At the end of the decade the Bank of Italy, realizing the consequences of its policy, raised internal interest rates to make domestic investment more attractive.

---

*Italian labor contracts are normally made for a three-year period.

In that period industrial investment was concentrated in the public sector. IRI's and ENI's proportion of total investment increased regularly, making the economy more dependent on the public sector and on state subsidies granted to private firms. To a substantial degree new investment came from bank loans. The big expansion of fixed indebtedness would create difficult problems during the slowdown of the 1970s. The state issued bonds, bought mostly by government-controlled banks. Increasingly, the state provided direct grants to public sector firms for capital investment, to substitute for the scantiness of profits available for reinvestment, and to reduce the price of money. The Bank of Italy slowly lost control over the money supply.[2]

Other than industry, critical areas of the Italian economy remained relatively neglected. Agriculture was not modernized at a rate comparable to that of other member states of the EEC, nor was the food-processing industry improving in efficiency. Public investments in education, sanitation, public transportation, and housing were insufficient. Italy was extremely competitive with other countries in the production and sale of consumer goods requiring medium-level technology but weak in those dependent on advanced technology. Both public and private sectors of industry preferred to buy the results of applied research done in other countries, through licensing and royalty agreements, rather than to set up research laboratories on a large scale in Italy. The failure to make research and development an important part of the educational-scientific enterprise and the low level of support for basic research resulted in a brain drain of young scientists and technologists who found better opportunities abroad. In the long run this neglect reduced the competitive position of the economic system.

The pattern in growth and distribution of firms shifted. The total number of industrial workers remained stable, but after 1966 the proportion working in big firms (over 500 employees) began to decline while the proportion in medium-sized (between 100 and 500 employees) and small industries (fewer than 100 employees) grew. Greater specialization made the smaller units flexible and profitable. The large number of tiny shops (employing fewer than ten) of an artisan and handicraft nature, always present on the Italian scene, continued to survive.

These tiny operations had always been prominent in the commercial and services sectors. With the overall stability of the industrial labor force, with the continuing exodus of manpower from agriculture, and with the expansion of the working-age population, it is not surprising that the services sector was under pressure to absorb the demand for jobs. In the late 1960s the major portion of the limited growth in national employment occurred here and in public administration. In neither area, however, did expansion contribute to efficiency. The center-left governments of the period had put on their agenda the reform of the public administration and the reform of the markets and distribution networks in Italy. Pressures to expand jobs in these sectors, however, led to poor service in the public administration and high retail prices. Naturally, general discontent rose among the people, who, if unable to get much for their money in the way of goods and services, then demanded higher wages and salaries.

A major formal goal of the center-left coalition was the establishment of a system of national planning to give direction and coherence to economic growth. The development of a five-year plan was a principal Socialist condition for joining the government. Because the new coalition came into existence in a period of economic slowdown, Moro had successfully persuaded the Socialists that recovery was necessary before new experiments could be introduced. With the recovery of 1965, Socialist pressure for planning became the prime issue of the political debate.[3]

The DC had committed itself to planning, but was cautious and hesitant about implementing its promise. Its election losses of 1963 had often been attributed to the reform commitment as well as to the 1962 nationalization of the electric power industry. A large portion of the rank-and-file party members and of the DC electorate had opposed the opening to the left in any case, and these political considerations were additional reasons for DC politicians to proceed slowly. To make the experiment more palatable to a suspicious electorate, they avoided the word "planning" and substituted the word "programming." Planning, especially on a five-year basis, had too many Marxist and bolshevik associations. In addition, the programming was supposed to be democratic, although nobody knew precisely what the phrase "democratic programming" really meant. Generically, it was supposed to mean participation. But by whom?

Legislation in 1965 created an interministerial committee to supervise and approve the first five-year program for 1966-70. This committee of the economic ministers was chaired by the minister of the budget. The programming machinery was located in the Budget Ministry. An advisory committee of experts was formed to give technical advice to the cabinet ministers as well as to oversee the programming operations. The technical committee proved to be a most political body, composed of representatives from the major industrial, commercial, and agricultural trade associations, from the principal trade union confederations, plus a number of university economists. Even the economists, however, had party identifications. Consequently, the program that emerged was more a result of political bargaining than a scientific product of the best economic and statistical minds in Italy. This was participatory democratic programming.

The five-year plan was finally passed by parliament in early 1967. The basic goals of the program were five: (1) to produce a growth of national income to achieve full employment at higher levels of well-being; (2) to increase agricultural productivity to meet the growing domestic demand for foodstuffs and to expand exports; (3) to reduce the gap between agricultural and nonagricultural incomes and to eliminate underemployment in agriculture; (4) to create new jobs in the south outside agriculture, particularly in industry; and (5) to expand investment in the public services— education, health, scientific research, and public transportation— without at the same time blocking all expansion of private consumption. There were no annual quotas, no specific production goals by economic sector; instead the five years were treated as a whole and the goals were set in the form of average percentage increases. The following projections of average annual growth, widely divorced from reality, were developed:

Industrial production—7 percent
Agricultural production—2.85 percent
Services—4.5 percent
Public administration—3.65 percent

It was expected that over the five-year period there would be a gradual increase in the proportion of the gross national product devoted to public as against private consumption; a higher share of national income would be allocated to health, education, and welfare. Underlying the program was the assumption that the pre-1964 rate of growth would be restored, and part of the increase in gross national product would be available to achieve these goals. A second underlying assumption was that the government and the public administration could function effectively, could organize and implement the necessary decisions, and could induce the required investments. Both assumptions were wrong.

When the program was published, Fanfani, a former prime minister and professor of economic history, called it a dream book. Before we laugh too hard at the dream book, however, we should reflect that this was a first attempt, that there was neither experience nor a political tradition or a civic culture to support the planning process.

During early discussions of planning, the imposition of obligatory programs had been rejected. By the time programming became a real political possibility, the private business community, the leaders of the public sector industries, and the DC party had already made it clear that at the most they would accept only indicative programming. The Socialists knew this when they entered the center-left coalitions but expected that the specific indicators for the future would be taken seriously. Since the underlying assumptions supporting the programming were erroneous—the resources were not available in sufficient quantity, nor was the political will or administrative effectiveness present—and since the indicators produced by the programming process were faulty, the program soon collapsed. Executives in both the private and public sectors continued to make decisions based on either market considerations or on whatever inducements were granted to them by the government on an ad hoc basis.

No second five-year program has yet appeared. The technical staff set up in the Budget Ministry has remained in existence, however, since in Italy no jobs are ever abolished; and it continues to produce a variety of studies, projections, and analyses that usually meet the fate of such exercises in all governments.

It would be wrong to conclude that the collapse of the programming effort left no benefits to Italian society. There were limited improvements in governmental budgetary procedures. For the first time one office in a single ministry was required to correlate its plans with another office in the same ministry. For the first time ministries were forced to think beyond the preparation of the next year's budget. The same held true for organized groups outside the government. The habit of depending on improvisation and ad hoc adjustment to events was disturbed slightly.

In the place of economic reform the Christian Democrats substituted the further expansion and colonization of the public sector industries. In effect, the attempt to make a more efficient socioeconomic system was abandoned in favor of a welfare economy: the concessions of grants, subsidies, and public expenditures to every claimant to the governmental largesse. Some claimants were naturally more favored than others. Most favored was a group that its critics called the "state bourgeoisie." Included in this group were executives and managers of the public sector industries and of government-controlled banks and financial holding companies, and the speculators and adventurers who put together large conglomerates with grants from the state and loans from these banks. The speculators made fortunes on the deals they promoted rather than on the productivity of the enterprises they controlled. They were supported by the government because they were supposed to promote economic growth, particularly in the south and in the islands. The legal basis of their operations was a 1965 law favoring industrial concentration. The preferred loci of their intervention were the chemical, petrochemical, and synthetic fibers industries.[4]

The speculators owed their fortunes to their close relations with the parties of the center-left coalition. They expressed their gratitude with financial contributions to these parties and to the factions and party leaders. They were shrewd enough not to neglect the opposition. Likewise, the executives and managers appointed to important positions in the public sector owed their appointments to their political associations. In the distribution of positions the Christian Democrats got the lion's share, but the Socialists also received a portion of the patronage; the two smaller parties of the coalition, Social Democratic and Republican, got the remaining crumbs. The state bourgeoisie were thus both beneficiaries and benefactors of the political system.

New factories were built and new jobs created, but the jobs in the plants were filled on the basis of political connections. Inadequate management, poor labor discipline, and mistaken product priorities did not make for profitable operations. Gradually in the late 1960s the deficits in the public sector began to increase. This sector had been reasonably effective and profitable in the 1950s and early 1960s. It had helped to stimulate the economic miracle and had supported the expansion of private industry and of exports. In the south, especially, the larger share of big business was in state-controlled firms. In the later 1960s, however, their qualitative decline contrasted with their quantitative growth. The costs of the qualitative decline would not become conspicuous until the 1970s when scandalous losses were revealed. Since jobs once created must be kept going at all costs, no big firm, private or public, is allowed to fail. So in the 1970s the banks would rescue the unprofitable operations.

Naturally not every public sector firm is unprofitable, nor is every executive or every worker unqualified. The scandals that made the newspaper headlines concentrated on the failures, not the successes. One prominent failure was the takeover of the huge Montedison chemical complex by a combination of IRI, ENI, and Istituto Mobiliare Italiano (IMI), a government investment bank. The rivals in these three government institutions first squeezed out the former private management of Montedison and then engaged in a power struggle for control among themselves that left the conglomerate floundering in a sea of debt.

Another failure was the decision taken in 1967 to construct an Alfa Romeo automobile plant (Alfa Sud) in the Naples area. Alfa Romeo is a public sector firm, part of the IRI group. Fiat, the largest private business in Italy, unsuccessfully opposed the project. The PSI supported the new plant, although it was not part of the five-year program. The PCI was persuaded to endorse it as a contribution to southern development, in spite of the Communist position ostensibly emphasizing mass over personal transportation. The government decision was based on the expected continuation of booming automobile demand. Numerous delays and bad planning postponed the completion of the plant until 1972. The political hiring policies and the lack of control over production lines meant that the first and every subsequent car manufactured by Alfa Sud has been produced at a loss. The current management now hopes that the plant may break even by 1983.

In the late 1950s the government decided to build a modern steel plant at Taranto, at the instep of the Italian boot. The plant began operations in 1964 and was successful. Because it made money, another decision was made in the late 1960s to double its size. By the time the addition was completed in 1974, a worldwide depression had hit the steel industry, so that this enlarged plant, along with others already in existence, was struggling to survive.

These examples illustrate a combination of bad policy, bad timing, and bad luck. This is not the whole story of the Italian economy in the last half of the 1960s, however. In the Veneto and Emilia-Romagna, for example, economic growth converted these regions from a semirural to a modern industrial and commercial society. To a lesser degree this was also true in Tuscany and Lazio. Here growth resulted from the initiative of many small and medium-sized firms, almost all of them private, many of them created by former peasants. This geographical expansion diluted the previous concentration of industry in the northwest industrial triangle—Genoa, Turin, and Milan. Here (except in southern Lazio) economic progress occurred without the special benefits and assistance of government agencies like the Southern Italy Fund. Many of these new operations were oriented to the then flourishing export market.

Government policies did not aid agriculture effectively. The establishment of the Common Agricultural Program (CAP) of the European Economic Community did no good for Italian agriculture or for Italian and other European consumers. The program subsidized the high prices and growing surpluses of dairy products and meat animals, foodstuffs produced in excess quantities in France,

West Germany, and the Netherlands. Italy was a major importer of these products from its EEC partners, although it could have obtained them at lower prices outside the EEC. The Mediterranean fruits and vegetables produced by Italy received no comparable support. Through both higher prices and financial contributions Italy had to pay the cost to keep the CAP solvent. The Italian government made feeble efforts to change the rules. Acceptance of the unfair burden could be rationalized as the price for the gains the EEC provided in nonagricultural sectors.[5]

The EEC was not totally neglectful of Italian agriculture. Its grants to Italy for agricultural restructuring and development were underutilized because Italian public administration was too inefficient to exploit them properly. Italy's weak participation in European regional affairs and inadequate functioning at home cost both farmers and the citizenry at large a high price.

In spite of limited involvement in the regular functioning of European regional institutions, Italy did take some action to promote its political interests in Europe. It unsuccessfully supported British applications for entry into the EEC, but the French vetoes of the United Kingdom's requests for admission could not be overridden. British membership was no economic threat to Italian interests, and the Italians believed that the British could play a useful role in helping offset France-German domination of the community.

On an opposite tack the Italian government moved to block Austria's efforts to become associated with the EEC although it had no objection in principle to Austria's application for associate membership. Italy was engaged, however, in a dispute with the Vienna government over the South Tyrol. Austria was accused of permitting its territory to be used as a base by anti-Italian terrorists from the German-speaking Tyrolese inhabitants of the province of Bolzano and was also charged with encouraging separatist sentiment. Austria denied both accusations but did support the claims of the South Tyrol People's Party (SVP) that Italy was not living up to the stipulations of the De Gasperi-Gruber agreement of 1946, the accord that regulated Italian treatment of the German-speaking inhabitants. The dispute dragged on through most of the 1960s, with charges and countercharges, negotiations and collapses of negotiations. It was during one of these breakdowns that the Italians vetoed Austria's application to the EEC. In 1969 an agreement between Rome and Vienna was reached. The Italian government expanded the rights of the German-speaking Tyrolese and the powers of the Bolzano provincial government dominated by the SVP. The Italian veto of Austria's application for associate status in the EEC was withdrawn. Interestingly, throughout the whole period of the dispute there is no indication that trade between the two countries was affected.

The U.S.-Soviet joint presentation of the nuclear non-proliferation treaty raised a number of doubts in the Italian government, doubts spurred mainly, though not exclusively, by economic considerations. Renouncing the establishment of a nuclear weapons system did not bother Italians on the grounds of high politics. They had no illusions that they were, or could be, a great power, and they had no intention of investing in nuclear weapons. They did fear, however, that adherence ot the proposed treaty might deprive them of the economic benefits of the spinoff from military atomic research. They thought the treaty might interfere with their own peaceful nuclear research, thereby impairing economic growth and placing the country at a competitive disadvantage vis-à-vis the atomic powers. They also preferred that the inspection functions incorporated into the treaty be carried out by Euratom, an EEC organization, rather than by the United Nations International Atomic Energy Agency. In addition, Italians worried about the prospect of being potential victims of nuclear blackmail. All these considerations led Italy to delay acceptance of the treaty in 1966 and 1967.

Since other European countries, particularly West Germany, shared these same concerns, negotiations dragged on until 1968 before reaching a satisfactory conclusion that enabled Italy to adhere to the non-proliferation treaty. In that year the super-powers guaranteed the non-nuclear states that the benefits of nuclear research for peaceful purposes would be transferred to them. They also gave assurances against nuclear blackmail (for whatever these assurances are worth). A compromise was reached on inspection procedures whereby the International Atomic Energy Agency retained overall responsibility, but in Western Europe Euratom functioned as the operating agency of this United Nations organization.

Italy endorsed United Nations action to promote the economic development of Third and Fourth World countries. The governments of the center-left coalition made many rousing declarations of responsibility to the poorer nations of the world. The Socialist Party, in particular, asserted the moral responsibility of Italy and other Western countries. But these declarations and assertions produced little concrete assistance. Italy was engaged in a major effort to expand foreign commerce, an effort that included the underdeveloped countries, but it concentrated on trade, not aid. Of all the advanced, developed members of the Organization for Economic Cooperation and Development (OECD), Italy and Japan were and still are the two countries giving the lowest amount of foreign aid as a proportion of GNP. In its pursuit of trade Italy had established a commercial office in Peking in 1964 and had concluded trade agreements with the Communist government while maintaining formal diplomatic relations with the Nationalist government on Taiwan. In 1970 Italy broke with the Nationalists and gave de jure recognition to the Communist Chinese regime.

The year 1969 brought to an end twenty years of continuous economic growth that had transformed Italy in many ways but had left it vulnerable to future setbacks. The margins of flexibility of the economic system had been reduced. The country was more than ever a transformer of raw materials imported from abroad. It was increasingly an importer of foodstuffs and technological innovation. The state capitalism was neither robust nor efficient. National economic programming had failed. The early dynamism of its entrepreneurial leadership was dissipating. Its earlier advantages of low-cost labor and newly achieved economies of scale were ending. It still had widespread weak and backward sectors, in agriculture, in retail distribution, in investment goods, and in construction and real estate. These contradictions were to plague it throughout the next decade.

In the aftermath of the failure of economic programming, in the insufficient growth of the domestic economy, Italian commentators with a propensity for conspiracy theses found political explanations for the poor performance of the center-left governments. Since exports were increasing, there was no real danger of balance of payments crises. There was surplus capacity in various industries. The Bank of Italy had sustained and guaranteed the sale of treasury bonds to the banks and the investing public between 1966 and 1969, limiting the pressure on the treasury to expand the monetary base. Consequently there was little likelihood of significant price increases at home. Therefore, these analysts conclude, the Christian Democrats held back on programming and stronger economic stimulants because the resulting sociopolitical changes could threaten their domination of Italian society. The welfare economy that they promoted instead consolidated DC hegemony, produced a solution to the exacerbated rivalries of party factions by providing them with patronage and financial support, kept the Socialists quiet by sharing some of the spoils, and postponed the hard decisions to another decade. The Socialists acquiesced, according to this interpretation, because they had been bought off.[6] They had fallen victim to the historic Italian vice of transformism.

This argument has some validity but is insufficient. It neglected some Italian economic history and certain current political necessities. The Italian people, and the financial managers of the Bank of Italy in particular, still had an historic fear of inflation and of deficits in international accounts. This fear was an inheritance from the wild inflation of the late 1940s and the incipient inflation of the 1961-63 boom. The past preyed on the minds of the decision makers, who preferred not to run risks that might threaten the stability of the lira. The lira was to be defended; that was the prime objective. Furthermore, Moro never had strong support in his own camp for the reform program to which he was publicly committed; his position would have been undermined by his DC rivals if he had pushed faster and harder. In the next decade the priorities would be changed.

NOTES

1. Michele Salvati, *Il sistema economico italiano: Analisi di una crisi* (Bologna: Il Mulino, 1975), p. 41.

2. Mariano D'Antonio, *Sviluppo e crisi del capitalismo italiano 1951-1972* (Bari: De Donato, 1973), pp. 227-31.

3. Joseph LaPalombara, *Italy: The Politics of Planning*, National Planning Series, No. 7 (Syracuse: Syracuse University Press, 1966).

4. Giorgio Galli, *Storia della Democrazia Cristiana* (Bari: Laterza, 1978), pp. 249-66.

5. F. Roy Willis, *Italy Chooses Europe* (New York: Oxford University Press, 1971).

6. Galli, *Storia della Democrazia Christiana*, pp. 249-66.

14
THE ROLE OF
THE SOCIALISTS

The Socialists rationalized their entry into the center-left coalitions of the 1960s on both socioeconomic and political grounds. The reforms that they expected from the coalitions were supposed to transform Italian society by providing more social justice for more people. In the process the Communists would be isolated; the Socialists would attract large blocs of voters away from the PCI, and once more become the largest party of the left. Great numbers of formerly Communist voters would now shift to a party unequivocally committed to parliamentary democracy and the European and Atlantic communities. The Italian political system, therefore, would be strengthened as domestic political institutions gained a previously lacking legitimacy among the masses. The pro-Western foreign policies of the earlier centrist coalitions would be reinforced. Even the preeminent electoral position of the Christian Democrats could be threatened. A future alternation of governments was now possible, an alternation to provide flexibility and choice within the framework of democratic institutions.

These anticipations remained unrealized, but the center-left was far from the total failure later judgments assigned to it. The political isolation of the Communist Party remained incomplete. True, at the national level the PSI was in the government rather than in the opposition with the PCI, but the splinter Socialists who had created PSIUP in 1964 continued to cooperate with the Communists. At provincial and communal levels Socialists abandoned many alliances with the Communists in favor of coalitions with the Christian Democrats. Nevertheless, a minority of local governments, particularly in the Red Belt regions of Emilia-Romagna, Tuscany, and

Umbria, continued to be based on Communist-Socialist collaboration.

It was at the trade union level, however, that the effort to isolate the PCI failed miserably. Almost all the Socialist trade unionists, both leaders and rank-and-file members, remained in the Communist-dominated CGIL. In social, cultural, professional, and student groups Socialists usually found it easier to get along with Communists than with Catholics. The center-left, consequently, failed to push the Communists into the cold.

Socialist participation in the government produced little visible change in foreign policy. There was much talk about a moral obligation to the underdeveloped countries of the Third World, but it remained merely talk. Italian contributions to Third World economic development were, and still are, the smallest in proportion to gross national product of any advanced modern country. There was no reason that the fact should have been otherwise, given the priority of the claim of the underdeveloped parts of Italy. Both public and private businesses in Italy continued to search for new export markets and for more sources of raw materials and foodstuffs, to say nothing of additional contracts to build roads, dams, factories, pipe lines, etc. This search, of course, was independent of the nature of the coalition running the government.

The Socialists abandoned whatever earlier reservations they had had about the European Economic Community, but Italian participation in the EEC remained essentially passive, limited to weak efforts at protecting national interests. The Common Agricultural Policy of the EEC developed in the 1960s imposed a high price on Italian agriculture and consumers, for the center-left coalition defended Italy's interests ineffectively. Rhetoric about promoting further regional integration did little to counteract the nationalist involution of the EEC brought about by French President Charles de Gaulle. The Italians did resist resolutely the French efforts to turn Western Europe against the United States and NATO. Along with the West Germans they insisted upon the compatibility of the two alliances,[1] and there is little doubt that if they had ever been forced to a showdown, they would have chosen the Atlantic link over the European one. Hostility to the United States among various Italian opinion leaders because of the Vietnam war made it difficult for center-left governments to be conspicuously pro-United States, but in the 1960s a choice between the United States and Europe was not required. The Italian government favored British admission to the EEC, but could do nothing in the face of French vetoes. Nor could the Socialists persuade the left wing of the British Labour Party to abandon its hostility to the Common Market. Joint membership in the Socialist International was a useless lever for the PSI.

Center-left cabinets had their domestic disappointments also. Socialists in the government did not achieve effective decentralization. In the late 1960s parliament established regional planning commissions for nonexistent regional governments, but these commissions had no more success than the national programming committee had. Instead they became a focus of rivalry among the factions of the government parties, an additional occasion for patronage, and a potential power base in case the commissions should amount to something in the future. In some of the more advanced regions they produced useful studies and plans that could be stored away for later use.

The Christian Democrats were responsible for the center-left failure in the 1960s to create regional governments for the 15 regular regions. The DC demanded a guarantee that the Socialists would not form coalitions in the Red Belt with the PCI. In the face of the Socialist refusal to give this guarantee, the DC delayed fulfilling its pledge to implement regionalism. The issue would not be resolved until the next decade.

Of the three major economic reforms that the center-left attempted, national programming failed. A second was the nationalization of the electric power industry, undertaken in 1962 to induce the Socialists to enter the government. Depending on their ideological predilections, Italian economists still debate whether this was an improvement or a regression. The 1964 law providing for the gradual elimination of sharecropping was eminently successful, economically and socially. The former sharecroppers and, even more, those of their children who remained on the land, were slowly transformed into commercial farmers, who were better educated and who applied modern techniques and modern machinery to the improvement of agriculture.

The coalitions were also able to take some of the regressivity out of the Italian tax system. Italian statistics on income, on tax burdens, on tax evasion are unreliable. What appears clear, however, is that the proportion of government income derived from progressive direct taxes gradually increased while the proportion received from regressive indirect taxes decreased. The changes were minor, however; the tax system as a whole still remains substantially regressive.

Socialist participation in the successive cabinets of the period was responsible for a significant revision of secondary education. A unified lower middle school (grades six through eight) with a common curriculum was created to replace separate academic and vocational schools. Completion of this school satisfied the constitutional requirement for compulsory education to the age of 14.

The upper middle schools continued to exist as separate types: classic *liceo*, scientific *liceo*, normal school for training elementary school teachers, and commercial, vocational, and fine arts schools. The first two years of their curricula were now unified, to expose all Italian school children to a common basic curriculum until the age of 16. At this age a student could transfer from one type of school to another with essential prerequisites completed. The last two or three years in the upper middle schools (some have four, others five, years) continued to provide the differentiated offerings of the past. The selectivity process that controlled a young person's future had thereby been postponed. Instead of determining career choices at age 11, the reformed school system delayed critical decisions for five years when, presumably, they could be made on the basis of more training and maturity.

In the 1960s secondary school attendance was rising rapidly. The number of classrooms and teachers fell short of demand. Double shifts became common, teachers without credentials for tenure were hired, and the stresses on pupils, parents, and teachers grew. There is general agreement that the level of education improved for the mass of young people coming from families that had never before received much formal education. There is also general agreement that the quality of education was diluted from the standards required of educated elites of previous generations.

School expansion also took place at the beginning levels. There had been few public kindergartens and nursery schools. Almost all of those then existing were privately operated, the vast majority by the Catholic Church. Their expense limited access to the children of the well-to-do. The Socialists pushed for more public kindergartens and nursery schools to make them available to more of the preschool population and to reduce the role of the Church in the educational process. The DC moved slowly, to protect Church interests. It compromised by enlarging public opportunities and then increased government grants to Church schools so that they could expand in number. On more than one occasion the question of public funding for parochial schools brought the center-left coalitions to the verge of collapse.

In the long run the changes in the school system were the most important of the reforms effected by the center-left. The overall expansion of education was related to the economic development and modernization of the country. Quantity was stressed at the expense of quality. The declining reputation of the public schools among educated parents led them to prefer private schools. Whereas in the past the private schools had been looked upon as refuges for young people incapable of handling the rigors of the public *liceo*, they now became the choice of the families who could afford them. This reversal of judgments took place among anticlerical intellectuals of the left as well as conservatives and Catholics. Political postures were not permitted to control private adjustments to the conditions of contemporary life.

The 1960s witnessed the temporary political unification of the two principal socialist parties. With Socialists and Social Democrats partners in coalitions at national and local levels, it was natural to raise the question of reunification. Since the split in 1947 their relations more often than not had been affected by attitudes of rivalry and hostility. In 1956 the Socialist and Social Democratic leaders, Pietro Nenni and Giuseppe Saragat, had met at Pralognan to discuss reunification. The increasing divergences between the PSI and the Communists laid the premises for the conversation. Nothing was resolved at that time. Ten years later, in 1966, the process was renewed. A personal obstacle—who the leader of the united party would be—had been removed in 1964 when Saragat was elected to the presidency of the Italian republic. Programmatic and organizational obstacles were successfully negotiated this time. At a conference held between October 28 and 30, 1966, the new party was formed and named the Unified Socialist Party (PSU). PSIUP, in a number of ways more leftist than the Communists, remained outside the union.

The rank and file of the PSI and PSDI had not demanded unification. Consequently, the PSU was joined only at the top. The former Social Democrats became separate, identifiable factions within the new party, in competition with other Socialist factions for posts, power, and rewards. Social Democrats feared absorption into the larger PSI organization. This worry aggravated their personal concerns about future leadership roles. They feared a takeover, not a merger. The history of the rivalries and antagonisms since the split of 1947 could not be overcome quickly. The Social Democrats could feel that the circumstances of reunification justified their policies since 1947; the Socialists could feel proud of their historic tradition and larger organized base.

An effort to develop new programs and policies appropriate for a modern industrial society might have consolidated the new political formation. Such an effort could, perhaps, successfully attract growing numbers of young voters who had weak identifications with other political parties. The leadership of the PSU had neither the capacity nor the will to make the attempt. They produced nothing comparable to the 1959 Bad Godesberg program of the German Social Democratic Party, a program that modernized the basis of German socialism and provided that party's electoral successes in the 1960s. Instead, the Italian Socialists spent their time and effort in tactical maneuvering and personal rivalries. A party that might have challenged successfully both the Christian Democrats and the Communists never emerged.

Nevertheless the potentiality of a new and serious challenger induced the two largest parties to react in various ways. The Communists denounced the Socialists for splitting the working class, particularly in many cities where the PSU abandoned former local coalitions with the PCI. The Communists also made friendly approaches to left-wing Catholic political factions and social groups. The PCI continued to pursue its goal of avoiding isolation. The DC, worried by the prospect of growing Socialist influence, gave the PSU more patronage, instead of intensifying and accelerating the reform program. On the contrary, it sought to close its own ranks by providing places in the government and jobs in the public services to conservative Christian Democrats who had opposed the opening to the left throughout the decade. This consolidation then made the PSU leadership more suspicious of the sincerity of the DC commitment to reform.

Both the DC and the PSU were divided internally over the two major international events of the period, the Vietnam war and the Six-Day Arab-Israeli War of 1967. In each party left-wing groups were pro-North Vietnam and pro-Arab, as was the PCI. The official position of the center-left government was pro-United States and pro-Israel. These differences were used primarily for domestic political purposes; on the part of the PCI to undercut the unity of the PSU and the coalition government, in the other two major parties as maneuvering tools by the factions in their incessant struggles. Thus, Foreign Minister Fanfani expressed veiled sympathies for the Arab states with various proposals for mediation. His intrusion into the Vietnam war was more overt. The United States found his effort to arrange an Italian mediation irritating and uncomfortable. These activities served to undercut the position of Prime Minister Moro and also to lay the basis for Fanfani's 1971 campaign for the presidency of the republic. Fanfani could hope to get Communist and other anti-United States votes in support of his prospective candidacy. The backing that the United States was giving to the dictatorship of the colonels in Greece served to fan anti-United States feelings in Italy. More and more, parliamentary representatives of the majority coalition underlined the obvious fact that Italy's commitment to the Atlantic community was limited geographically to Europe and implied no support for U.S. policies beyond the Atlantic area.

To offset the anti-U.S. atmosphere President Saragat paid a state visit to the United States in September 1967, accompanied by Foreign Minister Fanfani. The traditional friendship between the two countries was reaffirmed. Presumably suggestions were made to President Lyndon B. Johnson about reducing the U.S. commitment in the war in Southeast Asia. Since Saragat was considering running for reelection, Fanfani's position was thereby defined. Saragat's pro-U.S. stance, however, made him more unpopular among the left-wing factions of his own PSU.

Strains within the PSU were matched by strains between Socialists and their Christian Democratic allies. Two major scandals found each on opposite sides of the issues. In the summer of 1965 the former minister of finance, Giuseppe Trabucchi, Christian Democrat, was charged with corruption while in office. He was accused of accepting large bribes that presumably went to his party. Since he was still a deputy, it was necessary for his accusers to get his parliamentary immunity lifted in order to bring him into court. The DC defeated this move, but found itself abandoned by its Socialist, Social Democratic, and Republican allies.

More serious was the charge made in 1967 by two Socialist journalists that General Giovanni De Lorenzo had been plotting a coup d'état in the summer of 1964. Since Antonio Segni, then president of Italy, was implicated, the Christian Democratic Party had to defend its honor. Although the courts finally exonerated De Lorenzo, certain aspects of the issue remain a mystery. Many Socialists joined the call for a parliamentary investigation of the affair, but the government refused, claiming that state secrets were involved. Here Moro was acting to defend the image of his own party for the following years's elections, and in this he succeeded. A subsequent public criticism of the two journalists by President Saragat further divided the factions in the PSU.[2]

The question of divorce added another stress to the cohesion of the governing coalition. In 1965 the Socialist deputy, Loris Fortuna, introduced a divorce bill in the Chamber of Deputies. Although it was a private member bill, the issue immediately put the DC at odds with its lay partners. The Catholic Church opposed any divorce bill absolutely, no matter how stringent its provisions, and the DC had no option but to defend the Church's position. The issue thereby became one of party, drawn out for years before it was resolved.

In this climate the country went into the 1968 parliamentary election on May 19 and 20. The DC gained slightly; in the Chamber of Deputies its proportion rose from 38.3 percent of the total vote to 39.1 percent. The conservative parties, Liberal, Monarchist, and Missini, all declined. PSIUP received 4.5 percent, retaining 23 of its 24 Chamber seats. The big gainer was the PCI, which increased from 25.3 to 26.9 percent of the electorate and received 11 more seats in the Chamber. The big loser was the PSU. It lost almost 25 percent of the vote that the PSI and PSDI together had totaled in 1963. Part of their former voters went over to PSIUP, but it was obvious that another part had gone to the Communists and, in small measure, to the DC[3] (see Table 16).

Moro and his party could be pleased with the outcome. They had reassured their moderate electorate that there was no danger from the alliance with the Socialists. They had recouped part of their 1963 losses to the Liberals. The PSU no longer loomed as a possible threat to their leading position. What the DC had failed to do was to block the continued advance of the Communists. The PCI received the largest vote in its history to that point. Analysis of the election results indicated that it was making headway, especially among the young voters, which augured well for the party's future. The PCI had staved off the attempt to isolate it and to steal its electorate.

Inside the PSU the atmosphere was bitter. Erstwhile Social Democrats and former PSI leaders could agree that the basic cause of their electoral defeat was their failure to achieve significant reforms. They could agree on little else, however, and mutual recriminations increased. The PSU had been only partially unified at best; the election returns brought the unification process to a halt. Many Socialists blamed Moro and his strategy of delay for their failure. Others, however, believed Moro to be sincere in his commitment to reform, recognizing that he could not move too far ahead of his own traditional electorate. The latter Socialist group, led by Nenni, felt that Moro had to be supported in the effort to reorganize a new center-left coalition, since there was still a good majority in parliament. The alternative would be a return to weak center-right governments like those of the 1950s, with the Socialists again in opposition. Neither the country nor the Socialists would benefit. Within the Socialists, Moro's enemies won out, arguing that the PSU would have to remain outside the government while it reassessed its position. On May 31, 1968, the Central Committee of the PSU voted to cut its ties to the center-left coalition. The era of the Moro-Nenni-Saragat triumvirate had ended.

Three weeks later Giovanni Leone, speaker of the Chamber of Deputies, formed a one-party DC minority cabinet as a caretaker for

TABLE 16: Results of Four Elections to the Italian Chamber of Deputies, 1968-79

Parties*	May 9, 1968 Valid Votes			May 7, 1972 Valid Votes			June 20, 1976 Valid Votes			June 3, 1979 Valid Votes		
	Number	Percent	Seats	Number	Percent	Seats	Number	Percent	Seats	Number	Percent	Seats
Christian Democrat (DC)	12,441,553	39.1	266	12,919,270	38.7	266	14,209,519	38.7	262	14,007,594	38.3	262
Communist (PCI)	8,557,404	26.9	177	9,072,454	27.1	179	12,614,650	34.4	228	11,107,883	30.4	201
Unified Socialist (PSU)	4,605,832	14.5	91	—	—	—	—	—	—	—	—	—
Socialist (PSI)	—	—	—	3,210,427	9.6	61	3,540,309	9.6	57	3,586,256	9.8	62
Italian Social Movement (MSI)	1,414,794	4.5	24	2,896,762	8.7	56	2,238,339	6.1	35	1,924,251	5.3	30
Social Democrat (PSDI)	—	—	—	1,717,539	5.1	29	1,239,492	3.4	15	1,403,873	3.8	20
Republican (PRI)	626,567	2.0	9	954,597	2.9	15	1,135,546	3.1	14	1,106,766	3.0	16
Socialist Party of Proletarian Unity (PSIUP)	1,414,544	4.4	23	648,763	1.9	—	—	—	—	—	—	—
Proletarian Democracy (DP)	—	—	—	—	—	—	557,025	1.5	6	501,431	1.4	6
Liberal (PLI)	1,851,060	5.8	31	1,297,105	3.9	20	480,122	1.3	5	708,022	1.9	9
Monarchist (PDIUM)	414,423	1.3	6	—	—	—	—	—	—	—	—	—
Radical (PR)	—	—	—	—	—	—	394,439	1.1	4	1,259,362	3.4	18

*In addition, local ethnic and linguistic parties have a few deputies.

Sources: Istituto Centrale di Statistica, Annucrio Statistico Itaiiano 1977 (Rome: Published by the Institute, 1977), p. 100; Annuario Statistico Italiano 1979, p. 94.

221

the summer holidays, while the Socialists were deciding what to do. A PSU party congress called in October to resolve the issue of participation was divided into five factions. Two of them, originally Social Democratic for the most part, plus some former PSI autonomists led by Nenni, succeeded in getting 51 percent of the votes at the congress. Included in this group was Antonio Mancini, leader of the Socialist organization in Calabria. The group gained temporary control of the party organization, further irritating many of the former PSI wing. The internal equilibrium of the PSU was precarious.

Provisionally almost all of the factions agreed that they had no choice but to continue the coalition. The exception was the small Riccardo Lombardi group, hostile to the center-left since 1963. As a result the Leone government resigned on November 19. In less than a month the Christian Democrat, Mariano Rumor, formed a new cabinet. All the principal PSU leaders participated in the government in a move designed to hold the party together.

The new government reformed the pension system, but accomplished little else because renewed strife erupted inside the PSU in the spring of 1969. Involved were policy issues such as bringing the Communists, who were themselves evolving rapidly, into the center-left. Another dispute concerned the role of the police in an atmosphere of increasing violence. But personal rivalries and fears were more important. Saragat hoped to obtain reelection in 1971, but found many PSU leaders hostile. Ministers from PSI factions envisioned a future Socialist prime minister and were willing to compensate the DC by giving it the presidency of the republic. They knew that Fanfani had his eye on the post and thought he might be willing to support a Socialist candidate for prime minister. In this climate Mancini and his followers shifted to an alliance with Francesco De Martino, leader of those Socialists hostile to the Social Democrats. The Social Democrats felt their position threatened both in the government and inside the PSU. Efforts to mediate between the contenders failed. On July 3, 1969, the party split. The Socialists resurrected their old title, PSI. De Martino became secretary-general of the party. The Social Democrats continued using the PSU label for a while and then returned to their traditional PSDI label.[4]

Some of those who went over to the PSDI had come from the old PSI. Others originally from the PSDI now entered the PSI. Leading trade unionists, chief of whom was Italo Viglianesi, secretary-general of the UIL, joined the PSI. The loss of much of their trade union component isolated the Social Democrats even more from the organized workers' movement.

The reunification of Italian socialism had lasted fewer than three years. Unlike Christian Democrats and Communists, the Socialists were incapable of maintaining that minimum of unity in diversity necessary to keep a large party together in the complexity of modern Italy. The policy issues over which disagreement existed do not appear sufficiently serious to explain the rupture. Instead, the personal ambitions and animosities of leaders, the maneuverings of factions, and the distribution of patronage played the significant roles. As a result, a strong third force between Catholicism and communism failed to emerge.

NOTES

1. Primo Vannicelli, *Italy, NATO, and the European Community: The Interplay of Foreign Policy and Domestic Politics* (Cambridge: Harvard University, Center for International Affairs, 1974), pp. 47-51.

2. Giorgio Galli, *Storia della Democrazia Cristiana* (Bari: Laterza, 1978), pp. 280-81.

3. Giuseppe Mammarella, *L'Italia dalla caduta del fascismo ad oggi* (Bologna: Il Mulino, 1978), pp. 426-27.

4. Giuseppe Tamburrano, *Storia e cronaca del centro sinistra* (Milano: Feltrinelli, 1973).

15
THE EVOLUTION OF
THE COMMUNISTS

In the early 1960s the PCI had already endorsed reformism, as a method, if not as a goal. Palmiro Togliatti had wondered publicly if the class struggle, in its orthodox Marxist version, made sense in the modern developed countries. Asserting openly that if it came to power it would respect parliamentary democracy and a multiparty system, the party then qualified such affirmations in a number of ways. It insisted it was still a revolutionary party because the ultimate goal was the transformation of society, even though this transformation was to be achieved gradually over a substantial period of time by democratic means. Italian communism was not interested merely in making the welfare capitalist state work better, which it claimed the social democrats of the Western world had settled for. It limited its acceptance of the multiparty system to those parties seeking socialist goals. The PCI continued to preach the hegemony of the working class, a concept initiated by its patron saint, Antonio Gramsci. This was supposed to be different from the dictatorship of the proletariat, but nobody, including Communists, could agree on just what it meant.

On one criterion there was clear agreement: the internal unity and cohesion of the party must be maintained. The organizational principle of democratic centralism was not to be challenged. Debate and discussion were to be promoted, but organized groups and factions were still proscribed. Giorgio Amendola, a leading Communist, had suggested the possibility of majority and minority votes within party decision-making organizations, but the suggestion was dropped. Nor was there any noticeable sentiment for cutting the ties to the international communist movement, as the Yugoslavs had done in 1948 and the Chinese after 1960. These ties were not those of subordination to Moscow, for as early as 1957 Togliatti had made it clear that the Communist Party of the Soviet Union was no longer the guiding party for the international movement. But the continuation of symbolic and probably financial links distinguished the PCI from even left-wing socialist parties, in Italy and elsewhere. The PCI, in other words, remained a party "different from the others."

In the middle 1960s the major foreign relations problem of the PCI was the Soviet-Chinese rivalry within the international movement. The Italian Party was caught between two fires. On the one hand it challenged the Soviet Party's effort to excommunicate the Chinese. Since it was defending the right of Italians to determine their own path to socialism it had to endorse a similar right for the Chinese, even though formal contacts with the Chinese Party were practically nonexistent. On the other hand, the Chinese way, at least at the verbal level, was an extremist revolutionary one, at the opposite pole from the reformist procedures advocated by the Italians. As a result the PCI found itself on the receiving end of a barrage of Chinese attacks and insults, denounced as revisionist and an enemy of the true revolutionary spirit. The outbreak of the cultural revolution in China in 1967 aggravated tensions. Nevertheless, the PCI continued to object to all efforts by the Soviets to call a world conference of Communist parties to read the Chinese out of the international movement. Together with the Romanian and a few other Communist parties, it blocked such Soviet efforts in 1968 and 1969. The PCI was aware that what could be done to China might, in the future, be done to it.[1] Only ten years later, in 1978, a different Chinese Communist government made an initial opening to the Italians for the reestablishment of normal relations. In 1979, after the visit of the Chinese president, Hua Kuo Feng, to Rome at the end of a European tour, the premises were laid for a resumption of regular contacts between the two parties. The Italians insisted that such a resumption excluded any obligation to endorse the Chinese position of intense hostility to the Soviet Union.

In Italian foreign policy affairs the PCI maintained its already established positions. It had publicly endorsed Italy's membership in the European Economic Community in 1962, reversing its negative vote of 1957. This shift did not gain the PCI one of its ambitions, immediate membership in the Italian delegation to the European Parliament at Strasburg. Part of the price it demanded in December 1964 for supporting Saragat's successful candidacy for president of the republic was participation in the Italian delegation. The Italian parliament, not the president, chose the delegation, however, and the most Saragat could do was to use his influence in his party and its allies. This took time, so that it was not until 1969 that a PCI group, led by Giorgio Amendola, was included in the Italian contingent.

Italy's other major foreign policy commitment, membership in NATO, continued to be the object of PCI hostility. The Communists could do nothing but denounce the alliance, so they did that vigorously, repeating their slogan "Italy out of NATO and NATO out of Italy." As the United States got mired down in the Vietnam war after 1965, the Communists were able to use the war to mobilize numerous anti-U.S. demonstrations and to involve non-Communists in their anti-U.S. campaign. This was one more technique of escaping the isolation that the center-left policies of the time were supposed to achieve.

For the Communists, as for the other Italian parties, foreign policy was a tool of domestic politics, and their domestic relationships primarily concerned the Catholic and Socialist camps. Pope John XXIII and Vatican Council II had created ferment in the Catholic world, even within traditionalist Italian Catholicism. As the Pope extended his hands to non-Catholics and to nonbelievers, they were obliged to respond and, if possible, to understand him. Since Togliatti had always tried to moderate the inherent anticlericalism and anti-Catholicism of the Italian left, the Pope's policies stimulated him to a renewed effort. In 1964 Togliatti urged his party to recognize that a religious faith can stimulate aspirations for a Socialist society. In his Yalta memorial to Khrushchev that year, he called on the international movement to recognize the contribution the forces of religion and the Church could make to the cause of the working class.

Most members of the PCI were and are anticlerical and antireligious. For them relations with the Catholic world could be at best an arrangement—not even a marriage—of convenience. In the mid sixties a leading Communist, Pietro Ingrao, argued that efforts should be made to promote such arrangements with the left-wing anticapitalist elements of the Catholic world and of the DC. It was of little importance whether their anticapitalist views originated from a corporativist or from a social Christian tradition. Amendola, arguing a contrary line, advocated reaching out to the Socialist and even Social Democratic camp instead of the Catholic one. In 1964 Amendola asserted that traditionally conceived communism had failed in the Western world. What was needed, therefore, was a new party of the working class, neither Communist nor Social Democratic. The outlines of this new party were vague. The goal was socialist democracy, but what that meant in the way of concrete policies and organizational arrangements was unclear.

For two years the debate between these two strategies divided the PCI leadership. The political forces to which the strategies were directed remained suspicious, when not hostile. The Catholics found it difficult to take at face value the PCI abandonment of hostility toward religion just as many Socialists found it hard to believe in the PCI conversion to socialist democracy. Both strategies were part of the general Communist policy of avoiding isolation. Ingrao's was the safer for his party in that it did not propose more than a deal between political powers, each of which would be able to preserve its nature and identity. Amendola's was the riskier for it would require all partners to abandon historic natures and identities, to create something new and untried. In the end neither strategy prevailed; the debate petered out as elements of each position were fitted into the continuing process of adjustment to the center-left in Italy and to the larger European world beyond the frontiers.

Luigi Longo, secretary-general of the PCI after Togliatti's death, continued the trends set in motion by his predecessor. In reaching out to the Catholic world he asserted at the Eleventh Party Congress in 1966, "Just as we are against the confessional state, so are we against state atheism. And is it not possible, is it not necessary to seek together points of agreement and of collaboration so that we may succeed in building together a new society?"[2] In reaching out to and beyond Socialists and Social Democrats in 1968, the party leaders insisted that their long-run strategic objective was socialist democracy, to be achieved through the union of all working and democratic forces, secular and Catholic, with a plurality of parties, organizations, and social groupings. The following year at the Twelfth Party Congress, Longo described his party's goal as:

> ... a socialist society rich in democratic articulations, based on a popular consensus, on the direct and active participation of the masses, on the laic, nonideological character of the state. An objective, that is, of a socialist society, decentralized, nonbureaucratic, in which religious liberty, the freedom of culture, of science and of art, the freedom of information, of expression and circulation of ideas. [We] will make socialism in Italy, with the presence of a plurality of parties and social organizations committed to a free and democratic dialectic of differing positions, something qualitatively different from the experiences hitherto known and fully corresponding to the traditions and the will of our people.[3]

This claim to the inheritance of the bourgeois democratic revolutions of the eighteenth and nineteenth centuries was made by a party still calling itself Marxist-Leninist. That the inheritance corresponded to the traditions of the Italian people was debatable, for those traditions could as easily be described as authoritarian, dogmatic, and oligarchical. Indeed, the Communist Party still exhibited these characteristics along with other Italian political parties and social and religious organizations. The claim was, nevertheless, a recognition of changing social and cultural conditions and of the appeal of democratic symbols to growing numbers of Italians who were benefiting from the modernization and secularization of Italian society. Blue-collar workers and alienated intellectuals were the traditional groups in European society to whom Marxism had made its appeal; in Italy landless farm laborers and sharecroppers had also responded. Now the peasants' share of the labor force was shrinking rapidly. The number of blue-collar workers in industry had peaked in the middle 1960s and then began a slow decline. The middle classes had always been relatively numerous in twentieth-century Italy so that after World War II Togliatti had excluded small owners, artisans, white-collar employees, and professionals from the ranks of the class enemy. In the middle 1960s the number of small and middle-sized firms was increasing so that the PCI found it beneficial to enlarge its appeal to include their owners and managers. The class enemy was now further limited to the small number of large private monopolists. Since a substantial and growing number of the large firms were publicly controlled, this left very few enemies in principle. The evolution of doctrinal positions, the open acceptance of the legal and political tradition of the bourgeois revolutions, was linked in part to the policy of expanding Communist penetration into the growing instead of the shrinking sectors of Italian society.

This penetration did not increase party membership. During the middle and late 1960s the number of party cardholders remained relatively stable at approximately 1.6 million. The social composition of party members gradually changed, however, partly as the result of the normal processes of aging and death and partly as a result of the upgrading of the educational levels and skills of the Italian people. An increasing share of the membership, particularly of the activists, came from the middle class.

The gradual growth in the size of the PCI electorate was demonstrated in the 1968 parliamentary election. The 1.6 percent increase in its popular vote for the Chamber of Deputies resulting in the addition of 11 seats in the Chamber indicated that the center-left had failed to erode the PCI's constituency. The Communists' gain among young voters roughly equaled the attractiveness of the DC to the youth cohorts. The Communists held their traditional constituency, even that part of it opposed to the recent developments in party doctrine, and at the same time they gained ground in sectors of society hitherto suspicious of the party's objectives.

In the 1960s these suspicions had hardly disappeared. In spite of the claims Communists made for the Italian way to socialism, disbelief in their claims was based on a variety of fears about the real nature of the PCI:

a) it is the enemy of religion;

b) it is not committed to the rules of representative democracy, no matter what it says about the democratic way to socialism;

c) it is the agent of a foreign power (the Soviet Union);

d) it is ready to use violence to gain its ends;

e) its internal cohesion and discipline (democratic centralism) is dangerous to the country;

f) it is the enemy of private property.[4]

The changes in Communist doctrine were the result of many considerations: not only judgments about the direction of events in Italy and the Western world and disappointments over developments in Eastern Europe and in East Asia, but also an attempt to meet and to allay the suspicions that so much of the Italian electorate felt toward the PCI. The slowness of the increase in the Communist vote indicated that for many people those fears were still alive.

Events in Czechoslovakia in early 1968 were momentous for the Italian Communist Party. The victory of the party group led by Alexander Dubcek opened the way in Czechoslovakia for a new set of policies that were later labeled "Communism with a human face." The orthodox command economy was abandoned for a socialist market economy. Censorship was loosened, public dissent permitted, and the role of the political police restricted. As successive reforms were instituted during the "Prague Spring," the outside world had the chance to see that there were certain Communists who had different perceptions of the meaning of their doctrines.

Not surprisingly important leadership groups and other intellectuals within the PCI quickly developed a strong emotional commitment to the success of the Prague experiment. Czech Communists were natural allies for the PCI in the international Communist movement. Their example indicated a path that other fraternal parties might take. They provided a way to show skeptics that liberal principles were not merely false propaganda put out by Communists seeking power but were taken seriously by Communists who were in power.

The PCI was seriously shocked in August 1968 by the Soviet-led invasion of Czechoslovakia. Not only did the executive bureau of the PCI criticize the Soviet Union openly but it also did not withdraw the criticism despite the protests of many local and sectional leaders of the party who were still emotionally identified with Russia. In 1956 the PCI had rationalized the Soviet invasion of Hungary. In 1968 it rejected the Soviet justification of its attack on an ally, just as it later rejected the Brezhnev Doctrine, with its assertion of the right to intervene in the internal affairs of the countries of the socialist world.

The negative reaction in Italy to the invasion of Czechoslovakia was widespread throughout all sectors of the political world. President Saragat and the Christian Democratic cabinet condemned the Warsaw Pact outright. The Chamber of Deputies did likewise in a special session of August 29. The PCI, after the initial criticism of Soviet behavior, moderated and differentiated its position from the other parties by blaming all the trouble on the policy of military blocs to which Italy contributed with its membership in NATO. Some of its leaders thought the party had gone too far in its initial reaction. They worried about their relations with the Soviet Union in the international Communist movement. Furthermore, they had second thoughts about the importance of the myth of the Soviet Union to the party rank and file, the myth of the Communist fatherland as the bulwark of international socialism.

Nevertheless, the destruction of communism with a human face in Czechoslovakia, coupled with the enunciation of the Brezhnev Doctrine, created obvious potential dangers for the future of the PCI. On paper the Italian way to socialism was more liberal and deviant than anything produced during the Prague Spring. If Dubcek's reforms were intolerable to the Warsaw Pact countries, what could a future democratic socialism in Italy face? Was such a regime possible in a Europe dominated by the Soviet Union?

August 1968, therefore, led the Italian Communists to a reappraisal of the international situation in Europe and the larger Western world. For almost twenty years the PCI had opposed NATO and Italy's membership in the alliance. Now NATO was seen to have virtues formerly unperceived. The shift in perception was gradual. Years of opposition to the alliance had to be overcome. Internal resistance had to be persuaded. The Vietnam war was still being waged full force with all the anti-U.S. hostilities it produced in Italy and elsewhere. Nevertheless, the process of reevaluation had begun. In the usual pattern it moved slowly. In 1969 the NATO treaty came up for renewal, as its own terms provided. The Christian Democratic-led government renewed it with little hesitation. The Communists still formally opposed renewal. Although a few elaborate articles were written by Communist intellectuals in criticism of the pact, no major campaign was organized, no enormous propaganda effort was launched against the government's foreign policy. A start had been made.

NOTES

1. Donald L. M. Blackmer, *Unity in Diversity: Italian Communism and the Communist World* (Cambridge: M.I.T. Press, 1968).

2. Quoted in *Il Crociato*, February 2, 1966.

3. See resolutions of the executive bureau of the PCI of July 17, 1968, and the speech of Longo to the Twelfth Congress of the PCI, 1969. Reprinted in *Almanacco PCI '76*, pp. 251-52.

4. Giacomo Sani, "Mass Level Constraints on Political Realignments: Perception of Anti-System Parties in Italy," *British Journal of Political Science*, January 1976, pp. 1-31.

16
THE CHANGING SOCIAL CLIMATE

The years between 1968 and 1970 mark a turning point in postwar Italian history. The series of center-left coalitions, a relatively stable political formula, was breaking down because of the Socialist electoral losses of 1968 and the split of the PSU in 1969. The PSI was now torn between perpetuation of the formula and a return to association with the Communists, a return made more attractive by the evolution of the PCI. Two decades of continuous economic growth were coming to an end. External markets that had been a major stimulus to this growth were changing their character. Now foreign competition and growing protectionism started to challenge Italian sales expansion. At the same time world prices of raw materials and foodstuffs, upon which Italy was increasingly dependent, began to rise steadily, bringing about a slow deterioration in Italy's terms of trade.

These political and economic developments were not immediately critical. What struck Italy with full force, instead, was a social explosion initiated in the universities that then spread to other parts of society. The student movement erupted in early 1968. The May revolt in the Parisian universities stimulated the Italian students further, although in no single week did the violence in Italy equal the intensity of May Week in France. Behind the surge of drama and excitement lay growing academic frustrations, national disappointments, and international myths. Together they produced an outburst of Catholic and Marxist utopianism that temporarily swept the universities and quickly spread to the senior secondary schools. The foci of the movement were in the huge urban universities of central and northern Italy: Rome, Turin, Milan, and Padua. The smaller provincial universities, though not immune, were less vulnerable.

For several years young Italians had been affected by international mythologies, particularly those of the Third World revolutions. The Cuban revolution and the figures of Fidel Castro and Che Guevara; the cultural revolution in China and the figures of Mao Tse-tung and Lin Piao; the Vietnamese war of the North against the South and against United States intervention, a struggle led by Ho Chi Minh—all provided mythologies and charismatic heroes to stir youthful imaginations. Closer to home the Prague Spring with its hopes and final delusions was an additional stimulant. The civil rights movement and anti-Vietnam war campaigns in United States universities set further examples. Unlike U.S. students, however, the Italians faced neither a race problem nor a wartime military draft. In the heated utopian atmosphere the distance of the myths made them more attractive. The Frankfurt school of social thought, particularly Herbert Marcuse's amalgam of Marxism and Freudianism, provided an explanation of the despised modern industrial world that made the serious study of Marx, Freud, or that world unnecessary.

The student movement initially contended with issues that were much more immediate. The inadequacies of the Italian university system were all too visible. An unexpectedly rapid increase in the numbers of students between 1964 and 1968 exposed the faculties and the inadequate facilities to tremendous pressures. Many students found it impossible to attend courses in the overcrowded buildings and classrooms. There were far too few teachers. Medicine, law, architecture, the social sciences, and the humanities bore the brunt of the expanded enrollments. The physical and biological sciences, engineering, and agriculture were less crowded. The large urban universities suffered more than the provincial ones. Antiquated curricula and autocratic academicism—anachronistic approaches and illogical requirements—aggravated the problems created by huge numbers.

Many students experienced financial difficulties and were concerned that the degree they hoped to acquire would have questionable value after graduation. The shift in values and manners and the enlarged gap between the students and their parents made the younger generation more dependent on each other for reference groups and role models.

The attack on the universities was physical as well as moral. Classes were disrupted. Professors could not teach. Buildings were vandalized and sometimes wrecked. Contrary to the ancient Italian tradition that university precincts were beyond the normal jurisdiction of the regular authorities, the police were brought in to restore order. Some universities were closed for months at a time. Activist students made sporadic attempts to create counter-courses or counter-universities. Academic standards were denounced. The examination of individual students was rejected in favor of group examinations with the same grades for all. Everybody was to pass because discrimination on the basis of traditional criteria was intolerable. The right to enroll automatically included the right to graduate. Professors were sometimes threatened with death if a student was failed. Most of these demands did not survive the tense years between 1968 and 1970. Outside the university the suspicion of the quality of the degrees conferred after 1968 worked against the graduates.

It became apparent that the student movement could do little to change the university immediately, so the students shifted their attack to society at large. The activists concluded that the university was simply a functional agent of the power elites dominating Italy and the world: a machine producing graduates as replacement parts to fit into the slots assigned by the establishment to solidify and perpetuate the status quo. That the Italian universities, like other university systems of the Western world, traditionally and currently performed the role of critic and opponent of established ideas and institutions went unrecognized by the student movement. The activists replaced their goal of reforming the higher educational system with their ambition to achieve the revolutionary overthrow of industrial society, its values, its economic and political orders.

Student activists saw society's supreme value as consumerism; the rejection of the consumer society became their major theme. In the name of a higher liberty and of greater equality they also attacked the constituted powers, the judicial order, and the family. Throughout the country's history most Italians had never been fortunate enough to participate in a consumer society; the change in their condition was very recent and far from complete.

Large numbers of students did not follow the activists in the shift of the attack from the university to the overthrow of the social order. Inside the university the pressures to conform to the latest activist fashion, the fear of being ostracized by their peers, led them to participate in the movement, whatever their doubts. It was part of being modern and being young, and the youth cult was an important part of the myth (as it had been for futurism and fascism). The external aspects of the youth movement were the easiest to assimilate and many students became prisoners of the latest fads in personal life style and mass culture. Abandoning the universities to agitate in factories was something else, however; and only the most militant went out to challenge the larger world.

The utopianism of the student movement had both positive and negative aspects. The extraordinary, if short lived, confidence of the student revolt was based on the optimism of a generation that had never personally known world wars or great depressions. In the lifetime of these students much had changed and much greater change appeared feasible. The positive consequences of decisive action were taken for granted. On the other hand, the movement had no thoughtful and articulated ideal model to replace detested reality, no strategy of action and no organization. Student action deteriorated into interminable debates in assemblies. No authority to make decisions was granted to any one person or group. Only the entire assembly could decide. Incapable of distinguishing between authoritarianism and authority, the assemblies after a time split into rival groups that directed most of their energies against each other. All the activists considered themselves to be to the left, whatever their spiritual or ideological origins. As they fractured into splinter groups the confusion of political identities increased. One group at the University of Rome took the name of Nazi-Maoist. As the clashes among them grew, some groups would be identified as neo-Fascist, others as Communists of various leanings.[1]

In the general confusion one thing was clear. The traditional parties with their regular youth groups had lost all control of organized student life. The Catholic, Communist, Socialist, and other youth organizations were all pushed aside for the time being because of their links to the defenders of the status quo. Students who had a Catholic Action tradition from secondary school, university, or Catholic workers organizations found their original spiritual home intolerable. The ferment in Catholic life spurred by Pope John XXIII and Vatican Council II was soon considered anachronistic and insufficient. The Christian Democratic Party, hesitating over even limited reforms, was rejected. Some of the future leaders of terrorist organizations had strong Catholic institutional origins. Renato Curcio, founder of the Red Brigades, had attended the Catholic Higher School of Sociological Studies at Trento. Antonio Negri, who later became the key intellectual theorist of terrorist activity, emerged from the left wing of the Catholic Federation of University Students.

Marxist students, Socialist and Communist, similarly repudiated their original political homes. As the PSI entered the center-left coalitions with bourgeois parties, as it united with the PSDI between 1966 and 1969, young Socialists who considered these moves a betrayal of the Socialist tradition might find a home in PSIUP or move out of Socialist party organizations completely. Likewise, young Communists could feel that the evolution of their party in the 1960s had culminated in its complete abandonment of revolutionary goals. The constant denunciation of the PCI as revisionist by the Chinese Communists reinforced this belief.

The Communist movement had always had critics to its left, outside and inside the party, who strongly opposed the strategy pursued by Togliatti in the postwar years. Whether they were labeled Bordigaists, after Amedeo Bordiga, the first secretary of the party in 1921, or Trotskyites, their numbers were insignificant and their impact marginal. In the early 1960s domestic and international developments stimulated new critical groups who elaborated their own reinterpretations of Marxism. They went back to the pre-1848 Marx of the philosophical manuscripts and the German ideology to emphasize his humanism rather than his scientific and economic determinism. Marx's ideas of alienation fascinated them for they were in the mood to feel alienated. These young ex-PCI and ex-PSI intellectuals founded and published new reviews with small circulations but much verve. Such publications as *Quaderni Rossi, Classe operaia, Giovane critica, Quaderni Piacentini* treated themes and issues that later formed some of the ideas of the student movement and young trade union extremists. From them came the suggestions for counter-universities, for an alternative culture. From them came the shift to the attack on the larger society, for these groups were a decade ahead of the students.[2] Some of them organized the Communist Party of Italy (Marxist-Leninist), which was suspected of receiving Chinese money.

The ferment outside the PCI had its counterpart within the party. A minority of regular party members, including some parliamentarians and members of the Central Committee such as Rossana Rossanda, Lucio Magri, Luigi Pintor, and Aldo Natoli, had protested their party's strategy and what they considered its excessive opportunism. Infected by the currents circulating in the political atmosphere, opposed to the policies of gradualism and their party's opening to non-Marxist social groups, they advocated a return to a revolutionary strategy and the traditional emphasis on the proletariat. Their dissidence became increasingly open, the wider party membership was made aware of their criticism, and they began to take on the characteristics of a faction. In early 1969 they published a new review, *Manifesto*, in which they proposed a line admittedly close to that of the Chinese Communist Party. They denied any official relations with that party, however, and repudiated suspicions of Chinese financial support. The new publication brought the conflict to a head. Charged by the top party leadership with the Leninist sin of fractionalism, the dissidents were expelled from the PCI in the middle of 1969. They would later organize a small party named Manifesto, which became one of the more prominent groups of the extra-parliamentary left—those groups outside parliamentary politics and contemptuous of it.

Some of the leaders of the student movement entered the new party; some joined the groups associated with the little magazines. The action was shifting away from the schools. By 1970 the student movement was dying as a nationwide phenomenon, although student discontent continued in a variety of forms. Its one lasting impact on higher education was a change of admission policies legislated in 1970. All requirements for admission to specific faculties were eliminated.* Any graduate of any five-year senior high school could enter any faculty of any state university. Since Italian universities are not liberal arts colleges,† but rather professional schools, this change meant that the universities were flooded with students unprepared for the courses of study they were selecting. Together with the continuing expansion of enrollments in the 1970s, only slightly relieved by the creation of new universities and the addition of new faculties to already existing institutions, the problems of Italian higher education became even more unmanageable than before.

The excitement of these years stimulated changes in the position of women. They had received the vote in 1946. The 1948 constitution provided for the equality of the sexes. The historic Latin tradition of male domination of public life, however, had left little scope for women outside the roles of wife and mother, the protector of the family and the home. Peasant women had labored in the fields for centuries, but only gradually had certain social roles outside the family become acceptable. Early in the twentieth century professions such as nursing and teaching, particularly at the elementary level, had become standard women's fields. The beginnings of the industrial revolution before World War I brought women into the factories in small numbers, especially in the textile industry. As in other countries women moved into office work, or into shopkeeping, to supplement their traditional jobs as seamstresses and dressmakers. As late as the 1950s women received, on the whole, less formal education than men and even in the 1960s there were far fewer females than males among the increasing numbers of university students.

---

*A faculty of an Italian university is the counterpart of a school or college of a U.S. university. For example, Italians refer to the Faculty of Law of the University of Rome.

†The liberal arts preparation is offered in the classic and scientific *licei*.

A small number of women had been active in cultural and public life since the late nineteenth century but their ranks grew slowly. It took years to implement the formal emancipation embodied in the republican constitution. The accumulated corpus of legislation and court decisions that discriminated against women had to be replaced piecemeal. In the 1960s these efforts started to bear fruit. Women began to appear in greater numbers at the directive levels of the state bureaucracy, to receive appointments to the judiciary, and later to the diplomatic service. At the upper levels of politics they remained few. A small number had been elected to the parliament of 1948, but in subsequent elections their numbers shrank. The first woman cabinet minister, Tina Anselmi, was not appointed until 1976.

Secularization and modernization of Italian society accelerated in the 1960s. The impact of Pope John XXIII and Vatican Council II was evident even though no new doctrines specifically changing the position of women in the Church or society were promulgated. Italian women, traditionally responsive to ecclesiastical influence, were moving away from clerical control, particularly the younger generations. The election patterns of 1963 and 1968 were one indication. The growing ferment over woman's role in the family, and the question of the indissolubility of the family, was another. In the latter part of the 1960s, public policy on the family was fought out over the issue of divorce.

The struggle began in 1965 when the Socialist deputy Loris Fortuna introduced a divorce bill in the Chamber of Deputies. It was a private member bill, rather than a party one, for these were the years of the center-left coalitions, and the PSI was cautious about upsetting its relations with its Christian Democratic ally. Other lay parties were equally careful for similar reasons. The Communists were chary on two grounds. If they pushed the divorce issue their strategy of making contacts with the Catholic world, of engaging in dialogue with Catholic intellectuals, of attempting to allay the fears of the Church hierarchy about future Communist intentions, would be undercut. In addition a large part of the rank-and-file party membership, the electoral sympathizers, as distinct from party activists and intellectuals, were quite traditionalist in social perspectives and personal morality. Opinion polls taken at the time indicated that a majority of the public, especially of the women, opposed divorce. As a result the Fortuna bill made little initial headway.

Throughout the postwar period the political parties had always had women's affiliates that were expected to deal with women's issues and to function as informational and electoral agencies for their party sponsors. Like similar groups elsewhere they spoke mainly to the already converted. Taking their cues from the parties that supported them, they also treated the divorce issue with caution. They too were aware of the findings of the public opinion polls. When the currents released by the student movement and the extraparliamentary groups began to sweep Italy in the late 1960s, the women's political associations were unprepared, just as the party youth organizations had been caught short. They found themselves outflanked by a small but growing and aggressive feminist movement, independent of political party ties.

The changed atmosphere brought the Fortuna bill back to life. Antonio Baslini of the Liberal Party became an additional formal sponsor in 1968. All the lay parties rallied behind the bill. The Christian Democrats led the government but, except for the support of the Monarchists and neo-Fascist Missini, they now found themselves isolated in their opposition to divorce. The Catholic Church, cautious since the days of Pope John XXIII about openly intervening in Italian politics, mounted a public campaign to oppose the bill. The Church called it unconstitutional, a violation of Article 7, which incorporated the Lateran Accords of 1929 into the constitution. In 1967 the parliamentary Committee on Constitutional Affairs had decided that the divorce bill would not require an amendment to the constitution. In 1970 this judgment was upheld in a decision of the Constitutional Court. To make the bill more palatable to the Catholic community, amendments were inserted to restrict its scope. The amended bill was passed by the Senate in October 1970 and sent to the Chamber of Deputies for approval. Again the Vatican intervened. Pope Paul VI denounced the pending legislation vigorously. Nevertheless, on November 30 the Chamber passed the amended bill and sent it to President Saragat for his signature. On December 18, 1970, the Fortuna-Baslini bill became law. Divorce, under heavily restrictive conditions, had come to Italy, one hundred years after the Italian kingdom had ended the temporal power of the popes.

In this atmosphere of radical social change, political terrorism overtook the country. In the immediate aftermath of the second world war, the country had witnessed occasional violence. Later pan-German or pan-Austrian activists had committed isolated terrorist acts in the South Tyrol—bombings of utilities and power lines for the most part—to reinforce demands for separation from Italy. At their worst these had been random or spasmodic acts of violence. Following the disorders of the student movement in 1968 terrorism became a key political tactic of extremist groups holding a variety of political positions but a shared antagonism to the parliamentary republic. They would be given or would themselves assume labels such as right-wing Fascist or extremist Communist, but their contempt for order and the rules of the democratic game gave them much in common, even when attacking each other. Their kind of terrorism was different in nature and degree from what had been experienced before.

In a few months at the end of 1968 and in early 1969 a growing number of minor episodes threatened public order. The serious violence began in the spring. On April 25, 1969, the twenty-fourth anniversary of the liberation of northern Italy from Nazi-Fascist rule, two bombs exploded in Milan, wounding nineteen people. On August 9, 1969, explosives were set off on eight trains in various parts of Italy, mostly in the north. In autumn 1969 violence in the factories increased in connection with the negotiation of new trade union contracts. Clashes between students and police or between workers and police intensified, and in October and November of that year a student and a police agent lost their lives.

December 12, 1969 inaugurated a new era. On that day during normal business hours a highly destructive bomb was set off in the branch of the Bank of Agriculture on Piazza Fontana in Milan, killing 16 and injuring 90 people. The same day three bombs exploded in Rome, injuring 16 persons though no lives were lost. The bombing in Piazza Fontana set off a spiral of terrorist acts that had not ended ten years later. The investigation of the crime dragged on. An anarchist, Pietro Valpreda, was initially arrested and charged; the evidence against him was weak but he was held for years. The parties of the left accused the police and the government of using him as a scapegoat to protect the true miscreants, alleged to be extreme neo-Fascists who were acting on secret military or police intelligence instructions. The left charged that a "strategy of tension" was being orchestrated by unnamed powers located in high places. After Valpreda was released for lack of evidence the search continued. Finally two young former neo-Fascists, Franco Freda and Giovanni Ventura, were arrested for the crime. In February 1979, almost ten years later, they were found guilty and sentenced to life imprisonment.

NOTES

1. Gianni Statera, *Death of a Utopia: The Development and Decline of Student Movements in Europe* (New York: Oxford University Press, 1975).

2. Massimo Teodori, *The New Left: A Documentary History* (Indianapolis: Bobbs-Merrill, 1969).

17
TRADE UNION DEVELOPMENTS

The Italian trade union confederations had been weak and ineffective throughout the 1950s. Their weakness was the result of the divisions within the trade union movement that were based on political affiliations. Even more it was a consequence of chronic high unemployment. An additional source of debility was the concentration of bargaining power at the national level. Collective bargaining was conducted between the national headquarters and the highest-level organizations of employers such as Confindustria. Agreements at the firm or plant level were illegal, although, in fact, they did occur. During the 1950s average real wages had risen more slowly than average productivity, permitting the growth of profits, which, in turn, were invested in economic expansion.

During the years of the economic miracle, between 1959 and 1963, inemployment almost disappeared. Wage increases became more numerous and more generous. The bargaining power of the unions increased because of favorable economic conditions and because the trade unions concentrated more on the bread-and-butter questions of wages and working conditions and less on the rivalries engendered by their political party linkages. Rival unions collaborated informally. The 1962 round of negotiations for the renewal of the standard three-year contracts produced some good settlements and initiated changes in relationships and procedures. For the first time the contracts provided for plant-level bargaining on a restricted number of issues within well-defined rules. The big change came later, in 1968 and 1969, when the procedures were revised to provide for across-the-board collective bargaining with the firm.[1]

A consequence of the shift in locus of collective bargaining negotiations was the weakening of the power of the large employer associations, particularly the most important of them, Confindustria. The Confederation of Industries had already been hurt by the detachment of the publicly controlled corporations from the association in 1957, and their reorganization into the association called Intersind. In 1962 Intersind settled first with the unions on terms that Confindustria had rejected. Next the Fiat Corporation broke the united front of the private industrialists and reached its own agreement with the metal mechanics union. Finally, in February 1963, Confindustria settled with the unions on the basis of conditions already agreed to by Intersind and Fiat. For the first time the increases in salary were larger than the increase in productivity.[2] The 1968 changes were a logical outgrowth of the trends begun earlier.

Bargaining at the plant level benefited the workers in the more profitable firms and industries. It encouraged differentiation of rewards and increased the gaps among trade union members and between them and nonmembers. During the same period, however, through both labor contracts and legislation, certain previously accepted differentiations were eliminated. Separate salary scales based on sex were abolished. In 1969 salary scales based on geographical zones were outlawed. In 1973 separate scales based on age were eliminated; in the same year wage scales were equalized between white-collar and blue-collar workers.

The elimination of the differences based on geographical zones was done in the name of justice for the southern workers. In bringing their wages to the level of the rest of the country, however, the program for the development of the south was threatened. For many industries the only attraction the south had been able to offer was lower labor costs, and this advantage was now wiped out. To preserve the southern development program, the government passed new laws shifting the costs of financing certain welfare and fringe benefits from the firms' wage package to the national treasury. In other words, the general public, rather than the businesses, would bear the cost. By compensating the firms for the higher wages to be paid, the inducement to invest in the south would remain. At the same time it was expected that the increase in southern incomes would raise the demand for goods and services and further stimulate economic growth.

The gains the workers obtained over the decade were offset to an extent by short-run cyclical fluctuations and by long-run structural trends. The economic downturn in the years from 1963 through 1965 brought an end to the period of relatively full employment and concomitant increases in wages. The trade unions entered the 1965-66 round of contract negotiations in a much weaker position; the resulting agreements reflected this situation. The wage and salary increases gained were small, averaging about 5 percent, with specialized and skilled workers doing a little better. The unions achieved only limited success in preventing layoffs, whether on an individual or a collective basis, either through contract provisions or through legislation. By 1968 they did gain new laws setting unemployment compensation in industry at 80 percent of wages for three months, with retention of full family allowances. This legislation cushioned the material hardships if not the psychological blow of losing a position.

If the workers received little from the 1965-66 collective bargaining agreements, the union organizations achieved important gains. The most significant was the checkoff. Union dues would be deducted from the member's paycheck, thereby providing the unions with a steady and large source of income that they had never had before. Throughout the early postwar period the unions had been dependent on the voluntary payment of dues. In their competitive struggles for membership they did not expel delinquents. The resultant poverty of the organizations kept them dependent for financial support on the political parties with which they were associated. The non-Communist-dominated union confederations, CISL and UIL, were also receiving funds from the American and international trade union movements and also indirectly from the CIA. The achievement of a regular income through the checkoff established an important prerequisite for the subsequent efforts of the trade unions to cut their ties with the political parties and foreign sources of support.

In addition to the financial gains the unions acquired the right to have union newspapers posted on plant bulletin boards, the use of plant offices for union business, and similar benefits that collectively augmented the presence of the trade unions in the plants.

The emergence of national democratic programming found the unions ambivalent at best. CISL and UIL, identified with the political parties of the center-left coalition, were reserved in their expressions of opinion, but CGIL was openly hostile. The Socialist minority in CGIL, although linked to the second largest party of the coalition, was unable or unwilling to restrain the Communist majority from its critical attacks. All the unions could applaud the plan's priority on achieving full employment. They objected to, and CGIL openly opposed, the initial version of the plan that included provisions for an incomes policy. These provisions would have limited wage settlements to the average increase in labor productivity to keep prices and labor costs stable. The unions considered an incomes policy a euphemism for a wage freeze without any corresponding limitations imposed on employers. The Italian trade union movement never accepted an incomes policy in principle. By 1969 events made it irrelevant. Confindustria accepted the idea of programming reluctantly, but opposed the plan that emerged in 1966 for reasons opposite to those of the unions. It centered its attack on the priority given to full employment rather than to economic efficiency.

Democratic programming required the collaboration of the trade union movement as well as business. That was inherent in the nature of the plans and in the planning machinery, since representatives of the union confederations sat on the committees participating in the development of the plans. The cool reception the trade union organizations gave to programming indicated the varying degrees of their unwillingness to become integrated into the political and economic system.

CGIL was still the largest confederation throughout the 1960s, although its membership was declining. Meanwhile CISL succeeded in achieving a slow but steady growth during the decade. The membership of UIL remained stagnant. Despite differing philosophical and political origins and despite the competition for membership, the major confederations had found it beneficial to collaborate on concrete issues in their negotiations with employers and their associations. Unity of action on specific problems might be extended to broader approaches. The possibility of reunification of the divided union movement emerged. The larger cultural and political atmosphere encouraged such a hope. The influence of Pope John XXIII and Vatican Council II, particularly the Vatican's extension of friendship to nonbelievers and encouragement of dialogue with those of differing philosophical inspiration, provided a favorable context. The formation of the center-left coalition and the political collaboration between Catholics and Socialists was another positive factor.

The links between the confederations and the political parties remained a stumbling block. If reunification were to materialize, these links would have to be severed to guarantee that the reunified confederation could not be dominated and manipulated by a political party. A critical element of this linkage was the leading position held by trade union officials in party and governmental organizations. At the top of the union hierarchy were officers who were also members of parliament, of the central committees and national councils, and of the executive boards of the political parties. Further down the hierarchy union officials held office in the provincial party federations or in provincial and municipal governments. CISL supported Forze nuove, a well-identified faction within the DC. Furthermore, top officers such as Giulio Pastore and Carlo Donat Cattin were cabinet ministers in numerous DC and center-left governments.

It was CISL that initiated the moves to loosen the ties with the government and subsequently with the DC. At its 1965 convention the delegates resolved that CISL officers could not hold posts in the cabinet, whether as ministers or undersecretaries. Pastore, who was quite old, retired. Donat Cattin resigned his office in CISL, preferring to remain the leader of Forze nuove. In subsequent years the ban was extended so that by 1969 CISL officers were precluded from running for parliament or for provincial, municipal, and regional councils (in the five special regions). They were also forbidden to be officers in the apparatus of the political parties. Beyond these prohibitions the 1969 convention also ordered that CISL no longer urge its members to vote for DC.

An analagous process was at work in ACLI, the Christian Association of Italian Workers. This organization was not a trade union but an educational and social agency linked to the Catholic Action Society, which is under the guidance of the bishops. In the late 1960s ACLI, led by the dynamic Catholic activist Livio Labor, was moving to the left. In June 1969 a majority at its annual convention voted to cut ACLI's ties to the Catholic Action Society and to abolish the practice of having chaplains attached to the association's chapters. Ties to the DC would also be cut. ACLI members would no longer run for political office on DC election lists. The association announced that its members were free to vote for whichever party they wished. Resistance to these developments by more traditional elements induced Labor to resign from ACLI to form a new political movement of the extreme left, ACPOL, the Christian Association for Labor Political Action. He was to convert it later into a political party for the 1972 parliamentary elections.[3]

Parallel developments were taking place in UIL, historically tied to the Social Democrats and, to a lesser degree, the Republicans. The unification of the Socialists and Social Democrats into the PSU in 1966 had created a situation in which PSU trade unionists were now divided, some in CGIL and others in UIL. The unification agreement permitted Socialist trade unionists to choose their trade union confederation. By the time of the PSU split in July 1969 a left-wing group led by Giorgio Benevento had gained control of UIL. After the split most of the UIL leaders and members decided not to return to the PSDI but to join the PSI. In the same year UIL also forbade its officials to hold political party or governmental offices.

CGIL, predominately Communist with a PSI minority, was the slowest to make the move initiated by CISL. Ties to the political parties were historic and strong. For many Communist unionists the party, not the union, was the mother. Union office was part of a party career. In this period the PCI endorsed the principle of trade union unity and independence but found it hard to put the endorsement into practice. The developments in the other confederations forced the issue, however; and CGIL went part of the way traveled by the others. Overcoming the resistance of orthodox Communist labor leaders such as its president, Agostino Novella, CGIL voted at its 1969 convention to prohibit its top leaders from being members of parliament or holding party office at the national level. Luciano Lama and other top CGIL Communists resigned from the Chamber of Deputies and from the Executive Bureau of the PCI. Below the national level, however, joint officeholding was still permitted.[4]

These developments did not mean, of course, that either the voting habits of union members or their personal or political relations were drastically altered. Union leaders might no longer be subject to party discipline, inside or outside a legislature, but reciprocal influences continued. The degree of separation varied, but in all three confederations, in CGIL least of all, the union leaders established an autonomy from the parties that enabled them to propose policies and take actions during the 1970s that would have been most unlikely at an earlier time. The premises had been laid for unity of action and for prospective reunification, but obstacles remained.

Among these obstacles was the evolution of economic conditions in Italy in the late 1960s, particularly in the manufacturing industries. The economic revival that began at the end of 1965 led to increased industrial productivity but to little increase in industrial employment. The improved productivity was the result of a reorganization of work procedures and a speedup of industrial techniques. Industrial employment reached a peak in 1966 and from that time forward remained relatively stable. Industrial patterns were changing, however. The number of large firms (over 500 employees) remained stationary, while the number of medium-sized (100 to 500 employees) and small (10 to 100 employees) firms grew. The tiny artisan-level shops (fewer than 10 employees) were as numerous as ever. Consequently, a larger proportion of the labor force employed in manufacturing was working for the small and medium-sized firms and a smaller proportion in the large firms.

Meanwhile, big industry was experiencing a concentration of control. Government-controlled businesses were being brought under one or more of the principal super-holding agencies: IRI and ENI, plus the nationalized electric power trust, National Electric Power Agency (ENEL). In the private sector five or six major conglomerates emerged, of which Fiat was the largest. There were also large conglomerates, such as Montedison, in which ownership was almost equally divided between private stockholders and government super-holding agencies. Moreover, the large manufacturing plants were contracting out various parts of the production process more commonly than before. The strongholds of the union movement had always been in the large manufacturing plants, and contracting out, which the unions had little success in blocking, complicated their problems of organizing and controlling the work force.

The stagnation of the overall size of the work force employed in industry did not mean a low turnover rate. As many workers left manufacturing for service jobs, a new influx of rural immigrants to the industrial cities replaced them, exacerbating the life of urbanites and immigrants alike: creating more congestion, more housing problems, and more social, educational, and recreational problems. The rural immigrants were less skilled than their predecessors and less accustomed to the discipline of the factory system. By 1967 unskilled workers comprised 23.9 percent of all industrial workers, with 25.8 percent in the manufacturing plants. In the automobile industry they comprised 45.6 percent of the total, with 65 percent unskilled workers at the Fiat plants in Turin.[5]

The vexations of life and of work in the large industrial centers and the limited gains obtained by the unions in the 1965-66 round of collective bargaining negotiations provided the background for the growing unrest in the industrial plants. It was the infection of the violence of the student movement in 1968 and 1969, however, that precipitated the upheavals in the factories. The example of the substantial gains achieved by the French workers in May and June 1968 when they linked their strikes to the French student uprising provided an additional stimulus.

Extremist Italian students had shifted their focus of activities from the universities to the plants as part of their attack on all social and political structures. Most of the workers were indifferent to the ideas and goals of the student agitators but were susceptible to the atmosphere of revolt. The students preached strange mixtures of classical Marxism, Catholic romanticism inherited from the worker-priest movement, revolutionary syndicalism, and Marcusian new-left slogans. By late 1968 the first "unitary rank-and-file committees" were being formed in the plants by young workers and students to press the workers' demands; these committees not only existed apart from union control, but also in many respects they were anti-union.

With the 1969 negotiations for renewal of the labor contracts, the struggle came to a climax in the "hot autumn" of that year. The conflict was more persistent and more violent than at any time since the occupation of the factories in 1920. More hours of work were lost; more people were involved than at any previous period of contract renewals. In many cases the workers engaged in wildcat strikes or blocked a section of a plant or a whole plant, leaving their union leaders far behind. Strikes were prolonged beyond the length of time fixed by the unions; demands were raised beyond the original claims of the leadership. Extremist assemblies composed of worker and student members condemned bosses and unions alike, shouting slogans such as "more money, less work" or "a contract is a piece of paper."

In these circumstances the major labor confederations were forced to join their worker antagonists, adopt many of the demands of the rank-and-file committees, and participate in the upheavals in order to regain their positions. CGIL was the first to adjust; the others followed. In the process the confederations collaborated with one another in the elections of workers' delegates to factory councils and to unitary assemblies. This collaboration to regain control of the situation helped overcome traditional divisions among the confederations and further stimulated the movement toward trade union unity.

Employers were outraged and frightened, but found little support from the DC minority government. The one-party DC cabinet, now headed by Mariano Rumor, was too weak to control labor unrest and maintain order. The PCI and PSI naturally supported the unions, and the Rumor cabinet was concerned to obtain a settlement on almost any terms. Throughout the 1960s the minister of labor had played an increasingly important role in collective bargaining negotiations. During the hot autumn the minister of labor was Carlo Donat Cattin, formerly of CISL, who exerted the strongest pressures to overcome employer resistance. He directed his initial efforts to the firms in the public sector of the economy, grouped together in Intersind. They capitulated first, under political pressure, and this capitulation made it harder for Confindustria to hold out. Employers' worries about their ability to absorb the increased costs of production were assuaged by government promises to subsidize their losses. By the end of 1969 the hot autumn was over, but its effects would be felt in 1970 and the next decade.

Organized labor's gains were the highest ever achieved at any one time. In 1970, the first year under the new agreements, industrial wages rose 18.3 percent. In 1971 and 1972 they increased further, by 9.8 percent and 9.0 percent respectively. The indexing mechanism linking wage increases to the cost of living was improved. There was a general acceptance of the forty-hour work week, controls on overtime work, and a simplification of the different levels and distinctions among categories of workers. The overall result was to reduce the wage spread among specialized, skilled, semi-skilled, and unskilled workers, a result contrary to the 1966 settlements. The principal beneficiaries, however, were the full-time workers in the large plants. Gaps in wages and benefits actually widened between the lucky and unlucky ones: between those with jobs in the large firms and those in the small firms, between factory workers and cottage labor, between those holding secure jobs and those whose employment was precarious, between full-time and part-time workers.

In 1970 parliament passed a comprehensive body of labor legislation reflecting the atmosphere and the outcome of the hot autumn. It legislated many of the gains achieved in collective bargaining agreements and extended them to other categories of the labor force. It gave the workers almost complete protection from employer control: for example, the number of days of permissible sick leave was greatly expanded, while employers were prevented from checking on the validity of the absence. The law established the principle of just cause for individual or group firings or layoffs, laying the burden of proof on the employer. The results of the law and of the atmosphere were an increase in absenteeism, a reduction of discipline in the plants, and a general decline of productivity.[6]

The hot autumn brought victory to the major trade unions. Recovering from their initial loss of control over the workers they reasserted their presence and influence, both in the factories and in the larger society. Membership grew; for example, CGIL had 2.63 million members in 1969 and counted 3.44 million members by 1973.[7] The collaboration of the confederations during the crisis furthered the progress toward reunification. On May 1, 1970, the unions held one joint May Day celebration. In October of the same year they met to discuss formal reunification but discovered that this goal was still premature. The following year they met again, found that considerable differences still remained over the question of political affiliations, but agreed in principle to unite by 1973. In that year, however, the remaining divergences blocked the final step. Instead, they agreed to establish a federation of the confederations, which they named CGIL-CISL-UIL, a compromise that was to endure despite varying strains and disappointments.

Although unity eluded the three confederations, they collaborated on political action. Extending their scope from traditional subjects of union action the confederations agreed, beginning in 1970, to concentrate their efforts on modifying government social policies. They decided to bypass the political parties and parliament to achieve social reform. The primary fields of their activity were health, education, housing, social security, and transportation. Their primary weapon, the strike, was used generously in 1970. In October of that year the cabinet agreed to establish one national health service to replace a number of separate health programs, to build more public housing, to improve public transportation, to expand the school system, and to raise old-age pensions. All these reforms were justifiable; they were also expensive. Not surprisingly, their implementation was delayed and the scope of the promises reduced.

For the unions the emphasis on social reforms was, in a sense, a continuation on a national scale, in the larger society, of the struggle in the factories. The mass of unionized workers could be pleased with the immediate and concrete results of their action. For the small number of extremists, however, the hot autumn had been intended to launch an attack to overthrow the system. The unions' shift in emphasis to social reform appeared to the extremists to be a cooptation of the workers into the system. Workers' participation in the making of governmental social and economic policies results in their defending those policies. This reduces their fighting spirit and hostility to the political and economic order, when on the contrary, the workers should always be on the attack. Consequently the revolutionary minority opposed, but without success, the emergence of the trade union movement as an active autonomous protagonist in the political process. Since the unions and most of the workers could not support the revolutionaries, the extremist minority turned to disruptive and terrorist tactics, trying to achieve a state of permanent conflict, in the plants and in the broader society.

NOTES

1. Vittorio Foa, "Sindacati e classe operaia," in *L'Italia contemporanea 1945-1975*, ed. Valerio Castronovo (Turin: Einaudi, 1976), p. 267.

2. Gloria Pirzio Ammassari, *La politica della Confindustria* (Naples: Liguori, 1976), pp. 108-11.

3. Giuseppe Mammarella, *L'Italia dalla caduta del fascismo ad oggi* (Bologna: Il Mulino, 1978), p. 455.

4. Peter Weitz, "The CGIL and the PCI: From Subordination to Independent Political Force," in *Communism in Italy and France*, ed. Donald L. M. Blackmer and Sidney Tarrow (Princeton: Princeton University Press, 1975), pp. 541-71.

5. Foa, "Sindacati e classe operaia," p. 273.

6. Giorgio Galli, "La politica italiana," in AA. VV., *Dal '68 a oggi come siamo e come eravamo* (Bari: Laterza, 1979), p. 73.

7. Foa, "Sindacati e classe operaia," p. 261.

18
POLITICAL STRESSES

The minority Christian Democratic cabinet that had ineffectually faced the violence of the hot autumn of 1969 came into being after the Socialist split had caused the breakdown of the center-left coalition. Prime Minister Rumor failed to reconstitute the coalition because the aftermath of their rupture left the two Socialist parties intensely hostile to each other. The bombing in the Piazza Fontana, however, which appeared to threaten the survival of the political system, made it incumbent on the politicians to create a more broadly based cabinet. Negotiations were begun to that end.

The alternative was to dissolve parliament and call new elections. Liberals and Social Democrats favored this choice, expecting that a popular reaction to the disorders of the two previous years would work in their favor. For the same reason the Socialists and Communists were resolutely opposed. Because the Christian Democrats were weak and divided they had no desire to face an election in the spring of 1970, especially since provincial and local elections regularly scheduled for the summer could provide an indication of the humor of the electorate. In retrospect it is now clear that dissolving parliament in the 1969-70 winter would have exacerbated the tensions and atmosphere of crisis. In any case, the Christian Democratic refusal put an end to talk of parliamentary dissolution: attention shifted to the necessity of constructing another coalition government.

A return to the centrist coalitions of the 1950s, bringing the Liberal Party back into the government to replace the Socialists, was numerically possible. Although the Social Democrats were initially favorable, the idea encountered resistance from their former partners. Gradually but inexorably, a reconstitution of the four-party center-left government emerged as the only feasible solution. Between January and March attempts by Rumor, Moro, and Fanfani to form a cabinet failed. The critical issue was the relationship of the center-left to the Communists, in parliament and in the country. Social Democrats and many Christian Democrats insisted on isolating the Communists at all governmental levels. But in numerous local administrations the Socialists had been allied to the Communists rather than to center-left parties before and during the heyday of the center-left. In several localities Communists and Socialists in a popular front coalition provided the only numerical majority. If the two left parties did not form a government the local administrations would have had to be taken over by a prefectural commissioner until new elections were called. In addition the left factions within the Socialist Party were tepid at best to a reconstitution of the four-party coalition. For these reasons the PSI had no intention of making a radical change now. The impasse was resolved by the Christian Democratic secretary-general, Arnaldo Forlani, whose elastic and ambiguous formula emphasized the obligation of center-left consistency and gave the Socialists the freedom to make the choices they wished after the forthcoming local elections.

During the peak period of the center-left coalitions the historic strains over church-state issues, although somewhat moderated, persisted between Socialists and Christian Democrats. In the late 1960s special privileges of the Vatican came under increasing attack from the left. In 1967 the Socialists challenged the Vatican's non-payment of income taxes on dividends from Italian investments. These dated from the Lateran Accords of 1929 under which the Italian state had made a large financial reimbursement to the Holy See in settlement of the Roman Question. The Vatican became the controlling stockholder in several large firms, such as the Società Generale Immobiliare, the largest real estate company in Italy. It was the most important minority stockholder in the IRI Banco di Roma. Although Italian law did not exempt the Church from paying income taxes on its earnings in Italy, successive DC treasury ministers used administrative fiat to waive the Holy See's financial obligation to the national state. In 1967 the Socialists forced the DC hand on this question. The Christian Democrats conceded. Informed that it would have to start paying taxes, the Vatican began to sell off its Italian stockholdings and to invest the proceeds outside the country.

The wrangling on this issue stimulated the secular forces to agitate for revision of the Concordat between Italy and the Holy See.

Because the Concordat is an international treaty, its revision requires the consent of both parties. At the end of the decade the government appointed a special committee of ecclesiastical experts to study the question. The Vatican did the same. In the meantime, the 1970 vote in the Chamber on the Fortuna-Baslini divorce bill and the Vatican's intervention to block the vote created a new obstacle to resolution of the government crisis. The most the DC, in a minority on this issue, could do was to delay Senate passage until the fall. Fanfani tried to form a government based on a commitment by the prospective lay partners to pass a bill implementing the process of a referendum, which would then be used to attempt an overturn of the anticipated divorce law. Fanfani also insisted that the secretaries-general of the four parties participate personally in the cabinet to form a directorate with him to guarantee the stability of his government and the loyal backing of the parties. Fearing the subordination of the secretaries to the prime minister, the other parties, and the DC as well, rejected his proposed innovation. Fanfani withdrew and Rumor again came to the fore, proposing Forlani's compromise and Fanfani's linkage of the divorce bill to the referendum act. On this basis Rumor was finally able to establish a new cabinet on March 27, 1970, consisting of 17 Christian Democrats, six Socialists, three Social Democrats, and one Republican. The cabinet received votes of confidence from the two houses of parliament on April 10 and April 17. The crisis had been one of the lengthiest and most difficult of the postwar period.[1]

The duration of the cabinet crisis in no degree matched the period of inaction on the referendum question. Article 75 of the 1948 constitution provided for the institution of a popular referendum to repeal laws, in whole or in part. For 22 years successive Italian governments had blocked the required implementing legislation, defeating all opposition attempts to institute a referendum. As long as the DC dominated parliament, it was determined to keep control over the legislative process. Now, while the Christian Democrats were losing control and passage of a divorce bill appeared inevitable, a series of opinion polls indicated that a popular majority in the country, especially strong among women, opposed divorce. The DC parliamentarians rapidly shifted their tactics, and in the spring of 1970 legislation to implement a referendum was passed.

Further blows to Catholic doctrine were in store for the DC and the Holy See to be delivered by the Constitutional Court. In December 1970 the Court overthrew the historic law on adultery on the grounds that it discriminated against women, violating their constitutional right to equal treatment. Three months later, on grounds of freedom of speech and freedom of the press, the Court overturned a 1926 Fascist law that prohibited the publication and dissemination of information on birth control. Both decisions reflected the growing secularization of Italian public life.

In the spring of 1970 parliament passed two other important laws, the labor relations act described earlier and the final bill instituting governments for the 15 regular regions. Here again it took 22 years to implement a provision of the constitution completely (Articles 115 to 133). The five special regional governments had been created in the early postwar period because of the presence of either linguistic minorities, as in the Vald'Aosta, Trentino-Alto Adige, and Friuli-Venezia Guilia, or separatist movements, as in Sicily and Sardinia. Then the process of establishing regional governments had ground to a halt, in spite of a Christian Democratic tradition favoring decentralization and regionalism that went back to the earlier years of the twentieth century. The Communist and Socialist movements had no such tradition; on the contrary they reflected the Jacobin preference for the unitary centralized state. The Christian Democrats, in continuous control of the national government, had no interest in creating institutions that might weaken this control, and therefore ignored the constitution and their own tradition. The Marxist parties became entrenched in the Red Belt—the regions of Emilia-Romagna, Tuscany, and Umbria—while their prospects for victory at the national level dwindled. So they reversed their positions and became champions of regionalism, hoping for gains below the national level.

When center-left coalition governments emerged in the 1960s the Socialists included implementation of the constitutional provisions for the regions among their conditions for participation. It was not a critical condition, however, and the DC was successful in postponing action. In the late 1960s a number of Christian Democrats rediscovered their regionalist heritage and in 1968 parliament passed a law providing for the establishment of governments in the 15 normal regions. Since the law made no provisions for election procedures or for financing these governments, it was useless. Violence in the final years of the decade, particularly in the hot autumn of 1969, was probably the determining factor in the Christian Democratic decision to pass the financing act and the electoral law in the spring of 1970. The first election to establish regional councils was set for June 7 of that year. The elected councils then had to draft regional constitutions and get them approved by the national parliament. At the same time they had to build a bureaucracy that, in large part, was composed of employees transferred from the national government.

The time consumed in these necessary first steps meant that the governments did not begin to operate until the spring of 1972.

The regional governments were organized on a parliamentary system. The regional council, a unicameral legislature elected by proportional representation with the preference vote, would create a cabinet, the *giunta*, led by the president of the region. The president, the equivalent of a prime minister at the national level, and his *giunta* would need a vote of confidence from the regional council. The term of office of the council was five years.

The parties devoted the late spring of 1970 to the election campaign. In addition to the 15 new regional councils, large numbers of provincial and communal governments were up for their regular elections. June 7, therefore, would be the first important indication of how the Italian public felt about the upheavals of the preceding two years. The novelty and significance of the new level of government were lost in an atmosphere of debate over national political issues, including the capacity of the government to maintain law and order.

This last theme was emphasized particularly by the neo-Fascists. After the death in 1969 of its leader, Arturo Michelini, who represented the moderate wing, the MSI had become more extremist. Succeeding him as secretary-general was Giorgio Almirante, the spokesman of the revolutionary faction, who favored policies analogous to the squadrist activities of Fascism in 1921-22, before the march on Rome. Almirante had been an official in the Republic of Salò, Mussolini's government of the Fascist Social Republic set up behind the Nazi lines in northern Italy during 1943-44. His emphasis was on national socialism. Some of the student groups active in 1968 and 1969 were offshoots of his wing of the party. At the same time that neo-Fascist elements were contributing to the terrorism, the MSI was denouncing the government for its failure to maintain law and order. It expected to benefit electorally from the average citizen's fears and frustrations.

Missini expectations were fulfilled in part. In the June 7 election it received 5.2 percent of the vote, in comparison to the 4.3 percent it received in the 1968 parliamentary election in the 15 regions, a noticeable but not exceptional gain. The PCI vote remained static compared to 1968, although the party usually did better in administrative than in parliamentary elections. The DC vote declined a little; it usually did poorer in administrative elections. The conspicuous gainers were the Social Democrats and the Socialists, running separately after their split of the previous year. They regained almost all the votes they had had in 1964, before they merged in 1966. This election confirmed their split, if only in purely vote-getting terms. But the sources of their gains were from different parts of the electorate. The PSDI benefited from the law-and-order reaction, while the PSI, in moving to the left after 1969, recaptured votes from PSIUP, its 1964 leftist offshoot. The Italian Socialist Party of Proletarian Unity was declining; its reason for existence became obsolete once the PSI moved again toward collaboration with the PCI.

The 1970 elections demonstrated once more the basic stability of the Italian electorate. For a party to gain or lose 1 percent of the total vote is considered noteworthy. For a small party like the MSI, with only slightly more than 4 percent of the vote, the gain of almost one percentage point meant an increase of 21 percent over its previous vote, enough to stimulate its militants to continued activity. Another, and important, consequence of the election was the significant shift in the composition of many local governments. In the three Red Belt regions the Socialists joined with the Communists to form popular front regional governments, while in most of the other regions they allied with the DC and smaller parties to form center-left coalitions. In several provinces and communes, however, the Socialists switched from center-left to popular front coalitions, thereby bringing the Communists into control of a number of local governments for the first time since the 1950s. The complexion of local government in Italy changed noticeably because of this shift in local alliances.[2]

The regional capitals were established in the principal cities of the regions, Milan in Lombardy, Rome in Lazio, Naples in Campania, for example. In two regions, however, rivalries between cities for location of the capital provoked riots. At stake were not only local patriotism but also jobs, contracts, real estate investments, and commercial growth, all associated with the establishment of government agencies and offices. In the Abruzzi the competitors were the cities of L'Aquila and Pescara. Rioting broke out in L'Aquila when it appeared that Pescara might be selected. Several party headquarters were assaulted and burned. Conceding to the violence, the government chose L'Aquila.

Far more serious was the situation in Calabria. There, at the toe of Italy's boot, three cities vied for the honor: Cosenza, Catanzaro, and Reggio Calabria. No one of them clearly dominated in size or historical tradition. Catanzaro, most centrally located, was initially designated as the capital. Protests from the other two cities forced the government not only to reconsider its choice but to enter into political negotiations to find a satisfactory compromise. Cosenza was compensated by the national government's promise to establish the new University of Calabria there.

In Reggio the situation was much worse. Rioting began in July 1970 and continued sporadically until February 1971. Barricades were set up in the streets. The neo-Fascists seized every opportunity to exploit the tensions and the hopes of the unemployed for jobs to fan the flames of discontent. Carabinieri battalions were brought to the city to restore order. After they were withdrawn rioting erupted again. Finally, the politicians found solutions that had no intrinsic justification other than to give something to each. The executive branch of the regional government—the *giunta* and the administrative agencies—was located at Catanzaro, but the regional council was established at Reggio Calabria. Moreover, IRI was to construct a major steel mill on the outskirts of Reggio, providing thousands of jobs in the area. Whether Italy needed another large steel mill, whether Reggio was the suitable location for it, were irrelevant questions; the politicians wanted only to get rid of a hot potato.

Subsequently, the government bought up large stretches of fertile farm land outside Reggio Calabria. Installation of the mill's infrastructure was begun. Then in the middle of the 1970s the worldwide steel depression began. Italy's existing mills were operating at only 60 percent of capacity. Work on the site was halted, but the government refused to admit that the mill would have to be abandoned. Only in 1979 in a manner as inconspicuous as possible did the government announce the cancellation of the steel mill in favor of other unspecified industries to be established at the Reggio site. Billions of lire had been wasted, and thousands of acres of fertile farm land destroyed.

The government that had administered the June 7, 1970 election survived it by only a month. On July 6 Prime Minister Rumor suddenly resigned, one day before a general strike scheduled by the unions to back up their demands for social reform. Rumor's cabinet, lasting a little over three months, had one of the shortest lives in postwar Italian history. In addition to the problems created by the continuing ferment among the workers, Rumor faced dissension within his own party; within his faction, the Dorotei; and between the Social Democrats and Socialists in his cabinet. Under the stimulus of the upheavals of 1969, the Social Democrats had shifted to a more conservative stance, to which they attributed their electoral gains. Meanwhile, the Socialists had shifted to the left, increasing their participation in local popular front coalitions. Their new secretary-general, Giacomo Mancini, was also trying to exploit student and worker militancy to his party's benefit; he interpreted his party's electoral gains as approval of his strategy. The Social Democrats accused the Socialists of violating the agreement of the early spring that had made the most recent center-left coalition possible. It is not surprising that Rumor felt he had had enough.

President Saragat first asked Giulio Andreotti, a competitor of Rumor within the Dorotei faction, to form a new center-left cabinet. The Socialists opposed him because they considered him too conservative. The Social Democrats feared him because they believed he had no ideological scruples and could easily make a public or covert deal with the PCI in spite of his conservatism. Andreotti withdrew his candidacy to be succeeded by Emilio Colombo, another Dorotei leader. Concern over economic conditions induced the parties to put aside their hostilities. Colombo quickly put together another center-left government that, by early August, easily obtained the confidence of both houses of parliament. Colombo had had many years of experience as treasury minister but this was his first investiture as prime minister.

The Colombo cabinet had to face changes in the psychological atmosphere. Although it was still possible to launch a demonstration against the U.S. war in Vietnam, the wave of extremism was petering out. Nevertheless tensions were rising throughout the country. Rioting in L'Aquila and Reggio Calabria revived historic southern feelings of resentment against the national government. In the north common criminality and violence increased. Vatican intervention in the parliamentary conflict over the divorce law strained relations between the DC and its lay partners.

The limited cohesion of the coalition parties was eroded throughout the last half of 1970 and all of 1971. The economic decline affected the political atmosphere. Christian Democratic factions were already beginning to maneuver in anticipation of the election of a new president of the republic, to be held at the end of 1971. In these circumstances the operations of the Colombo cabinet were reduced to little more than routine administration. In February 1971 the Republicans withdrew from the government, charging it with inaction and failure to control public expenditures. The Social Democrats and Socialists continued their squabbling, as the latter party edged closer to the Communists. The PCI was encouraging this evolution by avoiding intransigent attacks on the majority, in some cases actually helping the government (including the DC) by prudent abstentions.

Behind the PCI's soft approach was its increasing apprehension of widespread political unrest, which especially in the south benefited the neo-Fascists. For off-year local elections held in June 1971 in several cities and provinces scattered throughout Italy, the Missini conducted a vigorous and expensive campaign that paid off in a doubling and in some cases a tripling of its vote. It became the second largest party in the city of Catania (Sicily). MSI gains were most conspicuous in the south, where the DC and Liberals suffered significant losses to them. Christian Democracy, shaken by its defeat, made every effort to regain its influence and recover from the setback by shifting to a conservative stance. The shift was particularly important because of the forthcoming presidential election.

The seven-year term of office of President Saragat expired in December 1971. The president is elected by both houses of parliament in joint session, with added delegates from the regions. The Social Democratic president was old and sick but a candidate for reelection nonetheless. The DC, however, was determined to gain the office, but its lay partners opposed the leading party's ambition to control both the government and the presidency. The politicians spent the last half of 1971 completely on election maneuvering.

The presidential election was more than routine because the violence of recent years and the instability of cabinets had raised the question of institutional reform from the level of academic to political interest. Although parliamentary democracy had performed badly in Italy, in neighboring France a strong presidential republic appeared to manage problems efficiently. Connected with the election of the president, therefore, was the issue of the role the president should play and the powers a president should exercise.

Political forces fearful of the emergence of "a man on horseback" focused their concern on personal attributes; it was important that the winning candidate not be an ambitious person tempted to create a new and different political order. The 1948 constitution was a kind of social contract among Catholic, Marxist, and lay-liberal forces. Since DC domination of the political system was becoming shaky, the Marxist forces not surprisingly looked upon the establishment of a powerful president as a means to consolidate Christian Democratic control at their expense, perhaps a threat to their very survival. Many DC politicians also were suspicious of a presidential republic. They had operated the parliamentary system to their advantage for several decades; they knew all the techniques of maneuver and compromise; they had doubts about the utility of pushing the left into a position of intransigence. Although the parliamentary system was serving the country badly, the alternative could be worse.

Restructuring parliament drew some attention. Some commentators considered the Senate an unnecessary duplication of the Chamber of Deputies and advocated its abolition. It was difficult to imagine, however, that the Senate would vote itself out of existence. Others suggested that the Senate be elected on a corporatist rather than territorial basis to represent the various organized economic interests of the nation. Since most parliamentarians were old enough to remember Mussolini's corporate state, this suggestion received short shrift.

As the debate proceeded it became clear that neither a presidential republic nor parliamentary reform had significant political support. Italy needed a more effective executive but strengthening the authority of the prime minister and his cabinet depended on political forces and the personal qualities of leaders, not on institutional engineering.

Parliament assembled to elect a president on December 9, 1971. Saragat had the support of the Social Democrats, Republicans, and Liberals. Fanfani, presiding officer of the Senate, was the official DC candidate. Unofficially, Moro was available in case Fanfani faltered. The Socialists put forward their former secretary-general, De Martino, who had PCI support also since he would not necessarily reject a government supported by the Communists.

A two-thirds majority is required for election on the first three ballots; after that a simple majority is sufficient. Although the balloting is secret, it became apparent quickly that Fanfani was being deserted by some of his own Christian Democrats. Vote followed vote; days passed without a result. Moro, regarded with sympathy by the Marxist parties, had at least half of his own party against him. To break the stalemate, after the inconclusive twentieth ballot on December 21 the Christian Democrats put forward a compromise candidate, Giovanni Leone. The small parties that had endorsed Saragat promised to support Leone, but this was still not enough for victory. The Socialists substituted 80-year-old Nenni for De Martino. On the twenty-third ballot, held on December 24, Leone was elected. He took the oath of office on December 29. Almirante later claimed that MSI votes gave Leone the margin of victory.

Leone had been the speaker of the Chamber of Deputies and an interim prime minister. He had led caretaker minority DC cabinets after various breakdowns of center-left coalitions. He was not considered an important politician, nor was he a leader of a key faction of the DC. He was deemed safe; no one could imagine him, as they could Fanfani, trying to overturn the parliamentary system to establish a presidential regime.

The protracted election had left its mark on the country. As the Italian population watched one ballot follow another on television, the election process, the representative assemblies, and the parliamentary system fell into further disrepute. The situation was farcical, if not tragic. The two most important parties of the coalition, the DC and PSI, had opposed each other from beginning to end. Could the center-left coalition last much longer?

But when parliament reassembled on January 18, 1972, it was not Christian Democratic-Socialist conflict that brought the government down. The Republican Party had withdrawn from the cabinet the previous spring but had continued to support the center-left coalition as part of the majority in parliament. The PRI now removed its support, proclaiming that a new government was needed to take effective action on the nation's economic and social ills. The Republicans were especially worried about the rapid growth of public expenditures and the increasing deficit in the national budget. Prime Minister Colombo immediately presented his cabinet's resignation to President Leone.

Colombo then made some hesitant and feeble efforts to restore a four-party coalition, but differences between proponents of rigorous and of expansive economic policies led to failure. Leone then called on Andreotti. After going through similar motions Andreotti, with the president's approval, formed a one-party minority Christian Democratic cabinet that received the necessary endorsement of the former allies in parliament, and on February 18 was sworn into office. Ten days later Leone dissolved parliament, scheduling elections for May 7, 1972. For the first time in the history of the Italian republic parliament had been terminated before the completion of its five-year term.

Parliamentary support for Andreotti's caretaker government had been granted in anticipation of dissolution. For months sentiment had been growing among the parties for a new election. The main reason was the ubiquitous divorce issue. That question had returned to haunt the political compromise when militant Catholic groups gathered more than enough signatures to petition for a popular vote to repeal the divorce law. The referendum was scheduled for the spring of 1972. A feature of the referendum law provided for suspension of the popular vote if parliament was dissolved. Public opinion polls gave no clear indication of the outcome of the referendum. In the meantime the campaign would split the country apart. The DC would be in conflict with its smaller lay partners. Because the only other party in the country against the divorce law was the MSI, the DC would be uncomfortably coupled in the public mind with the neo-Fascists. For some time the PCI had been making approaches to the Christian Democrats, offering compromise amendments to the divorce law that the Catholic forces found unacceptable. The tensions generated by a nationwide referendum campaign would not only nullify the Communist approaches but also undermine the solidity of Communist supporters. The PCI drew votes from a large contingent of sympathizers whose attitudes on private-life and family questions were quite traditional.

The Socialists had done well in the regional and administrative elections of the two previous years and would hope for greater parliamentary representation. For a combination of reasons, therefore, the early dissolution of parliament seemed to the major parties to be a lesser evil than a referendum.

For more than two months the political life of the country was bound up in the parliamentary election campaign. The tiny Monarchist Party merged with the Neo-Fascists to form the Italian Social Movement-National Right (MSI-DN). The Manifesto faction, expelled from the PCI in 1969, launched its own slate, as did the dissident ACLI group led by Livio Labor. Other small extremist parties ran, for example, a group calling itself the Marxist-Leninist Communist Party.

The DC election strategy, bearing down heavily on the theme of law and order, stressed the centrality of the party to the political life of the country. In pinpointing its centrist position the DC was tacitly drawing back from the center-left policy it had pursued over the previous decade. The Communists fought their campaign on two fronts, trying to reach secular moderate and leftist Catholics with the theme of law and order and at the same time reemphasizing the revolutionary heritage to counter the attacks of the extra-parliamentary left. The PSI accentuated reform, the importance of leftist unity, and the gains of the unions in recent years.

The neo-Fascists also played a double game. Under Almirante's leadership they emphasized respectability and law and order, playing down the violence of the nationalistic terrorist groups they had indirectly encouraged. On the MSI-DN electoral slate could be found high-level military officers and traditional bureaucrats together with squadrist and neo-Nazi elements.

The results of the May 7 election thwarted the hopes of the extremists, especially those of the left. None of the extra-parliamentary groups succeeded in electing a single deputy or senator. The DC and PCI made slight gains compared to their 1968 parliamentary vote. The Social Democrats held their own. The limited Republican gains came principally at the expense of the Liberals. The PSI maintained the position it had won in the regional elections of 1970.

The MSI-DN made clear-cut but not extraordinary advances. The newly created party obtained 8.7 percent of the vote, far from the high point, 12.7 percent, that the Monarchists and neo-Fascists had reached separately in 1953. Nevertheless, the election doubled their representation in parliament over 1968. The third-largest party in Rome, the MSI-DN was also strong in some southern centers like Reggio Calabria and Catania.

The 1972 election gave a death blow to PSIUP. Having separated from the PSI in 1964 after the latter party joined the center-left, in the early 1970s, PSIUP found its supporters turning to the PSI or PCI. It received 1.9 percent of the votes on May 7 but they were so dispersed that not a single one of its 23 deputies was reelected. It elected 11 senators only because they ran on a joint ticket with the Communists. In a party congress held in July 1972 the PSIUP voted to dissolve. Almost two-thirds of the delegates joined the Communists, fewer than one-third returned to the PSI. A tiny minority, preferring to continue a separate existence, formed a new party, the Democratic Party of Proletarian Unity (PDUP). In the same period the dissident ACLI movement led by Livio Labor dissolved. Labor himself joined the Socialist Party.[3]

The years between 1968 and 1972 had witnessed the most destablizing events in postwar Italian history. Yet this ferment appeared to have little effect on the voting behavior of the electorate. The extremist movements demonstrated that they were more noisy than large. Of course, the constancy of the election returns, particularly for the large parties, hid internal changes that cancelled each other out. For example, the Communist gains from former PSIUP voters at the national level helped to compensate the PCI for losses to the neo-Fascists in the south. The DC had reasserted its critical role in the center of the political spectrum, showing once again its ability to mobilize voters' preferences for stability. Its task now was to organize a government capable of dealing with the changes occurring on the national and international economic scenes.

NOTES

1. Giuseppe Mammarella, *L'Italia dalla caduta del fascismo ad oggi* (Bologna: Il Mulino, 1978), pp. 465-68.

2. See the illustrated figure in Norman Kogan, "The Italian Communist Party: The Modern Prince at the Crossroads," in *Eurocommunism and Détente*, ed. Rudolf L. Tökés (New York: New York University Press, 1978), p. 88.

3. Norman Kogan, "Italy," in *World Topics Year Book 1973*, ed. Marilyn Robb Trier (Lake Bluff, Ill.: Tangley Oaks Educational Center, 1973), pp. 279-82.

19
ECONOMIC CRISES IN THE 1970s

A marked deterioration in the economic situation beginning in 1970 heightened political and social tensions in Italy. The downturn started sooner and the consequences were worse than in almost all of the other industrialized countries. For most of the next ten years the economy on the whole suffered high rates of inflation, major balance of payments difficulties, consequent severe devaluation of the lira, and low rates of real economic growth. In 1975, for the first time since World War II, the country underwent a recession rather than just a decline in its growth rate. The economic history of the decade was one of stop and go. Table 17 indicating the annual percentage changes in real gross national product, illustrates the pattern. With the exception of the slowdown in 1964-65, the real increases in the 1960s had been more than 5 percent a year. However, in the 1970s only three years, 1973, 1976, and 1979, saw a real GNP growth of more than 5 percent over the previous year.

World market prices of raw materials and foodstuffs, on which Italy was heavily dependent, had begun climbing in the years 1968-69. The consequences of the hot autumn began to be felt in 1970 as production costs rose faster than productivity. Self-financing of new investments had begun to drop in the late 1960s but the rate of decline accelerated in the early 1970s. Although the economy started to slow down in the summer of 1970, prices continued to rise. Table 18 shows the annual increases in consumer prices over the decade.

Faced with growing inflationary pressures the cabinet issued an executive decree in early September 1970 imposing new taxes, especially on consumption items. In addition, the decree changed various appropriations. When parliament returned from its summer

TABLE 17: Annual Changes in Real GNP in Italy, 1960-79

Year	Percentage Change Over Previous Year	Year	Percentage Change Over Previous Year
1960	—	1970	+5.0
1961	+8.2	1971	+1.6
1962	+6.2	1972	+3.1
1963	+5.6	1973	+6.9
1964	+2.6	1974	+3.7
1965	+3.2	1975	-3.9
1966	+5.8	1976	+5.5
1967	+7.0	1977	+2.1
1968	+6.3	1978	+3.0
1969	+5.7	1979	+5.6

Sources: Commercial Office of the Italian Embassy, Washington, D.C., *Italy, An Economic Profile, 1978*, p. 1; *Italy, An Economic Profile, 1979*, p. 1.

vacation it broke into an uproar over this usurpation of legislative powers. Under the Italian constitution the government may issue decrees in cases of an extreme emergency. Parliament then has 60 days to ratify or reject. Considering the cabinet's decree an abuse of its constitutional powers, parliament rejected the decree. The government then introduced a new decree with slightly changed language, thereby giving the taxes another 60 days of life. The opposition joined the allies of the DC to propose a deal: Parliament would ratify the decree if the Christian Democrats would let the divorce bill come to a vote. On November 28 the decree was ratified and on November 30 the Chamber of Deputies passed the divorce bill.

Confronted with continuing price rises the government imposed price controls on selected food items and certain basic supplies on September 22, 1971. Since no wage freeze was imposed, pressure on prices continued.

In August 1970 the United States had cut the dollar loose from gold and abandoned the dollar exchange standard. A year later, on August 15, 1971, the U.S. government devalued the dollar by 10 percent and, in addition, imposed a 10 percent surtax on imports. All exporters to the United States, including Italy, suffered from this increase in protectionism. Moreover, Italy was already under pressure to restrict its sales of shoes, textiles, and clothing in the American market. The United States had threatened to impose import quotas on these items if the Italians did not exercise self-restraint. In July 1971 Italy had reluctantly agreed to set its own limit on footwear sold to the United States. The drop in the value of the dollar

TABLE 18: Percentage Change in Consumer Prices for All Goods and Services in Italy, 1970–79

Year	1970	1971	1972	1973	1974	1975	1976	1977	1978	1979
Percentage Change	+5.0	+4.8	+5.7	+10.8	+19.1	+17.0	+16.8	+17.0	+12.1	+19.0

Sources: Commercial Office of the Italian Embassy, Washington, D.C., *Italy, An Economic Profile, 1975,* p. 3; and *Italy, An Economic Profile, 1978,* p. 2; *Italy, An Economic Profile, 1979,* p. 1.

TABLE 19: Italy's Balance of Payments on the International Market, 1970–79

Year	1970	1971	1972	1973	1974	1975	1976	1977	1978	1979
Overall balance[a]	+356	+783	-1,281	-356	-5,518	-2,055	-1,235	+1,960	+8,244	+2,195

[a]in millions of dollars.
Sources: Commercial Office of the Italian Embassy, Washington, D.C., *Italy, An Economic Profile, 1975,* p. 5; *Italy, An Economic Profile, 1978,* p. 5; *Italy, An Economic Profile, 1979,* p. 5.

the next month was a financial blow to the Italian treasury, which held a large amount of dollar reserves. Not surprisingly, in September the Italian government called for a new international currency exchange standard to replace the dollar reserve standard, a monetary system that would not be dominated by the currency of any one country. In subsequent years the International Monetary Fund did establish a system of special drawing rights (SDR), but neither the new system nor any other system has replaced the dollar as the principal reserve currency.

In the previous decade Italy had accumulated one of the largest reserves of gold and foreign exchange in the world. Still running a surplus in its current account in 1970 and 1971, the Italian government did not start to worry about its balance of payments soon enough. From 1972 to 1974 the country depleted its reserves severely. Table 19 summarizes Italy's annual payments balance for most of the 1970s. The deficits of 1972 and 1973 are the result of food and commodity price explosions. Since Italy imports 94 percent of its oil, mainly from the Middle East and North Africa, the massive deficit of 1974 is the consequence of the fourfold increase in the price of petroleum imposed by the Organization of Petroleum Exporting Countries (OPEC). The terms of trade had turned against Italy as the prices of its imports rose faster than the prices of its exports.

Italy's export problems resulted not only from occasional and sporadic protectionist impositions by other countries. New competitors emerged on the international market to challenge leading Italian export industries such as automobiles, shoes, and clothing. The last two industries met the challenge by concentrating on high quality and high style. The automobile industry was protected inside the Common Market but had trade difficulties elsewhere. Fiat rapidly diversified into nonautomotive products, but state-owned Alfa-Romeo was losing money heavily, particularly after 1972 when its Neapolitan plant, Alfa-Sud, came into production.

The 1972 trade union contract negotiations did not give rise to another hot autumn. In manufacturing, union gains above automatically indexed increases were modest. Without calling a major strike the metal mechanics union achieved the key settlement in October. The economic downturn and growing unemployment explain the restraint shown by the manufacturing unions. The situation was different in the services sector, where wages were inelastic. Throughout the fall and into 1973 price increases heightened discontent. In 1973 Italy's double-digit inflation was the highest in Western Europe. Wildcat strikes plagued the hotel and restaurant businesses and the public services: railways, municipal transportation, garbage collection, mail deliveries, and electric power utilities. To add to the public unease, student demonstrators, Fascist and anti-Fascist, clashed in the city squares.

To offset the downturn the government had begun to pump money into the economy. By the end of 1972 and beginning of 1973 business was reviving, at the expense, however, of a large increase in private and public indebtedness. Profits had been declining for several years. By 1972 most big firms were losing money, or at best breaking even. Self-financed investments dwindled. In the private sector the alternative was to borrow from the banks. By 1973 the indebtedness of private sector firms had increased to 70 percent of total financing. Public firms used the endowment funds granted by the state to meet current expenses. These funds were supplements to all sorts of indirect subsidies already granted to firms in both sectors.

A substantial rise in government expenditures without a corresponding increase in tax revenues swelled the national debt. Subsidies to business were only one source of the increasing deficits. Until 1971 the public administration had operated at a surplus. Not only the national administration was spending more, so also were the local governments and the social security institutions. The governments were expanding services and were also hiring more employees to offset unemployment. By 1973 the proportion of government employees at all levels, from national to local, was one of the highest in Western Europe. Almost 30 percent of Italian workers were on a government payroll, as compared to 19 percent in West Germany, 14 percent in Belgium, and 13 percent in France. The deficits of the social security institutions from 1972 on were even higher than those of the local governments. These deficits reflected greatly improved health and pension benefits gained by the unions and subsequently extended to others by business and by the government. The national treasury had to cover the losses at all levels of public administration; the treasury cash deficit rose from 4.5 percent of gross domestic product in 1970 to 14.5 percent in 1975.[1]

In the main, the Bank of Italy financed the treasury deficits. The Bank had no choice but to expand the money supply, even though in doing so it lost control of the money supply. The resulting high rate of inflation was the subject of a major debate among economists. Although almost all of them agreed that the external forces, the increase of prices on world markets, was only a secondary cause, they disagreed over the major domestic sources of price increases. One school blamed the huge increase in labor costs of production after the 1969 union settlements, requiring governmental validation and large amounts of public funds to help businesses cover the costs of the higher wages and fringe benefits. The unions, in other words, imposed a burden on the country inconsistent with achieving price stability, full employment, and balance in the external accounts. The other school argued that excessive monetary expansion was the major cause of inflation and stagnation. It appears that in the early period, 1970-72, monetary expansion was overdone; it more than validated the increased labor costs in the effort to stimulate the economy. From 1973 on, however, both labor costs and money supply were pushing each other upward.[2].

The 1973 economic revival strained Italy's currency. The lira was already shaky in January. The Andreotti government, afraid to devalue openly, instituted a system of two rates, commercial and financial. Ordinary business transactions and tourist exchanges applied a rate of 580 lire to the dollar, at the same time that banks and other financial institutions could get 605 lire to the dollar. In February the U.S. dollar declined another 10 percent. Common Market treasury ministers met hurriedly. The majority decided to institute a common float against the dollar, called the snake and linked, essentially, to the strong German mark. Italy, Great Britain, and Ireland refused to join the snake. In the opinion of the Italian treasury minister, Giovanni Malagodi (Liberal Party) the lira was too weak to be revalued upward, which would be the result of participating in the common float. Consequently the lira fell independently almost as far as the dollar, 7 to 8 percent. Exports became more competitive but imports became more expensive, boosting prices in Italy. In June both the United States and the European Economic Community made loans to Italy to bolster the lira. Throughout the year, however, the lira's value fluctuated with the dollar.

By the summer of 1973 the economy was booming once more and so were prices. In July there were bread riots in Naples. The government reimposed selective price and rent freezes and began a credit squeeze. There were emergency importations of wheat, the appearance of black markets, and sporadic gasoline and fuel oil shortages.

Then in October came the Yom Kippur War between Israel and its Arab neighbors and the aftermath, the OPEC oil embargo. The government instituted a ban on driving in private cars on Sundays and holidays and other measures to reduce oil and gas consumption. Communists, Christian Democrats, and others clamored for a reconsideration of Italy's evenhanded foreign policy. The head of ENI, the National Hydrocarbons Agency, testified before the Foreign Affairs

Committee of the Chamber of Deputies that it was time for Italy to take a pro-Arab position. In the spring of 1974 ENI began making arrangements with Arab oil producers separate from oil-consuming nations' efforts at common action. One week after ENI completed an agreement with Libya, the Italian government called on Israel to return to the 1967 frontiers.

On December 25 the Arab oil producers ended the embargo for their customer nations except the United States and the Netherlands. The full impact of the fourfold increase in petroleum prices was felt in 1974. In Italy the automobile industry was hit hardest. Fiat had started losing money in 1973 for the first time in the postwar period, but 1974 losses were far worse. For much of the year Fiat operated on a three-day work week. The workers received supplements to their reduced wages from the unemployment compensation system so that they actually received between 80 and 90 percent of their full-time wages. The impact of the oil price rise was felt not only in the automotive industry but also in the manufacturing of plastics, fertilizers, and other petroleum by-products. At the end of 1973 British Petroleum sold its Italian subsidiary to the Monti Oil Company, a private firm. Early in 1974 ENI bought out most of the Italian operations of Royal Dutch Shell. Over the course of the year 70 percent of Italy's foreign payments went for oil.

When the lira began to float downward in early 1973, intervention by the Bank of Italy to support it had kept the decline moderate. During the first five months of 1974, the Bank lost foreign exchange at the rate of $1 billion a month. Italian commercial bank borrowing in the Eurocurrency market had reached $7 billion. At this point the cabinet turned to governmental and intergovernmental lenders. The United States extended and increased its loans of the previous year. In February 1974 the IMF provided a standby credit of $1.2 billion. Italy borrowed more money from the EEC in the late spring and in August from the German central bank, the Bundesbank. Its total borrowings that year amounted to $5.9 billion.

The loans had been granted on condition that Italy limit domestic credit expansion and the size of the treasury deficit. Negotiations for the loans provoked a political crisis and the fall of the fourth Rumor government. The PSI was particularly reluctant to support deflationary measures, but had little choice. A fifth Rumor cabinet was formed; it accepted the restrictive loan conditions.

Efforts were made to reduce low-priority imports. On April 30, as a temporary emergency measure, the government required financial deposits from importers of finished goods. These restrictions were a violation of the spirit of both the EEC and GATT, but were technically legal since both the regional and international agencies provided for emergency exceptions. Although Italy's trading partners were unhappy, they had no choice but to accept the *fait accompli.*

Slowly and halfheartedly the government began to apply deflationary measures whose effects would begin to be felt in the last half of 1974. A strong policy of fiscal and monetary stabilization was carried out. Limits were imposed on bank lending and interest rates were raised. By June short-term interest rates went above 20 percent on an annual basis. On June 27 the government increased a wide range of direct and indirect taxes by $5 billion. At the same time it revised the tax collection system to make it both more equitable and more efficient. Grants to local governments and to public and semi-public institutions, such as museums, galleries, and opera houses, were reduced. This cutback was not so much in numbers of jobs as in hours of work.

The effects took time to appear. The rate of inflation, previously above 20 percent, began to decline by the end of 1974. As the deficit in the balance of payments dropped, consequent upon a sharp fall in imports and a slight rise in exports, the lira strengthened. Investments fell. Part-time work increased at the expense of full-time jobs. The full impact of the belt tightening was indicated in 1975 by the first absolute drop in GNP since World War II.

To compensate for the downturn in 1975, economic policy gradually became expansionist. In March the import deposit scheme and bank credit ceilings were terminated. The large Communist advances in the regional elections of June 1975 alarmed the government into more decisive reflation. In August a large spending package was adopted. The money supply was expanded. Interest rates dropped so that by December 1975 the annual rate for short-term bills had fallen to 8 percent. In the last quarter of 1975, at the same time recovery began, the balance of payments worsened rapidly. Foreign exchange reserves were critically low.

A political and economic crisis erupted in the first weeks of January 1976. The two-party DC-PRI Moro cabinet, dependent on support from the PSI, collapsed over the issues of abortion, relations with the PCI, and economic policy. On January 20 when the country had only a caretaker government, a foreign exchange crisis exploded. Between January 20 and the end of May the lira dropped from 688 to almost 900 to the dollar. The foreign exchange market in Italy had been closed for several months. Although the lira made a slight recovery, nevertheless by the end of 1976 it had depreciated about 20 percent over the year. In May the caretaker government revived the import deposit scheme. The following October the new Andreotti one-party DC government then in power instituted a tax on foreign exchange purchases to reduce the run on foreign exchange. At the same time it asked for extensions on repayment of some of the country's foreign debts. Italy applied for a new loan from the European Community. Negotiations for more stand-by credit from the IMF lasted until the following spring.

In addition to the emergency steps already taken, the government introduced a new system of exchange controls and another tight money policy. In the fall a new fiscal policy required more taxes and a rise in utility rates. The expansionist policy adopted earlier, in 1975, to overcome the recession had stimulated a rapid growth of the economy in 1976 (see Table 17) but at the price of a continuing high rate of inflation and a devalued currency.

The stop-and-go economic policies followed by successive Italian cabinets in the first half of the 1970s had little effect on the workers in the protected sectors of the Italian economy. Between 1970 and 1976 real wages in industry rose 41 percent, while real gross domestic product grew less than 19 percent. The wage share of net national income grew from 59.5 percent in 1970 to 69.7 percent in 1976. Income per worker rose faster than output per worker. Since prices did not go up as fast as wages, rising unit labor costs accompanied declining profits. Organized labor had demonstrated its power to extract real income increases despite a relatively stagnant economy. Included were substantial improvements in fringe benefits. By the middle 1970s the ratio of fringe benefits to direct wages was higher in Italy than in other OECD countries. Management suffered little from the redistribution of income from profits to wages thanks to governmental support for distressed firms.

The 1972 labor contract renewals set the conditions for an almost 25 percent increase in wages every year between 1973 and 1976. In January 1975 the unions negotiated an agreement with Confindustria to change the indexing formula. Whereas by 1975 the old system increased wages only about half of the consumer price increases, after 1975 the new formula automatically raised wages almost 100 percent of price increases. It also provided for quarterly rather than annual or semiannual indexing. With the wage package completely guaranteed against inflation, union negotiators in the 1975 round of collective bargaining could concentrate on getting even more. They succeeded; in 1976 and 1977 wages rose at an annual rate of 34 percent. The government adopted the 1975 formula for pensions and other social insurance payments. In addition the beneficiaries received one-time adjustments to compensate in part for past slippage in value.

Confindustria endorsed the serious efforts the trade unions made in the early 1970s to improve governmental social programs. The industrialists hoped that more effective programs would reduce government waste and make labor more satisfied, cooperative, and productive. These were vain hopes. Morale in the plants did not improve. There were growing restrictions on management's freedom to manage: to define and assign tasks; to hire, transfer, or lay off; to schedule overtime or multiple shifts; to maintain discipline; to determine products, production rates, and markets.

Key spokesmen of management reemphasized the country's need for efficiently managed and profitable firms. By the end of 1972 Giovanni Agnelli, head of Fiat, was insisting on the necessity for productivity, distinguishing between "productive forces" in business and labor alike and "parasitic groups" who contributed little to the economy for the income they gained.[3] In April 1973 his younger brother Umberto reiterated these themes at a symposium organized by the research group, Il Mulino, of Bologna. At that symposium Giorgio Amendola, a leading Communist, not only noted that workers had to produce but indicated also that his party colleagues realized the effects of the indexing mechanism and wage increases on the economy of the country, and on those Italians who were outside the protected part of that economy.

The unprotected were many: the unemployed, the partially employed, and those working in the submerged economy. Unemployment was especially concentrated among the young. In 1976 14.4 percent of the 15- to 24-year-olds were unemployed. This was one of the highest rates among developed Westernized countries. There were also large numbers of people partially or seasonally employed in both urban and rural work forces.

The submerged economy is composed of illegal unlicensed operations that typically pay lower than standard wages, avoid fringe benefits, and escape taxation. A small submerged economy has always existed in Italy; in the 1970s it grew rapidly as legitimate business sought to escape increasing rigidities and costs of operation.

The high labor costs of big firms reduced their incentive to hire new employees. Industry had two alternatives. One was to increase capital intensity by substituting capital for labor. Fiat, for example, installed a highly automated assembly line process in 1975. The other was to subcontract many processes to small producers and suppliers. The latter were either small, highly advanced, and efficient specialty producers able to pay the high wages and fringe benefits of the legitimate economy, or firms in the submerged economy particularly in labor-intensive fields.

The practice of subcontracting had received passive encouragement from changes in the tax laws. On January 1, 1973, in line with EEC policies Italy substituted the value added tax, *Imposta sul valore aggiunto* (IVA), for the old multiple-stage sales tax, *Imposta generale sul esercizio* (IGE). The IGE had encouraged vertical integration since the tax was paid only when a product or good was sold to a customer, whereas IVA provided no such benefit to concentration.

Based on small artisan-level shops and cottage industries, and located primarily in central and southern Italy, the submerged economy provided jobs for moonlighters and pensioners seeking additional income, for female workers, especially those who could work at home, for workers listed as officially unemployed who collected unemployment compensation simultaneously, and for legal or illegal aliens. The workers gained untaxed income and flexible work schedules based on part-time or cottage labor. Moonlighters and pensioners did not want full-time jobs in the submerged economy. Many housewives, because of their family responsibilities, could not take a full-time job in the legitimate economy even if one were available.[4] Neither could illegal aliens.

The advantage to the employers was obvious; they paid lower than standard wages, and escaped paying fringe benefits and taxes. Some workers, however, had fringe benefits from their regular full-time jobs. Pensioners were protected, also. Housewives whose husbands had regular jobs were covered by those fringe benefits. Public employees at all levels of governmental departments were massively involved in moonlighting, often at the expense of their regular work. The working hours of government employees were from 8:00 a.m. to 2:00 p.m., six days a week, when they came and left on time. They had the afternoons and evenings to moonlight. When required to work by their ministry in the afternoon they had to be paid overtime. Herein lies a partial explanation of the breakdown of public services.

The growth of the submerged economy not only lost tax revenues to the state but also reduced the validity of Italian statistical records. Data collected by the national government's Central Statistical Office, Istituto centrale di statistica (ISTAT), could not include the illegal sectors of the economy. It was obvious that gross national product and national income were higher than the official figures indicated. How much higher was uncertain and could be only a matter of speculation.

Italian agriculture was affected by the spreading submerged economy. In the mid-1970s it was estimated that 35 percent of agricultural production came from the part-time labor of farmers who had full-time jobs outside agriculture. They worked on the farms before or after hours and on weekends. During the planting and harvesting seasons they contributed to growing industrial absenteeism by calling in sick on their regular jobs to work full time on the farm.[5]

After the middle 1960s a process of agricultural consolidation began in Italy as more and more farms were abandoned in the flight to the cities. Although it is true that the efficiency of Italian agriculture increased and farm wages and income rose, the growing non-farm income of rural families made the real improvement in their lot. Work in the expanded cottage industry supplemented wages from urban jobs and farming. By the middle of the 1970s the economic position of rural families was improving significantly in comparison with both their own recent past and the position of working families in industry.

The ups and downs in the economy aggravated the political strife that in turn exacerbated the economic problems. The center-left formula was becoming more unwieldy. Government stability became more difficult to maintain. Alternatives to the basic center-left formula were being urged with increasing insistence, but the political system was not yet ready to consider them.[6]

NOTES

1. Raymond Lubitz, "The Italian Economic Crises of the 1970's," paper presented at the Annual Meeting of the American Political Science Association, Washington, D.C., September 1-4, 1977, pp. 3-5.

2. *Ibid.*, pp. 13-18.

3. See the interview by Agnelli in the weekly newspaper *L'Espresso*, November 19, 1972.

4. Nora Federici, "Il costume," in *Dal '68 a oggi, come siamo e come eravamo*, pp. 286-93.

5. *Ibid.*, p. 292.

6. A conference held at the Casa Italiana, Columbia University, in October 1978 stimulated a number of excellent papers on the economic situation. The following, all mimeographed, may be cited: Gardner Ackley, "Italy in the 1970s: Down the Drain to Bangladesh?"; Pietro Alessandrini, "Structural Aspects of the Italian Economic 'Crisis'"; Marcello Colitti, "Italy in the '70s and '80s: Premises for an Outline of a Forward Looking Industrial Policy"; Raymond Lubitz, "The Italian Economic Crisis"; Cesare Sacchi, "The Response of the Italian Industry to Increasing Structural Constraints."

20
POLITICAL UPHEAVALS

The results of the 1972 parliamentary election made difficulties for both the DC and PSI. The two parties moved farther apart, for the Christian Democrats had emphasized conservative appeals while the Socialists had put forward leftist proposals. Under the circumstances the DC chose to return to the centrist coalitions of the 1950s. Giulio Andreotti, identified at that time as a conservative, organized a cabinet that brought the Liberal Party into the government for the first time since 1957. The Social Democrats joined the DC and the PLI in the cabinet. The Republicans remained outside because of their rivalry with and hostility to the Liberals, but promised to support the coalition as part of the parliamentary majority. The secretary-general of the PLI, Giovanni Malagodi, was appointed to a post critical for economic policy, minister of the treasury. Several prominent Christian Democrats from factions usually considered progressive refused appointments in a cabinet that included Liberals. Their refusal forecast trouble for the government.

Governmental policy emphasized the restoration of law and order, the revival of the economy, and social and educational reforms. In fact economic policy received primary attention. Included in a program of easy public spending were substantial salary increases for high-level bureaucrats in the public service. Compared to persons holding analogous positions in private or public sector firms, the bureaucrats were substantially disadvantaged. Their raises evoked protests from the left parties and the general public. The unions representing lower levels of the public service agitated for similar increases that when granted enlarged the public deficit.

Meanwhile the PSI was rethinking its strategy after its relative electoral failure. Important Socialist factional leaders were fearful that centrism might become firmly reestablished, that the political system could learn to get along without their participation in the majority. At a PSI party congress held from November 8 to 14, 1972, the two factions led by Pietro Nenni and Francesco De Martino, favoring a return to the center-left, obtained 58 percent of the votes. The two opposing factions led by Giacomo Mancini and Riccardo Lombardi received 42 percent. The PSI then expressed a qualified readiness to discuss the possibility of its return to the government with the DC leadership. Andreotti was not eager to seize the opportunity, however; and as the year ended the centrist coalition was still in office.

Over questions unimportant in themselves, dissident Christian Democrats were using their votes to demonstrate their opposition to their own cabinet leadership. The shift in the Socialist position stimulated left-wing Christian Democrats to more aggressive behavior. By March and April 1973 increasing numbers of DC politicians were publicly calling for a return to the center-left coalition. The same spring the government was put in a minority on several secret ballots. In Italian parliamentary procedure the loss of a vote on an important issue is not considered a judgment of no confidence. Rather, a formal motion of no confidence must be introduced and voted upon in a roll call. When on April 12 the harassed prime minister called for a formal vote of confidence the snipers within his own party voted with him and the cabinet was upheld.

Andreotti timed his no confidence motion well. In the first place, he exploited the imminence of his formal visit to the United States, scheduled for the next week. Nobody wanted a government crisis that would cancel the visit in embarrassing circumstances. Furthermore, the Christian Democrats had scheduled a national party congress in early June; even the most disaffected were willing to postpone a cabinet crisis until the conclusion of the congress. Elections of delegates would indicate the relative strength of the numerous factions into which the party was divided. The proceedings of the congress would provide more clues for the formation of a new government.

Andreotti's visit to the United States appeared to reap little beyond the ceremonial benefit of a warm greeting in Washington. Although the trip was pronounced a great success, it did nothing to bolster his position at home. The issue that finally precipitated the cabinet crisis was unrelated to international policy. It was, instead, a struggle over control of the national radio-television monopoly, Radio-televisione italiana (RAI). RAI was dominated by the Fanfani faction of the Christian Democratic Party. Other parties and other factions of the DC had attempted for years to break this domination, but without success. As the DC became less able to control its allies, pressures mounted to distribute access to the monopoly among other political interests. The development of cable television intensified the pressures. Other parties saw opportunities to erode the effects of DC control over RAI through independent cable television. The regional governments also had a direct interest in the issue. Accusing the national network of deliberately ignoring their existence, they hoped that decentralized cable television would give them more visibility. The regional governments also wished to regulate local television stations and collect license fees to bolster their revenues.

The Republican Party wanted to decentralize the national network and open television to private stations. Presumably the coalition partners had come to some understandings. Then in April 1973 Giovanni Gioia, minister of telecommunications and a leader of the Fanfani faction, prevented the operation of a private cable television station in the city of Biella (Piedmont). Ugo La Malfa, head of the Republican Party, accused Gioia of violating the understanding and called for his resignation. Upon Gioia's refusal La Malfa announced in the last week of May that his party no longer supported the government. Andreotti postponed resigning until after the DC congress scheduled for June 6-10.

The radio-television issue remained unresolved until the following year. The Constitutional Court then pronounced the state monopoly illegal, a violation of the constitutional provisions protecting freedom of speech and the press. Nevertheless, it refused to permit the establishment of privately owned networks and did not order the dissolution of the state network. In subsequent years individual private radio and television stations went into operation all over the country. Some were owned in a camouflaged manner by political parties, others by extremist groups, by regional or local governments, and by commercial interests. In a political agreement, control of the two national television channels was apportioned between the Christian Democrats, who retained control over Channel 1, and the Socialists, who obtained domination of Channel 2. Late in 1979 a third, high culture channel began operating.

Delegates to the DC congress in June 1973 had to face two issues, the composition of the next government and the revolt of the next generation of political leaders. Throughout the postwar period the party had been dominated by a group of top leaders who had come to prominence at an early age. Now elderly, they nevertheless refused to give up positions of power. The generation of middle-aged and politically frustrated Christian Democrats made an unsuccessful attempt to take over party leadership. Senior factional leaders, Moro, Fanfani, and Rumor, agreed among themselves to reorganize the party and government. Forlani, a former Fanfani man, was replaced as secretary-general of the DC by Fanfani himself.

They decided to terminate the centrist experiment and return to the center-left. On June 12 Andreotti's cabinet resigned. President Leone assigned to Rumor the task of organizing a new one, excluding the Liberals. In a month Rumor put together a four-party coalition of the center-left consisting of 29 ministers and 57 undersecretaries and including the leaders of almost all the factions of the four parties. Since there are only 20 ministries, nine ministers served without portfolio. Among the ministers were 17 Christian Democrats, six Socialists, four Social Democrats, and two Republicans. Andreotti and Forlani refused cabinet posts as did the two Socialists, Mancini and Lombardi, who had preferred to have their party support the government in parliament without participating in it.

In this fourth Rumor government a troika consisting of Colombo (DC), minister of finance; Giolitti (PSI), minister of the budget; and La Malfa (PRI), minister of the treasury, was set up to make economic policy. Their stated goals were to contain inflation, reinforce the shaky lira, and control public expenditures. Endorsing these goals the PCI announced that it would follow a constructive and responsible opposition.

For some time the Communists had been hinting that they were ready to pursue a domestic policy that would be more pro-government and a foreign policy that would be more pro-Western. Their inclusion in the Italian delegation to the European Parliament since 1969 provided them with the opportunity to take an active role on EEC issues. They tried unsuccessfully to persuade the French Communist Party (PCF) to revise its hostility to the European Community. Although the PCF did consent in 1973 to become part of the French delegation at Strasbourg, it continued its negative behavior in the European Parliament. Also unsuccessfully, the Italian Communists attempted to persuade the left wing of the British Labour Party to drop its anti-EEC stance. More effectively the PCI pursued the improvement of relations with the French Socialist and German Social Democratic Parties. In 1971 it played a useful role in helping Willi Brandt to accomplish his *ost-politik* strategy of reconciliation with East Germany and the Soviet Union. It also sought more friendly relations with other Western European Socialist parties.

By 1972 although anti-NATO slogans were still the standard

stock in trade of the extra-parliamentary left, they had disappeared from Communist rhetoric. At a meeting of the PCI Central Committee in January 1973 Secretary-General Enrico Berlinguer asserted in a discussion of European policy that Europe should be neither anti-Soviet nor anti-U.S. At the same time, however, he vigorously attacked the Italian government for having secretly conceded a nuclear submarine base in Sardinia to the United States. Exposure of the concession brought down the wrath of the left. The Communists were later to say that they did not oppose the base itself, but rather the government's handling of negotiations behind parliament's back.

In the spring of 1973 the PCI responded to a renewal of street violence by intensifying its attack on student demonstrators and extra-parliamentary groups. Behind this strategy lay a fear of the consequences of deterioration of public order for the party and for Italy. The collapse of public order in the years preceding Mussolini's 1922 march on Rome was a history lesson the Communist leaders had learned well. The similarities to the current situation were uncomfortably close. Since 1968-69 the politically moderate public had reacted against the growing violence to give electoral gains to the DC and MSI-DN in 1970-72. Berlinguer, initially favorable to the student movement and inclined to exploit the instability created by the events of 1968-69, changed his strategy in the early 1970s. PCI leaders became convinced that they would be isolated if they followed a strategy of frontal attack on the social structure. In any case, since the late 1940s the PCI had avoided radicalizing politically sensitive situations. The Italian way to socialism was a pessimistic judgment on the success of a revolutionary strategy.

It was apparent in the early 1970s that the DC had a popular base that in all likelihood would remain stable. Years of Communist appeals to the Catholic masses had produced limited results. PCI efforts to provoke a schism between progressive and conservative sections of the DC had failed. If Communists were to avoid political danger, if they were to play a vigorous role in policy making, they would have to come to terms with all of the factions of the DC.[1]

The U.S.-assisted coup d'état in Chile that overthrew the Salvador Allende regime in September crystallized the strategic issue for the Italian left. The extra-parliamentary groups insisted that the fate of Allende proved the impossibility of a peaceful way to socialism; only a revolutionary strategy could be victorious. The PCI leadership thought otherwise. In three articles published in *Rinascita* a few weeks later, Berlinguer reflected on the events in Chile: U.S. intervention was not the key issue. Rather, the radicalization of the situation by extremist elements in Allende's camp had pushed the moderate Center into the arms of the Right. The lesson for Italy was obvious. It too had a large moderate Center that could endorse progressive reforms but that also could be frightened into the arms of militarists or neo-Fascists. To avoid the fate of Chile the anti-Fascist unity during the war and early postwar years had to be restored. An "historic compromise" was required between the Marxist and Catholic camps, between the PCI and the DC as a whole. The Socialist idea of a left alternative to DC rule was rejected. Berlinguer opposed forming a leftist coalition government even if it were to win as much as 51 percent of the votes. It could not survive a frontal attack of the frightened 49 percent and at the same time realize its program of a democratic transformation of society.[2]

The offer of the historic compromise stimulated much discussion and analysis but little immediate action. In line with the trend of the party and with the policy of trade union unity, CGIL engaged in a partial withdrawal from the Soviet-dominated World Federation of Trade Unions (WFTU). It adopted an associate status in the WFTU and a similar one in the European Confederation of Free Trade Unions (ECFTU).[3]

In the fall of 1973 the Rumor government had to deal with double-digit inflation and in the last months of the year with the OPEC oil embargo. The European countries were in a state of disarray in the face of the challenge. Like the others Italy's response was to make the best arrangement for itself while at the same time giving verbal support to U.S. efforts to organize a unified front of consumer countries. In the spring of 1974 the restrictions on the use of private automobiles were relaxed and were completely removed before the beginning of the summer holiday season.

In the fall of 1973 conflict grew between the Republicans and Socialists over fiscal policy and the negotiations for an IMF loan. Committed to a policy of austerity, La Malfa was ready to accept the IMF conditions for restricting credit and reducing budgetary deficits. Giolitti rejected this approach, insisting on an expansionist rather than a deflationary economic policy. The DC was divided between the two viewpoints. The dispute throughout the winter delayed completion of the negotiations. It was a hard winter. In addition to the economic problems there were growing violence, the beginning of a wave of kidnapping for both political and ordinary criminal motives, and spreading rumors of neo-Fascist or military coups.

By early 1974 agitation was mounting to expand the powers of the police to handle growing criminal activity. This issue was added to the economic one to divide the contesting parties further. The DC,

PRI, and PSDI wanted stronger police powers; the PSI and PCI charged that democratic liberties would be threatened. The deadlock on both economic and internal security issues provoked La Malfa's resignation from the government in early February. A week later the press exposed a new scandal: the association of petroleum refiners and distributors, which included public and private firms, Italian and multinational, had been making payoffs for a number of years to all the political parties, in the opposition as well as in the government, in return for favorable legislation and administrative regulations. Some of the current cabinet ministers were personally involved.

Popular indignation required a political response. A bill was quickly introduced to provide public financing for the parties from the national treasury. Contributions from state-controlled firms were forbidden. All the parties except the Liberal Party supported the bill. The law was promulgated on May 2, 1974, granting annual funds to all parties that received more than 2 percent of the vote in parliamentary elections. Exceptions were made in favor of the local parties representing linguistic minorities in the special regions. The money was distributed to the parties in proportion to the size of their vote in the previous parliamentary election. The total distribution would be included in the annual budget passed by parliament. A large part of the public was highly critical of the bill as yet another example of political exploitation of the taxpayers. Few people believed that under-the-table contributions from important interests would end, however illegal.

In short order La Malfa's departure from the cabinet led to the resignation of the Rumor government. On March 6 President Leone asked Rumor to form another government and he was quickly successful. By March 14 the cabinet was in place. It was an almost exact replica of its predecessor, which had resigned two weeks earlier. The same men held the same posts. Only the two Republican ministers were replaced, for the PRI remained outside, even though it agreed to support the cabinet in parliament. Among the first acts of the new cabinet was to abolish the double market for lire that had been introduced in January 1973. Compromising between Republicans and Socialists, the cabinet adopted a deflationary monetary policy and an inflationary fiscal policy.

The immediate question facing the politicians was not economic policy but the divorce issue. The referendum that had been staved off in 1972 by dissolving parliament was again on the agenda. Since another dissolution was inconceivable, the referendum date was set for May 12 and 13. After the divorce bill passed in 1970 the public attitude had veered away from the Catholic position. In September 1971 the Italian Confederation of Catholic University Students endorsed the divorce law, called for the separation of Church and State, and called for the abolition of the Concordat between Italy and the Holy See. It challenged the dogma of papal infallibility in areas of faith and morals and the principle of hierarchy. In October 38 Catholic committees of priests and rebel parishes publicly dissented from the doctrine of church hierarchy and called for a revision of clerical structures. Denouncing the Concordat between Church and State, they characterized the campaign against the divorce law as "clerical-Fascist."

Over the years a succession of public opinion polls indicated that the anti-divorce majority was declining. By spring 1974 the polls indicated that the anti and pro opinions were about evenly matched throughout the general population. The wording of the referendum asked the public if it was for or against repeal of the Fortuna-Baslini law. A "yes" vote was for repeal of the law and therefore against divorce. A "no" vote was against repeal and therefore for divorce.

In the two months prior to the voting, the Church threw all its weight in favor of a yes vote. Dissident priests who opposed the campaign or who supported divorce were suspended from their duties. A small number of Catholic intellectuals who had organized a group called "Catholics for No!" were harassed. The MSI-DN was the only party allied to the DC in the campaign. DC Secretary-General Fanfani converted the question into a party issue by embarking on an anti-Communist crusade to make a pro-divorce position seem a pro-Communist position. As the referendum date approached, both sides became increasingly strident.

The results astonished everyone. The vote was 59 percent in favor of no, 41 percent for yes. Pro-divorce sentiment was 3 to 2. Not even the most acute observers had suspected the degree of secularization of the electorate. The no vote was strongest in the traditional Red Belt regions. The yes vote, while stronger in the DC strongholds of the northeast and south, was still much lower than the vote the DC had received in those areas in the previous parliamentary election of 1972.

The public, recognizing that the law had not destroyed the Italian family, had learned to take divorce in stride. In the previous three years divorces numbered 17,164 in 1971, 31,717 in 1972, and 22,500 in 1973. In those years 76 percent of the divorces were granted to couples who had already been separated over 20 years, and 22 percent to couples separated from ten to 20 years. Only 2 percent of the divorces went to couples separated fewer than ten years. Those families had been destroyed long before the Fortuna-Baslini bill became law.[4]

The referendum was a political defeat for Fanfani. The next month he suffered another in the elections for the Sardinian regional council. The DC vote dropped as the left vote increased. At the end of June a group of dissident Catholics met in Rome to threaten the DC with the creation of a second Catholic political party. Nothing came of it, although a number of individual dissidents migrated to several other parties.

In the meantime the Rumor cabinet had fallen on June 11, the victim of an accumulation of political, economic, and personal strains. It had lasted for three months. Unhappy about the government's acceptance in April of the IMF credit and restrictive fiscal conditions, the PSI was becoming more rigid. The Socialists interpreted the votes of May and June as a signal that the country was moving to the left. They therefore became more demanding. Rumor was tired and simply quit. None of the major DC politicians wanted to succeed him, not Fanfani, not Moro, not Andreotti. President Leone rejected the government's resignation. A few small concessions were made to the PSI to ease credit policy. At the same time certain taxes and controlled prices were raised.* Rumor, head of a weak government, stayed in office because nobody else was willing to accept responsibility for unpopular policies, but the country was left with all of its internal conflicts unresolved.

Despite Fanfani's anti-Communist crusade the PCI did not use the result of the divorce referendum to launch a general attack on the DC. Instead, in early September the party made a public demand to become part of the majority without insisting on direct participation in the cabinet. The Communists announced openly what had been cautiously emerging for a couple of years: they had no objection to Italy's continuing membership in NATO. Giovanni Agnelli, chairman of Fiat and president of Confindustria, reacted immediately to the Communist demand for parliamentary recognition. On September 5 he opposed Communist participation in the majority and rejected PCI assurances about its international commitments, warning of the danger to free and efficient private enterprise. Shortly afterward, U.S. Secretary of State Henry Kissinger publicly disapproved of admitting the Communists to the Italian majority.

The PSI, however, disagreed with both Agnelli and Kissinger. It

---

*The government sets the retail prices of certain items such as gasoline, electric power, bread, and milk.

was cautiously coming to Berlinguer's conclusion that Communist participation was essential if the government were to face the trying conditions of the country effectively. On September 30 Mario Tanassi, secretary-general of the PSDI, attacked the PSI for its intransigence on economic policy and its ambiguity on relations with the PCI. He openly forecast a cabinet crisis and raised the prospect of dissolving parliament. In effect, he was saying that the center-left formula was ending, since without the Socialists that coalition did not have a majority. The other choices were a return to centrism, acceptance of the historic compromise, or new elections. On October 3 the cabinet fell. It was the last one that included the Socialists until 1980.

The Rumor governments of 1974 had not only administered the divorce referendum and managed the law establishing the financing of political parties from public funds. They also put through a constitutional law reducing the minimum voting age for the Chamber of Deputies and for regional and local governments from 21 years to 18 years. (The minimum age for voting for senators was left at 25.) These same governments had also made initial efforts to lessen Italy's overwhelming dependence on imported petroleum. They made the decision to build more nuclear powered electric generating stations; parliament finally adopted a policy to build 12 nuclear-powered facilities. By the end of 1979, however, only two had been constructed and were not yet in operation because of the opposition of the anti-nuclear movement and public concerns about their security in an age of terrorism.

The latest crisis lasted for two months until finally in December 1974 Moro formed a two-party cabinet of Christian Democrats and Republicans with La Malfa as deputy prime minister. It was a minority government dependent on the external support of the Social Democrats and Socialists. Moro's program emphasized an economic policy of retrenchment and sacrifice, and reaffirmed Italy's international commitments. The Communist offer was rejected, although in fact Moro was consulting behind the scenes with the PCI on policy questions.

Two events in Europe made good democrats happy. In April 1974 a revolutionary officers' group overturned the 50-year-old corporatist regime in Portugal. In the summer the military dictatorship in Greece collapsed as a result of its mistakes in Cyprus. The Junta in Athens had encouraged a rebellion of nationalist Greeks in Cyprus only to provoke a Turkish invasion of the island. The Turks were now occupying over 60 percent of Cyprus. Neither the Greek military regime nor its democratic successor nor the United States could get them out. Meanwhile, both Turks and Greeks were angry at the United States, and their commitments to NATO were unreliable. The new Greek government withdrew its troops from NATO and, like France earlier, announced it would participate only in the political alliance, not in the military command structure. It threatened to deny the U.S. Sixth Fleet use of Greek naval bases.

The disputes in the eastern Mediterranean, the uncertainty over Greek and Turkish intentions, made Italy more important to NATO. The Italian government, without Communist objections, promised to make more bases available to the Sixth Fleet if needed. Since the Greeks did not carry out their threat, Italian bases were not used immediately. Berlinguer was proposing a scheme in which all non-Mediterranean powers would withdraw their fleets from the Mediterranean. Inasmuch as the Russians had spent a decade in building up a strong naval position in that sea, it is doubtful that Berlinguer expected the Soviet government to reverse its policies at his request. It appears that he was rationalizing his party's acceptance of the U.S. military presence in the country.

The fall of the Greek military regime relieved the Italian left. The Greek colonels were suspected of having given financial support to neo-Fascist extremist groups in Italy. Moreover, the left feared the Greek regime as an attractive model for Italian military and national police forces. The fall of that regime removed a source of temptation.

These suspicions were not unfounded. In October 1974 Andreotti, then defense minister, consigned to the prosecutor of the republic a dossier on plots for coups d'état that Italian secret military intelligence agents had detected in recent years. High-level military officers were suspected of involvement, and in the late fall General Vito Miceli, the former head of military intelligence, was temporarily jailed on suspicion of participating in some of these plots, or at least of failure to notify his political superiors and to take appropriate action. He was later released when nothing concrete could be proved against him. In the meantime, political commentators suspected Andreotti of having released the information to acquire credit with the left parties for a future try at the position of prime minister.

On April 18, 1974 the Red Brigades came to national attention when they kidnapped the Genoese judge, Mario Sossi. They were an outgrowth of two of the New Left groups, Workers Power (Potere operaio) and Continuous Struggle (Lotta continua). Their leader, Renato Curcio, was believed to have spent some time in Czechoslovakia in 1972, training for violent action. The Czech Communist government hated the PCI intensely; the hatred was reciprocated.

The PCI had welcomed refugees from the destruction of the Prague Spring. The Red Brigades financed themselves by blackmail and bank robberies. They were believed to be linked to terrorist groups in West Germany, France, and the Middle East, and might have been receiving foreign funds. Before 1974 they had carried on propaganda attacks against the political system and had damaged industrial property sporadically. The kidnapping of the judge was an escalation of their strategy.

Other terrorist organizations were quick to react. A neo-Fascist gang, Black Order (Ordine nero), bombed a demonstration in Brescia on May 28, killing six persons and wounding 90. On August 4 the Black Order bombed a Florence-Bologna train as it emerged from a tunnel; 12 people were killed and 48 wounded. The neo-Fascists appeared to seek anonymous victims in crowds; the Red Brigades concentrated on specific targets, choosing most of their victims from the categories of magistrates, political leaders, police officers, business executives, and union leaders.

The Moro cabinet of December 1974 was consequently confronted with a debate on the question of law and order, which began when Oronzo Reale (PRI), the minister of justice, introduced a bill to reinforce the police and expand their powers. The key issue in this early stage of the parliamentary debate was the authority that the bill would give to the police to arrest suspected terrorists and hold them incommunicado for 48 hours. Reflecting their traditional suspicion of the police, the PSI and PCI were firmly opposed. This article was defeated but the debate continued for several months. During the spring, as the election campaign for the regional and local elections scheduled for June gathered momentum, there was an upsurge of terrorist violence. On May 7 parliament passed the Reale bill. It denied bail for extremist crimes, gave new power to the police to arrest suspects, increased police arms and equipment, and strengthened the punishment for attacks on police. The center-left parties supported the bill as did the MSI-DN, although the PSI voted against two of the articles. The PCI voted against the entire bill.

Nevertheless the Communists avoided conflict with the majority on most other issues. At their national party congress in March they reiterated their offer of an historic compromise. They reaffirmed their commitment to the government's pro-Western foreign policy. Events abroad, however, were sabotaging their strategy. In Portugal the Communists were preventing the Christian Democrats from participating in the national elections scheduled for April. The PCI denounced the Portuguese Communists for their Stalinist behavior, but to little good. After the Portuguese Socialist Party led by Mario

Soares won the election in April, the Portuguese Communists who had fared poorly joined extremist elements in the military. The Italian Communist Party and the Spanish Communist Party dissociated themselves from their Portuguese comrades. Nevertheless, the Italian Christian Democrats transferred the Portuguese lesson to their own country and the historic compromise remained more suspect than ever.

Most of the allies of the DC did not follow the DC in this rejection of the Communists. In the spring La Malfa began to allude to the necessity of associating the PCI in the governing process. Although his language was cautious the message was understood. The Socialists were taking a more polemical position against the DC. In response to pressure generated by the women's liberation movement and the tiny Radical Party, Fortuna introduced a liberal abortion bill in parliament with PSI backing. (The bill would have a difficult legislative career for the next three years.) The growing influence of left factions in the Socialist Party and the prospect for increased votes in the forthcoming regional elections stimulated the PSI in its tendency to abandon the center-left policy.

The June elections were the first in which the 18-to-21-year age group would vote. There were over five million new voters since 1972. In economic performance 1975 was the worst year of the decade, and the young were the most affected by unemployment. All the opinion polls forecast a leftward shift. The election results bore out the forecasts. The PCI was the big gainer, jumping 5.1 percent from its 1972 figure to a total of 33.4 percent of the vote. The PSI gained 2.2 percent. The PSDI and PRI had negligible increases. The DC was the big loser, dropping 3.1 percent from 1972. The PLI and the MSI-DN also experienced small declines. The DC vote was down to 35.3 percent of the total, just 1.9 percent higher than the PCI.

Undoubtedly a large number of young voters had opted for the Communists. The PCI interpreted its gains as a vote for reform, not revolution, a confirmation of its current line. The PSI judged its advances to be a reward for its dissociation from the center-left and a signal to continue on the new course. Not all the increases of the two leftist parties came from first-time voters, however. There were also shifts by previous electors from the moderate center and from the MSI-DN.

The significant consequence of the election returns was the major change in the composition of numerous regional and local governments. In addition to holding the three regions of Emilia-Romagna, Tuscany, and Umbria, leftist coalitions now took over the governments of Piedmont and Liguria. Several months later, due to a shift of the small lay parties, a leftist coalition gained power in the region of Lazio. Six of the 20 regions were now governed by coalitions led by the PCI, even when the president of the region was a Socialist. In other regions, for example the Marches, center-left alliances led by the DC became "open" to the leading opposition party, the PCI. This meant that while formally in opposition, the Communists were participating in program and policy formation.

Most of the major cities from Naples northward were taken over by leftist coalitions. Naples, Florence, Genoa, and Turin now had Communist mayors. In Milan a Socialist mayor led the leftist majority. Almost 45 percent of the provinces and a large number of smaller communes were controlled by the popular front.[5] The city of Rome was the principal exception because it did not have a municipal election in 1975. Its election came a year later, and there the popular front won again. The newly elected mayor of Rome was Giulio Carlo Argan, professor of art history at the University of Rome, an independent running on the Communist ticket. The surprisingly large number of offices captured by the PCI put a strain on its bureaucratic resources. The party was quickly forced to promote a new generation of local officials, many of whom had been party members for only a few years, and who had limited experience.

At the national level the election results were interpreted as the electorate's judgment of national party performance. The PSDI shifted to the left to join a number of popular front regional and local governments. To a lesser extent Republican Party politicians did the same. Giovanni Malagodi was forced out of the post of secretary-general of the Liberal Party to be replaced by the more progressive Valerio Zincone. The DC concluded that Fanfani's open hostility to the PCI and his strategy of conflict had produced nothing but losses: the divorce referendum of the previous year, the Sardinian regional election, and now the 1975 regional elections. Fanfani was pushed out as secretary-general. Although Benigno Zaccognini, who replaced him, was not a major factional leader, he was backed by Prime Minister Moro. These two men did not trust the Communists any more than Fanfani had, but they were forced to face the situation in which their allies were in revolt and the PCI was in a stronger position politically than ever before. They therefore maintained Moro's cautious approach to the Communists.

In these circumstances the PCI continued its line of seeking agreements with the DC. Its public advocacy of Eurocommunist principles was intensified and internationalized. On July 12, 1975 the Italian and Spanish Communist Parties issued a joint proclamation of Eurocommunist commitment to parliamentary democracy. The proclamation concluded with a condemnation of the Portuguese Communist Party and a declaration of support for the Portuguese government led by Mario Soares. Four months later, on November 15, Berlinguer and Georges Marchais, secretary-general of the French Communist Party, proclaimed their commitment to democratic socialism. Rejecting Soviet domination of the international workers' movement, they asserted the right of each party to pursue its own way to socialism. They announced that Soviet conditions for a meeting of the Communist parties of both Eastern and Western Europe were unsatisfactory.

During the fall the Italian Communists continued their offers of support to the center-left government. While making it clear that they did not seek entrance into the cabinet immediately, they insisted, however, that the crises of Italian society could not be solved without a serious PCI contribution to their solution. In the meantime the Communists asked to be consulted and to participate in the determination of policy at the national level, as they were already doing at regional and local levels. Moro rejected open PCI support, although he did admit that he was in communication with the Communist opposition. Writers in various Catholic religious periodicals and some bishops warned against any arrangement with the PCI. They admonished individual Catholic politicians against being seduced by Communist offers even when, for example, the PCI was trying to work out a compromise on the proposed abortion bill, a moral issue certain to tear the Catholic world apart.

The Socialists, having concluded that the election results endorsed their leftward swing, were worried that a direct DC-PCI agreement could bypass them and make their participation in any government irrelevant. During the months of October and November pressure built up within the PSI to withdraw its support for the center-left coalition and to go over to the opposition. At the end of the year Secretary-General De Martino announced in the party newspaper *Avanti* that the following week he would recommend to a meeting of the executive bureau of his party that it stop supporting the government. On January 7, 1976, the PSI abandoned its backing of the coalition and the cabinet resigned. The center-left, progressively shakier since 1969, had come to an end.

NOTES

1. See the essay by Sidney Hellman in *Italy at the Polls: The Parliamentary Elections of 1976*, ed. Howard O. Penniman (Washington: American Enterprise Institute for Public Policy Research, 1977).

2. Berlinguer's articles are reprinted in Enrico Berlinguer, *La questione communista* (Rome: Riuniti, 1975).

3. There is an interpretation of this move that sees it as being perfectly in line with the then current Soviet strategy, done with the Soviet government's approval, and not a pro-Western step at all.

4. Alberto Marradi, "Analisi del referendum sul divorzio," *Rivista italiana di scienza politica*, December 1974, pp. 589-644.

5. See the figure in Normal Kogan, "The Italian Communist Party: The Modern Prince at the Crossroads," in *Eurocommunism and Détente*, ed. Rudolf L. Tökés (New York: New York University Press, 1978), p. 88.

21
THE RISE AND FALL OF THE GRAND COALITION

The Moro cabinet that fell on January 7, 1976 had wrestled with the recession of 1975. It started the year by cutting costs. Subsidies to deficitary operations were reduced. For example, in March 1975 the government announced its intention to sell most of the fleet of trans-Atlantic passenger liners. Regular trans-Atlantic service had terminated in the spring of 1973, but the government had hoped to use the large ships for profitable cruises. By 1975 even this hope vanished. Later in the year the cabinet reversed economic policy and started to stimulate the economy. The upswing began at the end of 1975 and continued into 1976.

Negotiations at the end of 1975 for the renewal of collective bargaining agreements proved to be long and hard. Many negotiations, particularly in the important manufacturing and machine tool industries, were not concluded until the spring of 1976. Part of the problem was the divided union movement. Since the workers in manufacturing already had 100 percent indexing, CGIL wanted the unions to emphasize jobs for the unemployed and job security for those already working. CISL and the independent unions demanded all the additional wage increases they could get. Although a compromise was finally reached between the two positions, it was weighted toward the latter one. The political benefits of the settlements and of the economic upswing would be gained by successor governments.

In the meantime, the political atmosphere at the turn of the year was tense. The Communists upbraided the Socialists for pulling down the cabinet, charging them with risking the safety of the country. The PSI answered that its purpose was to bring the PCI into the government openly, the ostensible Communist goal. At this moment the PCI evidently preferred its arrangement of informal consultations with the DC. It also feared a dissolution of parliament and new elections for which the party was unprepared. The PCI wanted time to consolidate its gains of the previous June. The Socialists, on the contrary, thought new elections would benefit them. They expected to exploit their recent gains.

Just at this time two new scandals, both involving the United States, shook the political establishment. Congressman Otis Pike published an investigating committee report on the CIA, revealing U.S. financing of the Italian center-left political parties in the 1960s, especially the DC. The financing had ended in 1968, but the report noted that in 1970 and 1971 U.S. Ambassador Graham Martin wanted to renew it, concentrating on the Fanfani faction. He also evidently proposed channeling funds to General Vito Miceli, then head of the Italian secret intelligence forces. The report revealed that in 1971 the CIA opposed the ambassador's recommendations. President Nixon and Secretary of State Kissinger turned down the request.

The second scandal exposed bribes given in 1970 to leading Italian politicians by the Lockheed Aircraft Corporation. Suspicion was cast on a former prime minister, Rumor, and on Giovanni Leone, now president of the Republic. More directly involved were former defense ministers Mario Tanassi and Luigi Gui. By 1976 Tanassi was secretary-general of the PSDI and Gui a prominent member of the Moro faction in the DC. Tanassi and Gui were subsequently tried. In 1978 Tanassi was convicted and sentenced to a prison term, the first time in Italian history a cabinet minister was so punished. In 1979 Gui was acquitted.

The scandals in early 1976 made it imperative to organize a new government. After futile attempts to reconstitute a center-left coalition, on February 21 Moro created a one-party DC minority cabinet. It survived in parliament on the affirmative votes of the Christian Democrats and Social Democrats, with the PLI, the PRI, and the PSI abstaining. The Communists and neo-Fascists opposed. The life of this cabinet was unusually short. The following month three parties held their national congresses. The PSI was first. Concluding with resolutions denouncing both the center-left and the historic compromise, the Socialists established the long-range goal of a left alternative as official party policy. In the meantime, they called for an emergency government open to the Communists.

The Social Democratic congress was next. The party was reeling from the recent revelations. Tanassi was removed as secretary-general, and former president Saragat, leading a leftist faction, took control.

The DC began its congress on March 18. The key issue was the competition for secretary-general between Zaccagnini and his predecessor, Forlani. Zaccagnini won a narrow victory. Since he was backed by Moro the result was viewed as a limited endorsement of Moro's policy of progressive dialogue with the left. Moro's prestige was reinforced, but most of Zaccagnini's efforts had to remain concentrated on the continuing struggle with his internal party opposition. There was little time or energy left to work on a program that might have the support of the PSI and PCI.

The issue that precipitated the cabinet crisis had nothing to do with economic policy. Once again the abortion bill was before parliament. In April the DC blocked a liberalization of abortion rights, putting through an amendment to the Fortuna bill when many pro-abortion supporters were absent from the Chamber of Deputies. The amendment restricted the right of abortion to two circumstances only: when the life or health of the mother was in danger, and in case of rape. The Socialists seized the occasion to withdraw their abstention. They wanted new elections. The DC was ready since recent public opinion polls indicated the party was on the upgrade. On May 1 Moro resigned. His government had lasted a little over two months. President Leone dissolved parliament, setting the election date for June 20. The abortion bill was postponed for two more years. It was the second time the legislature was terminated before its normal term expired.

Before the campaign could get under way the region of Friuli in northeastern Italy was hit by a severe earthquake. The event took everyone's mind off electioneering for several weeks. The parties reached a tacit understanding to refrain from campaigning while rescue operations proceeded. When politicking was resumed little more than three weeks remained before the election. The usual increase in terrorist violence associated with an election period supplemented the violence of nature.

The major Communist gains of the previous year had focused attention on the PCI challenge. Public opinion polls in the intervening months revealed growing support for the party. Some showed the PCI equaling if not surpassing DC strength among the electorate. Communist Party membership, which had stabilized in the late 1960s at around 1.6 million party card holders, began to grow again. The party's appeal was strengthened by Berlinguer's address to a congress of the Communist Party of the Soviet Union in Moscow in February. He firmly reiterated the independence of the PCI from the Soviet Union. He reasserted in clear terms the PCI's commitment to a pluralist democratic parliamentary system. What he said was not new; it was where he said it that made the strong impression.

On June 15 Berlinguer gave an interview to the *Corriere della Sera* in which he reiterated party policy on domestic issues but elaborated on foreign policy. Answering a question on NATO he justified the organization on the grounds that its existence was essential to maintain a balance of power upon which the peace of Europe depended. It would be irresponsible to pull Italy out of NATO and undermine the balance. When his interviewer linked NATO to domestic considerations, Berlinguer admitted that the achievement of socialism in liberty in Italy would be more likely behind NATO's shield than without it. "I feel safer on this side."[1] He did not add that PCI concessions on foreign policy were useful as a part of future negotiations with the DC for entry into the government. The interview sparked much interest among political commentators, but it is doubtful that it had a significant impact on the Communist electorate. When a summary of the interview was printed in *L'Unità* this sentence by Berlinguer was omitted. It would have been difficult for many of the PCI faithful to swallow.

The June 20 election produced both expected and unexpected results (see Table 16). The Communists advanced on their success of the previous year but not with a gain of similar magnitude. Their increase in the south brought their progress in that part of the country into line with their earlier success elsewhere. The DC recouped its losses of 1975 and returned to its 1972 level. The big loser was the PSI, which had been responsible for the election in the first place. Rather than capitalizing on its gain in the 1975 regional election, it fell back to its 1972 position. The Social Democrats dropped badly, as did the Liberals. Neo-Fascist losses were smaller and the Republicans held their own. Undoubtedly the DC comeback was at the expense of the PSDI and PLI, while MSI losses were distributed between Christian Democrats and Communists. Since the Socialists had argued that it was necessary to bring the PCI into the government in order to face the economic situation effectively, those voters who were persuaded could feel that the best way to achieve this was to vote Communist. The DC, as earlier, emphasized both anti-Communist and progressive reformist themes to regain its position.

Two new arrivals appeared in the parliamentary scene, the Proletarian Democracy alliance, and the Radical Party, with six and four deputies respectively. The first was a coalition of extra-parliamentary groups: Manifesto, Workers' Vanguard, Workers' Power, and the Democratic Party of Proletarian Unity. The second was a libertarian party attractive to younger voters. It emphasized life style and civil rights issues: divorce, abortion, women's liberation, conscientious objection, Third World hunger. Led by a dramatic, theatrical figure, Marco Panella, it used television opportunities to great advantage. It provoked hostility from the PCI because of its competition for similar clienteles, and outrage from the DC because of its offense to traditional Catholic morality. Since it was small and had little organization it concentrated on publicity, shock effect, and the mass media to reach a wider public.

If the DC could feel pleased with its performance, many of its leaders were less so. Rumor, Moro, Andreotti, and other well-known names dropped noticeably in the personal preference votes they received although they were all reelected. In some cases relative unknowns or newcomers got more preference votes than senior leaders. This result indicated a form of protest voting among DC electors not ready to go so far as to abandon the party. It also indicated that party factions and collateral support groups were having difficulty in controlling their followers.

The most important consequence of the 1976 election was to eliminate two kinds of parliamentary combinations. For the first time since 1948 neither a centrist nor a center-right coalition was numerically possible. A traditional lever of DC maneuverability had been removed. For the first time a left alternative was numerically possible, in the Chamber if not in the Senate, if every party from Social Democratic to Proletarian Democracy joined together. If the Liberals were added, recreating the party lineup that supported the divorce law during the referendum, this coalition would have just half the Senate.[2] Since the left alternative was politically unacceptable to the largest of the left parties, the PCI, the only real choices were between some form of center-left or some form of government of national emergency. The DC preferred the former; the Communists pushed for the latter, demanding to become direct participants in a coalition government. Both the U.S. and West German governments publicly intervened to warn the Christian Democrats against admitting the PCI to the cabinet. Chancellor Helmut Schmidt threatened the Italians with a loss of loans if that option were chosen.

Before the issue could be joined, Andreotti, who was asked by President Leone to initiate negotiations, was blocked in his initial soundings by a Socialist crisis. At a meeting of the PSI central committee held the first week of July in Rome the embittered committee members threw out the whole senior leadership group. A number of forty-year-olds took over. Bettino Craxi, a Milanese leader from the former Autonomist faction, became secretary-general. Claudio Signorile of the leftist factions became deputy secretary-general. Enrico Manca represented what was left of the faction of the deposed leader Francesco De Martino. All factions were formally abolished, only to reappear shortly under new labels.

The PSI was in no mood to consider a return to the center-left. The PSDI and PLI were hostile to the DC because of the losses they suffered, which were blamed on the Christian Democrats. Andreotti delayed negotiations while the new parliament organized itself. The novelty was in the organizing process. All the parties of the "constitutional arch," from the PCI on one wing to the Liberals on the other, sat down to bargain over parliamentary offices. When the bargaining was finished, a minor revolution had occurred. The Communists held important posts in the parliamentary hierarchy. Pietro Ingrao, a leading member of the PCI executive bureau, was speaker of the Chamber of Deputies. The PCI obtained four committee chairmanships in the Chamber and three in the Senate, plus a number of deputy chairmanships. It was receiving open recognition of its new position. In addition, PCI experts and technicians benefited from the patronage available in the political system. Under party sponsorship they began to receive appointments to a variety of positions in the state and para-state agencies, as well as in public sector industries.

The DC, however, was far from ready to accept Communists in the cabinet. Its campaign had emphasized anti-Communist themes. Much of its electorate would find PCI participation in the cabinet intolerable. The number of Italians who considered the PCI beyond the pale was declining but those who still did were concentrated to a great extent among Christian Democratic voters. The smaller parties of the former center-left coalition had few or no objections. By 1976 Republicans, Social Democrats, and Socialists were allies of the PCI in a number of municipal and provincial governments. It was apparent that they expected a similar evolution at the national level.

Andreotti needed all his negotiating skill to find a way out of the impasse. The successful formula was that of "non-no confidence." He created once more a one-party minority Christian Democratic cabinet. All the other parties of the constitutional arch abstained: Liberals, Social Democrats, Republicans, Socialists, and Communists. The Missini, Proletarian Democrats, and Radicals opposed. The PCI abstention was determining. If the party had voted with the opposition, the cabinet would not have survived. For the first time since 1947 the Communists were not in opposition. Moro and Andreotti had to struggle with might and main to get disgruntled Christian Democrats to accept the PCI abstention, but Socialist hostility had eliminated the only other choice.

Novelties were not finished. When Andreotti presented his cabinet to the Senate in early August he announced a program that had been constructed in close consultation with the abstaining parties. He did not merely propose what his government intended to accomplish, he publicly set specific dates when particular laws would be put into effect. No previous prime minister had been forced to tie himself down to such a schedule. Most former programs had either dragged on for years or fallen by the wayside.

His program was an emergency one to handle current problems; it was not intended to achieve economic or political reforms. When the politicians returned in September from their summer holidays they had to wrestle with difficult problems. Although the economy was rising from the low point of 1975, the improvement had not reduced the rate of inflation or eliminated the deficit in the balance of payments. Italy was still constrained to borrow to meet foreign debts. Again, negotiations were begun with the International Monetary Fund to obtain standby credits. The discussions were long lasting and difficult, for the IMF was insisting once more on a deflationary policy. As a partial response the government did increase taxes, raise public utility rates, and tighten monetary policy. These steps received the approval of all the parties inside the constitutional arch. The big stumbling block was IMF insistence that the government deficit be significantly reduced. Too many parties with too many constituencies had a stake in continued spending. Agreement was reached only in April 1977. Four hundred fifty million standby drawing rights were granted. In its letter of intent to the IMF the government promised to limit credit expansion, control the size of the public deficit, restrain social security and local government deficits, and increase productivity. It eliminated a few holidays by switching them to Sundays. The successful negotiation of the loan was a signal to other lenders that Italy was creditworthy. A new loan was received from the EEC, and the international banking community was encouraged to look upon Italian borrowers with favor.

In 1976 the Italian economy had resurged strongly from the 1975 recession. Real GNP grew 5.5 percent, the third highest increase of the decade. The rate of inflation remained high, almost 17 percent. The deficit in the balance of payments continued although the size of the deficit was below each of the three preceding years (see Tables 17, 18, and 19). The country was recovering from the economic crisis but no important reforms were instituted that would substitute for stop-and-go policies.

With the Italian public loath to accept any sacrifices, the capacity of the cabinet to restrain government spending was limited. In January 1977 Berlinguer preached the necessity for austerity. His advocacy of belt-tightening and restraint in consumption was addressed to Italians of all social categories, but it was to be expected that his own constituencies might be the more receptive. He was warning the unions, in effect, to exercise restraint in wage demands. The reforms they had been seeking since early in the decade would need further scaling down over an extended time period. He was impressing on local governments, many of them based on popular front coalitions, that their plans for expensive municipal services would have to be postponed.

His words were received glumly. During the early months of 1977 the government tried to persuade the unions to change the indexing formula. At the end of March agreement was reached to make very minor changes in the way cost-of-living adjustments were calculated. It was a face-saving accord to satisfy the IMF, for 100 percent indexing for industrial workers remained basically untouched. The April agreement with the IMF was thus the expression of a policy that did not have public support. The general public was, of course, unaware of its existence.

Reluctantly, the trade unions bowed to the political pressures urging wage restraint. During the course of the year first CGIL and then the other major confederations admitted that wage increases were not an independent variable to be pursued in disregard of other economic considerations. They had to recognize the effects of labor costs on price levels and the profitability of firms. By the end of the year the triple federation CGIL-CISL-UIL adopted a formal policy of wage restraint over and above the untouchable indexing mechanism. The unions accepted the principle of increased labor mobility as a substitute for layoffs. They demanded the right to be consulted and to participate in management decisions, but not to codetermination. In practice neither the workers nor employers demonstrated any propensity to change their usual behavior.

An upturn of both private and political violence in 1977 aggravated the atmosphere of mistrust. Robberies, juvenile delinquency, and particularly kidnappings were increasing. Political violence erupted in two peak periods. In the spring university students rioted again, demonstrating in the centers of the major cities and closing down their universities for days at a time. It was the worst upheaval since 1968-69. These uprisings differed from the previous ones in two respects. First, the students were now armed and policemen were killed. Second, the violence was motivated by the desperation of prospective future unemployment or underemployment. In the late 1960s the demonstrators were optimistic, thinking they could remake the world. In 1977 they were pessimistic, fearful of their personal futures and isolated from a general public preoccupied with its own problems of daily existence.

In the early summer parliament voted increased powers to the police, expanding the right of the police to invade offices or private living quarters, to hold suspects on little or no evidence, and to close down the offices of political groups on the mere suspicion of harboring weapons or supporting terrorism. These revisions of public security laws were supported by all the parties of the constitutional arch, Socialists and Communists included. Just a few years earlier these two parties had fought against the Reale Law, far less drastic in content, calling it a violation of democratic rights and civil liberties. When the police began to use their new powers they were criticized for failure to maintain law and order democratically.

Student and terrorist behavior since the end of the 1960s had introduced a new element into Italian life. Italians are often volatile and excitable, and there have been movements in the squares that toppled governments. In the past, however, killings had been limited, and volatility usually stopped short of bloodshed. In the preceding two centuries Italians had not let political philosophy seriously govern personal conduct and deportment. Now, instead, the student movement imposed ideology on personal attitudes and behavior. Catholic extremists pursued a variety of directions as they felt their Catholic consciences being liberated. Some became secularized; others moved toward new mystical-religious movements inside and outside the Church. Secularized extremists formed a new terrestrial absolute in which faith in violence supplanted other faiths.

The New Left was going through a moral crisis with a consequent escalation of the level of terrorist violence. In part, the crisis was the result of a series of blows to its Third World heroes and models. The death of Che Guevara in Bolivia was one such blow. The overthrow of Allende's regime in Chile was another. Perhaps the collapse of the cultural revolution in China was the blow that the Italian New Left felt most keenly. The mysterious death of Lin Piao, who had theorized the international struggle of the rural periphery against the urban center, the overthrow of the Gang of Four in 1976, the normalization of the Chinese revolution—its domestic and foreign policies moderated and priority given to achieving an industrial society—all had a devastating impact on the Italian extremists. At home the PCI had disappointed them again in choosing not to radicalize the political atmosphere. In reaction the extremists considered it more necessary than ever to destroy industrial society, to take violent terroristic action. Remodeled Marxism, inspired by Marcuse in a utopian and eschatological key, was succeeded by an extreme form of nihilism that required the destruction of everything: the unions, the economic leaders, the entire industrial society, the political parties, and the very state. The main targets of the terrorists were union leaders, business executives, magistrates, police officials, and politicians.[3]

Nihilism emerged most vividly in 1977 among students who called themselves Autonomists and who conducted an open offensive against the PCI. They were the instigators of the spring uprisings in the universities. Their public advocacy of armed action made them auxiliaries of the terrorists and they were a source from which new terrorists could be recruited. They put the earlier extra-parliamentary New Left—Workers' Power, Continuous Struggle, Manifesto, and PDUP—in the embarrassing position of having to support a parliament in which they were present with their six deputies of Proletarian Democracy. Proletarian Democracy was divided over the Autonomists, and the divisions reduced its effectiveness in both parliamentary and extra-parliamentary arenas.

The dramatic German police seizure of a German terrorist-controlled airplane was followed by the suicide in prison of leaders of the Baader-Meinhof gang in the fall of 1977. Italian terrorists reacted violently. The authorities appeared incapable of controlling the terrorist groups in spite of the increased powers they had recently received.

The decline of order shook the fragile unity of the coalition supporting Andreotti's cabinet. After passage of the new police powers the parties decided that a reconfirmation of their agreement was needed. In July this new look produced a broad statement reaffirming the restrictive economic program that was making a number of politicians nervous. The only significant addition was a program of further decentralization. Additional transfers of authority to the regional governments were granted in the area of social welfare. They were given almost complete power to protect regional cultural resources, the environment, and agriculture. National libraries, major museums, and the portion of the nation's artistic patrimony of national importance remained the responsibility of the new Ministry of Cultural Affairs, created in 1975 from the cultural affairs division of the Ministry of Public Instruction. The regions were granted limited funds to do their new jobs. Successive delays, arguments over the machinery of devolution and over the application of the law, meant that by the end of the decade many parts of the transfer were still not operative.

In the field of agriculture the extension of regional powers came by a presidential decree of 1977. The autonomy of the regions was subject to serious de facto limitations, however, because of the EEC's Common Agricultural Program. CAP policies stressed concentration of landholdings and efficiency of production. They promoted large-scale commercial farming and discouraged small landholdings. Christian Democratic politicians, however, favored distributive policies to all agricultural categories, whether or not they were efficient or productive. Small peasant proprietors were an important DC clientele who had to be protected. The regions, consequently, found themselves constrained in their freedom to make farm policy.

On December 1 the parties of the constitutional arch supplemented their domestic policy statement with one on foreign policy. The PCI participated in its drafting, which reaffirmed NATO and the EEC as the cornerstones of Italian foreign policy. A Ministry of Defense White Book published the same year linked defense to foreign policy by tying together in six proposals the Atlantic, European, and Mediterranean aspects of Italy's security:
1. Promote détente;
2. Participate in NATO to maintain the East-West political and military balance of power;
3. Increase military cooperation with European allies, especially in the standardization of weapons;
4. Support UN efforts to promote peace and arms control;
5. Take a leading role to achieve political-military stability in the Mediterranean; and
6. Mobilize political support for military security.[4]

Most of these proposals were beyond Italy's political or economic power. Italians tended to vacillate between two extremes: overvaluation of their abilities to influence foreign affairs, particularly in the Mediterranean area and sporadically in other parts of the world; and fatalistic resignation believing that they could do nothing to save themselves. The myth of Italy's Mediterranean vocation persisted; they still saw Italy as the great mediator between the developed West and the Arab-African world. They justified this role on the basis of their country's geographical location and on its condition as a partially developed, partially underdeveloped nation. They, or at least their diplomats, knew that this role was not taken seriously abroad. Their solution, at least on paper, was to transfer the Mediterranean vocation to Western Europe as a collective entity. The problem was that Western Europe was not a collective entity.

In October 1977 Berlinguer went to Moscow to participate in the sixtieth anniversary celebration of the Bolshevik revolution. He reiterated the Eurocommunist themes he had stated in the Soviet capital the previous February. The consequences were soon felt back in Rome. In November La Malfa precipitated a cabinet crisis by announcing it was time to bring the PCI into a government of national emergency. After waiting a few weeks to observe the various reactions, Berlinguer called for the inclusion of his party in such a government. He threatened to withdraw his party's abstention. With the rug pulled out from under him Andreotti resigned on January 16, 1978. The prime minister told President Leone that Republican, Socialist, and Communist leaders had informed him that he could no longer count on their abstention.

Both conservatives and extremists were horrified at the prospect of PCI inclusion in the cabinet. The issue was mainly symbolic, for Communists were already part of the governing elites. All major policy decisions required clearance with the leaders of the abstaining parties. Inclusion in the cabinet would mean, however, final legitimation of the PCI in the political system. For the extremists this would be the ultimate confirmation of their charge that the PCI had betrayed the revolution and abandoned the proletariat.

As the crisis continued, opposition to a government of national emergency crystallized within DC ranks. It was reinforced by the public intervention of the Carter administration in the form of a U.S. declaration against including the PCI in the new government. The U.S. statement went further, expressing a hope that in the next election Communist strength would decline. PCI leaders resentfully interpreted this statement as a suggestion to the DC to dissolve parliament only a year and a half after the June 1976 election. The PCI had hoped that the Carter administration would follow a more elastic strategy toward Eurocommunism than had been pursued by the previous Republican administrations. Its hopes disappointed, it beat a limited retreat. By the end of January Berlinguer hinted that entry into the cabinet was not absolutely essential. This statement gave Moro, president of the Christian Democratic Party, the leeway he needed for negotiations. It took several weeks for Moro to work out a compromise, and much of his time and effort was directed to persuading his own party to accept it. The arrangement was revealed at the beginning of March. The new cabinet would again be a minority government led by Andreotti. The previously abstaining parties would now become part of the majority in parliament voting for the government. The Liberals opposed admission of the PCI to the majority and returned to the opposition. For the first time since 1947 the Communists were included in the parliamentary majority. The vote of confidence to endorse the new cabinet was scheduled for March 16.

On his way to parliament for the vote Aldo Moro was kidnapped by a band of the Red Brigades. His five police guards were killed. The event stunned the Italian people and the broader Western world. The new cabinet, composed overwhelmingly of the same persons as in the previous government, received an immediate vote of confidence. The kidnappers sent letters to political figures, newspapers, and Moro's family demanding the release from jail of 13 terrorist leaders awaiting trial or sentencing in exchange for the kidnapped leader. The government rejected the blackmail and demanded Moro's release. The political leadership was in a terrible dilemma. To succumb to blackmail exposed other leaders to future kidnapping. It would admit that the life of a political leader was worth saving, but not the lives of policemen, judges, journalists, and businessmen. The terrorist movement would partake in the political process. Yet humanitarian pleas from the victim, his family, and his associates were difficult to resist. Ties of long friendship bound many of the political leaders to their kidnapped colleague.

The government and the parties held firm, backed by the understanding received from the Vatican. The next month, however, Socialist leader Bettino Craxi broke ranks. After some kind of undisclosed contact with unnamed extremists he announced a vague formula that would presumably obtain Moro's release without formally giving in to terrorist demands. To other politicians Craxi's proposals appeared to be a political maneuver to curry support for his party among the extra-parliamentary left and other groups, through a humanitarian gesture. Some of his party associates condemned him for negotiating behind the back of the government, thereby splitting the solidarity of the parties. Craxi's formula, in any case, proved to be in vain.

On May 9, 54 days after the kidnapping, Moro's body was found in the trunk of an automobile abandoned on a street in Rome approximately halfway between the national headquarters of the Christian Democratic and Communist Parties. His family bitterly rejected a state funeral and buried him in the cemetery of a small village where he had a summer home. A few days later a state memorial service was held in Rome, attended by the leaders of all the parties and high representatives of the Holy See.

A terrible period in Italian life had ended. If the Red Brigades hoped to undermine the system, the results contradicted their hopes. The republic was temporarily reinforced. The population as a whole rallied to the support of the state, as did all the important political, economic, and social groups. A few benighted intellectuals advanced the slogan "Neither with the State nor with the terrorists," but the vast majority of them, whatever their criticism of and hostility toward the political order, preferred it to the extremist alternative.

During the crisis cabinet functions were at a standstill. Policy-making had halted, major decisions were postponed, and only routine administration continued. The police and internal intelligence networks had been demonstrated inadequate to their tasks. Francesco Cossiga, minister of the interior, resigned since he bore ultimate political responsibility for the failures of the internal security forces. He was a member of Moro's DC faction.

When political activity resumed a number of items already on the agenda had to be faced. The first was the long-simmering abortion issue, the culmination of a decade of debate and change in the field of family relations. In 1970 the divorce law had been passed; in 1971 the Constitutional Court had declared the old Fascist laws prohibiting the advertising and sale of contraceptives unconstitutional. In 1974 the referendum had upheld the divorce law. In 1975 family legislation was revised. The minimum age to marry for both sexes was set at 18. Equal rights for both husband and wife within the family were established. Illegitimate children were granted equality of status with legitimate ones. Family planning agencies were organized under auspices of the regional governments. Also, in 1975 the Constitutional Court declared unconstitutional some of the articles of an old anti-abortion law that dated from the Fascist period. The Court decision stimulated lay parties to introduce a new pro-abortion bill. The DC had fought off the lay offensive for three years. By 1978 the abortion question could no longer be escaped except by dissolving parliament once more. Social workers estimated that an average of 400,000 illegal abortions took place every year.

The DC was isolated once again, except for the MSI-DN. In the vain hope that concessions might soften resistance to it, the bill was amended to permit conscientious objection from doctors, nurses, midwives, and hospitals not wishing to perform abortions. On June 9 a very liberal abortion bill was passed, almost abortion on demand.[5] The Church immediately began a campaign to sign up as many conscientious objectors as possible. Some intransigent Catholics wanted to circulate petitions for a referendum to repeal the law, but cooler heads, mindful of the results of the divorce referendum, discouraged hasty action.

Referendum time was again on the calendar. The tiny Radical Party, which made a career of using referenda as a political and propaganda weapon, had months earlier gathered sufficient signatures to challenge two laws, the Reale Law extending police powers, and the 1974 law on public financing of political parties. At the time, the PCI and PSI had opposed the Reale legislation as an unconstitutional violation of civil liberties and democratic rights. Subsequent experience with terrorism induced a reversal of their position. On June 12, a little more than one month after Moro's murder, 77 percent of the electorate voted against repeal of the expanded police powers. Almost all the parties opposed repeal of the law on public financing, for obvious reasons. A bare 54 percent of the electorate opposed this repeal, but it was enough to enable the parties to continue feeding at the public trough.

Hardly were the results of the two referenda known when a new crisis hit the country. On June 15 President Leone resigned, six months before the end of his term of office. He was under accusations of earlier tax fraud, of collaboration with key defendants in the Lockheed bribery scandal, perhaps of his own involvement in the scandal. The PCI urged him to resign in the face of these charges of corruption, but it was the pressure put on him by his own DC party that was the culminating factor. The Christian Democrats wanted to avoid a presidential election campaign at the end of the year in such disadvantageous circumstances. Fanfani, presiding officer of the Senate, became interim president of the Republic until parliament elected Leone's successor. On July 9 it took 16 ballots to elect Sandro Pertini, an 82-year-old Socialist and a former speaker of the Chamber of Deputies. The country had faced two major crises and sharp policy clashes in four months. The government had held, the institutions had survived, the political system had shown its resilience.

The parliamentary coalition that backed the cabinet had lost its elan. Its victories were crucial, but negative; it had staved off potential disaster. It had been put together, however, to handle a different national emergency, not the one that erupted in March but the one the country had been experiencing for years: the economic crisis. How critical was the economic situation in 1978? Fortunately for the country, not very critical at all. The deflationary policy of 1977 had reduced imports while exports grew, producing a good surplus in the balance of payments. By the end of 1977 the slow growth of the GNP was speeding up. Agitation by business and labor organizations and by the political parties had induced the cabinet to increase public spending, ignoring its earlier promise to the IMF to keep the government budget under control.

The downfall of the Andreotti cabinet in January 1978 plus the subsequent months of political crises had no effect on an economy that was picking up steam. Italy benefited from an improvement in its terms of trade. Its principal customers were prosperous, particularly the most important one, West Germany. It was buying the raw materials, foodstuffs, and equipment with weak American dollars. Spending soft dollars on imports and earning hard marks from exports, Italy in 1978 had the biggest balance of payments surplus in its history, over $8 billion on current account. As a result, the exchange rate of the lira stabilized against the major trading currencies. The accumulation of foreign exchange reserves enabled the government to repay ahead of schedule an EEC loan of over $1 billion, thereby boosting the country's international credit rating. In September the discount rate was lowered by 1 percent to stimulate investments.

Two encouraging domestic indicators revealed the decline of the rates of inflation and of unemployment. In 1978 the inflation rate was 12 percent, a substantial reduction from the previous year, although still much higher than the low rates in Switzerland, West Germany, and the Netherlands. In central and northern Italy unemployment was disappearing, although it was still present in the south, especially among the young. These brighter conditions were reflected in a consumer buying spree, a return of foreign investors to Italian markets, and a revival of the Milan stock exchange, which had been in the doldrums for most of the decade.

Dark spots remained. The enormous budget deficit of the national government threatened renewed inflationary pressures. *Business Week* reported a survey of 750 of the biggest firms in the world outside the United States, showing that only 7 percent lost money in 1978. Of the 7 percent the Italian record was the worst. Nineteen large Italian firms were included in the survey. Fiat and a few banks made money. The four worst cases were public sector enterprises, ENI plus three IRI companies, Alfa-Romeo (automobiles), Italsider (steel), and Snia Viscosa (artificial fibers). Together they lost more than $1 billion that year.[6] It was clear that the economic spurt and export boom were coming from medium and small firms and from the thriving, submerged economy.

Improving economic conditions were not attributable to major reforms or important policy decisions made by the indirect grand coalition. There was nothing different about the political process even if the Communists were part of the majority. With Moro gone the sectors of the DC never reconciled to Moro's arrangement increased their resistance to the application of his formula of dialogue with the PCI. In the summer of 1978 the Socialists began a short-lived ideological campaign against the Communists, questioning the PCI's commitment to democratic socialism and its true independence from Moscow. Although not repudiating the PSI goal of a left alternative, Craxi postponed it.

The Communist leadership was under attack not only from other parties but also from within its own ranks. It had little to show for its strategy, receiving acceptance neither from the Catholic world as an integral part of domestic society, nor from the larger community of Western nations, nor from the Socialist parties of Western Europe so assiduously courted. For their own domestic reasons these parties had to avoid open acceptance of PCI claims even if they did believe them. The same was true of the U.S. government, which rebuffed all PCI efforts to establish normal ties. Within the PCI Central Committee, among middle- and lower-level activists and party members, the leadership was charged with being too accommodating and submissive to the DC. The electoral successes of 1975 and 1976 had expanded the Communist presence in the political world but achieved little else.

The historic compromise was accepted by most party members but not wholeheartedly nor enthusiastically. For card-carrying Communists the DC and the Catholic world were still the main enemies. After World War II Togliatti had extended the hand of friendship to the Church. The PCI welcomes religious believers to its ranks. Nevertheless, very few party members were believers. Most persisted in their anticlerical sentiments. They swallowed the historic compromise as a step toward the goal they really preferred, a coalition of the left that would push the DC into the opposition.[7] This goal was already realized at local levels in numerous popular front governments. It was aided by the Christian Democratic party, which forbade its local DC organizations to join any government with the PCI.

Party membership had increased during the heady years of voting successes. Card holders rose from 1.6 million to slightly over 1.8 million as the PCI strove to consolidate election victories. The increase was in no degree proportionate to the voting gains, indicating that numerous PCI voters had yet to be converted into strong party identifiers or Marxist militants. The youth vote was particularly volatile. The new members came mainly from middle-class groups and contributed to the extraordinary turnover of local and regional leadership. By the late summer of 1978 public opinion surveys revealed considerable dissatisfaction and unrest among both members and supporters.

In the fall of 1978 the PCI leadership responded to these various pressures. Berlinguer, without abandoning the historic compromise, revised the formulation to make it more elastic, bringing in the possibility of an alternation of majorities. His language turned in a more orthodox direction as he reminded the public that the PCI was a

Marxist-Leninist party. Criticism of the Soviet Union was restrained. Communist leaders attacked the DC cabinet for failing to promote more fundamental reforms. The principal DC contribution in this direction was the Pandolfi Plan, put forward in 1978 by the treasury minister Filippo Pandolfi. It was a three-year plan for 1979-81 calling for:

1. A steady reduction in the rate of inflation;
2. The stabilization of the lira with other West European currencies;
3. An implementation of the 1977 law on industrial reconversion by gradually increasing investments to restructure production;
4. A gradual increase in imports as production capacity rose; and
5. The continued growth of exports.

It was not a plan but a statement of propositions. Both the PCI and PSI rejected Pandolfi's proposals, claiming that they put the sacrifices on the workers. The DC accused the left of irresponsibility. Point 2 required collaboration with other West European countries. That same fall the West German government proposed to its EEC partners a revived European snake, which would tie the several currencies to the leading one, the German mark. In 1973 Italy had stayed out of the first snake but this time Prime Minister Andreotti was anxious to participate. He feared the political marginalization of his country if it turned down the opportunity once more. Resistance was strong from the unions, many business groups, and Paolo Baffi, governor of the Bank of Italy. They were fearful that a possible upward revaluation of the lira would threaten Italian exports. To keep prices and production costs down at home would require a discipline of work, a restraint on wage demands, an improved level of efficiency, in other words, an austerity that few believed the Italians could meet. Britain and Ireland faced the same challenge. To make acceptance easier the other EEC countries granted Italy, Ireland, and Britain for an unlimited transition period, a broader band than was available to the others within which their currencies could fluctuate. Over Communist protests the Andreotti government chose to join the new snake. As long as the country was running surpluses in its balance of payments the threat to the value of the lira remained moot. The currency agreement was to go into effect on January 1, 1979. Britain decided not to join. Due to a last minute snag created by the French, the formal institution of the snake was postponed to March 15, 1979. In the meantime the countries that joined conducted themselves as if the snake were in operation.

The PCI did not appreciate these kinds of reforms. By the end of the year it was hinting it was not afraid to return to the opposition. In January 1979 its antagonism grew more open. It charged the DC with reneging on interparty agreements. It then asserted that the existing arrangement was untenable; being in the parliamentary majority was not enough. It wanted direct participation in the cabinet or else it would return to the opposition. On January 12, 1979 the Carter administration in Washington intervened to warn the DC against accepting the PCI into the government. The warning was unnecessary. The PCI knew its demand would be rejected and preferred at this time to return to the opposition. On January 31 the PCI withdrew from the majority. Prime Minister Andreotti submitted his cabinet's resignation to President Pertini, who made the standard request of him to stay on in a caretaker capacity until a new government was formed. The indirect grand coalition had collapsed. Another, and really serious, crisis had begun.

Luckily for the country it did not face an economic crisis at the same time. On the contrary, the economy was booming. The problem was that nobody was sure just how much. In March 1979 the government's Central Statistical Institute admitted openly that its economic and financial data were deficient. The figures did not include the submerged economy. The Institute announced that it would recalculate all its financial reports going back to 1975. It would assume that the submerged economy contributed 10 percent to GNP. The announcement provoked a storm of protest from numerous economists. Many charged that 10 percent was a gross underassumption; the real contribution of the submerged economy was closer to 25 or 30 percent. Others claimed the figures for the whole decade of the 1970s needed recalculating, pointing out that to begin in 1975 would destroy the comparability of pre-1975 and post-1975 reports. Still others claimed that the Institute's figures on the legal part of the economy were inadequate.

The disagreements continued over the question of unemployment rates. Officially, almost 8 percent of the labor force was unemployed. The government figures indicated that three out of four officially unemployed workers were under the age of 30. Most lived in the south. Again, economists and sociologists disputed the validity of these figures. In the fall of 1979 Professor Pasquale Saraceno reported to the Society for the Development of the South (SVIMEZ) that in the south alone the submerged economy was providing 1.1 million jobs. By the late 1970s whatever unemployment there was in the south resembled that in other parts of the country: older men past their prime, housewives looking for supplementary income, school dropouts, university graduates unwilling to take jobs beneath their dignity.

In central and northern Italy there were labor shortages. Craftsmen and artisans were difficult to find because not enough apprentices had obtained the required training and necessary skills. Plumbers, carpenters, electricians, and plasterers were in short supply. In another category workers to do very heavy work or dirty jobs were scarce. As a result, foreigners were moving into these positions, mostly from Third World countries of Africa and Asia. In 1979 an estimated 700,000 to 750,000 illegal aliens worked in Italy, doing the dirty jobs and heavy work that Italians were doing in West Germany, Switzerland, and the Low Countries. Some economists estimated that the real rate of unemployment in the country was at the most 2 percent, almost a condition of full employment.

These circumstances raised another question, just how poor was Italy, how poor was the south? In the north the levels of well-being seemed close to those of the countries of northwestern Europe. The impressive buying spree indicated that inflated prices were not stopping customers. The south was not as well off as the center or north, but how far behind was it? Nobody knew for sure. Between 1970 and 1977 consumption of industrial electric current rose in the south at an average annual rate of 9.6 percent compared with a national average of 4.0 percent. In the fall of 1979 ENEL reported that in the previous two years its sales of industrial electric power had again risen at a faster rate in the south than elsewhere in the country. Decentralization of industry was spreading. Medium-sized and smaller firms were moving, especially down the Adriatic coast from the Marches to Puglia.

The rigidities of the productive process in large enterprises were avoided by the flexible smaller ones. In the final years of the decade many small and medium-scale firms had carried out bold reconversion programs involving significant reductions in cost. They also benefited from a decline in both conflict and absenteeism. Examples could be found in the machine tool industry, the instrumentation industry, and in the private sector of the textile and apparel industries. There appeared to be little future for further expansion of the basic industries that had sparked Italy's second industrial revolution in the postwar years—heavy chemicals, oil refining, steel and automotive vehicles. The future appeared brighter for specialty production—sophisticated chemicals, high-fashion items, advanced mechanical products.

The automobile industry, which had led the Italian industrial explosion, was now falling behind its European competitors. Alfa Romeo suffered severe losses. Its southern subsidiary, Alfa-Sud, was a financial disaster. In 1979 Fiat lost money on its automobile business; its profits as a conglomerate came from its non-automotive operations. It entered the 1980 production year with a large inventory of unsold cars. In the spring of 1980 its chairman, Giovanni Agnelli, forecast a 30 percent cutback of automobile production and large-scale layoffs for the fall. When fall arrived Agnelli's forecast became a reality. The automotive unions struck the Fiat plants for 35 days before a settlement was reached on October 17, 1980. Fiat withdrew its threat of immediate dismissals, but the unions accepted the right of the firm to lay off 23,000 workers during the next three years if circumstances required it. The government promised that unemployment compensation to affected workers would come close to their working wages. The union had been forced, however, to accept the principle of the firm's right to lay off workers when business is bad. Other major industries immediately served notice that they would have to reduce their work forces.

Agnelli had noted in earlier years that Italian auto workers were 35 to 40 percent less efficient than German auto workers; yet they were paid almost as much. At the same time he fought to keep Japanese autos out of the European market, opposing a government-proposed solution to the Alfa-Sud crisis that involved a joint venture agreement with Nissan Motors of Japan. His negative comparison of Italian labor productivity in the auto industry could be matched in the chemical and other industries. In the summer of 1979 Professor Romano Prodi, former minister of industry, generalized the comparison, claiming that for many practically identical items German productivity was 40 percent higher. About half the difference was the result of more hours effectively worked, the other half the result of higher productivity per hour.[8]

The productivity of big firms had been declining throughout the 1970s while labor costs increased. In spite of the fiscalization of some fringe benefits, the remaining benefits paid by the firms were the highest in the EEC as a percentage of labor cost. Between 1968 and 1978 labor costs in Italy increased 450.1 percent while productivity increased 336.5 percent (both in current lire). Of the increase in labor costs, 74.8 percent was due to higher money wages, and 25.2 percent was the result of fewer hours worked. In the negotiations that began in the fall of 1978 for renewal of the collective bargaining agreements, production efficiency was a critical issue, even more than wages. The negotiations extended into 1979 and in the manufacturing industries were not concluded until the summer of that year. During that period strikes and work stoppages were frequent. The wage increases gained in the 1979 contracts over and above the automatic indexing were minor. The unions fought to have the length of the work week reduced without cuts in pay. They joined together with trade union confederations in other EEC countries to make this a continent-wide goal. They wished to avoid worsening any member country's competitive position vis-à-vis the others. The employers agreed in principle to a gradual reduction of the work week if the workers would really work when they were supposed to be on the job. Management also accepted the obligation to inform regional union offices of its overall plans and the prospects for employment. The unions, in turn, accepted the principle of labor mobility, as long as mobility did not mean layoffs. They insisted on being consulted when work assignments, schedules, and locations were rearranged. On both sides there was much dissimulation. Italian employers are not psychologically accustomed to consulting with their employees. The workers, imbued with a traditional Italian attitude of protectiveness toward particular jobs, were certain to resist movement from one department to another, from one location to another. They suspected methodological innovations. In spite of promises by management they feared the loss of jobs.

These were real fears. In the fall of 1979 the Olivetti Office Machines Company announced it would have to lay off up to 3,000 surplus workers. The unions immediately threatened retaliatory action. As of the end of the year the layoffs had not yet taken place. That same fall Fiat fired 69 workers for destruction and violence in the plants. A few days later Alfa Romeo fired four workers in its Milan plant for excessive absenteeism. The union immediately called protest strikes, but few of the workers responded. The fired Fiat workers were well identified as extremist troublemakers who, moreover, were hostile to the unions. The unions called the strikes because they had to go through the motions of being on the side of the proletariat against the bosses. Because Fiat had not specified in detail the acts committed by the dismissed workers, a labor court ordered the firm to restore their jobs. At the end of the year, however, they were still not back in the plants. The whole pattern of events revealed that the leaders of big business had gone on the offensive to restore discipline and efficiency to production.

Unquestionably the union federation of the confederations was in trouble. Internal strains were pulling the confederation apart as the leaders disagreed over the viability of their 1977 commitment to restraint. CGIL, led by Luciano Lama, remained the most moderate of the three confederations, while CISL, led by Pierre Carniti, was the most belligerent in supporting rank-and-file demands. Externally the confederations were losing membership, both to independent unions, which claimed the most of everything for their members, and to no unions as workers moved to rural factories. The unions were strongest in the big plants in the large urban centers. Even where they were present their reduced capacity to control their members meant they failed to limit the damage done by wildcat strikes and by slowdowns. By the fall of 1979 the PSI, which almost always backed the unions in its efforts to gain political supporters, warned the unions that if they could not control unauthorized strikes the government would have to step in.

By comparative standards the organized workers in the protected sectors of the Italian economy had little cause for complaint. From 1975 to 1979 Italian workers gained the second highest increase in real income within the EEC. Only workers of Luxembourg did slightly better. Wages and salaries were particularly high in the fields of fuel and power, credit and insurance, transportation, and communications. This was the case not only in comparison with other fields inside Italy but also in comparison with the same fields in other European countries. Inside Italy there was a substantial narrowing in income gaps between white-collar and blue-collar workers. There was also a notable upward leveling of women's wages to men's wages (in the regular economy), and of less-skilled workers to more-skilled workers. In the fall of 1979 even Luciano Lama admitted that the flattening of the reward ladder was discouraging incentive and productivity. The redistribution of income was not limited to urban workers. By the last half of the 1970s farm labor wages were closer to wages in manufacturing and construction. These changes reduced the gap between countryside and urban centers, between peasants and workers, between North and South.

Table 20 reveals which trades and professions gained or lost over the decade. In this table the increase in the cost of living in the 1970s is indicated by an index figure of 1.00.

It is clear that civil service employees at the administrative levels had taken a severe cut in their real incomes. The low morale, the absenteeism, the moonlighting, the inefficiency of public services are partially explained in Table 20. Italy had more appropriations unspent than any other country of the EEC because of the slowness of the bureaucracy and the technicalities of bureaucratic requirements. In the fall of 1979 the procurator of the Court of Accounts, an agency similar in some respects to the U.S. General Accounting Office, issued a report denouncing the intolerably low levels of efficiency of the civil service. He condemned the mediocre quality of services rendered, the absenteeism, the spreading laxity that was a rule of life in all sectors of the civil service.

In the spring of 1979 the government had announced a new wage scale for executive-level bureaucrats, military officers, magistrates,

TABLE 20: Consequences of Indexing and Wage Increases in the 1970s for Selected Employee Categories

Category	Ratio of Wage Increases to Cost of Living Rise
Workers in industry and commerce	1.66
Farm laborers	1.65
Transport workers	1.54
White-collar employees in industry	1.39
White-collar employees in commerce	0.83
Professors	0.81
Deputy office managers	0.74
Chief train conductors	0.63
Elementary school teachers	0.63
Section chiefs, public administration	0.51
School principals	0.51
Principal secretaries, public administration	0.42
Executives in the public administration	0.30
Higher executives in the public administration	0.22

Source: *Corriere della Sera*, September 2, 1979.

diplomats, and school administrators. The salary increases were substantial, intended to restore a position that had deteriorated badly. The increases provoked strong protests from the unions that represented the sub-executive levels of the public service. The workers at these levels had received wage increases slightly higher than the cost of living, much better on a relative basis than their superiors. Negotiations with the government over a new contract took all spring and summer. By fall the unions had won a substantial victory. The new agreement gave the lower-level public employees 100 percent indexing revised quarterly, almost identical to the 1975 agreement between the industrial unions and Confindustria. In addition, the government workers obtained a one-time, across-the-board wage increase. The cabinet presented the new agreement as an act of justice to an important segment of the labor force. The government announced that it expected to pay for the increases through more rigorous tax collections. The estimated budget deficit for 1979 was about 16 percent of GNP.

The efficiency of tax collections had improved in the late 1970s but much evasion still remained. The overall tax burden was 5 to 6 percent below the average of other OECD countries. The distribution of tax returns had shifted. In the early 1970s only a third of the returns came from direct taxes, two-thirds from indirect taxes. By the end of 1979 the ratio was around 50-50. It was estimated that 4 million Italians who received incomes paid no taxes at all. Many of these were self-employed. There was an unestimated number who made false declarations, understating their income. A large number of firms, particularly small and medium-sized companies, paid part of their salaries illegally, in cash that never got into official pay envelopes. The bigger the firm, the less this was true. The most honest were the Italian subsidiaries of foreign multinationals, where almost the entire pay appeared in the legal paycheck. Cheating, in other words, was not a behavior restricted to the wealthy.

Foreign firms were coming into Italy as the economy improved, reversing the process of disinvestment that had occurred earlier in the decade. Italy continued to put its external accounts in order. Once again, in 1979 it had a surplus in its balance of payments on current account, although not as large a surplus as the year before. The big jump in petroleum prices imposed by OPEC in the middle of 1979 created a bigger drain on foreign exchange. Nevertheless Italy once more repaid some of its foreign debt earlier than scheduled. Its trading relations with its EEC partners were closer than ever. In 1979 46.5 percent of Italy's foreign trade was with the other eight countries of the EEC. Forty-five percent of its imports came from EEC nations and 48 percent of its exports went to them. West Germany and France, in that order, were Italy's two most important trading partners. Over 60 percent of Italy's foreign trade was with the advanced, developed countries. The Italian demand for imported meat, dairy products, poultry, corn, and wheat had boomed in spite of a doubling of farm production in the postwar period. The doubling took place while the labor force in agriculture declined from 45 percent to under 15 percent. During the same years much agricultural land was abandoned or taken over by spreading urbanism and highways.

In 1979 foreign trade produced over 50 percent of Italy's GNP. The country's main exports were still in the sectors of its traditional strengths: textiles, clothing, shoes, wines, wood furniture—many of which could be manufactured in the submerged economy. It needed from abroad, in addition to basic raw materials, advanced technology, patents, and know-how. These could be acquired through joint ventures or through multinationals. Even the PCI had abandoned its hostility to multinationals. Italy could not compete with other advanced countries by devaluating its currency, as it had done in earlier years. In 1979 the lira was linked to the German mark through the renewed European snake. Nor could it compete on the basis of low-wage labor typical of semideveloped countries. By 1979 its labor force distribution approached that of a postindustrial society: 14.5 percent in agriculture, 37.5 percent in industry, 48.0 percent in tertiary services.[9] The dualism in Italy was less between north and south, or city and country, or capital and labor, than between the protected and the unprotected.

A shift of industry was transferring people from the large urban centers to the smaller cities and towns. From 1975 forward in nine of the 10 largest Italian cities there was more out-migration than in-migration. Florence was the only exception. The decentralization of the economy extended the historic industrial triangle from Genoa, Milan, and Turin to the northeast and center. Regions such as the Veneto, Emilia-Romagna, Tuscany, and the Marches witnessed the growth of flourishing commercial and manufacturing centers. Elsewhere in the country there were expanding pockets of industry: in the provinces south of Rome, in the region surrounding Naples, in the southeastern industrial triangle of Bari-Brindisi-Taranto, and on the east coast of Sicily.

The decade of the 1970s had been a decade of stop-and-go, of floating, or of laissez-faire tempered by public subsidies. In 1978 and 1979 the government would again instruct the banks to form consortia to reorganize the giant chemical firms in order to protect jobs. Nevertheless, on the whole, the decade had been a moderate economic success. In spite of the inflation imported from abroad and aggravated at home, most Italians were better off at the end of the ten years than at the beginning. The submerged economy had absorbed tensions that otherwise would have been acute. There had been a revival of private enterprise as entrepreneurs of small and medium-sized firms demonstrated a remarkable readiness to adapt, and a speed of adaptation, to new conditions. Even some of the big companies had moved to adjust to new circumstances. In some instances the unions collaborated; more often they protested. But in a number of cases these protests were just for the record. The fragmentation of Italian society permitted an exceptional degree of elasticity that enabled it to survive urban disorder, administrative inefficiency, and even terrorism.[10]

But could it survive parliamentary breakdown? The collapse of the informal grand coalition on January 31, 1979, left the country once more with a caretaker government. Prime Minister Andreotti made several efforts to reconstitute the parliamentary majority but failed. The PCI insisted: either inclusion in the cabinet or a return to the opposition. President Pertini called on other political leaders, such as La Malfa, to try to form a government. It was the first time since 1945 that a non-Christian Democrat was asked to make the attempt. Neither La Malfa nor the others succeeded. Two months of stalemate made new elections inevitable. Andreotti organized a minority three-party coalition of the DC, PRI, and PSDI, presented it to parliament, and openly invited a vote of no confidence. He got what he asked for, and on March 31 President Pertini dissolved parliament. It had lasted two and a half years. For the third time in the 1970s the legislature failed to complete its full term. The Christian Democrats were ready for new elections, for the public opinion polls indicated that they were gaining support while the Communists were losing ground. The three-party cabinet continued in a caretaker capacity to administer the coming election, set for June 3. The choice of that date created a fracture between Andreotti and Craxi, the leader of the PSI. The Socialists wanted a later date, after the first popular election of representatives to the European parliament, scheduled for June 10. Craxi expected that a strong showing of other Socialist parties in Western Europe would boost PSI prospects in Italy.

The election campaign was unexciting. Again terrorist activity increased in the attempt to radicalize the atmosphere. The election itself went off without incident. The results (see Table 16) produced few surprises. DC losses were minor, but unexpected because pre-election polls had forecast substantial gains. The PSI vote improved marginally, as did the vote for the Social Democrats and Liberals. The big gainer was the Radical Party, the big loser the PCI. The Radicals more than quadrupled their representation in the Chamber of Deputies. Their popular vote for the Chamber increased compared with 1976 from 1.1 to 3.4 percent of the total vote. The Communists dropped from 227 to 201 seats in the Chamber and from 34.4 to 30.4 percent of the total vote. It was the first time since World War II that the PCI vote had declined. The Radicals, led by the theatrical Marco Pannella, attracted young voters from the Communists with a campaign against nuclear power and for unilateral disarmament, the legalization of drugs, and women's liberation. The Communists lost votes all over the country, particularly in the south. Their losses were minor, however, in their historic Red Belt strongholds. They also lost to the increasing numbers of voters who cast blank ballots, and to nonvoters. For the first time turnout in a parliamentary election dropped below 90 percent of the registered voters, in comparison with the 93 to 94 percent turnout in previous elections. A week later Italians voted in the first direct election to the European parliament. The results followed the trend of the previous week. The turnout of 86 percent was the largest of all member countries of the EEC. The Socialist parties of Europe did not do as well as Craxi expected.

Forming a new government took most of the summer. Two types

of political majorities were possible: a cabinet of national emergency or a center-left cabinet. The PCI announced: either inclusion in the cabinet or a return to the opposition. That made the center-left the only alternative, for none of the DC factions was ready to include Communists in the government. They were willing, as in 1978, to accept the PCI as part of the parliamentary majority. A center-left cabinet would require the PSI to reverse every statement it had made since 1975. A number of DC leaders believed, however, that if Craxi were given the premiership the Socialists might be willing. Andreotti's initial efforts to form a new government were vetoed by Craxi, who would not even promise a Socialist abstention. Then President Pertini turned to Craxi and asked him to form a government. Part of the DC leadership was agreeable for it saw an opportunity to split the PSI and the PCI. Most of the DC leaders refused. Their party was four times larger than the Socialist Party in parliament. They had held the premiership uninterruptedly since 1945. After lengthy negotiations a truce cabinet was formed. Led by Francesco Cossiga, the minister of the interior in 1978 who had resigned after the death of Moro, it was a minority government of Christian Democrats, a few Social Democrats and Liberals, plus a very few nonparty experts. It survived on the abstention of Republicans and Socialists. The PCI returned to the opposition.

The new government faced difficult prospects. The rate of inflation, moving upward throughout the first half of the year, spurted when OPEC imposed major price increases in the summer of 1979. Italian consumption of petroleum products continued to grow. In March the government had promised its EEC partners to cut back petroleum usage by 5 percent from the previous year. By the end of the summer it was clear that Italian oil consumption was growing by 5 percent, not declining. Fuel supplies and electric power were tight. The government imposed higher prices on gasoline, on heating and diesel fuel, and on electricity, prices that became effective in the fall. These increases spread through the economy pushing up the inflation rate. When 1979 ended the consumer's price index was 19 percent higher than the previous year.

A succession of caretaker and truce governments was hardly the basis for running a modern society, although there are Italian cynics who maintain that Italy is better off when it has no government. In the fall of 1979 the debate was renewed over institutional reform. The same prescriptions as before were offered: a presidential republic, abolition of proportional representation, and reduction in the number of political parties. In October the PSI called on all the parties to join in the task of institutional reform. It quickly became apparent that no party would countenance any change threatening to its power position. The DC announced it would consider revising its own party rules to institute primaries to choose parliamentary candidates. After a month the discussion petered out. In the meantime the Socialists and Republicans announced that their abstentions had a time limit, the Christian Democratic party congress scheduled for January 1980.

The debate inside the DC in preparation for the congress soon revealed two contrasting positions. By the end of October Andreotti and Zaccagnini were arguing that sooner or later the Communists would have to be brought into the government. Andreotti suggested that the process could begin at local levels. Fanfani and Flaminio Piccoli proposed a renewed center-left coalition with the Socialists. In the meantime, the other parties watched and waited while Cossiga's government struggled with the continuing problem of terrorism and violence.

The courts and the special antiterrorist police squads commanded by the Carabinieri general Carlo Dalla Chiesa had had some successes in catching and convicting terrorists. The previous April a principal intellectual exponent of terrorism, Antonio Negri, professor of political theory at the University of Padua, was arrested and charged with involvement in the murder of Aldo Moro. Although the charge was later dropped he was kept in jail on a variety of other accusations. In May the government assigned army troops to guard public buildings, electrical power stations, and other sensitive installations. This made more police available for the antiterrorist campaign. Private violence was also continuing at a strong pace. In the summer several wealthy vacationers were kidnapped. The Mafia was expanding into parts of the country hitherto immune, on the heels of the spreading traffic in both soft and hard drugs. It was becoming evident that terrorist groups and organized crime were linked.

A different source of violence was reviving in the 1979 clashes in the South Tyrol between German-speaking and Italian-speaking residents. There was a growing self-consciousness of small ethnic groups on the frontiers of Italy and even in the continental boot. It was a development similar to the revived ethnic and regional consciousness in other European countries. In the South Tyrol, in the Val d'Aosta, in Trieste, in Sardinia, Calabria, and elsewhere, linguistic minorities were asserting their presence. Only in the South Tyrol, Val D'Aosta, and Trieste were they numerous enough to elect representatives to parliament. Some were appealing to the EEC to support claims for more autonomy.

In September the Cossiga government attacked the EEC's Common Agriculture Policy. The minister of agriculture charged that in 1978 his country had spent 1,248 billion lire more for food imports from the EEC than if it had purchased the same products from non-EEC countries. He protested once more the discrimination against Mediterranean farm products. His colleague, the minister of the treasury, insisted that Italy's contribution to the EEC budget was too high. Since the United Kingdom shared the same complaints the two countries agreed to cooperate in an effort to change EEC policies. In October the EEC retaliated when its High Commission announced an investigation of Italian government subsidies to public sector firms, asserting that these grants violated antitrust rules of the Common Market.

A more important internal dispute erupted in October when the Italian government accepted the U.S. proposal to upgrade medium-range nuclear missile installation in Europe. Brezhnev's threats and blandishments had been resisted. Italy agreed with West Germany that there was sufficient time to negotiate with the Soviet Union about nuclear parity in Europe before the new missiles would be installed in 1983. All the parties of the constitutional arch except the PCI supported the government's decision, although Craxi found some resistance among his own party leaders. The Communists took a stance equidistant between the Soviet Union and the United States, calling for immediate East-West negotiations before the decision to accept the new missiles was made. They also called on the Soviet Union to halt its installation of medium-range missiles. In essence, their position was similar to that adopted by the Dutch government and to the position of the left wing of the German Social Democratic Party.

The DC congress was postponed until the end of February 1980. At the congress the forces led by Piccoli and Fanfani obtained 56 percent of the delegates to the 44 percent who supported Zaccagnini and Andreotti. A week later the DC national council elected Piccoli the new secretary-general of the party. One week after that the Socialists announced they would vote against the government instead of abstaining. On March 19, 1980, Cossiga presented his cabinet's resignation to Pertini. The president quickly asked him to form another government. In a short time Cossiga created a center-left cabinet of Christian Democrats, Socialists, and Republicans. The PSDI decided to stay out. It was the first majority government in half a decade. Craxi stated that although his party did not repudiate the left alternative, it would have to be postponed to an indefinite future. A Christian Democrat was still prime minister. In the meantime the new center-left government might do better than the old ones of the 1960s.

The Communists were comfortable as the opposition, a role for which they had long experience. Their international posture, however, was not so comfortable. They attacked the Soviet invasion of Afghanistan at the end of 1979. They criticized the arrest of Andrei Sakharov by the Soviet government and his internal banishment to the city of Gorky. They refused to attend a conference of European Communist parties in Paris at the end of April 1980, a conference sponsored by the French and Polish parties with the endorsement of the CPSU. Instead they were actively engaged in meeting with European Socialist parties. In April Berlinguer paid a formal visit to China, concluding his stay with the reestablishment of friendly relations between the two Communist parties. He refused, however, to take sides in the Chinese-Soviet rivalry. At the same time the PCI was attacking the United States for not ratifying the Salt II treaty and for boycotting the Moscow Olympics. It accused President Carter of reviving the Cold War and called on European countries to resist both Soviet and U.S. influence. The balancing act of the Italian Communists on the international scene paralleled their domestic strategy of pursuing reform while at the same time calling themselves a revolutionary party.

As long as the country did not undergo a drastic shift in its internal political balance, the question of where the Communists would finally come down was not critical. The regional elections of June 1980 left the positions of the parties where they had been the previous year. The DC made modest gains over 1979; the PCI held its own. The PSI moved forward and interpreted its improvement as approval by its supporters for the renewed center-left policy. In organizing the new regional, provincial, and municipal administrations, however, it joined again with the PCI in almost all the popular front governments of the previous five years.

The country appeared immobilized in its old condition of stabilized instability. As long as the economy moved forward the prospect for a breakdown of its political system appeared remote. In the first half of 1980 the annual rate of real economic growth approached 6 percent. The rate of inflation was slightly more than 20 percent. Obviously most Italians, with the possible exception of the executives of the Bank of Italy, preferred to stay ahead of inflation, not to control it. The terrorists were not quiescent, however, and in the first four months of 1980 they committed over 20 assassinations. Numerous arrests followed each killing, and repeated unfounded claims were made that a breakthrough in the antiterrorist struggle had been achieved. The worst shock of all was the bombing of the waiting rooms of the Bologna railroad station on August 2. Eighty-four people died and over a hundred were wounded. Presumed neo-Fascist extremists were suspected of this single worst terrorist act in recent Italian history, but concrete evidence was scarce. The public was shocked and indignant. More extensive police powers adopted at the beginning of the year, the appointment of army generals as prefects in some key northern cities, had failed to stop the violence. Some intellectuals feared a future military takeover if order could not be maintained. The danger appeared remote from the minds of most Italians. In the summer more people went off on vacation than ever before. Life went on.

NOTES

1. *Corriere della Sera*, June 15, 1976.

2. Alberto Spreafico, "Analisi dei risultati elettorali del '76," *Quaderni dell' Osservatorio elettorale*, October 1977, p. 152.

3. Lucio Colletti, "Le ideologie," *Dal '68 a oggi* (Bari: Laterza, 1979) pp. 136-38, 147-66.

4. Admiral Franco Micali Baratelli, "Sicurezza e stabilità nel Mediterraneo," mimeographed paper read at the Conference on "Italy and the United States Face the International Order," sponsored by the Italian Society for International Organization, October 19-21, 1978.

5. Nora Federici, "Il Costume," *Dal '68 a oggi* (Bari: Laterza, 1979) pp. 314-15.

6. *Business Week*, July 23, 1979, p. 112.

7. Marzio Barbagli and Piergiorgio Corbetta, "Una tattica e due strategie. Inchiesta sulla base del PCI," *Il Mulino*, November-December 1978, pp. 922-67.

8. *Corriere della Sera*, July 16, 1979.

9. Tullio De Mauro, "La cultura," *Dal '68 a oggi* (Bari: Laterza, 1979) p. 184.

10. Giorgio Ruffolo, "L'Economia," *Dal '68 a oggi* (Bari: Laterza, 1979), pp. 259-65.

22
A TIME OF CHANGE

The cabinet reshuffling in October 1980 recreated the classic four-party center-left of the 1960s. Despite the stabilized instability of the political system, continuing social change could not be forestalled, especially after 1968-69. Neither stop-and-go economic policies nor political stalemate affected the evolution of birth and death rates, levels of education, literacy rates, or patterns of daily living.

Throughout the 1970s the number of marriages per year dropped steadily as more couples dispensed with legalizing their cohabitation. Family composition was changing. At the beginning of the 1970s two-thirds of all families were nuclear families; throughout the decade the extended family gradually continued to dissolve. Increasing numbers of people were living alone. It was estimated that in industrial centers this was the condition of 15 to 20 percent of the population; elsewhere the estimate was of 10 to 12 percent.[1]

Italian birth rates had been falling since 1964, but the rate of decline accelerated in the 1970s. In 1971 the birth rate per thousand people was 16.8. It fell steadily: to 14.8 in 1975, to 13.2 in 1977, and in 1978 the birth rate was down to 12.5 per thousand. In 1978 the birth rate in northern Italy fell below population zero for the first time. The rate in central Italy hovered on the margin, while the southern rate was somewhat above. The entire country was expected to reach population zero by the end of the 1980s.[2] The trend was already apparent in the schools. Elementary school enrollments were beginning to fall, and lower secondary school enrollments were stagnant.

The longevity of the population was increasing. Infant mortality rates were declining. In 1971 deaths before one year of age averaged 28.5 per thousand births. In 1978 the average fell to 16.8 deaths per thousand births. Adults were living longer, too. The decline in the adult death rate was particularly marked in the south. By 1978 the overall death rate was down to 15.2 in the center and north, 17.0 in the islands (Sicily and Sardinia), and 19.5 in the south.[3]

In the late 1970s the average age at death for males was over 70 years, for females over 76 years. By 1979 about 18 percent of the Italians were more than 65 years old. Gradual population growth in the country was due more to increased longevity than to the birth rate. In 1979 the total population was estimated at 57 million. Demographers projected that if present trends continued national population stability would be achieved by 1991. For that year a population of 60 million was forecast.

Increased longevity and reduced infant and adult death rates resulted from changing values and living conditions. Opinion polls revealed that throughout Italy people placed a high value on cleanliness in the home, on indoor plumbing, on refrigerators and washing machines, and on healthful diets. The decline in death rates continued despite inadequate public water and sewer systems and insufficient health and sanitation facilities. Meanwhile food consumption patterns were shifting. People were eating less pasta and bread, fewer fats, sugars, and soft drinks. Consumption of meat, poultry, dairy products, fruits, and vegetables soared. There was a slight decline in per capita consumption of wine, a decline linked at the same time to a more selective choice of types and years.

Regional variations in behavior and values had not disappeared, but were in decline. Especially among the youth the trend was toward national homogenization of behavior and of values. Habits of speech changed however slowly. An optimistic survey made in 1962 had estimated that about 18 percent of the population spoke standard Italian regularly and habitually. The remainder spoke local dialects. By the mid-1970s the proportion who habitually spoke Italian had risen to 25 percent. Another 33 percent spoke Italian when necessary, although they continued to speak dialect at home.

The school is a standard agency of nationalization. Prior to World War II very few Italians had spent much time in school, an important reason for the persistence of dialects. As late as 1957, 90 percent of the population had no more than five years of schooling. In the 1960s and 1970s school attendance leaped upward. The 1971 census revealed that 32 percent of Italians over the age of 14 were without any diploma. Another 44 percent had only the elementary school certificate received at the end of the fifth year. In 14 years the proportion of the people with no more than five years of schooling had fallen from 90 to 76 percent. In 1978 almost 100 percent of elementary-school-age children were attending school. Of them 98 percent went on to the lower secondary school. In 1978, 92.1 percent of the 13- and 14-year-olds were attending the lower secondary school, up from 55.7 percent in 1972-73. Education is compulsory only until age 14, yet by the end of the 1970s over 50 percent of the lower secondary school graduates were going on to the *licei*, scientific, technological, or other specialized schools. The numbers graduating from these upper secondary schools had increased tremendously. In 1967 only 19.6 percent of all 19-year-olds had graduated from an upper secondary school. By 1978 the figure was 41.6 percent. In that year about 30 percent of them entered the universities.[4]

The establishment of the open university admissions policy in 1970 had stimulated a large increase in university enrollments. Throughout the 1970s the government failed to expand the university system sufficiently to accommodate the growing student body. Nor did appropriations for universities keep pace with the rate of monetary inflation. Inadequate funds combined with an exaggerated egalitarian ideology to foment academic disaster. By the late 1970s the number of dropouts was increasing and the overall size of the student body was stabilizing. From 1973 through 1979 only 23.4 percent of university students received degrees; 39.0 percent had given up, while the rest were continuing. For those attending the universities space and opportunities for serious study were inadequate. Enrollments in the major urban universities remained huge. In 1979 over 138,000 students were registered at the University of Rome. In October 1979 the Conference of University Rectors called for the termination of open admissions and the institution of a selection process. The recommendation was politically controversial, certain to stir bitter ideological debate, and unlikely to receive quick action in parliament.

Adult education was promoted by the labor law of 1970. Under union impetus a provision in the law granted workers the right to obtain schooling and specialized training with pay. Beginning with the academic year 1973-74 the regional governments sponsored adult education programs. Most of the courses were instituted to enable participants to obtain the lower secondary school diploma. As many as 30 million people were eligible; yet every year only a few tens of thousands took the courses. Although precise figures are not available, it is certain that much functional illiteracy remained.

Not surprisingly, Italy has one of the lowest proportions of readers in Europe. Surveys taken in the 1950s indicated that 65 percent of the adult population never read a daily newspaper. Among the remaining 35 percent no distinction was made between regular and occasional readers. By 1978 daily newspaper readers had increased to about 53 percent of the adult population. A RAI-TV survey of that year found that while only 23.9 percent of Italians over the age of 15 read a newspaper regularly, 13.2 percent said they read one fairly frequently, and another 16.2 percent said they read one occasionally. The remaining 46.6 percent said they never read one. In 1977, 4.85 million copies of newspapers were sold per day, not even one copy for every 11 inhabitants. This ratio was little better than in the 1950s. Italy can be compared with Switzerland, where one copy is sold for every two inhabitants. The three papers with the largest circulation were the *Corriere della Sera* (Milan), *La Stampa* (Turin), and *L'Unità* (Rome and Milan). The first two were independent, that is, not owned by a political party; the third was the official organ of the Communist Party. The weeklies do better than the dailies. But the 1978 figure of 17 million copies sold weekly in Italy (population 57 million) compared poorly with the 32 million sold in West Germany (population 62 million). Readers of books were also few. In 1978 only 28.2 percent of Italians over age 15 read a book that year. Over 42 percent of all Italian families did not have a single book in the house. This percentage was even higher in the south.[5]

In the 1970s the labor force included more women and included them in more job categories. Government surveys indicated that women composed 26.8 percent of the labor force in 1972 and 32.4 percent in 1978. Undoubtedly these were underestimates since the large numbers of women working in the submerged economy were not counted. In 1977, almost 30 years after the constitution came into force, a law was finally passed imposing equal treatment for women in all careers. Women were beginning to appear in heavy industry in jobs where they had never before been present; they became crane operators and train conductors. The trend was evident in other employment categories as well.

Both internally and internationally the migration of the labor force declined considerably in the 1970s. The reduced demand for workers was caused in part by the economic slowdown in Italy and in northwestern Europe. From 1973 on, more Italians were returning to Italy than were emigrating. Italian workers were the victims of a perverse effect of the Common Market. As citizens of an EEC country they were protected by job rules and employment regulations not available to Balkan, Iberian, or Levantine workers. They had the right to seek employment anywhere in the EEC, but employers in northwestern Europe preferred to hire workers who were more vulnerable, who could be sent home once a contract expired.

The modernizing process in Italy resembled the process in other countries of the Western World. The accumulation of durable consumer goods had effects in Italy similar to those of its northwestern European neighbors. Mass acquisitions of refrigerators, washing machines, and modern kitchens and bathrooms came quickly after the diffusion of electric power networks throughout the country. The rapid spread of radio and television and of the family automobile served to destroy the historic isolation of the various regions. The government was losing its domination over the listening and viewing public. In the last half of the 1970s private radio and television stations made major inroads on the audiences formerly monopolized by the government-controlled networks. Surveys indicated that by the end of the decade 40 percent of the total radio audience was listening to private radio stations. By 1979 there was one automobile for every 3.4 inhabitants of the nation, plus 5 million motorcycles and motorbikes. People were traveling; the boom in the tourist and vacation industry was not just the result of the foreign tourist invasion of the country.

The spreading secularization of society reflected cultural as well as physical mobility. Ways of looking at religion were also in flux. Church attendance continued to decline. Among those people who were getting married the number married only in civil ceremonies rose—from less than 2 percent of all marriages in the immediate postwar period to about 12 percent by the end of the 1970s. Interest in religion took a variety of forms; exploration of oriental mystical movements, activities by evangelical groups such as Jehovah's Witnesses, new types of Catholic communities and practices, and deviations from the institutional, hierarchical Church. In all cases these new directions were taken by small groups who were, however, sufficiently numerous to be subjects of interest to the press. At the same time the Church was recouping some of its influence. Since the split in the early 1970s between ACLI and the Church hierarchy, there had been a rethinking and reconciliation between the two, though ACLI still avoided political formulas and alliances. Discussions between the Church and the government concerning revision of the Concordat moved slowly. The deaths of two popes created delays. The Holy See posed no objection to eliminating the designation of the Roman Catholic Church as the official state church. It was ready to give up the description of Rome as a sacred city; after all, the municipality had a Communist mayor. But no agreement could be reached on the question of religious teaching in the public schools, nor could the dispute over the taxation of nonreligious Church property be resolved. Secular groups who wanted to exclude only religious structures from property taxation would not define Catholic schools or hospitals as religious structures. Consequently, negotiations continued into the 1980s.

Negative effects of modernization were spreading. Several problems of contemporary urban life afflicted the nation, with the authorities apparently incapable of bringing them under control. Nonpolitical crimes proliferated. In 1968 records showed 16.7 criminal acts per 1,000 inhabitants. In the next decade the murder rate doubled, thefts more than tripled, and extortion and kidnapping increased 600 percent. These increases resulted partly from better statistics and more publicity and partly from a genuine increase in criminal behavior. There was a big increase in the 1970s of the consumption of both soft and hard drugs. The streets of the cities were not as safe as in the past; apartment dwellers barricaded themselves behind multilocked doors.

Resource conservation and antipollution programs existed on paper but were neglected in fact. Fertile land was disappearing and forests were few. The great floods of the Arno River and Venice Lagoon in 1966 produced little subsequent action to prevent repetitions. In 1979 the northwestern regions of Lombardy, Piedmont, and Liguria were flooded. In 1976 parliament passed a law to control pollution and to repurify water. In 1977 Italy entered into treaty agreements with other countries of the Mediterranean basin to stop polluting the waters and continental shelf of the Mediterranean Sea. By 1979 parliament suspended the 1976 law because so little had been done by municipalities, provinces, regions, and private and public firms to control pollution and to repair earlier damage. The response of all these organizations was that they lacked the money. In 1979 many beaches were closed to bathers because of polluted waters. The failure to invest in conservation and antipollution measures threatened economic growth as well as the livability of city and countryside.

The trade unions had made social reforms a primary target of political action in the 1970s. High priority among these reforms was assigned to more and improved housing, especially public housing. Although Italy needed 400,000 new dwelling units a year for many years to meet a stored-up demand, at the end of the decade only 150,000 to 160,000 were being built annually. In 1979 public housing construction was only 3 percent of total housing construction. Funds for public housing are scarce when the government has a huge budget deficit and gives a higher priority to subsidizing unprofitable industries.

Italy was living through developments and problems that were the same as in other advanced societies. Its population, like other populations, was asserting what Daniel Bell has called the "revolution of rising entitlements." This revolution is most successful when more entitlements can be financed out of economic growth. In the 1970s economic growth was present though spotty. The rate of inflation was one of the highest among the advanced countries, but a good share of the population was able to keep ahead of it. For many families this required two or more incomes, a requirement not unique to Italy. The submerged economy helped pull the nation through some difficult years. Could it continue to do so?

This was both a moral and an economic question. Although the government was losing tax revenues from illegal employers and their workers, the losses were partially offset since the public treasury did not have to support a larger burden of welfare expenditures. But the workers in the submerged economy were exploited and without protection. The rigidities of the protected labor market sector contributed to the growth of the unprotected sector, since an unemployed worker could always argue that exploited work was better than no work.

The economy as a whole had become increasingly dependent on foreign trade and therefore increasingly vulnerable to upheavals and disruptions in that trade. As foreign protectionist pressures rose, the Italians faced a potential loss of markets. As high rates of domestic inflation pushed prices and costs upward Italian producers became vulnerable to foreign competition not only in their own markets but even more so in external markets. In the fall of 1980 the export boom was in danger. Some large firms were pressuring the government to abandon the snake entered into just the year before, to devalue the lira in order to keep the firms competitive abroad. Other firms, and critical economists as well, suggested as an alternative to devaluation that the government assume more of workers' fringe benefits now paid by employers: for devaluation would feed inflation at home and its stimulus to exports could be only temporary. Surpluses in the balance of payments on current account were replaced by deficits. The Iraq-Iran war threatened Italy with another dramatic increase in petroleum prices. The government budgetary deficit was rising significantly. The lira was weakening. Once again the economy was endangered.

The political system had muddled through more than a decade of expediency. No legislature after 1968 had completed its full five-year term of office. The 1968 legislature lasted four years, the 1972 legislature four years, and the 1976 legislature three years. Throughout the 1970s no stable political formula underlay the successive cabinets. Most goverments were either minority governments, care-taker governments, or truce governments. Sometimes they had majority support in parliament; at other times they depended on abstentions. It is true that even the occasional majority government rarely accomplished more than the others. And the period was not devoid of some important legislation: the labor law of 1970, the establishment of governments for the regular regions in 1970, the divorce law of 1970, the reduction of the voting age for the Chamber of Deputies in 1974, public financing of political parties in 1974, the abortion law of 1978, and the various internal security laws of which the Reale Law is best known. Additional legislation to improve security brought few results, for both private and political violence continued to increase, and crime continued to spread. The growing sense of insecurity in the large urban centers reflected not only the inadequacies of the various police forces but also the fragility of social structures.

The hope that decentralization would bind the population more closely to the political system was disappointed. The financial dependence of the regional and local governments on the national government and the many functions they were mandated to perform effectively undercut decentralization and left them little autonomy. None of the regions had truly formulated a regional development program on the basis of which it could ask the central government for necessary resources. There was no framework for making re-gional policy decisions.

In the name of participatory democracy parliament passed legislation in 1976 and 1977 creating neighborhood committees and school committees of students, teachers, parents, and administrators that had no power. They were advisory; in one case to the municipal governments, in the other to the provincial superintendents of schools, who in turn were officials of the Ministry of Public Instruc-tion. These community organizations fell almost completely under the domination of the left and extra-parliamentary left parties. Under party manipulation they drove out participants from other sectors of the population. The experiment was a failure.

No Italian government had found formulas to control inflation, stimulate steady economic growth, or distribute the financial re-wards in a politically equitable manner. Neither had other govern-ments, but many others were less vulnerable to the economic hurri-canes circulating throughout the world. The revolution of rising entitlements prevented any government from imposing a policy of personal austerity. In Italy, every social group was certain that it alone would pay the price of retrenchment while all the others would continue to take care of themselves. The Christian Democrats and Socialists were unwilling to deny almost any claimant a share of the public treasury. The Republicans and Communists talked about austerity and fiscal responsibility. The Republicans, however, were a tiny party without much political impact. The Communists retreated every time a subsidy was requested to preserve jobs. In August 1979 Berlinguer reiterated that austerity was not to be borne by wage earners alone but must be endured by all social groups. While it is true that the unprotected—the unemployed, the aliens, the underemployed—were well acquainted with austerity in spite of the existence of the welfare state, Italian society as a whole lacked sufficient cohesion to integrate its social groups in any policy of sacrifice.

The leftist formula of democratic programming was nothing more than a variant on the existing mixed economy of limited laissez-faire supplemented by government subsidies. By the late 1970s the PCI had little taste for more government nationalization of industry and no illusions about the inadequacies of a command economy.[6] The DC policy of buying and holding the support of clientelistic groups through the distribution of favors depended on having available resources. The slower growth of the economy in the 1970s reduced but did not eliminate these resources.

A different approach to the nation's economic problems would have to come from a political coalition other than the one centered on Christian Democracy. In the early 1970s the Socialists had proposed the left alternative as the long-run goal. It was the only possible alternative within the framework of the existing political system. The Communists had instead opted for the historic compromise, involving a long-run agreement with the DC coupled with a hope of changing the nature of Christian Democracy. By 1979 the PCI was thinking more favorably of the left alternative. Whether such an alternative would really postulate a different kind of economic order and attempt to implement it remained speculative. Descriptions of the economic content of the system Communists called democratic socialism were vague and abstract. Communist leaders really did not know what democratic socialism would be like. All they knew was that it would be different from any socialist system in existence.

In the spring of 1980 the PSI returned to the formula of the center-left. When the cabinet was reshuffled in October 1980 the Social Democrats were included in the governing coalition, thereby recreating the four-party alignment of Christian Democratic, Socialist, Social Democratic, and Republican parties. In the same month the Socialists and Social Democrats announced their agreement to consult, to collaborate, and to establish joint positions on policy although they denied any intention of reuniting in the immediate future. The two parties affirmed their clear adherence to the values of "Western Socialism." Whatever these values may be, since World War II they have not included open collaboration with Communists except in France and Italy. With this agreement Craxi not only undercut the left wing of his own party but also made it clear that the Socialists were abandoning the left alternative at the national level when the Communists had become more interested in it. The PCI was in a cul-de-sac; neither the historic compromise nor the left alternative was realizable.

But the left alternative flourished at sub-national levels. As a result of regional and local elections in June 1980 almost all of the popular front governments were reconstituted in the regions, provinces, and municipalities where they were functioning already. Social Democrats and Republicans participated in some of these governments. That the open historic compromise did not replace the left alternative at these levels was owing to DC refusal to allow its local units to participate in these coalitions, not to exclusionary policies followed by Communists and Socialists. Though the DC would not govern together with the PCI at any level of government, it was ready to invite Communist collaboration—a necessary condition to maintaining what social peace there was in the country. In the 1960s the old center-left had been promoted as a way to isolate and undercut the PCI. The new center-left of 1980 had no such aspiration. The DC, in any case, expected to continue its leading role in national affairs, reasonably confident that no other party or combination of parties was able or willing to challenge its leadership.

The leadership of the DC was being challenged in one respect, however, and by its largest ally, the PSI. The Socialists already had the presidency of the republic; in addition, Craxi had ambitions to obtain the position of prime minister for his party. Italy's increasing troubles could provide a suitable occasion. By the fall of 1980 the economic boom was faltering. The exchange value of the lira, especially in relation to the American dollar, was declining. A new oil scandal broke out. At the end of November a major earthquake devastated several mountain areas east of Naples and killed over 3,000 people. The slowness of governmental rescue efforts brought public criticism from President Pertini, from opposition parties, and from the DC's Socialist ally, who accused the DC of failure to implement legislation passed ten years earlier for the creation of regional emergency centers.

In the spring of 1981 at the Palermo party congress, Craxi consolidated control over his own party in preparation for launching a campaign for leadership of the government. He renamed his faction the Reformist faction to emphasize moderation and redefined the Socialist program as one of Liberal Socialism, a euphemism for Social Democracy.

In a national referendum on May 18, 1981 the Italian people voted by a margin of 68 percent to 32 percent to continue the existing liberal abortion law. Although the Church, not the DC, had led the struggle to overthrow the law, the DC nevertheless suffered from the results.

At the end of May the eruption of a scandal connected to the secret Masonic lodge, Propaganda 2, brought the government down. Secret organizations are illegal in Italy. Rumors had been circulating for several years about this lodge, and the scandal came to a head when the Grand Master of the lodge, Licio Gelli, was charged with financial corruption and political conspiracy. He fled the country but was captured abroad in 1982. A former Mason accused him of plotting a military coup. Under pressure from the opposition parties and the press, Arnaldo Forlani, the DC prime minister, reluctantly released the names of lodge members. The list included cabinet ministers and undersecretaries, parliamentarians, high military officers, career diplomats, bureaucrats, and prestigious business executives.

Socialist pressure forced the resignation of the Forlani government on May 26. Craxi's efforts to get the prime minister's post were opposed by Christian Democrats. Their resistance crumbled after local elections held on June 22, 1981 revealed DC losses in most of Italy. At the end of July a compromise brought in the secretary general of the small Republican Party, Giovanni Spadolini, as prime minister. It was the first time since 1945 that a non-Christian Democrat was head of the government. Fifteen DC cabinet ministers remained in office. Neither of the two larger parties in the cabinet, the Christian Democrats and the Socialists, looked upon the compromise as more than temporary.

Spadolini proved quite skillful at keeping his larger allies at bay. The Christian Democrats were demoralized because of their voting losses and the scandals. At a party conference toward the end of November, repeated calls were made for the rejuvenation of the party, for an end to scandals, and for a new morality. Younger leaders and fresh ideas were demanded. Some delegates suggested that it was time for the party to disassociate itself from the Catholic Church; others reasserted the importance of Church connections. The Socialists, confident that the times were moving in their direction, waited for the opportune moment to achieve their goal of a takeover of cabinet leadership.

High rates of inflation, increasing unemployment, and the declining lira pushed the Spadolini government into strong action. A choice was made for a policy of moderate austerity. Government spending was cut for a variety of social programs. The goal was to reduce the annual rate of inflation from 21 percent to 16 percent.

The Communists, in the meantime, were in opposition while continuing to call for a new alignment of political forces. Their major problem came from Eastern Europe. The imposition of martial law by the Polish military on December 13, 1981 produced a violent reaction among PCI leaders. Both the Polish and Russian governments were held responsible for the Polish crackdown. In a series of attacks levied against the CPSU, Berlinguer and his leading associates demanded the restoration of liberties in Poland, while asserting that the capacity for renewal and development of Eastern European societies, a renewal launched with the October Revolution, was exhausted. The Soviet system of leadership and the Polish program of economic development had both failed. Not all PCI leaders endorsed this attack on the USSR. Some, such as Armando Cossutta, called for a continuation of Soviet ties. Berlinguer had the majority of the leadership on his side, and this majority stood by him even after *Pravda* on January 24, 1982 attacked the PCI in a violent language not used since the days of the Soviet polemics against the Chinese. It stopped just short of reading the PCI out of the international Communist movement.

Berlinguer had rejected the logic of military blocs and had asserted that there was no need for Italy to identify with either the USSR or the United States. He did not, however, call for Italian withdrawal from NATO, only for more autonomy for Western Europe within NATO. In fact, the Spadolini government was collaborating closely with the United States. It reaffirmed the Italian acceptance of a new generation of intermediate-range ballistic missiles based on Italian soil. In the spring of 1982 it contributed troops, with France and the United States, to the joint force set up to police and protect the withdrawal of Israeli troops from the Sinai desert. In the fall of 1982 Italy, again with France and the United States, sent troops to police and protect the Lebanese capital of Beirut after the Israeli destruction of PLO military units.

Italy's major differences with the United States were in the area of foreign trade. The Italians, along with other Western Europeans, opposed American efforts to limit steel exports to the United States, and participated in the compromise settlement reached in October *pol parties* (handwritten margin note)

1982. Italy was involved in the construction of the natural gas pipeline from Siberia to Western Europe. The ENI had signed contracts with the Soviet government to buy natural gas and to furnish pumping equipment, pipe, and other supplies. Italy had been buying some natural gas from the Soviet Union since the 1950s and did not view increased purchases with alarm. In November 1982 Spadolini visited Washington to overcome American opposition to the pipeline. The issue was resolved when President Reagan dropped American opposition in December.

Spadolini's problems with the recession absorbed most of his energies. Again, the dynamism of the submerged economy helped to moderate the recession's effects. By the end of 1982 the annual rate of inflation had been practically reduced to the target of 16 percent.

Spadolini's cabinet allies finally caused his downfall. In August 1982 Craxi had brought the government down in an effort to obtain the prime ministership. Spadolini skillfully outmaneuvered Craxi, using his personal popularity to isolate the PSI. Spadolini reconstructed the identical cabinet that Craxi had overturned. By the middle of November another crisis was brewing, again over the issue of austerity versus renewed spending to refloat the economy. The cabinet resigned and President Pertini called on the Christian Democrat Amintore Fanfani to organize a government. On December 2, 1982 a new coalition was formed with the parties of the previous cabinet, except for the Republicans. Fanfani promised to stimulate the economy and reduce further the rate of inflation. The DC had once more demonstrated its critical role. No combination of parties could substitute for it.

The absence of a credible opposition to the DC created what some commentators called the "blocked political system." The blockage was blamed as a major cause of the extremist strategy of terror in the 1970s. No clear-cut choices could emerge to reduce the tension. There were no decisive victories for either a democratic left or a democratic right.[7] That the extremists of the Red Brigades or Front Line would have accepted the policies of the only feasible alternative centered on the Communist Party is highly doubtful. In spite of their libertarian Marxist doctrines, their behavior and their language were more Fascist than anything else. The PCI accused the extra-parliamentary left, especially the extremists of the autonomist university-student movement, of behaving like Fascists. In cautious academic language a scholar of the Fascist period wrote:

As the Fascist period recedes in time, many attitudes which it

favoured are becoming fashionable again: we have only to think of
the spawning of irrationalism, voluntarism, anti-intellectualism,
the exaltation of youth over maturity, spontaneity over organization, of actions which are dictated by emotional frustration over
those which are based on rational analysis.[8]

Whether or not there is an alternation in the roles of government
and opposition, the leading parties in an open political system must
establish understandings among themselves about the rules of the
political game. The center-left was one kind of understanding, the
indirect grand coalition another. The mutual decision to concede
each other's role as leader of the government or the opposition, each
with its privileges, is yet another understanding and one the DC and
PCI have been accused of making tacitly. All of these game plans
require compromises that must be arranged by the political leadership.

The political leadership was hampered in the management of the
political process by continuing residual differences of values and
attitudes rooted within their followers. Although the direct intervention of the Church hierarchy in political affairs had declined, many
of the DC electoral supporters still held the traditional values of
family, doctrinaire authority, intolerance of differences, and confor-
mity to the standard criteria of respectability. The PCI, on the other
hand, had to manage an important sector of its rank and file that was
still tied to the maximalist revolutionary tradition, to residual
dogmas, and to millenarian visions of charismatic forces capable of
launching revolutions. There remained a continuing suspicion of the
Church and hostility to the Christian Democrats. Many Communist
and Socialist supporters shared some of the positions of the extra-
parliamentary left. Nevertheless a significant minority of left-wing
voters espoused conservative values, particularly on life-style issues
such as personal behavior, dress, parental authority, and stability of
institutions.[9] Berlinguer was justified in his fears that radicalizing
the political atmosphere in Italy would drive large numbers of
moderates into the hands of the right, for he also risked the same
threat from a part of his own following.

The Communist Party's Italian way to socialism had to operate
within these limiting contradictions. It accepted the alternation of
majorities in the country but rejected alternation inside the party. It
accepted a pluralism of values, religions, and philosophies, and
asserted the hegemony of the proletariat, insisting that these were
not incompatible concepts.[10] It wavered between minimizing and
emphasizing its Marxist-Leninist origins and remained ambiguous

in its relations with the Soviet Union. The party wanted to get the political and economic system in Italy functioning again. The leaders did not believe "so much the worse, so much the better." Yet they insisted that the party's goal was not to reform the system but to transform it.

In 1964 Giorgio Amendola called for a new, unified party of the working class, neither communist in the orthodox sense, nor social democratic. At the time he hoped that Socialists and Social Democrats would join Communists in the creation of this new party.[11] His hopes were unrealized, but in subsequent years his own party evolved in the direction he had projected. But was the evolution enough? For some of its supporters it was too much; for sectors of the Socialist electorate the PCI had hoped but had failed to reach, it was not enough. These Socialists wanted to see the PCI social-democratized and to see a clear-cut split between it and the Soviet Union. The PCI would not, or could not, take these steps so in 1979 it lost votes from among those who thought it had gone too far, and failed to gain votes from those it had hoped to attract. At the same time most Communist leaders rejected even a partial return to orthodoxy. The PCI was Eurocommunist, they believed, because Eurocommunism was the only kind of communism relevant to advanced modern societies. Italy was such a society and would remain one.

No such debates over identity disturbed the sleep of Christian Democracy. Its leaders wrangled over power and possessions. Whatever clashes, and they were many, marked the rivalries of the factions, they were no longer motivated by distinctions of program. Between those rejecting and those accepting the eventual inclusion of the PCI in a government, policy differences centered on the costs to the DC of such a prospect. There were also differences of opinion between those who felt Italy could be governed without the Communists but not against them, and those who believed the country could also be governed against the PCI. In the Communist Party there were differences between those who thought that a left alternative might be formed in the future without the DC, but not against the DC, and those who still chose an historic compromise. In all cases, however, these debates and the political developments that produced them revealed the incomplete integration of the PCI into the Italian political system.

Moreover, neither Eurocommunist nor Social Catholic doctrines were adequate for a modern consumer society. The solidity of electoral support for the parties was beginning to erode. In the 1979 parliamentary election the voter turnout fell to just below 90 percent of the eligible electorate for the first time. The turnout in the 1980 regional elections dropped to 88.5 percent, the lowest in the entire postwar period. Furthermore, an increasing number of those who did vote cast invalid or blank ballots. Although these developments were interpreted by politicians and political analysts as a protest against the parties and the political system, they must be understood in context. Italy still has one of the highest voter turnouts in the modern democratic world. However much the parties lagged at the ideological level, they remained skillful at the electoral level.

The electorate manifested a growing fluidity. The south had always been more politically volatile than other parts of the country, but fluidity in party identification was extending to other zones over and above any political influence attributable to southern migration. The electorate was becoming gradually freer of dogmatic or sub-cultural origins. Voters' electoral choices were reflecting more weight given to judgments on policies and performance and less emphasis on tradition and identity. The change was hidden by compensating shifts in voting choices that resulted in the overall stability of the final election returns, but nevertheless the change in voting behavior was there.

Even so, high percentages of voters and overall stability of the vote could not hide popular discontent. The masses of the people and educated opinion leaders alike believed that the political system functioned disgracefully, producing frustration, disaffection, and impotence.[12] Public opinion polls revealed the disillusion with political parties, which was particularly marked among the youth. Another indication of popular dismay was the response to the 1978 referendum on the law providing for the public financing of the political parties; 46 percent voted against the law. A general hostility to the parties buttressed a widespread belief in the existence of a fracture between the political elites and the population as a whole. Even supporters of the two major parties, the DC and the PCI, held this opinion. People had daily reminders of governmental malfunctioning in the inadequacies of the postal system and in the hours spent waiting in the post offices, the banks, and administrative offices. Throughout most of the 1970s coins were lacking to make small change; hard candies and postage stamps served as substitutes for 5-, 10-, and even 50-lire pieces. By 1979 the overall situation was improving but had not yet been resolved. The people's patience with the low levels of public service was remarkable.

In spite of double-digit inflation and stop-and-go economic policies the vast majority of the population was materially far better off than ever before, but industry in Italy was not. Even though the vitality and dynamism of the small and medium-sized firms in the private sector was striking, nevertheless the same could not be said for large industries, either public or private. Their pessimistic prognosis of their future in Italy led them to shift their investments during the 1970s to foreign countries.

During the same decade organized labor's power reached its apex, in the workplace and in its influence on social policy. By the end of the period it appeared that this power was beginning to decline. Management was again asserting its right to manage; to modify production methods that might require workers to shift jobs or to use new techniques; to fire for excessive absenteeism; to lay workers off when business declined. At the same time the government was imposing austerity programs, increasing taxes and prices, while squeezing consumer standards of living.

Discipline might be returning in the factories but people were more free in their private and social lives than ever before. The changing condition of women was one example of the increased personal liberty. The heightened informality of dress and social intercourse was another. In a contrary direction the population in the large urban centers became afraid of being out on the streets at night. The extension of police powers in the antiterrorist campaign was a potential threat to civil rights and to democracy, although on the whole there had been few abuses of these powers. Postwar governmental policies had produced many positive results, yet these gains had done little to strengthen national political identity.

There was a pervasive sense of discontent that went beyond the political sphere. Italians were not happy with their lives as a whole, in spite of the real improvements in their conditions. A cross-national survey taken in 1977 by Gallup International Research Institutes revealed widely differing responses by Western populations to questions concerning life satisfactions. In the United States 69 percent of the citizens were highly satisfied with life as a whole, as were 67 percent of the Danes, 59 percent of the Irish, 57 percent of the Dutch, 51 percent of the Belgians, 50 percent of the British, 41 percent of the West Germans, and 26 percent of the French. Only 17 percent of the Italians were highly satisfied with life as a whole.[13]

The political system deserves part of the blame for the low level of satisfaction with life. But it also deserves part of the credit for having raised the expectations and hopes of a people many of whom had never before enjoyed the luxury of aspiration. That Italians were dissatisfied with the everyday realities of life indicated the new criteria that they had adopted in contemporary times. Unrealized higher popular expectations could be potentially dangerous, but the people as a whole were demonstrating remarkable patience. The reradicalization of Italy after 1968 proved to be quite limited in real political impact or in penetration of most of the population.

The political leaders of the large parties had for the most part avoided polarizing slogans and intransigent behavior. They were rivals and competitors, but they had resisted the urgings of extremist supporters to decimate opponents. As a result most of the significant political and interest group elites had developed a real stake in the parliamentary republic. Thus the government survived, even if it did not govern very well.

The political system and the political leadership enjoyed little esteem, but when the system was struck at its very heart by the kidnapping and assassination of Aldo Moro the people rallied to it. They backed the state, not its enemies nor those who were indifferent. Perhaps their sense of national political identity was not as weak as their responses to pollsters indicated. Perhaps there was more consensus and less fragmentation than they expressed. The people had survived difficult tests with remarkable resilience. They continued to be Italy's real heroes.

NOTES

1. Nora Federici, "Il costume," pp. 277-81.
2. *Ibid.*, pp. 274-75.
3. Tullio De Mauro, "La cultura," p. 181.
4. *Ibid.*, pp. 191-200.
5. *Ibid.*, pp. 207-10, 215-16.
6. Lucio Libertini, "The Problem of the PCI," p. 3, mimeographed paper presented at the conference on "Italy and Eurocommunism, Western Europe at the Crossroads," June 7-9, 1977.
7. Giorgio Galli is a vigorous exponent of this position. See his book, *Storia della Democrazia Cristiana* and his chapter in *Dall '68 a oggi, come siamo e come eravamo.*
8. Giulio C. Lepschy, "The Language of Mussolini," *The Journal of Italian History*, Winter 1978, p. 531.
9. Gabriele Calvi, "La frattura tra valori e scelte politiche in Italia," *Rivista italiana di scienza politica*, April 1980, pp. 125-47.
10. Giorgio Napolitano, *Intervista sul PCI*, ed. Eric J. Hobsbawn (Bari: Laterza, 1976), pp. 72-73.
11. Giorgio Amendola, "Ipotesi sulla riunificazione," *Rinascita*, November 28, 1964, pp. 8-9.
12. Norman Kogan, Carlo Mongardini, Mario P. Salani, and Maurizio Maravalle, *Realtà e immagine della politica estera italiana* (Milan: Giuffrè, 1980).
13. *Public Opinion*, July/August 1978, p. 21.

BIBLIOGRAPHY

Acquaviva, Sabino S. *Guerriglia e guerra rivoluzionaria in Italia.* Milan: Rizzoli, 1978.

Alberoni, Francesco. *Italia in transformazione.* Bologna: Il Mulino, 1976.

Allum, P. A. *Italy—Republic Without Government?* New York: Norton, 1973.

———. *Politics and Society in Post-War Naples.* Cambridge: Cambridge University Press, 1973.

Ammassari, Gloria Pirzio. *La politica della Confindustria.* Naples: Liguori, 1976.

Andreatta, Nino. *Una economia bloccata, 1969-1973.* Bologna: Il Mulino, 1973.

Barnes, Samuel H. *Party Democracy: Politics in an Italian Socialist Federation.* New Haven: Yale University Press, 1967.

———. *Representation in Italy: Institutionalized Tradition and Electoral Choice.* Chicago: University of Chicago Press, 1977.

Belloni, Frank P., and Dennis C. Beller, editors. *Faction Politics: Political Parties and Factionalism in Comparative Perspective.* Santa Barbara: ABC-Clio Press, 1978.

Berlinguer, Enrico. *La questione comunista.* Rome: Riuniti, 1975.

Blackmer, Donald L. M. *Unity in Diversity, Italian Communism and the Communist World.* Cambridge, Mass.: MIT Press, 1968.

Blackmer, Donald L. M., and Sidney Tarrow, editors. *Communism in Italy and France.* Princeton: Princeton University Press, 1975.

Blackmer, Donald L. M., and Annie Kriegel. *The International Role of the Communist Parties of Italy and France.* Cambridge, Mass.: Center for International Affairs, Harvard University, 1975.

Caciagli, Mario, and Alberto Spreafico, editors. *Un sistema politico alla prova.* Bologna: Il Mulino, 1975.

Carli, Guido. *Intervista sul capitalismo italiano.* Bari: Laterza, 1977.

Castronovo, Valerio, editor. *L'Italia contemporanea 1945-1975.* Turin: Einaudi, 1976.

Clark, Burton R. *Academic Power in Italy: Bureaucracy and Oligarchy in a National University System.* Chicago: University of Chicago Press, 1977.

Contini, B. *Lo sviluppo di una economia parallela.* Milan: Comunità, 1979.

Dal '68 a oggi, Come siamo e come eravamo. Bari: Laterza, 1979.

D'Angelo, Massimo, Giuseppe Sacco, and Gian Andrea Sandri. *La cooperazione industriale tra Italia e paesi in via di sviluppo.* Bologna: Il Mulino, 1979.

D'Antonio, Mariano. *Sviluppo e crisi del capitalismo italiano 1950-1972*. Bari: De Donato, 1973.

Di Palma, Giuseppe. *Political Syncretism in Italy: Historical Coalition Strategies and the Present Crisis*. Berkeley: Institute of International Studies, University of California, 1978.

——. *Surviving Without Governing: The Italian Parties in Parliament*. Berkeley: University of California Press, 1976.

Di Renzo, Gordon J. *Personality, Power and Politics*. Notre Dame: University of Notre Dame Press, 1967.

Dogan, Mattei, and Orazio M. Petracca. *Partiti politici e strutture sociali in Italia*. Milan: Comunità, 1968.

Evans, Robert H. *A Venetian Community, an Italian Village*. Notre Dame: University of Notre Dame Press, 1976.

Farneti, Paolo, editor. *Il sistema politico italiano*. Bologna: Il Mulino, 1973.

Filo della Torre, Paolo, Edward Mortimer, and Jonathan Story, editors. *Eurocommunism: Myth or Reality?* Harmondsworth: Penguin Books, 1979.

Forte, Francesco. *La strategie delle riforme*. Milan: Etas Kompass, 1968.

Franco, Giampiero, editor. *Sviluppo e crisi dell'economia italiana*. Milan: Etas Libri, 1979.

Fried, Robert C. *Planning the Eternal City*. New Haven: Yale University Press, 1973.

Fua, Giorgio. *Occupazione e capacità produttive: La realtà italiana*. Bologna: Il Mulino, 1976.

Galli, Giorgio. *Il bipartitismo imperfetto*. Bologna: Il Mulino, 1966.

——. *Storia della Democrazia Cristiana*. Bari: Laterza, 1978.

Galli, Giorgio, and Alfonso Prandi. *Patterns of Political Participation in Italy*. New Haven: Yale University Press, 1970.

Gorresio, Vittorio. *Berlinguer*. Milan: Feltrinelli, 1976.

Graziano, Luigi, and Sidney Tarrow, editors. *La crisi italiana*. 2 vols. Turin: Einaudi, 1979.

Grindrod, Muriel. *Italy*. New York: Praeger, 1968.

Istituto Affari Internazionali. *L'Italia nella politica internazionale*. 7 vols. Milan: Comunità, 1974-1980.

Italy, Presidency of the Council of Ministers. *The State Participation System in Italy*. Rome: Istituto Poligrafico dello Stato, 1977.

Keefe, Eugene K., editor. *Area Handbook for Italy*. Washington: Government Printing Office, 1977.

Kogan, Norman, Carlo Mongardini, Mario P. Salani, and Maurizio Maravalle. *Realtà e immagine della politica estera italiana*. Milan: Giuffrè, 1980.

LaPalombara, Joseph. *Italy: The Politics of Planning*. National Planning Series, No. 7. Syracuse: Syracuse University Press, 1966.

LaPalombara, Joseph, and Stephen Blank. *Multinational Corporations and National Elites: A Study in Tensions*. New York: The Conference Board, 1976.

Levi, Arrigo. *Un'idea dell'Italia*. Milan: Mondadori, 1979.

L'Italia negli ultimi trent'anni, Rassegna critica degli studi. Bologna: Il Mulino, 1978.

Low-Beer, John R. *Protest and Participation: The New Working Class in Italy.* Cambridge: Cambridge University Press, 1978.

Magister, Sandro. *La politica vaticana e l'Italia, 1943-1978.* Rome: Riuniti, 1979.

Mammarella, Giuseppe. *Il partito comunista italiano 1945-1975.* Florence: Vallecchi, 1976.

——. *L'Italia dalla caduta del fascismo ad oggi.* Bologna: Il Mulino, 1978.

Napolitano, Giorgio. *Intervista sul PCI.* Edited by Eric J. Hobsbawm. Bari: Laterza, 1976.

Negri, Antonio. *Il dominio e il sabottagio: Sul metodo marxista della trasformazione sociale.* Milan: Feltrinelli, 1977.

Nichols, Peter. *Italia, Italia.* London: Macmillan, 1973.

——. *The Politics of the Vatican.* New York: Praeger, 1968.

Parisi, Arturo, and Gianfranco Pasquino, editors. *Continuità e mutamento elettorale in Italia.* Bologna: Il Mulino, 1977.

Pedrazzi, Luigi. *La politica scolastica del centro-sinistra.* Bologna: Il Mulino, 1972.

Peggio, Eugenio. *La crisi economica italiana.* Milan: Rizzoli, 1976.

Penniman, Howard R., editor. *Italy at the Polls: The Parliamentary Elections of 1976.* Washington: American Enterprise Institute for Public Policy Research, 1977.

Posner, M. W., and S. J. Woolf. *Italian Public Enterprise.* Cambridge, Mass.: Harvard University Press, 1967.

Putnam, Robert D. *The Beliefs of Politicians, Ideology, Conflict, and Democracy in Britain and Italy.* New Haven: Yale University Press, 1973.

Ranney, Austin, and Giovanni Sartori, editors. *Eurocommunism: The Italian Case.* Washington: American Enterprise Institute for Public Policy Research, 1978.

Ronchey, Alberto. *Accade in Italia, 1968-1977.* Milan: Rizzoli, 1977.

Salvati, Michele. *Il sistema economico italiano: analisi di una crisi.* Bologna: Il Mulino, 1975.

Sartori, Giovanni, editor. *Correnti, frazionalismo e fazioni nei partiti italiani.* Bologna: Il Mulino, 1973.

Scandaletti, Paolo. *La fine del compromesso.* Venice: Marsilio, 1979.

Silj, Alessandro. *Never Again Without a Rifle: The Origins of Italian Terrorism.* New York: Karz, 1979.

Statera, Gianni. *Death of a Utopia.* New York: Oxford University Press, 1975.

Sylos Labini, Paolo. *Saggio sulle classi sociali.* Bari: Laterza, 1974.

Tamburrano, Giuseppe. *Storia e cronaca del centro-sinistra.* Milan: Feltrinelli, 1971.

Tannenbaum, Edward R., and Emiliana P. Noether, editors. *Modern Italy, A Topical History Since 1861.* New York: New York University Press, 1974.

Teodori, Massimo, editor. *Per l'alternativa.* Milan: Feltrinelli, 1975.

——. *The New Left: A Documentary History.* Indianapolis: Bobbs-Merrill, 1969.

Tökés, Rudolf L., editor. *Eurocommunism and Détente.* New York: New York University Press, 1978.

Trent'anni della CGIL (1944-1974). Rome: Sindacale Italiana, 1975.

Vannicelli, Primo. *Italy, NATO and the European Community.* Cambridge, Mass.: Center for International Affairs, Harvard University, 1974.

Vettori, G. *La sinistra extraparlaméntare in Italia.* Rome: Newton Compton Italiana, 1973.

Willis, F. Roy. *Italy Chooses Europe.* New York: Oxford University Press, 1971.

Wiskemann, Elizabeth. *Italy Since 1945.* New York: St. Martin's Press, 1971.

Zagari, Mario. *Superare le sfide.* Milan: Rizzoli, 1976.

Zariski, Raphael. *Italy: The Politics of Uneven Development.* Hinsdale, Ill.: Dryden, 1972.

Zuckerman, Alan S. *The Politics of Faction: Christian Democratic Rule in Italy.* New Haven: Yale University Press, 1979.

INDEX

abortion: conflict over, 306;
conscientious objection, 306;
political impact, 291; precipitates
cabinet crisis, 295; referendum
results, 335
Abruzzi, 257
academic standards: attacks on, 233–34
Acerbo Law, 64
ACLI (Christian Association of Italian
Workers), 329; and Catholic Action
Society, 245; and DC, 245;
denounces "dialogue," 196; helps
southern immigrants, 142n; and
trade unions, 50 (see also Catholic
Action society, Italian)
ACPOL (Christian Association for Labor
Political Action), 245
Action Party: disappearance, 26, 34;
origins, 16; republicanism, 22
adultery, 254
Afghanistan: Soviet invasion, 323
Africa: trade with, 132; North, 145
AGIP (Italian General Petroleum
Agency), 54, 94, 95
AGIP-Nucleare, 123
Agnelli, Giovanni: emphasizes
productivity, 274; layoffs of
workers, 313; opposes PCI, 285
Agnelli, Senator Giovanni: founder of
Fiat, 144
Agnelli, Umberto, 274
agriculture: agrarian pacts, 109–10;
Cossiga's policy, 322; difficulties, 55;
exodus from land, 137; fluctuations,
53–54; governmental policy change,
137–38; growth, 130; improvement,
189; income, 203; land expropriation,
141; modernization, 202; number of

farms declines, 317; part-time
farmers, 276; peasants, 45–47, 80;
reforms, 45–50, 58, 64, 137;
sharecropping, 109–10, 172, 191; and
social status, 58–59; wheat prices,
122
Air Force, Italian, 13
Albania, 2, 9, 11, 13
Alexander, Sir Harold, 1
Alfa Romeo: firings, 314; losses, 208,
268, 308, 312; problems, 208
Alfa-Sud, 312–13
Algeria, 114n
aliens: in work force, 312
Allende, Salvador, 281, 301
Allied Commission, 19, 25, 26
Allied Military Government: blocks
CLN, 20; lire in circulation, 31;
removes controls, 23; resists purge,
19
Almirante, Giorgio: backs Leone, 261;
election strategy, 263, radicalizes
MSI, 256
Alps: boundaries in, 6–7
Alto Adige (see South Tyrol)
Amendola, Giorgio: on Communist
weaknesses, 193–94; to European
Parliament, 226; on new party,
226–27, 338; on PCI reform, 224; on
productivity, 274; supports Socialist
candidates, 195; thesis of, 196
Andreotti, Giulio, 153, 285; accepts
revised snake, 310; angers Craxi,
319; brings PLI into cabinet, 277;
defends foreign exchange holdings,
272–73; and exchange rates, 270;
exposes military plotting, 287; forms
cabinets, 262, 298–99, 304, 319; loses

347

Cairo, 118
Calabria, 257; ethnic consciousness, 321;
    riots in, 46; University of, 258
Calamandrei, Piero, 64, 80n
Campania, 257
Capodichino airport, 117
Carabinieri, 13, 74
Carli, Guido, 187–88
Carniti, Pierre, 314
Carretto, Carlo, 62
carristi, 172–73, 185; attack Nenni, 169;
    dissent, 125–26; oppose opening to
    the left, 164; schism of, 176, 186;
    Socialist Party current, 83; strength,
    91–92
Cassa per il Mezzogiorno (see Southern
    Italy Fund)
Castro, Fidel: myth, 233
Catania: and MSI, 260, 264
Catanzaro: regional capital, 257–58
Catholic Action Society, Italian: and
    ACLI, 245; anticommunism of, 112;
    decline, 165–67; and Fanfani, 123;
    under Fascism, 17–18; on liberal
    Catholics, 79; opposes détente, 151;
    opposes Socialists, 117, 155;
    political role, 59–62; pressure on
    Christian Democrats, 94; reaction to
    general strike, 38; revival, 196
Catholic Church (see Roman Catholic
    Church)
Cattaneo, Carlo, 34
celeri: repression by, 58
censorship, 79–80, 173–74
center-left coalition: collapses, 286;
    divisions in, 177; failure, 213;
    recreated, 252–53, 322–23, 333–34;
    and regionalism, 215; rules, 337
Central Statistical Institute (ISTAT),
    275; inadequate statistics, 311
centrism: opposition to, 171;
    reappearance, 161–62
Centrismo Popolare, 195n
CGIL (Italian General Confederation of
    Labor), 197; accepts wage restraint,
    306, 314; attacks on, 78–79; attacks
    incomes policy, 199; and business,
    76; calls general strike, 37; and
    carristi, 83, 92; continued worker
    support, 214; creation, 36–37; and
    EEC, 100, 134–35; emphasizes jobs,
    293; foments agricultural unrest, 46;

and hot autumn, 248; and Hungary,
    90; partial withdrawal from WFTU,
    282; and PCI, 249; and planning, 243;
    revival, 142; size, 244; Socialist
    losses in, 186
CGIL-CISL-UIL: confederation
    established, 249; wage policy, 306
Chamber of Deputies: duplication by
    Senate, 260–61; elections to, 64
Chambers of Commerce, 97
Chambers of Labor, 197
Chardin, Pierre Teilhard de, 79
chemical industry: reorganized, 318
Chile: coup d'état, 281–82
Christian Association of Italian Workers
    (see ACLI)
Christian Democratic Party (DC), 213,
    218; and abortion, 306; on big
    business, 97; and center-left, 171,
    277; and CISL, 245; condemns
    Warsaw Pact, 230; and
    Confindustria, 123; conservative
    drift, 277; in Constituent Assembly,
    26; contributions to, 98; control
    weakens, 260; and Craxi, 320;
    critical role, 337; defends Trabucchi,
    219; differences within, 164, 195–96,
    338–39; and dissidents, 285; and
    divorce, 219, 239, 284; early growth,
    16–18; and election of 1948, 33; on
    election laws, 64, 162; election
    results, 192, 219–20; 260, 263–64;
    289, 296, 319, 335; election strategy,
    263; electoral effectiveness, 264; on
    electric power, 176; elects Fanfani
    secretary-general, 73; and
    emergency decrees, 266; evolution,
    128; factionalism, 212, 259; and
    Fascists, 19, 23, 160; gains, 40, 65,
    113–15; helps immigrants, 142n; and
    hot autumn, 248; on institutional
    question, 22; integration of, 82–83;
    on judicial reform, 104–7; and
    Liberal Party, 176, 179; and Leone,
    307; and local consortia, 139; losses,
    35, 60, 163, 182; and Mafia, 192;
    maneuverability, 297; and
    Monarchists, 26; on monetary
    controls, 57; and MSI, 262; on
    multilateral atomic force, 184; and
    NATO, 84, 230; on neo-Atlanticism,
    101–2; on neutralism, 43; new

ABOUT THE AUTHOR

NORMAN KOGAN is Professor of Political Science at The University of Connecticut, Storrs. He has also been a Fulbright research professor and Fulbright senior lecturer at the University of Rome, Italy. From 1967 to 1976 he was executive secretary-treasurer of the Society for Italian Historical Studies. From 1975 to 1977 he was president of the Conference Group on Italian Politics. He is a member of the Board of Editors of *Comparative Politics* and of the Board of Directors of the America-Italy Society. In 1971 he was made a Knight in the Order of Merit of the Italian Republic by the president of the Republic. The Society for Italian Historical Studies awarded him its Citation for Outstanding Scholarly Achievement in the Field of Italian Studies in 1981.

Professor Kogan has published in the fields of political science and history. His books include: *Italy and the Allies* (Cambridge, Mass.: Harvard University Press, 1956); *The Government of Italy* (New York: Crowell, 1962); *The Politics of Italian Foreign Policy* (New York: Praeger, 1963); *A Political History of Postwar Italy*, Vol. I (New York: Praeger, 1966) and Vol. II (New York: Praeger, 1981). In addition, he has published chapters in edited volumes. His articles have appeared in *The Western Political Quarterly*, *The Journal of Politics*, *Comparative Politics*, *International Journal*, *Polity*, *Studies in Comparative Communism*, *European Review*, *Italian Quarterly*, *The Yale Law Journal*, *Indiana Law Journal*, *Il Ponte*, *Il Mondo*, and *Il Movimento di Liberazione in Italia*.

Professor Kogan holds a B.A. and a Ph.D. from the University of Chicago.